The Best AMERICAN ESSAYS® 2002

Edited and with an Introduction
by Stephen Jay Gould

Robert Atwan, Series Editor

HOUGHTON MIFFLIN COMPANY

BOSTON • NEW YORK   2002

Visit our Web site: www.houghtonmifflinbooks.com.

ISSN 0888-3742
ISBN 0-618-21388-0
ISBN 0-618-04932-0 (pbk.)

Printed in the United States of America

DOC 10 9 8 7 6 5 4 3 2 1

The Best American Essays is a registered trademark of Houghton Mifflin Company.

Contents

Foreword

"Unfortunately, there's some very bad news," Stephen Jay Gould announced at the end of last March while leaving a message on my answering machine to say that he had completed making all the final selections for this year's book. He added that he would be checking into the hospital the following Monday for what he fully expected would be "a quite serious procedure." Less than two months later, this truly amazing person would be gone. He promised to finish the introduction before undergoing the surgery. And he did.

A native New Yorker, who at the time lived within a mile of Ground Zero, Gould had been emotionally devastated by the terrorist assault of September 11, 2001 — which as he notes in his introduction came one hundred years to the day after his grandfather landed at Ellis Island. Gould had planned to commemorate his family's centennial on that day by visiting his grandfather's site of entry. Almost immediately after the attacks, he wrote four short, reflective essays on 9/11 that he managed to include in his last collection, *I Have Landed,* which appeared shortly before his death. Although he saw the attacks as an instance of "spectacularly destructive evil," he optimistically believed that the terrorist "vision of inspired fear" would never prevail over the "overwhelming weight of human decency" we find everywhere around us.

As he read through the one hundred or so essays I'd sent him, Gould at one point observed how everything seemed "shaped by 9/11," regardless of whether an essay was written before or after. Later, I realized how every few years, ever since I launched this annual essay series in 1985, some pivotal event dominates the national attention and dramatically narrows our literary scope. In 1995 it seemed that half the essays I read dealt either directly or tangentially with the O. J. Simpson trial. The nation couldn't stop talking about it, and many distinguished writers weighed in with insightful and sometimes brilliant commentary. Something similar occurred toward the end of 2000, when the American political process was put on hold during the most bizarre presidential election in our history. Yet coverage of these events — as influential and absorbing as they still are — did not necessarily find their way into the volumes that featured the best essays of those years.

But the terrorist attacks of September 11, 2001, and their aftermath were altogether another story. The written response was overwhelming, and not merely because of the massive news coverage that instantly went into operation. The coverage, commentary, and reportage one could expect; what was unexpected was their astonishingly high quality. I had assumed that thoughtful essays would take months of reflection and deliberation, that the "literature of 9/11" was several years away. I was surprised to see it taking shape before my eyes. As Stephen Jay Gould mentions in his introduction, we could have assembled an entire volume of 9/11 essays. Perhaps two or three volumes, I should add.

And yet, when I consider the responses to 9/11 more carefully, I realize that I should have expected an abundance of fine essays. The essay always seems to revitalize in times of war and conflict — and it's usually with the return of peace and prosperity that fiction and poetry renew their literary stature. The First World War resulted in eruption of essays and introduced the work of some of our finest nonfiction writers, many of whom, like Randolph Bourne, took up the pacifist cause. Then the postwar years saw the flourishing of some of our most celebrated poets and novelists, those members of the "lost generation." This was true too in the Second World War (E. B. White published his greatest essay collection in 1942), and it was especially true during Vietnam. It seems to me no coincidence that the Vietnam years saw the emergence of the New Journalism, an exciting and innovative brand of nonfiction pioneered by one of the writers included in this volume, John Sack.

I can't prove this theory about essays in time of war. The idea occurred to me while reading Czeslaw Milosz's brilliant long poem *A Treatise on Poetry*, which arrived in the mail just a day or so before the 9/11 carnage. Though he promotes the value of poetry in difficult times, Milosz prefaces his "treatise" with the recognition that in our time "serious combat, where life is at stake, / is fought in prose." Even if that's accurate — at least in a general sense — I'm not sure why. Perhaps in times of conflict and crisis people want to be in the presence of less mediated voices — we need more debate and directives, we desire more public discourse. We instinctively turn to writing that displays a greater sense of immediacy and urgency. "These are the times that try men's souls," Thomas Paine memorably wrote in 1776, in what would be the first essay of *The American Crisis*. At that moment in history, radicalism and nationalism could go hand in hand.

A few weeks after the attacks of 9/11, I hosted a reading of essays from the newly published 2001 volume at Wordsworth bookstore in Cambridge, just a block away, incidentally, from the hotel where, earlier in September, my son and I (we had just moved a sofa into his freshman dorm) stepped out of the garage elevator into the lobby and exchanged uneasy glances with two unfashionably dressed Middle Eastern men who three days later would fly their suicide mission into the twin towers of the World Trade Center. I was apprehensive about the reading, thinking that anything written before 9/11 might now appear irrelevant, naïve, or just hopelessly dated to an audience saturated with minute-by-minute coverage of wreckage and terrorism.

Milosz's words, however, had stayed with me, and I cited them, suggesting that in these times the essay was perhaps the most suitable and effective mode of response. Here is what I said: "Whatever other consequences they entail, there can be little doubt that the attacks of September 11 will have enormous cultural repercussions, and among these will be a reemergence of the essay as a broadly relevant, even indispensable, genre — a vital source of voices, ideas, and personal histories that the public will turn to with perhaps greater attention than ever before."

A few months later, I found my observations about the essay independently corroborated by Peter Beinart in *The New Republic*, who pointed out that an increasing seriousness in the press after 9/11 has resulted in the reemergence of the "non-reported, non-narrative, political or historical" analytical essay, a genre that in his opinion had gone "deeply out of fashion in the 1990's." The "new gravity" that Beinart now sees in the magazine world is evidenced in this volume, not only by his own magazine's contribution (Mario Vargas Llosa's "Why Literature?") but by the large number of serious and informed essays on education, culture, history, music, and vital contemporary issues. Even the personal essays, with their prevailing medical topics, are grounded in matters of life and death, issues that we now know represented something more to Gould at the time than age-old literary themes.

The Best American Essays features a selection of the year's outstanding essays, essays of literary achievement that show an awareness of craft and forcefulness of thought. Hundreds of essays are gathered annually from a wide variety of national and regional publications. These essays are then screened, and approximately one hundred are turned over to a distinguished guest editor, who may add a few personal discoveries and who makes the final selections.

To qualify for selection, the essay must be a work of respectable literary quality, intended as a fully developed, independent essay on a subject of general interest (not specialized scholarship), originally written in English (or translated by the author) for publication in an American periodical during the calendar year. Magazine editors who want to be sure their contributors will be considered each year should include the series on their complimentary subscription list (Robert Atwan, Series Editor, *The Best American Essays*, P.O. Box 220, Readville, MA 02137). Writers, editors, and readers interested in the essay series can also contact me by writing to: Robert Atwan, Director, The Blue Hills Writing Institute, Curry College, 1071 Blue Hill Avenue, Milton, MA 02186-2395, or by visiting www.curry.edu and looking for the writing institute under "Continuing Education." Writers and editors are welcome to submit published essays from any American periodical for consideration; unpublished work does not qualify for the series and cannot be reviewed or evaluated.

I appreciate the assistance I received on this book from Matthew Howard and Ellen Thibault. As always, I'm grateful for the help and guidance I receive from various people at Houghton Mifflin, especially Erin Edmison, Larry Cooper, Liz Duvall, Eric

Chinski, and Janet Silver. All of us were saddened to hear of Stephen Jay Gould's serious illness, and then so very soon after we were all grieved to learn of his death. We join in dedicating this seventeenth volume in the series to the memory of this brilliant scientist, thrilling thinker, incomparable essayist, and steadfast humanist.

R.A.

Introduction:
To Open a Millennium

ACCORDING TO calendrical conventions, the third millennium of our era began on January 1, 2000, or on January 1, 2001, by equally defendable modes of reckoning. Either way, we all acknowledge that our favored decimal mode of numeration reflects nothing more than a convention, however sensible, based on our evolutionary complement of digits. Thus, although we count time by decades and centuries, the beginnings of such units cannot transcend the arbitrary and often bear no interesting relationship to the press of actual history.

Many commentators have stated — quite correctly in my view — that the twentieth century did not truly begin in 1900 or 1901, by any standard of historical continuity, but rather at the end of World War I, the great shatterer of illusions about progress and human betterment. We now face a similar problem for the inception of this millennium, one that must be addressed before proceeding with any collection of essays to honor a year for its inception. Forget the old argument about January 1, 2000 or 2001 (and I even devoted an entire book, albeit short, to this subject). To our great misfortune (that is, provided we can assure that events of similar magnitude do not dog the rest of our days), I suspect that future chroniclers will date the inception of the third millennium from September 11, 2001. Any collector of essays for this fateful year must therefore, up front and first of all, address this issue.

I was tempted to make a collection solely of 9/11 pieces (so many good ones already, and so many more yet to come), but neither decency nor common morality permitted such a course. We simply cannot allow evil madmen to define history in this way. Moreover, the event occurred late enough in the year to preclude the kind of pervasiveness that might summon such a temptation. But 9/11 stories must be here, and you will find some of the first of the best.

As another point about the need to focus on 9/11, no other event of my life so immediately became part of everyone's experience. (I think we may finally be able to retire that old question, Where were you the moment JFK was shot?) So we all have personal stories as well, and we need to share them, if only to keep the mantra of "never again" as active as we possibly can. For myself, and in briefest epitome, I live less than a mile from Ground Zero, and if the towers had fallen due north instead of downward, my home would have been flattened. I spent my sixtieth birthday in Italy, on September 10, the day before the attack. Flying back to New York on the day itself, I ended up spending an unplanned five days in Halifax, where my plane was diverted, among some of the kindest people I have ever encountered. Finally, in the weirdest coincidence of my life (the kind of event that makes the religious believe, although I remain a confirmed skeptic), I remembered that the history of my family in America had begun with the arrival of my grandfather. I own the grammar book that he purchased for a nickel soon after his immigration at age thirteen, and I have affirmed the correct date (for I have a copy of the ship's manifest for his arrival at Ellis Island) of the minimally elegant inscription that he wrote on the title page: "I have landed. September 11, 1901."

One truly final point and then I promise to move on. History's verdict remains to be assigned, but we tend to designate our important days by the events they commemorate, not simply by the date itself. Only one exception to this pattern now exists, the one date that must stand by and for itself: July 4. I can't help wondering (as seems to be the case so far, but we cannot yet tell) if this beginning of our millennium will enter American history as the second example, known either as September 11 or 9/11. I don't know how to root about this matter, for or against. As a devoted baseball fan, I do believe in the necessity of rooting. Several years ago, I promised Bob Atwan that I would take on one of the yearly "best" volumes as soon as I finished my magnum opus, *The Structure of Evolutionary Theory* (published in March 2002 by Harvard University Press, 1,433 pages, at the unbeatable hardback price of $39.95). I cringed when he sent me about one hundred essays for my selection, and exploded in premonitory fear for an odd reason that I rarely confess: I am a committed intellectual, and I like to read, but in a funny sense the last book that truly inspired me was probably *The Little Engine That Could*, first encountered more than half a century ago. Still, a promise is a promise, and so I proceeded. And, thank goodness for affirmations of prior hope, I actually enjoyed the task.

My overall impressions are scarcely worth the length of the following sentence, and I will surely not detail the reasons for most of my individual choices herein. But — and I guess because I primarily write, rather than read, essays — I was astonished by the single most salient character of the choices considered together. I knew that "confessional writing" now enjoys quite a vogue, but I had no idea how pervasive the practice of personal storytelling has become among our finest writers. I can't help asking myself (although all lives are, by definition, interesting, for what else do we have?): why in heaven's name should I care about the travails of X or Y unless some clear generality about human life and nature emerges thereby? I'm glad that trout fishing defined someone's boyhood, and I'm sad that parental dementia now dominates someone's midlife, but what can we do in life but play the hand we have been dealt? (And if I may be confessional for a moment, the line that most moved me in all these essays came from the pen of an author who stated, so truly, for I live this life every day, that nothing can be harder than the undesired responsibility for raising a child with severe handicaps). Still, I hope that the current popularity of confessional writing soon begins to abate.

I have made no attempt to gather my choices into subgroupings, but I offer a few comments in three categories to close this introduction. First, among the confessional writings, the number of medical pieces rather stunned me — as if we have come to the point where everyone with a serious illness (meaning all of us, at some point in our lives) feels some compunction to share the load. I particularly appreciated Barbara Ehrenreich's cancer tale for its wonderfully appropriate cynicism and honesty in the face of what nonprofessionals can and cannot do — for, contrary to hope and wishes turning into horses, we cannot will ourselves into betterment, and dreams of such mental control ultimately do not help. I also loved Atul Gawande's essay on the decline of autopsies (a truly scholarly piece within the more confessional genre) and the number of mistakes made by doctors that autopsies reveal.

In a second, political category, I did not know of Gore Vidal's odd relationship with the late Mr. McVeigh, and I found the tale fascinating. I struggled with John Sack's account of his contacts with Holocaust deniers and finally included it because, while I disagree with his decision to speak at their meetings, the deniers do remain (unlike the actual perpetrators) within the category of human beings, and I supposed that we therefore need to understand them as well as we can. Amy Kolen's essay on the Triangle fire, although entirely meritorious in se, did get a nod for personal reasons too. My grandmother was a shirtwaist worker, on the job at a different sweatshop on the day of the fire. My current office, in the very same building now owned by NYU, occupies a corner of one of the floors that burned on that fateful day. And — how can one possibly avoid so saying — the horrific image of young women jumping to their deaths resonated with every sentient person on 9/11, as history repeated itself when many trapped people decided (consciously or not, we can never know) to make their end with the same final gesture of freedom.

The 9/11 essays, of course, also fall into this political category. Rudolph Chelminski may win no literary prizes, but no New Yorker can forget the day that the Blondin of our times walked between the towers. Adam Mayblum may not be a professional writer, but his on-the-scene account touched me, as did Richard Price and Anne Hudson-Price's record of street voices in the aftermath of the tragedy. I loved the juxtaposition of David Halberstam's and Christopher Hitchens's essays, the first from a longtime New Yorker who used 9/11 to make some kind of peace that he had not found with his life, the second from an Englishman who used the same event to come to terms after decades of struggle.

In a third, more scholarly category, I struggled with Andrew Levy's "The Anti-Jefferson," for it runs longer, and more seriously, than the conventional essay. But in the end I decided that it had to win entry for a primary historical principle too rarely stated. It tells the story of the most extensive voluntary manumission of slaves ever achieved in Virginia, and few people have heard of the hero, nor do we really know why he acted as he did. We need to define and understand the unasked questions if we ever hope to grasp the pains and realities of our past. A reader would have to be tone deaf not to be fascinated by Nicholas Delbanco's detailed story of the renovation of one of the world's great Strad cellos. Among the more academic pieces, Louis Menand's reminder that liberal arts colleges never really enjoyed a Golden Age strikes home, for Golden Age myths exist for everything we like, and hardly anything can be more pernicious. I appreciated Mario Vargas Llosa on the continuity of books, and I sure hope he's right. Jacques Barzun has never been one of my heroes, but anyone still writing so well in his mid-nineties deserves a place here, and someone has to stick up for the three R's, hickory stick or no.

STEPHEN JAY GOULD

The Best
AMERICAN
ESSAYS
2002

JACQUES BARZUN

The Tenth Muse

FROM HARPER'S MAGAZINE

SHE IS THE MUSE of popular culture, the tenth muse, the muse
who inspires the poems and tales and tunes that express the hearts
and minds of the people. Reliable reports say that she has disappeared, and this worries a good many observers. Their concerns
point in various directions, but together they confirm the impression that in the modern world there is no popular culture. Listen
to some of these complaints. The *New York Times* says that the
whole country argues about taste and concludes that "when it
comes to enforcing it, it's best to tread lightly, if at all." A book by
Thomas S. Hibbs entitled *Shows About Nothing* has the subtitle *Nihil-
ism in Popular Culture from "The Exorcist" to "Seinfeld."* Another, *Crowd
Culture,* by Bernard I. Bell, points out that although the culture
that offers "escape . . . into a dream world of carnality and brutality" is conspicuous, it is far from being acceptable as culture at all.
The columnist Leonard Pitts deplores the "insidious" message that
gangsta rap sends to the young. "You struggle to make [black
youth] hear you over the beat of a song" that rewards death by
drugs and gunshot, but it is difficult. On a broader plane, Joseph P.
Lawrence asks "What Is Culture?" in order to discuss whether popular culture is the contradiction of high culture or its foundation.
To decide, one must first make sure which of innumerable things
that flourish under the name is *the* popular culture of the times.

The issue is not confined to the United States. In England the director of the Barbican Arts Centre in London sees a dangerous
conflict: "Populism versus Elitism in the Arts," which is something
new and alarming because of its effect on where the money for art

goes. To save themselves, the high arts must engage in "outreach" and "educating" the public. Meanwhile, the warden of Goldsmiths College wonders "Should the Arts Be Popular?" He means, Should the distinction be erased by a merger of styles and genres?

In France the same topic has received attention, but the only extended treatment, in Mona Ozouf's book *La Muse démocratique*, treats the popular with disdain and invokes the works of Henry James as a shield against "the gray, dull, and vulgar world." His novels serve this purpose because they show up and condemn vulgarity while steadfastly upholding the true democratic ideal.

Ozouf's sheer avoidance could be labeled sheer elitism, but it also suggests the absence in the popular genres of those qualities that in the past "elitist" minds enjoyed and respected. If, to return to this country, one goes to the *Journal of Popular Culture*, one is likewise disappointed to find it silent on its declared subject. It deals with such topics as "Fairy Tale Elements in Jane Eyre," H. L. Mencken and Methodism, and Sir Thomas Browne's *Pseudodoxia Epidemica*. That Georges Simenon's Maigret novels and Maurice Sendak's books for children are also discussed does not conceal the remoteness of all such considerations from the reality on the streets.

Let us take a quick look at the popular. In music, it includes cowboy and country, rock and rap, and other offshoots of early-twentieth-century ragtime and jazz. These have subdivided endlessly, each with a special name, fine-drawn characteristics, and clannish devotees. In storytelling, the popular ranges from tough crime to pornography; in graphics, from the comic strip to pop art; and in magazines, from the supermarket level to the group-interest form that rises out of bodybuilding and housekeeping to the dizzy literary heights of *The New Yorker* and the *Paris Review*. The television screen features soap operas, legal or other dramatic episodes, and moneyed competitions, while the Internet offers games and pseudo-culture — a congeries of pastimes that, with some overlapping, cater to diverse publics. The newspapers record the diversity in review articles by different experts.

Can it be said that any of these entertainments expresses the hearts and minds of the people? Some think that rap lyrics echo a prevailing disgust with life and society at the end of an era. Sentimental balladry under various names depicts the world that simple

souls desire but nobody believes in. And even these two extremes
of feeling might qualify as popular culture if they sounded more
spontaneous, less like standardized products modified only to
compete within an industry.

Clearly, in the modern democratic society there is no art of and
by the people. True, the many new immigrant groups in Western
nations cling to their folk songs and dances, but one cannot expect
original departures or any spread of innovations from one ethnic
enclave to another.

That a popular culture can express the people as a whole is not a
fanciful idea; it has been done. The Athenian population, brought
up on Homer, flocked to the Greek drama. The illiterate medievals
listened to the tale of Beowulf (recently resuscitated by an Irish
poet), to the *Nibelungenlied,* to the stories of Tristan and Parsifal
and the Nordic sagas, while they could also "read" the Bible in the
stained glass and sculpture of their churches. Next, the Renaissance created the superb Spanish ballads that inspired Spanish poets down to Lorca, the English and Scottish border ballads, and a
vast collection of folk songs and tales. It developed the modern
form of the play, and a mixed crowd filled Shakespeare's Globe
Theatre. Rabelais and Cervantes wrote bestsellers. The age cultivated domestic music and made abundant use in church and at
home of the new art of painting in perspective. From far back,
then, popularity meant the people's recognition of their life and
soul in their art.

But have I not omitted the modern equivalent, the movies? I
kept them out of the list with the thought that they might prove
the one genre of ecumenical appeal. Hollywood films reach all
parts of the country, indeed travel to the ends of the earth, and
thus seem to express all humankind. But that is an illusion. A large
part of the output expresses chiefly the "carnality and brutality"
that many object to; the ratings system to protect the young makes
it plain that "the people" do not see their hopes and fears mir-
rored on the screen. A segment of the public avoids the lust and
mayhem and looks for the sophisticated work of the artist-pro-
ducer, native or foreign. Since, we are told, a commercial film must
aim at the mind of the thirteen-year-old, the failure to produce
films for adults endowed with common sense about what matters
to them is *anti*-populism. They patronize the movies and tolerate,

often with disgust, the routine offering, but they are in fact under-
nourished by it, and their best selves remain unexpressed.

What takes some explaining is why the ordinary people of Athens could appreciate Sophocles' *Antigone,* medieval peasants the
tale of Tannhäuser, and sixteenth-century Londoners the point-
edly named *As You Like It,* when these works and their like are now
deemed too difficult to appeal to the common taste. The cause is
not the language alone, which can be glossed or modernized. It is
the lack of certain mental and emotional habits. Not only has a verbal and oral tradition been broken but a mental power has been
lost: the capacity, developed from infancy by myths and other domestic lore, to enjoy things that are beyond the fully understood.
In Athens not everybody could gauge the sublime in the tragedies,
but all found something to be moved by and to remember. This
possessive curiosity seems nowadays in abeyance. Culture, in the
sense of all things of the mind, has been split, first in half, and then
the lower half into bits and pieces at once obvious and obsessive.

The first writer to deal seriously with this division used the then
recently coined terms "lowbrow" and "highbrow." In *America's Com-
ing-of-Age,* published in 1915, the critic of New England literature
Van Wyck Brooks ascribed the split to the Puritan dogma that the
Deity directs with equal concern the moral and the practical successes of mankind. This belief, according to Brooks, gives equal
value to cultural effort and to selfish opportunism — the low cunning of business, the identification of worth with money. Shrinking
back from this materialism, said Brooks, the first American geniuses in art and thought — Emerson and his peers — made culture "fastidious, refined, and aloof." Hence the division into high
and low.

The fact is clear but the explanation hard to accept. No Puritan
tradition swayed continental Europe, yet the same separation came
about there. Nor can one see how the Almighty could do other
than oversee all the doings of humanity, moral and material.
Brooks's view was but one form of the anti-bourgeois, anti-Puritan
animus current early in the century.

A more tenable origin of the unequal brows is the physical uprooting that occurred in late-eighteenth-century society — first, of
those who came to people this country and who faced the task of
building it from the ground up. This effort and its continual west-

ward movement interfered with the handing down of old traditions, which did not fit the immigrants' new experience. The generations born here intermarried, wanted to be Americans, and spoke English, not the language of their folktales. For a popular culture to thrive, it must be part of a continuous fabric of ideas and feelings from low to high, each level inspiring and borrowing from the next. The continuity enables the uneducated to find ports of entry into high art and encourages the geniuses to make use of popular creations in their masterpieces.

A different uprooting "brainwashed" the Europeans who stayed home. Its cause: the Industrial Revolution and the cities it produced. Factory and slum put an end to the rural pleasures of the people. The tumult of the city, of many cities with shifting populations, destroyed reflection in idle hours and bred barbarians. It is significant that jazz, the one wholly American form of music, came out of a segregated group in New Orleans, a town free of industry. Later, it was again the South that produced poets and novelists who for their materials and outlook drew on the rustic past and called themselves Agrarians. The rest of the country responded to the insights of varying depth embodied in the world of Faulkner or in *Gone with the Wind*.

If the question were put abruptly, Does the machine lower the mind? one would have to answer yes and no. In direct contact, it stretches the senses, sharpens the wits, and by multiplying human relations it has a civilizing effect that we call sophistication. But a contrary effect accompanies the broadened outlook. The machine's multiplying power turns out goods in huge quantities and demands masses of consumers. To please them all, products must satisfy the most elementary taste — or so those who make them believe, rightly or wrongly. The net result is the lowering required: when a television show pleases twelve million viewers, one that pleases only six million is a failure. It rings the curtain down, and the upshot: six million deprived and their taste debased. The tinny flavor of mass-produced entertainment is the outcome of this numerical compulsion.

For a true culture to arise and survive, a common core of ideas and feelings must exist. The gifted among the people then produce works that on their merits turn out to please beyond the immediate audience. Hence the quality of past popular culture: the ballad of Chevy Chase shows a finer sense of words and rhythm than gangsta rap, and its pathos trains the emotions to a finer sensibility.

Seeing the political danger from industrial barbarism, thinkers and lawgivers in the mid-nineteenth century decreed free education for all — to create political responsibility and also to extend economic opportunity. In this effort the United States took the lead. It established primary schools that assimilated the great tide of immigrants, and, what is most remarkable, by 1900 the American free public high school, compulsory for all, was providing a secondary education that embraced the cultural heritage. As late as the 1920s and 1930s, a high school senior had had three years of Latin and was parsing Virgil, had read some Dickens, Scott, Hawthorne, and George Eliot, and was being taken through Milton's shorter poems by a teacher who knew how to make them clear and moving. In the Oak Park High School that Ernest Hemingway attended, there was a Latin Club with a room specially assigned to it, where the students talked to one another in Latin.

I cite this as indicative of the lengths to which it was once possible to go. So cruel a discipline today would cause an outcry, and it is not needed for a popular culture. But something like it is called for. The early and mid-twentieth century devised various means to supply it. Night schools for adults, and the Carnegie and other educational foundations, special periodicals, book clubs, libraries, innumerable series of classics in cheap but good hardcover editions — these, together with the new nationwide radio, seconded the work of the high school. As for the colleges and universities, they uniformly maintained a curriculum with liberal-arts requirements. The academic and intellectual elites were bent on giving everybody a chance to reconnect with the heritage.

Among the persons engaged in this crusade, the great hero was the late Clifton Fadiman. Every aspect of his career and achievement illustrates the vicissitudes of the endeavor first proposed by Matthew Arnold under the heading *Culture and Anarchy*. Arnold's aim was to civilize the philistines and barbarians of England by making "the best that has been thought and known in the world current everywhere," affording not only enjoyment but also an upward mobility in taste.

Fadiman's dedication to this task was not an inspiration of youth but a mature second choice. As a senior at Columbia College in 1925, Clifton ("Kip" to his classmates) was the acknowledged intellectual leader of his class, the model scholar and writer. Every issue of the literary magazine *Morningside* contained one or more of his poems — often a sonnet — or an essay, a fragment of philosophy translated from the French, or an imaginary scene between figures in a tragedy by Sophocles. The poetry was Georgian in style and sometimes down-to-earth like Edgar Lee Masters's narratives. Nobody could doubt that Fadiman would soon become a name in contemporary letters. The expectation was confirmed when the Modern Library commissioned him to translate and introduce a volume of works by Nietzsche.

With an academic record that matched this extracurricular performance, he had good reason to expect what he most desired: an academic career. His college instructors had encouraged this ambition, notably John Erskine, then famed as a scholar and novelist and the father of the Great Books program. But when in graduate school Fadiman was interviewed by the head of the English department, he was told with blunt kindness that he could not hope for a post at Columbia: he was Jewish. This exclusionary custom was not limited to that department. All but two or three observed a tacit rule that was broken only in the late thirties when President Nicholas Murray Butler forced the tenure appointment of Lionel Trilling.

Facing a blank wall, Fadiman turned to literary journalism. He became a reviewer for *The Nation*, like Mark Van Doren, who, though newly made assistant professor, was a little suspect as a scholar because of this venture into the marketplace. Fadiman reviewed books for *The Nation* for seven years, and so acutely and attractively that *The New Yorker* recruited him as its chief critic. He occupied the post for a decade before Edmund Wilson. Concurrently, Fadiman was acting as reader — and soon as editor in chief — for Simon & Schuster, thus serving literature like George Meredith and T. S. Eliot while contributing to it.

As a seasoned judge of books, Fadiman was next taken on by the Book-of-the-Month Club. Its mission was to distribute new books of high merit to a wider public than was reached by the antique methods of trade publishers. The new club meant to offer more solid works than those supplied by the Literary Guild. It is at this point

— the year was 1944 — that Clifton Fadiman began to be conde-
scended to by academics and the literati. He was deemed to have
gone down one level in the cultural hierarchy measured by height
of brow.

This notion of brow levels requires explanation. Paradoxically, it
was ushered in by the success of free public schooling. Enlarged lit-
eracy fostered the mass newspaper. Artists and intellectuals were
appalled at its tone and contents and united to condemn the type
of mind it created, again by lowest appeal. Baudelaire called it sa-
tanic. Contempt followed hatred until a radical difference in human minds was accepted as a fact of nature; the code words "lowbrow" and "highbrow" have been traced as far back as 1906. One's
choices in books and pictures, hobbies and employment, showed
to which division of mankind one belonged. Anything popular
meant low; popular culture was deemed a contradiction in terms.
As time went on, the distance between the poles kept increasing
until art and "journalism" were worlds apart.

The caste system held in spite of disputes about particulars
(Dickens was a great genius — No! he was "a writer for chamber-
maids," etc.). Arguing about such double-tongued classics suggested that perhaps the chasm between the high and the low was
inhabited; a large contingent thrived there unabashed: the middle
brow. The astute observer Russell Lynes mapped the three zones
of mind in an entertaining essay published in *Harper's Magazine* in
1949. By Lynes's reckoning, Clifton Fadiman, the respected critic
and once certified highbrow, was déclassé. While he pursued his
chosen task, a writer for *Partisan Review,* whose name is now obscure and who has left no work of any moment, wrote an essay entitled "Masscult and Midcult" and branded Fadiman "the standard
bearer of middle-brow culture."

The inferior status assigned to Fadiman in midcareer sank even
further when he became the host of *Information, Please.* This was a
radio quiz program of the simple kind, without money prizes,
which sparked a conversation among half a dozen notables who in-
dulged in witty digressions. Like the later *Conversation,* which discussed current books and in which Fadiman also took part, this
program entertained, obscuring the fact that it was manned by
highbrows and widely enjoyed by that same breed. But popularity
was the fatal stain.

Popularity, though, is a relative term. A little after *Information,*

Please came *Invitation to Learning,* of which I was the moderator for two years. It brought together knowledgeable people as different from one another as Rex Stout and Bertrand Russell, who debated the message of a work by Tocqueville or Walt Whitman or some other classic author. The program was protected by William Paley, head of CBS, who kept it alive in spite of its reaching only two million listeners when "success" called for ten.

These not-at-all-learned broadcasts somehow escaped censure by the friends of intellectual purity, but other, comparable ventures aimed at large audiences were finally outlawed, at least in words. When, for example, Time-Life Records in the 1960s offered a series of LP albums anthologizing Western music since the sixteenth century accompanied by well-written commentary (which I was given the task of editing), various academics condemned the set because all the discs were from one company and thus not the best recorded performance of each work — as if these carpers would ever have agreed on the best.

The highbrow guardians failed to understand how the things they cherished depend on stirrings down below. A chance encounter with a novel, a symphony, a painting, will impel a young mind to go on — and up. Highbrows are self-made, and even before reaching that glorious state, one possessed by cultural passion may produce original work. The creative geniuses are not invariably cultivated minds. But they must at some point have felt the power of the real thing, no matter how simple. All Burns and Lorca needed were the ballads of their country. Others, more fully self-educated, become the appreciative listeners they need.

Here again, Clifton Fadiman's odyssey is relevant. He was the son of unpretentious people who lived modestly — at times precariously — in Brooklyn. Both Kip and his older brother, Edwin, early showed a lust for learning that the local Boys' High School nourished by the kind of curriculum described above. Edwin, the first to attend Columbia College, did well there and shared what he acquired. He would "assign" his course readings to Kip, so that when the younger brother entered the college as a freshman aged sixteen, he already had a command of English and American literature and a reading knowledge of French and German. No wonder that when I met him two years later, he impressed me and others of us as the bearer of all Western culture since the Greeks.

Being so young, he often felt scared (as he later confided), but

most of the time he was buoyant, full of humor, fond of puns —
anything but pedantic or solemnly learned, though he could be
impatient and abrupt with the slow-witted when they were stubborn. He rejoiced in how vast the universe of learning was; he read
with the speed of light and retained all that he ever set eyes on or
heard. Such is the typical tale in the social history of civilization.
The makers and carriers of art and thought come from nowhere in
particular; they are suddenly there. No social class, no "method,"
turns them out like marketable goods; but a fund of culture, plain
or subtle, simple or complex, must exist, alive in human beings, to
attract and impel other individuals.

While Fadiman was giving some of his time to radio programs,
he was also pursuing his Arnoldian mission, writing essays about
books and ideas that now fill half a dozen volumes. His introduc-
tions to classic and contemporary works number nearly fifty, some
of which, like the one to *The Pickwick Papers,* are small masterpieces. The anthologies he compiled number fifteen and range
from the stories of O. Henry to those of Henry James. One other,
An American Treasury, which brings together utterances of every
kind about America from colonial times to the present, is a highly
original sourcebook. Fadiman also kept the very young in mind.
He selected a dozen or more readings with comments for the use
of children, his expertise confirmed by his masterly monograph on
the history of children's literature in the fourteenth edition of the
Encyclopaedia Britannica. And for readers with a mathematical turn
of mind, he gathered two collections of articles, short stories, and
poems that display the curiosities of numbers.

What is sad to look back on is that Kip adopted for himself the
judgment passed on him by the highbrows. It was not explicit but
atmospheric. In conversation with close friends, literary or academic, who esteemed him highly, his one irritating trait was the re-
current depreciation of his work and his mind: "Of course I am not
qualified like you to speak on the subject," or, "I am only a rank
amateur in these things," when in fact he knew more on the topic
than any of his listeners. He was not ashamed but thought that he
ought to be. It is not far-fetched to say that feeling obliged to dis-
avow *height* is now a national habit. For example, *Time* magazine assures us that "high style isn't highbrow. In fact, it's everywhere, for
everyone, in everything from can openers to CD racks to cars"

(March 20, 2000). In vain did Arnold point out that "the social idea and the men of culture are the true apostles of equality."

The printed word did not monopolize Fadiman's multiform energies. He lectured on humanistic topics at colleges and universities, was roving reporter for the Metropolitan Opera and intermission speaker for the Boston Symphony. As consultant on the humanities for the Ford Foundation's Fund for the Advancement of Education and a trustee of the Council for Basic Education, Fadiman contributed to the "Back to Basics" reform of the schools. Robert Maynard Hutchins, when president of the University of Chicago, recognized the caliber and experience of the man when he appointed him to the editorial board of the *Encyclopaedia Britannica*. Fadiman served it as writer and editor for twenty years. His devotion to the life of the mind persisted until his death at ninety-five. Although blind toward the end, he continued to "read" by audiotape six books a month for the Book-of-the-Month Club, while he coedited a massive anthology of world poetry in English translation.

It is clear that if the hundredth part of this noble work had been done from some campus or other, Clifton Fadiman would have been regarded as a scholar and a teacher of the highest attainable brow. Put together, his lectures amounted to courses and his essays to scholarly criticism. The labor of it all was not entirely overlooked. He received several prizes, culminating in the 1993 National Book Award for Distinguished Contribution to American Letters. His obituaries were full of respect, but their tenor was that of one of the headlines: "An Erudite Guide to the Wisdom of Others." The judgment not only ignores the wisdom needed for unerring guidance; it perpetuates a false view of culture and how it is kept alive.

Right now, working to that end is out of the question. Those who still think that *something* ought to be imparted to the next generation are struggling to rescue the public schools. It is a national goal, a presidential priority, but achieving it is hindered by many things, of which one is the absence of a popular culture. For such a culture by definition lives both in the world and in the home, where it provides the young with a springboard into what is taught in school. Today, all agree that for a majority of children the gap between the domestic and the school mind is unbridgeable.

If the efforts to restore the effectiveness of the public school succeed, the battle will then be joined with the ruling caste in higher education, which is busy destroying the heritage of the Western world by teaching the young to find ugly motives behind its creation.

Meantime, a miscellaneous public rejoices in the thought that the Internet "puts the whole world of knowledge at your fingertips." A fair number of fingertips itch for that wealth and are gratified with information at low cost, even with misinformation. But the lust for knowing creates less demand in the digital bazaar than games and porn, while the available "art shows" arouse less envy than the noted dilettante's collection of bottle tops from 159 countries. In any case, "the world of knowledge" is not something in a warehouse. Knowledge lives by being known, not stored. Like religion, like a popular culture, it is a possession held in common as widely as possible. No layer of culture exists on that scale today, and nobody is preaching a revival of the midcentury crusade. As things stand, this is as it should be: first things first. We shall be fortunate if all the earnest agitation brings back to the people a common possession of the three R's.

RUDOLPH CHELMINSKI

Turning Point

FROM SMITHSONIAN

> What turned the tide of public regard [for the World Trade Center]
> was not the bigness of the place but the way it could be momentarily
> captured by fanciful gestures on a human scale. It was the French
> high-wire artist Philippe Petit crossing between the towers on a tight-
> rope in 1974 . . .
>
> — *New York Times,* September 13, 2001

WAS IT ONLY twenty-seven years ago? It seems a lifetime, or two,
has passed since that August morning in 1974 when Philippe Petit,
a slim, young Frenchman, upstaged Richard Nixon by performing
one of the few acts more sensational — in those faraway times —
than resigning the presidency of the United States.

A week before his twenty-sixth birthday, the nimble Petit clan-
destinely strung a cable between the not-yet-completed Twin Towers, already dominating lower Manhattan's skyline, and for the
better part of an hour walked back and forth over the void, demonstrating his astonishing obsession to one hundred thousand or so
wide-eyed gawkers gathered so far below.

I missed that performance, but last summer, just two weeks before the 1,360-foot-tall towers would come to symbolize a ghastly
new reality, I persuaded Petit to accompany me to the top and
show me how he did it and, perhaps, explain why. I was driven by a
long-standing curiosity. Ever since reading about his exploit in
New York, I had felt a kind of familiarity with this remarkable fellow. Years before, I had watched him at close range and much
lower altitude, in another city on the other side of the pond.

In the 1960s, the Montparnasse area of Paris was animated by a colorful fauna of celebrities, eccentrics, and artistic characters. On any given day, you might run into Giacometti walking bent forward like one of his skinny statues, Raymond Duncan (Isadora's brother) in his goofy sandals and Roman toga, or Jean-Paul Sartre morosely seeking the decline of capitalism in the Communist daily, *L'Humanité*. And after nightfall, if you hung around long enough, you were almost certain to see Philippe Petit.

When he might appear was anyone's guess, but his hangouts were pretty well known: the corner of Rue de Buci and Boulevard St. Germain; the sidewalk outside Les Deux Magots, or directly under the terrace windows of La Coupole. Silent and mysterious, this skinny, pasty-faced kid dressed in black would materialize unannounced on his unicycle, a shock of pale blond hair escaping from under a battered top hat. He would draw a circle of white chalk on the sidewalk, string a rope between two trees, hop up onto it, and, impassive and mute as a carp, go into an improvised show that combined mime, juggling, prestidigitation, and the precarious balancing act of loose-rope walking. After an hour or so he would pass the hat and, as wordlessly as he had arrived, disappear into the night.

Then, on a drizzly morning in June 1971, the kid in black suddenly showed up dancing on a barely perceptible wire between the massive towers of Notre Dame Cathedral. For nearly three hours, he walked back and forth, mugged, saluted, and juggled Indian clubs while angry gendarmes waited for him to come down. When he finally did, they arrested him for disturbing the peace.

Disturbing the peace was a good part of what it was all about, of course, because Petit was out to prove something. Notre Dame was his first great coup, the sensational stunt that was to become his trademark. It was also his first declaration of status: he was not a mere street entertainer but a performer, an artiste. Ever since that June morning, he has dedicated himself to demonstrating his passionate belief that the high wire — his approach to the high wire, that is — transcends the cheap hype of circus "daredevil" routines to become a creative statement of true theater, as valid as ballet or modern dance.

Getting that point across has never been easy. After gratifying Petit with a few front-page pictures, the French establishment gave a Gallic shrug, dismissed him as a youthful crank, and returned to more serious matters — like having lunch and talking politics. There was a very interesting story to be told about this young loner who had learned the art of the *funambule* (literally, "rope walker") all by himself as a teenager, but the Parisian press ignored it. Within a couple of days, his Notre Dame stunt was largely forgotten.

Stung, Petit resolved to take his art elsewhere and began a long vagabondage around the world, returning to Paris for brief spells before setting off again. Traveling as light as a medieval minstrel and living hand to mouth, he carried his mute personage from city to city, juggling for his supper. None of his onlookers could know that back in his tiny Parisian studio — a rented broom closet he had somehow converted into a dwelling — he had a folder marked "projects."

Two years after the Notre Dame caper, the skinny figure in black appeared with his balancing pole between the gigantic northern pylons of the Sydney Harbour Bridge in Australia. Petit had strung his cable there just as furtively as he had done at Notre Dame, but this time the police reacted with brainless if predictable fury, attempting to force him down by cutting one of his cavalettis, the lateral guy ropes that hold a sky walker's cable steady. Flung a foot up in the air when the cavaletti sprang free, Petit managed to land square on the cable and keep his balance. He came in and was manacled, led to court, and found guilty of the usual crimes. The owner of a Sydney circus offered to pay his $250 fine in return for a tightrope walk two days later over the lions' cage.

And then came the World Trade Center. Petit had been planning it ever since he was nineteen when, in a dentist's waiting room, he saw an article with an artist's rendering of the gigantic towers planned for New York's financial district. ("When I see three oranges I juggle," he once said, "and when I see two towers I walk.") He ripped the article from the magazine and slipped it into his projects file.

The World Trade Center would be the ultimate test of Petit's fanatically meticulous planning. For Notre Dame and Sydney, he had copied keys to open certain locks, picked others, and hacksawed his way through still others in order to sneak his heavy material up into place for the sky walk. But New York presented a much more complicated challenge. The World Trade Center buildings were fearfully higher than anything he had ever tackled, making it impossible to set up conventional cavalettis. And how to get a cable across the 140-foot gap between the South and North Towers, anyway, in the face of omnipresent security crews? There was one factor in Petit's favor: the buildings were still in the final stages of construction, and trucks were regularly delivering all sorts of material to the basement docks, to be transferred to a freight elevator and brought up to the floors by workers of all descriptions. Wearing hard hats, Petit and an accomplice hauled his gear to the top of the South Tower (his walking cable passed off as antenna equipment) while two other friends similarly made their way to the roof of the North Tower, armed with a bow and arrow and a spool of stout fishing line. Come nightfall, they shot the arrow and line across the 140-foot gap between the towers. Petit retrieved the line, pulled it over until he was in possession of the stronger nylon cord attached to it, then tied on the heavy rope that would be used to carry his steel walking cable over to the other side.

As Petit paid out the rope and then the cable, gravity took over. The cable ran wild, shooting uncontrollably through his hands and snaking down the side of the giant building before coming up short with a titanic *thwonk!* at the steel beam to which Petit had anchored it. On the North Tower, holding fast to the other end of the heavy rope, his friends were pulled perilously close to the roof's edge. Gradually, the four regained control and spent the rest of the night hours pulling the cable up, double-cinching the anchor points, getting it nearly level, tensioning it to three tons with a ratchet, and finally attaching a set of nearly horizontal cavalettis to the buildings. At a few minutes past seven A.M., August 7, 1974, just as the first construction workers were arriving on the rooftop, Petit seized his balancing pole and stepped out over the void.

The conditions weren't exactly ideal. Petit had not slept for forty-eight hours, and now he saw that the hurry-up rigging job he had carried out in the dark had resulted in a cable that zigzagged where the improvised cavalettis joined it. Sensitive to wind, temperature, and any sway of the buildings, it was also alive — swooping, rolling, and twisting. At slightly more than twenty-six feet, his balancing pole was longer and heavier — fifty-five pounds — than any he had ever used before. Greater weight meant greater stability, but such a heavy load is hard enough to tote around on terra firma, let alone on a thin wire in midair at an insane altitude. It would require an uncommon debauch of nervous energy, but energy was the one thing Petit had plenty of.

With his eyes riveted to the edge of the far tower — wire walkers aren't supposed to look down — Petit glided his buffalo-hide slippers along the cable, feeling his way until he was halfway across. He knelt, put his weight on one knee, and swung his right arm free. This was his "salute," the signature gesture of the high-wire artist. Each has his own, and each is an individual trademark creation. Arising, he continued to the North Tower, hopped off the wire, double-checked the cable's anchoring points, made a few adjustments, and hopped back on.

By now traffic had stopped in the environs of Wall Street, and Petit could already hear the first police and ambulance sirens as he nimbly set forth again. Off he went, humming and mumbling to himself, puffing grunts of concentration at tricky moments. Halfway across, he steadied, halted, then knelt again. And then, God in heaven, he lay down, placing his spine directly atop the cable and resting the balancing pole on his stomach. Breathless, in Zen-like calm, he lay there for a long moment, contemplating the red-eyed seabird hovering motionless above him.

Time to get up. But how do you do it, I asked Petit as we stood together on the roof of the South Tower, when the only thing between you and certain death is a cable under your body and fifty-five extra pounds lying on your belly?

"All the weight on the right foot," he replied with a shrug. "I draw my right foot back along the cable and move the balancing bar lower down below my belt. I get a little lift from the wire, because it is moving up and down. Then I do a sit-up and rise to a standing position, with all the weight on my right foot. It takes some practice."

He got up. Unable to resist the pleasure of seeing New York at his feet, he caressed the side of the building with a glance and slowly panned his eyes all the way down to the gridlocked traffic below. Then he flowed back to the South Tower. "I could hear the horns of cars below me," he recalled, relishing the memory. "I could hear the applause too. The *rumeur* [clamor] of the crowd rose up to me from four hundred meters below. No other show person has ever heard a sound like that."

Now, as he glided along north to south, a clutch of police of-

ficers, rescue crews, and security men hovered with arms outstretched to pull him in. But Petit hadn't finished. Inches from
their grasp, he did a wire walker's turnaround, slipping his feet
180 degrees and swinging his balancing bar around to face in the
other direction. He did his elegant "torero's" walk and his "prome-
nader's" walk; he knelt; he did another salute; he sat in casual repose, lord of his domain; he stood and balanced on one foot.

After seven crossings and forty-five minutes of air dancing, it began to rain. For his finale he ran along the cable to give himself up.
"Running, ah! ah!" he had written in one of his early books.
"That's the laughter of the wire walker." Then he ran into the arms
of waiting police.

Petit's astonishing star turn created a sensation the likes of
which few New Yorkers had ever seen. Years later, the art critic Cal-
vin Tompkins was still so impressed by what Petit had done that he
wrote in *The New Yorker:* "He achieved the almost unimaginable feat
of investing the World Trade Center . . . with a thrilling and terrible beauty."

Ever resourceful, Petit worked out a deal with the Manhattan district attorney. In lieu of punishment or fine, and as penance for his
artistic crime, he agreed to give a free performance in Central
Park. The following week he strung a 600-foot wire across Turtle
Pond, from a tree on one side to Belvedere Castle on the other.
And this time he nearly fell. He was wearing the same walking slippers and using the same balancing pole, but security was relaxed
among the fifteen thousand people who had come to watch him
perform, and kids began climbing and jumping on his cavalettis.
The wire twitched, and suddenly he felt himself going beyond the
point of return.

But he didn't go all the way down. Instinctively squirming as he
dropped, he hooked a leg over the wire. Somehow, he managed to
swing himself back up, get vertical, and carry on with the performance. The crowd applauded warmly, assuming it was all part of
the act, but Petit doesn't enjoy the memory. Falling is the wire
walker's shame, he says, and due only to a lack of concentration.

In the years since his World Trade Center triumph, Petit has dis-
dainfully turned away all offers to profit from it. "I could have become a millionaire," he told me. "Everyone was after me to endorse their products, but I was not going to walk a wire dressed in a

hamburger suit, and I was not going to say I succeeded because I was wearing such and such a shirt. " Continuing to operate as a stubbornly independent freelance artist, he has organized and starred in more than seventy performances around the world, all without safety nets. They have included choreographed strolls across the Louisiana Superdome in New Orleans, between the towers of the Laon Cathedral in France, and a "Peace Walk" between the Jewish and Arab quarters of Jerusalem. In 1989, on the bicentennial of the French Revolution, he took center stage in Paris — legally and officially this time — by walking the 2,300-foot gap between the Trocadéro esplanade on the Right Bank, over the Seine, and up to the second tier of the Eiffel Tower.

Today, at fifty-two, Petit is somewhat heavier than in his busking days in Paris, and his hair has turned a reddish blond, but neither his energy nor his overpowering self-confidence has waned in the least. He shares a pleasantly rustic farmhouse at the edge of the Catskills near Woodstock, New York, with his longtime companion, Kathy O'Donnell, daughter of a former Manhattan publishing executive. She handles the planning, producing, problem-solving, and money-raising aspects of Petit's enterprises while they both think up new high-wire projects and he painstakingly prepares them. Petit supplements his income from performances with, among other things, book royalties and fees from giving lectures and workshops.

His preferred place of study is his New York City office. Knowing what an artiste he is, you would not expect to find him in an ordinary building, and you would be right. Petit hangs out at the Cathedral of St. John the Divine, the world's biggest Gothic cathedral, at Amsterdam Avenue and 112th Street. His office is a balustraded aerie in the cathedral's triforium, the narrow gallery high above the vast nave. Behind a locked entryway, up a suitably medieval spiral staircase and then down a stone passageway, the rare visitor to his domain comes upon a sturdy door bearing a small framed sign: *Philippe Petit, Artist in Residence.* Behind that door, stowed as neatly as a yacht's navigational gear, lie his treasures: thousands of feet of rope coiled just so, all manner of rigging and tensioning equipment, floor-to-ceiling archives, maps and models of past and future walk projects, and shelves upon shelves of technical and reference books.

It was another of his coups that got him there. In 1980 he offered to walk the length of the nave to raise funds for the cathedral's building program. He was sure he had the perfect occasion for it: Ascension Day. The cathedral's then dean, the ebullient James Parks Morton, famous for his support of the arts, was enthusiastic, but his board of trustees vetoed the idea as too dangerous. Petit sneaked a cable crosswise over the nave and did his walk anyway. Once again the police came to arrest him, but Morton spoiled their day by announcing that Petit was artist in residence and the cathedral was his workplace. And so he came to be.

Over the years, taking his title seriously, Petit reciprocated by carrying out a dozen wire walks inside and outside the cathedral. He figures that by now he has raised half a million dollars for the still uncompleted cathedral's building program, and enjoys pointing out the small stone carving of a wire walker niched in among the saints in the main portal. "It is high art," Morton says of Petit's work. "There is a documented history of wire walkers in cathedrals and churches. It's not a new idea, but his walk here was his first in an American cathedral."

Sometimes after six P.M., when the lights go out, the big front door slams shut, and the cathedral closes down for the night, Petit is left alone in the mineral gloom of St. John with his writing, sketches, calculations, chess problems, poetry, and reveries. The comparison to Quasimodo is immediate and obvious, of course, but unlike Notre Dame's famous hunchback, Petit wants nothing more than to be seen, in the ever greater, more ambitious, and spectacular shows that fill his dreams. One night after he took me up to his cathedral office, he gazed longingly at a print of the Brooklyn Bridge — what a walk that could be! But there is, he assured me, plenty more in his projects file. A walk on Easter Island, from the famous carved heads to the volcano. Or the half-mile stretch over open water between the Sydney Harbour Bridge and the celebrated Opera House.

Even more than all these, though, there is one walk — *the* walk, the ultimate, the masterpiece — that has filled his dreams for more than a decade. It's the Grand Canyon. Prospecting in the heart of the Navajo nation by air in 1988, Petit discovered the ideal spot for crowning his career: a ruggedly beautiful landscape off the road from Flagstaff to Grand Canyon Village, where a noble mesa soars at the far end of a 1,200-foot gap from the canyon's edge. The gap is deeper than it is wide, 1,600 feet straight down to the Little Colorado River.

Petit's eyes glowed as he went through the mass of blueprints, maps, drawings, and models he has produced over all the years of planning the Canyon Walk. Only one thing is missing: money. Twice now, the money people have backed out at the last minute.

But none of that seemed to matter when I spoke to Petit a few days after the September 11 catastrophe struck. He could scarcely find words for his sorrow at the loss of so many lives, among them people he knew well — elevator operators, tour guides, maintenance workers. "I feel my house has been destroyed," he said. "Very often I would take family and friends there. It was my pride as a poet and a lover of beautiful things to show as many people as possible the audacity of those impossible monoliths."

Haunted, as we all are, by the images of the towers in their final moments, Petit told me it was his hope that they would be remembered not as they appeared then but as they were on that magical August day more than a generation ago, when he danced between them on a wire and made an entire city look up in awe. "In a very small way I helped frame them with glory," he said, "and I want to remember them in their glory."

BERNARD COOPER

Winner Take Nothing

FROM GQ

WHEN I received word informing me I'd won the PEN/Ernest Hemingway Award for my first book, I held the letter in trembling hands while the following thoughts, in precisely this order, shot through my head:

I won the Ernest Hemingway Award!

I don't deserve it.

My father has heard of Ernest Hemingway!

There I stood, elated by a last-ditch chance to impress my dad.

Not that my father disapproved of my being a writer; he understood it to the extent that he could understand my gambling with my life in order to pursue a profession he found frivolous and fiscally unsound. Whenever I mentioned to him that I'd had something published in a magazine or literary journal, the first question he'd ask was "How much they pay you?" A retired attorney, he probably thought of "they" as a faceless jury, twelve arbiters of taste. He'd pose this question with considerable enthusiasm, arching his white eyebrows, his face a picture of impending pride. Imagine telling a man who keeps a wad of twenties in a gold money clip shaped like a dollar sign that, after working on a piece of writing for months, you've been compensated with a complimentary copy of the publication. "You're kidding," he'd say, shaking his head as if I'd told him I'd been duped in a shell game.

Over the years, I'd cultivated a certain temperance when sharing literary news with my father: I'd come to consider it unfortunate but not devastating that he was unable to recognize the arc — or was it the bump? — of my career. Still, I ached to have him slap me on the back, wanted to hear his unstinting praise and in it the honeyed pronouncement: son.

To this end, I once gave him an essay of mine to read. It was a brief reminiscence about my mother, who, up until her death, dreamed of writing a book into which she'd cram every anecdote she could think of, starting with her emigration from Russia to the United States at the age of two. She never wrote so much as a word, but the persistence of her wish struck me as oddly noble, and the tone of the piece was, I believed, unmistakably fond. And so, one night at the Brass Pan, the restaurant where my father and I occasionally met for dinner, I handed him the pages, neatly stapled. Before I let go of the manuscript (feeling him tug it from across the table was the closest I'd come to his tangible enthusiasm), I told him I hoped he'd enjoy reading it.

Days went by. Weeks. Months. For nearly half a year, in all the times we saw each other or spoke on the phone, he never mentioned the essay, and pride prevented me from coming right out and asking whether he'd read it. If it hadn't been for a chokingly potent vodka tonic I drank during one of our dinners, I might not have asked him to this day.

"Dad, you've never mentioned the essay I wrote about Mom."

"Well," sighed my father, shrugging his shoulders. "What can I tell you? You wrote down your opinion."

In the dim light of the restaurant, he looked anything but adversarial, his brown eyes peering at me over the rim of his bifocals. I took another swig of vodka. My father, I had to admit, had managed perfectly well without literature, and I had no illusions that writing, especially mine, could enrich his life. At eighty-six he chiefly read *TV Guide*, a map by which he navigated nights in front of the Sony console, its huge screen the only source of light. He also subscribed to *Consumer Reports*, but largely, I think, to sustain through retirement the image he had of himself as a citizen with buying power. The issues were stacked on a shelf next to his law books — and a yellowing paperback copy of *The Snows of Kilimanjaro*.

My father wasn't the first person I called with news of the award, but when I dialed his number and invoked the name of Hemingway, his "Oh!" was as round and buoyant as a bubble. For a moment, I thought the elusive approval I'd wanted might be close at hand, compensation for his years of disinterest in my work. In much of that work, I'd tried to capture the moodiness with which he'd presided over my childhood: a C on my report card, say, could meet with his indifference or detonate his rage. One never knew what familial infraction or offhand remark might cause him to suddenly leave the room and brood for hours. He was also capable of lavish generosity and bursts of goofy humor, and whenever these traits prevailed, I finally felt at peace with a man whose livelihood was, as he liked to put it, suing the pants off people.

"Listen," he said, "we'll fly to New York for the award ceremony, share a room and take in some Broadway shows." I was stunned by his offer, and more than a little touched. Since he had no compunction about expressing bemusement at my small successes, it never occurred to me that he might need to take an active part in my large ones.

I told my father that nothing could make me happier than knowing he was proud of me, and terrific as a trip with him sounded, I wouldn't have time to go to Broadway shows or give him the attention he deserved. Besides, I'd already made plans to go with Brian, the man I'd lived with for many years, our hotel and flight already booked. I offered to take my father to the Brass Pan so we could celebrate properly, and suggested the three of us take a vacation together another time, when I could relax and we could really enjoy ourselves. "I hope you understand," I said.

After I stopped talking, I gave my little speech high marks; it had been, I thought, a good mixture of respect and autonomy. But the longer he remained silent, the more aware I became of the telephone's static, a sound growing vast, oceanic. "Dad?"

"Fine," he said. "If that's what you want."

The plane flight, as always, made me claustrophobic. But when panic finally gave way to the Valium I'd taken twenty minutes before takeoff, my hands and feet grew rubbery, the view of earth abstract.

Once inside the terminal at JFK, the firm ground acted as a conduit, diffusing fear. At the baggage claim, watching luggage spill onto the carousel, it finally dawned on me that I had survived the flight to receive an award. Sunlight burned through a bank of windows. People swarmed toward a fleet of cabs and were whisked away to meetings and reunions. Possibility charged the air, dense, electric. In my happiness, I turned to Brian and faced my father.

At first I thought I might be drugged or dreaming, though by then, only the mildest trace of Valium remained in my system. I looked at him and couldn't speak, the entire busy terminal contracting to a point the size of his face. Was he omnipresent like Santa Claus or God? Dad looked back and blithely smiled.

"Surprise," he said.

"How . . . ?" I sputtered.

"Your plane. I went first class."

Suddenly, I understood that all the questions he'd asked about the details of my trip — time of departure, name of the airline — questions I'd interpreted as paternal concern, were part of a perfectly executed plan.

Brian, who at first had been as incredulous as I, rushed in to fill the conspicuous silence. He shook my father's hand. "Are you staying at our hotel?" he asked.

I recalled with a start that we'd booked a room at a gay hotel. "I'm at the Warwick," said my father. "Quite a fancy place, according to the Automobile Club." Two familiar carryalls were making aimless circles in the periphery of my vision, and before I knew what I was doing, I yanked them off the carousel. Vacillating between guilt and fury, I felt like a small unstable electron. "We're leaving," I announced. I fled toward the taxi stand, leaving Brian no choice but to dash after me.

"Share a ride?" my father shouted. I didn't look back.

Once we settled into our hotel room, I began to worry that I'd acted rashly. Had I been a different person, I might have poked my father in the ribs and teased him for being a stubborn coot. But to be a different person I would have to have been raised by a different dad. Mine was an old Jewish genie who materialized wherever he willed and granted any wish — as long as it was his.

When I called the Warwick, my father answered on the second ring. "We'd better have a talk," I said.

"It's your dime."

"I thought you understood I wanted to do this on my own."

"Fine. I'll pack my goddamn bags and go home."

"No. I want you to stay now that you're here. I'm just trying to explain why I reacted the way I did at the airport."

"Now you explained it. Is that what you wanted to talk about?" There had to be more. During the cab ride, I'd rehearsed ways to tell him that his surprise was an intrusion disguised as kindness, a success usurped. But now I couldn't recall what I'd wanted to say or understand why we each found it so important to win the other's capitulation.

"We'll have lunch tomorrow," he said.

The dining room at the Warwick, with its ambient chimes of silverware and ice, offered a quiet retreat from the city. My father looked small and harmless as he sat waiting for us at a table. He peered around the spacious room, bifocals flashing, hands folded before him in a boyish pose, almost contrite. As Brian and I walked toward the table, it struck me that my father was not at all the giant of the nursery I was prone to imagine; when I didn't have the actual man before me, he ballooned into myth.

A somewhat leery conviviality arose as we sat down.

"So, Mr. Cooper," asked Brian, "what have you been doing?"

My father toyed with the silverware. "Nothing much. I watched a little TV."

"What did you watch, Dad?"

"How about that. I can't remember."

Brian and I looked at each other.

"Is there anybody you know in New York you could go to dinner with tonight?" Please, I prayed.

"I got relatives in Jersey. Or used to twenty years ago. I should look them up next time I'm here." His hearing aid squealed with feedback, and he fiddled with its tiny dial.

"The thing is, Dad, we can't go to dinner with you tonight."

"I know," he said curtly. "You're very busy."

The maître d' brought us huge glossy menus, the covers printed to look like marble. I opened mine, expecting an engraving of the Ten Commandments: Thou shalt honor thy father, who gazeth at the entrées. Without lifting his eyes from the menu, he waved his hand in a gesture of largesse. "Get whatever you want. Sky's the limit."

*

The next day, I added an additional paragraph to my acceptance speech. In it I thanked my father for reading me stories as a child. His rapt voice had transported me, I wrote, and his enthusiasm for telling tales had introduced me to the power of language. I wasn't certain whether my father had, in fact, read me stories as a child, but neither he nor I would object to the sentimental prospect. Collusion, after all, would be a kind of bond.

At the ceremony that evening, half a dozen awards were handed out. Almost every author who received one had written a speech identical to mine, a sort of apologia in which they expressed surprise at having won and either implied or insisted they were undeserving. The motif of modesty had been exhausted by the time I walked up to the podium, but I'd already revised my speech that morning and was too nervous to change it again. When I came to the part about my father, I looked up from the wrinkled sheet of paper, eager to find him and make eye contact, but I had to look back quickly for fear of losing my place. The paragraph I'd added struck me as a little schmaltzy, and I worried that my apparent sentimentality would discourage people in the audience from buying my book. In the end, it didn't really matter; my homage was meant for Dad's ears alone, and reading it aloud righted the night.

Or so I thought. Immediately after the ceremony, I found my father milling in the crowd and raced up to ask him how he'd liked my speech. "Couldn't hear a damn thing," he said, chuckling at his rotten luck. His hearing aid, unable to distinguish between foreground and background noises, had amplified both. From the rear of the auditorium, my dad could see me reading in the distance, but he heard ubiquitous coughs and whispers, crackling leather coats, the rubbery acoustics of someone chewing gum.

In the year that followed, I began to publish essays and memoirs in a few well-paying magazines. My income was still meager by any standard except my own, but at last I could speak my father's language, a lexicon of hard cold cash.

By that time, however, it had become difficult for him to react to news of my solvency with anything but the foggiest acknowledgment. At the mention of money, he'd look at me wistfully, nod his head, then look away. My father was going broke from the lawsuits he'd recently filed against neighbors and in-laws and strangers.

Vines and retaining walls trespassed his property. A relative missed a payment on a loan. An uninsured idiot dented his fender. Someone blundered, someone would pay, someone would rue the day he was born. He represented himself in court and lost each case. The judges were corrupt, he'd claim, his witnesses inarticulate. Defeat never seemed to give him pause or lessen his zeal for prosecution.

Dad remained fairly amiable during our dinners, and I found it flattering to be one of the few people in his life exempt from litigation. Some nights, when the waitress at the Brass Pan asked for his order, my father stiffened and eyed her with suspicion, tense as a man being cross-examined. She'd hover above him, pencil poised, while he blinked and slowly returned to his senses, finally lifting his tremulous hand and pointing to an entrée on the menu. His decline was apparent in visit after visit. Time took a belated toll, as though weariness had waited until now to irrevocably claim his face; his eyes were puzzled, hair unkempt, chin bristling with patches of stubble.

Eventually, he grew too distracted by his legal battles to return my phone calls. On the rare occasions when we spoke, he said he was too busy to meet me for dinner. More often than not, the answering machine picked up after several rings and played its unassailable refrain: I am not at home at this present time.

After months of an elusiveness he couldn't be coaxed out of, I drove over to my father's house one afternoon to ask why he hadn't returned my calls. Dad answered the door of his Spanish-style house, blinking, beleaguered, but glad to see me. At my insistence, we sat in the dining room to talk. Briefs and appeals and depositions were scattered across the mahogany table, his makeshift desk. Pencils and paper napkins saved his place in the law books he hadn't opened for years, piled now in precarious stacks.

"Are you sure you're not angry at me about something?" I asked. "Because if you are . . ."

My father laughed, fiddled with his hearing aid. "What makes you think I'm angry?"

"You're so . . . unavailable these days."

"How many times do I have to tell you? I'm busy. Swamped. Do you need me to spell it out for you?" He rose to his feet, and I thought he might start to sound out the letters. "You have no idea. No goddamn concept."

I stood too, trying to rise above the childlike vantage point that came with being seated. "All I'm saying is that you have to eat dinner anyway, and we might as well . . ."

"Who says?"

"What?"

"Who says I have to eat dinner? Where is it written? Is it written here?" He hefted a law book and let it slam back onto the table. Stray papers jumped and fluttered. I made a move to calm him down, but he began to prowl around the table, stirring up the sunlit dust. "Don't you ever tell me what to do!"

"Having dinner is not something to do! I mean, it is something to do, but I'm not telling you to do it." At a loss for logic, I was barking back.

"Don't you raise your voice at me!" He rushed up and grabbed the back of my shirt, a hank of fabric twisted in his grip. "I'm eighty-six years old," he shouted. "I'm an old man, and I can do whatever the hell I want whenever the hell I want." He pushed me toward the door, breathing hard, his face red and alien with effort.

"Dad?"

"That's right," he said. When he opened the door, the daylight was blinding. "Don't ever forget that I'm your father. Now get the hell out and don't come back."

Since high school, I've been both taller and stronger than my father, but just as we reached the threshold of the door it occurred to me that I might flatter him into relenting if I let my body be heaved outside as though from an admirable, manly force. Instead of resisting or fighting back, I yielded to his elderly arms.

Acquiescence didn't help. Before the door slammed shut behind me, I turned and glimpsed his indignant figure retreating within my childhood house. The door hit the jamb with a deafening bang, the birds falling silent for half a second before going back to their usual racket.

Daily I relived the particulars: the shirt taut across my chest, the heat of his breath on the back of my neck, the flood of light as the door swung wide. The sheer abruptness and implausibility of what had happened made me worry that perhaps I'd said something inadvertently thoughtless or cruel — a spark to his incendiary temper.

In lieu of an explanation, I started making hypothetical changes in the story. Suppose I hadn't mentioned dinner. Suppose I hadn't raised my voice. Suppose we'd stood instead of sat. Say the day had been cooler, the hour later, the dust motes churning in another direction. Would the outcome of my visit have been any different?

Several nights a week, I had to drive past my boyhood house on the way home from teaching, and the closer I came, the greater its magnetic pull. More than once, I turned the steering wheel at the last minute, aiming my car through a tunnel of trees and parking across the street from his house. The urge to spy on my father was unexplainable, as deep and murky as the darkness it required.

Throughout the first year of our estrangement, my entreaties and apologies and furious demands for contact were recited into his answering machine. On a few occasions, he picked up the phone and then slammed it down at the sound of my voice.

By the second year, resignation took hold. I'd lost the desire to drive by his house or reach him by phone. I recalled that afternoon less often, and when I did, I refused to probe the memory for meaning.

By the third year, his absence settled inside me like a stone, impervious to hope or hurt.

"I realize this phone call must come as an unpleasant surprise," the social worker told me. "But I believe your father's deterioration is significant enough to make legal guardianship a necessary step."

Mr. Gomez assured me that I didn't have to make up my mind right away; it would be several months before the case came before a judge. An anonymous caller had phoned Adult Protective Services to say my father needed help. If I assumed responsibility, my father's Social Security checks would be placed in a trust, and he'd need my permission for every expenditure: medicine, groceries, clothes.

"Careful monetary management is especially crucial in your father's case," said Mr. Gomez. "As you may know, the bank has begun foreclosure on his house."

"I had no idea."

Mr. Gomez cleared his throat. "On a positive note, I should also tell you that your father spoke with great pride about your many accomplishments. What's the name of the book you wrote? He couldn't remember."

I mumbled the title to Mr. Gomez, promised to give our discussion some thought, and said goodbye. I'd become so guarded against any emotion having to do with my father that the prospect of seeing him again roused only a dull ambivalence. After three years, I'd finally decided it was I who didn't want contact with him, a decision that redefined circumstance and made my exile bearable. And now, out of the blue, the county urged a reunion, reminding me (as if I needed to be reminded) that the man was my inescapable relation.

I'd been writing when the phone rang.

"Bernard?"

"Dad?" Saying the word made my mouth go dry.

"I sold the house, and the people who bought it want to move in pretty soon, so I've been cleaning out closets, and I came across all sorts of drawings and photos of yours. You wanna come get them? Is four-thirty good?"

"Four-thirty's good." My assent was automatic, though I wasn't sure I was ready to see him.

"OK. See you later."

"Wait," I blurted. "How have you been?"

"Fine. And you?"

Three years. "I'm fine too."

"Good," he said. "As long as you're fine." His harried voice softened. "Well," he said, "I'm really swamped."

After I'd hung up the phone, I realized he hadn't said hello.

I approached the house with apprehension; who knew what condition I'd find him in? His Cadillac sat in the driveway, dented and missing strips of chrome. Since I'd last spied on the house two years ago, the first-floor windows had been covered with bars. The front door stood behind a wrought-iron grate, and no matter how decorative its design, it made the house look forbidding, aloof.

No sooner had I rung the doorbell than my father appeared behind the bars, jangling keys like a castle keep. All the while, he burbled greetings in the high-pitched voice of his jovial persona. Arms folded across my chest, I couldn't act as if things had been normal, not without damaging a sense of reality that, especially in my father's presence, could founder and bend like a little boy's. "Come on in," he said, unlocking the grate. I found his hospitality suspicious, and much as I wanted to make amends, I also wanted to run the other way. I'd come to think of my boyhood house as a place I'd never visit again, and now that I stood on the verge of return, I practically had to astral-project and give myself a push from behind.

The house was even more crammed with memorabilia than I remembered. He must have strewn souvenirs about the rooms as he cleaned out the closets, a last-minute effort to make his mark on the home he had to forfeit. A velvet painting of JFK hung above the fireplace. A birdcage he'd won on a cruise contained a windup canary whose jerky movements and monotonous song he insisted on demonstrating as soon as I walked in the door. In a sign of either delight or dementia, he watched it warble with childlike glee.

Piled on the coffee table, old boxes contained the egg-tempera paintings I'd done in elementary school, the colors still vibrant though the paint had turned as powdery as talcum. Crude landscapes and blotchy figures called back the distant triumph of being able to shape the world and contain it on a piece of paper. Pictures from photo booths showed a mugging ten-year-old who bore as much resemblance to me now as I to my father; I wanted to warn that oblivious boy of what was to come. I couldn't look at the stuff for long, and I gathered up the boxes, ready to go.

"Sit," said my father. I did.

"What's new?"

"Lots."

"Written any more books of yours?"

"Yes."

"Have they won those Hemingway awards?"

"That's only for a first book."

"I see," he said. "Tell me what else has been going on." He leaned forward in the chair, cocked his good ear in my direction.

"Look, I appreciate your willingness to get together with me, but I think I deserve to know why you haven't spoken to me in three years."

His brows furrowed in puzzlement. "You live, things happen, you go on. That's the way it works."

"That's not the way it works for me."

"Well, the truth of the matter is that you were getting irritated with me about my hearing aid. You were always screaming, 'What? What? I can't hear you! Turn up your damn ear!'"

"First of all, Dad, *you're* the one who shouts 'What? I can't hear you.' Second, I'd never scold you because you're hard of hearing."

"I'm telling you, that's what happened."

"It didn't."

"Did."

"OK. Suppose it did. Is that any reason not to speak to me for three years?"

My father sat back, stared into space, gave the question due consideration. "Yes," he said, lurching forward. "Yes, it is." He looked at his feet, then back at me. "I've lived in this house for fifty years. Do you remember when we moved in?"

"I wasn't born yet."

"Do you remember what day it was?"

It seemed pointless to repeat myself. "Tuesday?" I guessed.

"No," he said. "It was your mother's birthday. Boy, that was a long time ago. I sold the place to two very nice guys. By the way, how's that friend of yours, what's his name?"

"Brian's fine, he . . ."

"What do I need all these rooms for, anyway? It was either sell the house or get kicked out on the street."

I shook my head in commiseration, pretending to know nothing about the foreclosure.

"Some crazy social worker said I shouldn't handle the sale myself. But I showed him. Closed escrow on my own, then told Hernandez to take a hike."

I stopped myself from blurting "Gomez."

"The kicker," he continued, "is that I paid someone to report me to the guy in the first place."

"What!"

"See," said my father. "You do shout 'What.'" He bristled a moment, shifted in his seat. "It was the only way to save myself. If they said I was soft in the head, the bank couldn't foreclose."

"Did you know that Gomez called me?"

"I figured he might." My father sighed. "I got a pretty penny for the place, but I owe a lot, too. There are liens and things. A second mortgage. I'm looking at a mobile home in Oxnard. Not the best,

but it's what I can afford. And it almost looks like a regular house.
You'll come up and visit." He stared at me a moment. "You sure
have grown since the last time I saw you."

"Dad, I've been this tall since high school."

"Taller than me?"

"For years," I said.

He shrugged his shoulders. "Then I guess I'm shrinking."

After loading the boxes into my car, I came back inside the kitchen
to say goodbye. "I have something for you," my father said. He
beamed at me and stepped aside. Atop the counter, a pink bakery
box yawned open to reveal an enormous cake, its circumference
studded with ripe strawberries. Slivered almonds, toasted gold, had
been evenly pressed into a mortar of thick white frosting, every
spare surface dotted with florets. In the center was written, in
goopy blue script, *Papa Loves Bernard.* For a second, I thought
there'd been some mistake. I'd never called my father Papa. Dad,
yes. Pop, perhaps. The nickname didn't mesh with the life I knew.
If the years of silence between us had an inverse, that cloying, lay-
ered cake was it.

My father had begun yanking open drawers and kitchen cabinets, offering me anything that might not fit into his new trailer,
which was just about most of what he owned: a punch-bowl set,
napkin rings — artifacts from his life with my mother, a life of
friends and fancy repasts. His barrage of offers was frenzied, desperate. All the while, I politely declined. "This is more than
enough," I said, gazing at the cake. I knew a bite would be dense
with sugar, a spongy glut. Yet it looked delectable sitting in his
kitchen, Betty Crocker's Sunday bonnet. While my father jetti-
soned old possessions, I swiped a finger across the frosting and debated whether to taste it.

NICHOLAS DELBANCO

The Countess of Stanlein Restored

FROM HARPER'S MAGAZINE

ON SEPTEMBER 22, 1998, the cellist Bernard Greenhouse
drove from his home in Massachusetts the five hours to Manhattan. On the car's rear seat reposed his prized possession, named in
honor of two of its previous owners: the Countess of Stanlein, *ex.*
Paganini Stradivarius violoncello of 1707. Strapped down and secure in its carrying case, the instrument traveled wherever Greenhouse went, and it had done so for years. This afternoon, however,
he was planning to realize a long-deterred dream and deposit the
"Strad" in New York.

It did require work. There were nicks and scratches scattered on
the surface, front and back. The varnish had darkened in spots; in
others the varnish had thinned. Some previous patches needed retouching; in places the edging had cracked. The glue by the sound
post — an old repair — leaked. Decades of pressure on the neck,
and from the downward force of the bridge feet beneath the taut-
stretched strings, had forced the f-holes into less than perfect sym-
metry; the ribs would need to be adjusted and the front plate
aligned.

Not all of this was visible, and only the discerning eye would notice or, noticing, object. The instrument had long been famous for
both its beauty and its tone. But Greenhouse is a perfectionist, and
previous repairs had been stopgap and partial, in the service of
utility. At the height of his career he performed — with the Bach
Aria Group, as a founding member of the Beaux Arts Trio, as a so-

loist, and on recordings — nearly two hundred times per year. From continent to continent, in all sorts of weather and playing conditions, the Countess of Stanlein had been his companion; he had carried her on boats and planes, in rented cars and taxicabs and trains, and always in a rush.

Now the career was winding down. No longer appearing routinely in concert, he owned several other instruments to practice on at home. At eighty-two, the cellist had the money and unscheduled time and the desire to "give back," as he put it, "something of value" to the world of music that had given him so much. This was to be, he reasoned, both a good deed and an investment. He knew just the man to do the job — René Morel, on West Fifty-fourth Street — and the work had been agreed upon and delivery date arranged.

Greenhouse had been a student of the late Pablo Casals. After the Second World War he traveled to Prades, in the French Pyrenees, where the Catalan cellist lived in retirement. As a protest against Generalísimo Franco, Casals accepted no public engagements but continued, in private, to work at his art; there, in the church of Saint-Michel de Cuxa, he recorded the six Unaccompanied Suites for Violoncello by Johann Sebastian Bach. There too, in 1946, he took on the young American as, in effect, an apprentice. More than a half century later, that audition stays vivid for Greenhouse:

"He started asking for the repertoire, and he requested many pieces. After an hour or more of my playing — during which he indicated nothing more than the piece and the passage he wanted me to play — he said, 'All right. Put down your cello, put it away, and we'll talk.' He said to me, 'Well, what you need is an apprenticeship to a great artist. I believe in the apprentice system. Stradivari, Guarneri, Amati: they turned out so many wonderful violin makers. And I believe the same thing can hold true in making musicians. If I knew of a great artist I could send you to, I would do so,' he said, 'because my mind is very much occupied with the Spanish Republican cause. But since I don't know whom to send you to — and if you agree to stay in the village and take a lesson at least once every two days — I will teach you.'"

Such a system of tutelage remains in place today: implicit in the idea of "master classes" and explicit in the trade of the luthier. This is a generic term for those who make and repair bowed stringed instruments, and the enterprise feels nearly medieval in its hierarchy of apprentice, journeyman laborer, master craftsman. Young men still clean the varnish rags or sweep wood shavings from the floor as did their predecessors centuries ago, and under much the same close, watchful supervision. Bernard Greenhouse met René Morel in the early 1950s, when the luthier was working for the legendary Fernando Sacconi in the New York shop of Rembert Wurlitzer; he commended the Frenchman thereafter to the dealer Jacques Français. In 1994, Morel struck out on his own, both as dealer and restorer. His long and narrow workroom is chockablock with wood and tools and objects in molds and on benches; his public rooms display memorabilia — signed concert posters and photographs of virtuosi — from the storied past.

What this luthier sells are violins and violas and cellos and bows of value and importance, and what he repairs is the crème de la crème. There are workaday instruments also, of course; nearly a thousand pass through the shop each year for sale or repair. A dealer's reputation, however, rests on the highest common denominator of stock, and to have handled the Countess of Stanlein is no small professional thing. Greenhouse and Morel admire each other cordially; they trust each other a little, and when the cellist delivered his instrument for the purpose of "restoration," he left with a two-by-three-inch numbered ticket as receipt.

The human animal makes lists. Instinctively we scan the charts for those who come first, second, last. We like to know the names of the ten best- or worst-dressed celebrities, the all-time all-star baseball team, the richest men or women and the twelve safest cities for family life and the millennium's five or five hundred most important citizens. We rank colleges and wines. In our obsessive calibration of achievement by degrees, there are tables and annotated lists of lists; it sometimes seems as though the need to establish a "top dog" or a "leader of the pack" stays programmed in the species. Hierarchy has its comforts, after all; we want to know where we belong and, by extrapolation, where we stand.

Such ranking in terms of artistic achievement is a thankless task. We may have heavyweight champions of the world and world leaders in automobile or oil production, but enter the domain of art and any assessment of primacy falls flat. Pick the "greatest" of composers and for every proponent of Bach there will be a Beethoven buff; urge Mozart as the supreme musical consciousness and you'll find an adept of Stravinsky and one of Schubert or Schumann and one of Paul Simon or Sting. Pick the "greatest" of visual artists and there will be votes cast in that beauty contest for Raphael and Rembrandt and Leonardo and Dürer and Grandma Moses and Andy Warhol and Monet. Even Shakespeare has detractors: those who would put him in context or believe that he couldn't be Shakespeare or prefer Milton instead. The marketplace requires multiplicity, and to insist that X outranks Y is to reveal mere personal preference or a set of cultural blinders; a declension of the "hundred best" books or "all-time favorite" love songs seems, on the face of it, inane.

For there can be no argument — no instructive disagreement — as to taste. *De gustibus non est disputandum* is a dictum accepted by all. Yet ask a hundred people to name the greatest of instrument makers, and ninety-five will agree. One name is preeminent, and those who challenge his reputation do so as iconoclasts. If you have heard of anyone you will have heard of Stradivari, and to propose Guadagnini or Gofriller or members of the Amati family as the most accomplished of luthiers is to cast a minority vote. (Guarneri "del Gesù" has his consequential advocates, and there are cognoscenti who prize his violins and violas above all others, but he died young and worked at speed and built, it would seem, only one cello.) I know of no artist or craftsman more universally honored than is Stradivari; his bowed, wooden, stringed instruments have long been celebrated as the Platonic ideal of the form.

Antonio Stradivari was born in or near Cremona, Italy, in 1644. The actual date and place of his birth have been lost, but various Stradivaris had prospered in Cremona for centuries before. (The Latin and Italian spelling of his patronymic — Stradivarius and Stradivari — are interchangeable; by convention the former refers to an instrument, the latter to its maker, but this is a distinction long since blurred. Indeed, the proper orthography was "Stradiuarius" until in the 1730s the luthier himself replaced the "u" with a Roman "v." One of his violin-making sons retained it; another returned to the "u.") Ottolinus Stradivari had been a *senator patriae* as early as 1127; in 1186 there was a senator named Egidius Stradivari; the lawyer Guglielmus Stradivertus died in 1439. In the 1630s and 1640s, however, bubonic plague swept through Cremona, and those who could afford to do so moved to the nearby countryside; during plague years record-keeping was in any case at risk. We know a good deal about the instrument maker nevertheless, and this itself attests to prominence. *Ricco come Stradivari* was a saying of the Cremonese vernacular, and it referred not to inheritance but to earnings. He did well. The master craftsman lived long and was proud of longevity; in 1736 he inscribed a violin now called the "Muntz" Stradivarius with a label in his own hand, claiming to be ninety-two years old. (His first such label, in which he describes himself as a pupil of Amati, was signed in 1666.) So our knowledge of the birth date is in effect retrospective, a matter of subtraction, and whether he was born in Cremona or Brescia or Bergamo remains, as of this writing, moot.

He worked till the day of his death, and that day *was* recorded. *In the year of our Lord one thousand seven hundred and thirty-seven, on the nineteenth day of the month of December, Signor Antonio Stradivari, a widower, aged about ninety-five years, having died yesterday, fortified by the Holy Sacraments and comforted by prayer for his soul until the moment he expired, I, Domenico Antonio Strancari, Parish Priest of this Church of S. Matteo, have escorted to-day his corpse with funeral pomp to the Church of the very Reverend Fathers of S. Domenico in Cremona, where he was buried.*

We think that we know what he looked like — tall, dark, fine-fingered — though there's no authenticated likeness; we're told that he wore a white cap routinely and a white leather apron at work. We believe that he was pious, self-effacing, not litigious. These last qualities, however, are more a function of evidence absent than present: for so long-lived and prosperous a citizen to have engaged in so few court proceedings must mean he stayed contentedly at home and in his shop. Lately his testament has been unearthed, and we know the size of his estate — in a word, considerable — and what he distributed where. The dates of his two marriages also have been recorded — to Francesca Ferraboschi, a widow, and, when he in turn became a widower, to Antonia Zambelli — then the names of his several children, their birth dates, and which of them grew up.

We deduce, from the signed label ("*Antonius Stradiuarius Cremonenfis, Alumnus Nicolaii Amati, Faciebat Anno 1666*"), that he was apprenticed to Nicolò Amati. We assume that he lived, as well as plied his trade, at Piazza Roma, No. 1. He probably hung his instruments to dry in the attic of this building, but the structure no longer exists. As is the case with Shakespeare, the provincial place that harbored him appeared at first indifferent: his bones were removed from the crypt of the church when the church itself was razed; his workshop, too, was leveled and his tools and patterns dispersed. Now Cremona celebrates its honored resident and ancient cottage industry with a museum of the violin, a festival devoted to violin making, and a tourism boom.

René Morel's hair is white and curly, his figure trim in a blue smock, and he rolls back his shirtsleeves meticulously and sports a close-barbered mustache. In his late sixties, Gallic and dapper, the luthier maintains his eleventh-floor workshop in New York's theater district. Outside the locked glass door of his studio young dancers and singers and actors rehearse, and he eyes them where they cluster in the hall. "Those girls are wearing dental floss, not even a G-string," he says. "*Ces jeunes gens là,*" he says, "they entertain me with their dream of entertainment. They have not the slightest idea how hard one has to work."

He himself, he says, works very hard; his father and grandfather made instruments, and he has been elected president of the Entente Internationale des Maîtres Luthiers et Archetiers d'Art — violin and bow makers. His assistants call him Maître, and he reports with pride that long ago Pablo Casals called him Maître Morel. He had been taken to the hotel where the famed artist was staying, then introduced as the young man who would "save" the cello Casals was to perform on that night. "And Sasha [Alexander Schneider] says, 'He's young, but you'll see what he can do for you.' So Casals comes up, and Martita, his wife, was with him. I turned red, yellow, and he called me Maître Morel. I was looking for a mousehole to hide in, I shook, I was very much in awe, and I said, 'Oh, Maestro Casals, if you call me Maître, then how may I address you?' 'You must call me Pablo,' he says."

In Morel's own atelier — its proper name is Morel & Gradoux-Matt Inc., since a Swiss luthier is his partner — dozens of instruments wait for repair. They range from the amateur's hand-me-down "cigar box" to the professional's ideal of excellence. In the former case he lets his assistants do the work, murmuring "*bien*" if he approves or pointing out what needs to be redone. In the latter instance — when the instrument is of particular interest or of particular value — he does the work himself. And restoration, it's worth repeating, differs from repair. Repair may be accomplished rapidly — a small adjustment of bridge or sound post in time for a concert, a brief application of glue and a clamp. But what he and Greenhouse contracted to do, within the limits of the possible, was full-fledged restoration, and this must be done with the instrument open, requiring patience and skill.

"When I was young," says Morel, "I could work twelve, fifteen hours at a time and never once be tired; my eyes were better then. But when you deal with restoration it cannot be hurried, it must not be rushed. To start with, we take it apart. Even so fine a lady as the Countess of Stanlein must be opened for examination. You insert the knife carefully, carefully, just here into the glue — you must know how to do it — and then you just go *pop!*"

What are the components of this resonating box? What kind of wood is it made of and in what proportion? If this truly represents the Platonic ideal of the form of a violoncello, then how may we best measure it and who established its shape? Here's a skeletal description of the instrument's anatomy:

The *top* (alternately called the *table, front plate,* or *belly*) is by tradition made of two pieces of matching spruce or pine glued together. Two f-holes — so called because of their shape — are carved on the top of the instrument on each side; these are the apertures through which the sound of the vibrating plates is produced. The inside of the top is graded from $\frac{3}{16}$ inch in the middle to $\frac{9}{64}$ inch at the edges, for a cello with a body length of $29\frac{1}{2}$ inches.

The *back* is usually made of two matching pieces of maple — a harder wood than spruce or pine — selected for the figuration in and pattern of the wood. The back itself is graded from $\frac{4}{16}$ inch at the center to $\frac{9}{64}$ inch at each edge. (Stradivari did not work, of course, in inches, but by convention in the English-speaking world these measurements are so registered.) A few cellos exist with one-piece backs. The *neck, peg box,* and *scroll* were originally shaped from one piece of maple. The necks of older cellos were shorter than today's, but because of the rise in pitch over the centuries, new, longer necks have had to be attached. When this is done, the peg box and scroll, an ornamental gesture on the part of the luthier, are retained if possible and replaced on the new neck.

There are *sides,* or *ribs* — six pieces of maple glued to the top and the back; there's a strip of light-colored wood glued between two strips of black wood to form one tripartite strip. This is called *purfling,* and six of these strips fit into a groove near the edge of each plate for purposes of decoration; too, they protect the plate's edge. There's an elaborately carved piece of lightweight maple called a *bridge;* its feet are set — not glued — between the f-holes, centered on the f-hole notches, and it supports the four strings.

Over time such functional ornaments as an *end button,* a *nut,* and a *tailpiece* have become standard component parts of the instrument also; the *end button* is a small, rounded piece of wood inserted into the end block with the cord of the tailpiece wrapped around it and a hole bored through the middle for a metal end pin. That end pin is adjustable, raising the instrument to its desired height and attaching to the floor. The carved, triangular *tailpiece* is intended to keep the strings taut. The *nut,* slightly higher than the fingerboard, is a small piece of ebony glued onto the neck with grooves for proper spacing of the strings.

Interior component parts include the *linings,* the *bass bar,* and the *sound post.* The *linings* comprise twelve narrow strips of pine glued to the edges of the sides in order to increase the surface to which the top and back will be glued. The *bass bar* must be cut to fit the curvature of the top, then glued to the inside of the top on the left-hand side — where the lowest of the four strings, the C-string, is positioned; therefore the bar is called "bass." The *sound post* is not glued but placed just in front of the bridge's right foot, with ends shaped exactly to fit the contours of the top and back of the instrument; it sends the vibration from plate to plate, and its adjustment is crucial to the sound produced.

The end purpose of all such arrangements is, of course, sonority. The issues of weight and volume and proportion have to do with both the quality and quantity of noise produced. Too heavy an instrument fails to respond; too light a one will sound tinny or thin. The relatively slender walls of a guitar, for instance, will necessarily yield a different kind of vibration than those of a cello; sound waves result from density as well as from the volume of air contained by the wood's carved shape. (This description derives from Elizabeth Cowling's *The Cello* [1975].)

*

I am the cellist's son-in-law; I have known him well by now for more than thirty years. In that time I have not known him to be separated from the instrument for more than a few weeks, when repair became imperative, and during that time — although playing a fine copy he had commissioned from the luthier Marten Cornelissen — he was restless. He admires the Cornelissen, as well as other instruments he owns (in particular a Contreras, known as the "Spanish Stradivarius"), but the Countess of Stanlein is his heart's darling, his pearl among white peas.

As with many other performers, stories attach to the matter of attachment: how Greenhouse lost the cello once, in transit, on a plane to Paris and found it in Vienna on the airport tarmac; how he left it in a taxi in Dubrovnik, and spent a sleepless night because the cabbie, once identified, said he himself required sleep and would return the cello in the morning; how he braved a machine-gun-wielding customs inspector in South America who wanted to subject the instrument to a strip search. (When Yo-Yo Ma misplaced his Montagnana in a New York taxi's trunk last year it became a cause célèbre and its recovery a cause for celebration. Now his recorded voice inside the cab offers passengers the "classical advice" to remember their belongings.)

In the early days of airplane travel the Countess of Stanlein could come along free; later a "companion" ticket would be issued at half price. ("How old is your son Cello, Mr. Greenhouse?" an official in Newark once asked.) Then, with the increase in airplane traffic and procedural regulations, the cello's ticket became full fare — it cannot, of course, be stowed in the hold — and now the instrument must travel in isolated splendor, strapped into its own wide, padded seat in first class. The Russian soloist Raya Garbousova claimed to have avoided that expensive inconvenience by calling her cello a "bass balalaika"; since airplane regulations made no mention of that instrument, she carried her Strad at no cost.

All such association entails accommodation, and habit entails a resistance to change. Since this musician and his cello have been inseparable for decades, performer and instrument fuse. Less a romantic vagary than a statement of fact, such a process is familiar to any practiced player; the idiosyncrasies of an instrument, perplexing to A, have become second nature to B. And Morel knows how Greenhouse reacts:

"He was so fixed on the bridge Maestro Sacconi had cut for him that he wouldn't let it be moved. You ask him if I'm lying. It's probably been there now for thirty years, and we spent fifteen years without moving the sound post either. Of all my customers this is the one who has remained the longest with the same material. But Bernie, when he was younger and I first heard him play, he and his cello were one and one only. I always say there is no one in the world who could master that sound. It's his sound with the cello; you give that cello to anybody else and it won't sound the same. He has a way with the flesh of the finger, the vibrato of the hand — I was flabbergasted, and I said to myself, That's it, that's the complete sound of this instrument."

The luthier's task, therefore, is twofold: to restore the physical object and not to alter the instrument's sound. This is a delicate balancing act, all the more so when musician and cello have been long-standing intimates. Unnumbered hours in rehearsal and performance make a millimeter's difference in the height of the bridge or the width of the neck loom large, and Greenhouse knows as if by instinct how to produce his particular tone.

He and his instrument are — as Morel says admiringly — "one."

The city of Cremona, capital of the Province of the same name, is of great antiquity, having been founded by the Romans in the year 218 B.C. . . . Whether or not Cremona is distinguished as the actual scene of the emergence of the true violin by the hands of Andrea Amati, founder of the Cremona School, or whether that honor should belong to the neighboring city of Brescia, where Gasparo da Salò also fashioned instruments of violin form in the sixteenth century, the significance of Cremona will ever remain of first magnitude in the story of the Violin.

So writes Ernest Doring in the impressively titled *How Many Strads? Our Heritage from the Master; A* Tribute *to the Memory of a* Great Genius, *compiled in the year marking the Tercentenary of his birth; being a Tabulation of Works Believed to Survive Produced in Cremona by Antonio Stradivari, Between 1666 and 1737, including relevant data and mention of his two sons, Francesco and Omobono.*

To return to the matter of "first magnitude" and ranking, it's no small mystery that this small town in the north of Italy should have provided the locus for so many of the world's important bowed wooden instruments. There are some who claim it was a function of the excellence of available timber, much of it shipped across the Adriatic; there are some who argue for the town apothecary and the varnish he produced; there are others who attribute this "genius of place" to the system of apprenticeship as such. Roughly between the latitudes of 44 and 46 degrees, from west of Milan to Venice and Udine (though the luthier David Tecchler lived in Rome, and the Gagliano family in Naples), a group of craftsmen prospered. Andrea and Nicolò Amati, Francesco Ruggeri, Andrea Guarneri, were working in Cremona before Stradivari was born; Guarneri "del Gesù," Carlo Bergonzi, Lorenzo Storioni, and G. B. Ceruti — this list is truncate, selective — continued after his death.

Most likely there is no single answer but a confluence of answers to the question of why then and there. The quality of wood and varnish, the nature of apprenticeship, and the exigencies of competition would each have played a role. But whatever the reason or reasons, in the seventeenth and eighteenth centuries a skill came to fruition in and near Cremona that has not been equaled since. Although genius itself may be neither explicable nor replicable, that part of the luthier's art which can be called pure craftsmanship can be in part transmitted — rather like the guild of stoneworkers, the Cosmati, who set the floors of churches and crypts with intricate inlaid geometrical patterns, then watched their trade die off.

This trade, however, thrives. More people play wooden stringed instruments more widely now than ever before, and there's a flourishing business in both construction and repair. The membership directory of the American Federation of Violin and Bow Makers (1998–99) lists members from Ames to Zygmuntowicz with offices from Arizona to Wisconsin. René Morel's workshop in Manhattan contains a polyglot transient or resident crew; his assistants speak Japanese, French, German, and Czech. Today the business is international not local, and performers cross borders habitually; there's no fixed center of the music-making world. Yet the young luthier still travels to Cremona as a pilgrim to a holy place and, in the museum where the master's tools and patterns and drawings and instruments have been reassembled, still visits as though at a shrine.

For a few years the "Cremonese" were eclipsed — at the turn of the nineteenth century, German instruments outranked the Italians in terms of purchase price — but ever since then, in Jane Austen's phrase, "it is a truth universally acknowledged, that a single" music lover "in possession of a good fortune, must be in want of" an instrument built in that time and place. And, if he or she be very rich or skilled or fortunate indeed, the instrument will likely come from Stradivari himself.

"This is not my biggest restoration," says Morel. "I have done much more difficult work than this, I have restored instruments that were considered garbage — when I was in my thirties there was no challenge I wouldn't take. When I heard Maestro Greenhouse play, while I was still at Wurlitzer, his sound always moved me; it wasn't the largest sound, but whenever he touched the string it was unforced. He is very much a perfectionist, very much a serious person, the same way he is with his music. He used to bring me the cello once a year to deal with the cracks and all that, and he said, 'Someday, René, you will work with this cello and restore it entirely.' And I said, 'It would be an honor for me one day to work for you.' And now that he wants his cello preserved, it is with this in mind that I am doing it. He's going to get my best" — the luthier spreads his hands and lifts his arms and shoulders — "not the second best."

One of the major challenges has to do with varnish — worn away since Stradivari's time and, inattentively, replaced. The luthier shakes his head and points to blackened patches where, he says, his predecessors took a housepainter's brush and went *slap, slap, drip.* Morel removes these accretions with pure denatured alcohol and a small sable retouching brush. Very carefully he paints the alcohol across the grain with two, three, or four strokes of the brush; he repeats this gesture often enough to soften the surface of the varnish but not enough to go through, then almost imperceptibly removes the loose new varnish with a scraper or sharp knife.

To take off all such recent coating requires, self-evidently, that Morel can distinguish between the varnish Stradivari used and that which has been added since 1707. "It's not only the eyes," he tells me, "but also the feeling, the texture of the varnish, and the minute the original comes up you know that that is it." The varnish on the cello's back is almost wholly original, and so is the coloration of the scroll. But the varnish of the top had been much thickened and retouched, and when I ask him — pointing to an area of two square inches by the f-hole — how long it will take to clean this particular area to his own satisfaction, he says he cannot count how many days; it's one of the difficult jobs.

"Bernie says to me — I used to call him Mister Greenhouse, Maestro Greenhouse, but then he says no, you must call me by the name my friends use, Bernie — 'Make sure, René, you're the one to do this.' Because you have to know when to stop. If you put a drop of alcohol on that Strad varnish it will go to the white in no time. So you ask me, how can I use alcohol here? If you play the instrument and ask Bernie how much pressure do you put on the bow, he will raise his shoulders and shrug. If a virtuoso is going to play a concerto and he doesn't have the strings in tune, then he shouldn't attempt the concerto. I use alcohol, pure alcohol. And the answer to how to do it is skill. Skill, experience, feelings, and concentration."

Windows line the workroom of Morel & Gradoux-Matt Inc.; unsheathed lamps increase the light. The room is narrow, high-ceilinged, and long; its shelves stock a jumble of shapes. Seventeen violins hang from a rack; there are dismembered instruments and cardboard boxes full of wood beneath the cluttered tables where the men bend to their work. They are in their twenties and thirties, convivial yet focused; they sport ponytails and paint-bespattered T-shirts and smell of resin, tobacco, and sweat. They rasp and sand and join and splice; they use clamps and calipers and scrapers and chisels and fine-pointed brushes and rags. There are boxes of spruce scraps, boxes of necks — labeled in black capital letters: CELLO, VIOLIN — a band saw, a poster of a Ferrari, cans of dental compound, rabbit glue, jam jars labeled *Chicory* and *Potassium dichromate,* with which they will varnish "white" wood. The radio plays. I expect to hear Haydn, Vivaldi perhaps — but what these craftsmen listen to is rock and roll, a DJ selling cameras and Reeboks and reporting on the weather and traffic in New Jersey.

Morel walks through. He moves from desk to desk, assistant to assistant, examining their labors' progress, joking about masking tape and how I will steal his trade secrets. Half the work they do, he tells me, is to repair what has been badly done in other shops. When it looks very bad, he says, it's often not so serious, and when it's very serious it's not always easy to see. He points to a patch near

the sound post, newly fitted and glued into place. Each cut begins
with a saw in order, as Morel explains, "to approximate dimension.
Then we use knives and rasps to remove most of the wood, and
then we get the shape, and then after this we use files and in the
end scrapers for very thin shavings. And then sandpaper, and after
sandpaper we wet the wood three times, because when you wet the
wood the grain rises, and it must be sanded back . . ."

Although the violin and violoncello have changed their shapes
with time — in the former case a little, in the latter quite consider-
ably — the pattern as such remains fixed. I mean by "pattern" the
quintessence of form and not its surface adjustment; the cello's
functional proportions were no doubt determined by trial and error, and that process continues today. Routinely someone claims to
have discovered the "secret" of a Stradivarius and to reproduce its
excellence in plastic or metal or by computer; routinely that someone is wrong. We may play electronic cellos, ergonomically friendly
cellos, reduced or outsized cellos, but these are understood as variations on a theme. (The change in the structure of bows is a separate but related subject; the beau ideal of a Tourte bow stands in
much the same relation to the run-of-the-mill version thereof as
does a Stradivarius to a factory-issued machine.) And it's perhaps
the case that contemporary instruments will "season" over time,
sounding more impressive to the auditor in three hundred years.
Still, the art and craft of the luthier attained its height in Cremona,
and most modern practitioners attempt to imitate, not alter, that
ideal.

It's as though Cézanne or Kandinsky sought only to paint in the
manner of Titian or Brueghel, as though the contemporary writer
tried only to write like the Greeks. For all practical purposes this
fidelity to the ancient mode of instrument production remains the
test of excellence, and I know no other métier of which this can be
said. Singers, athletes, architects, each profit from the new technologies; they take advantage of modern techniques. The luthier, too,
deploys special plastics, chemicals, calipers, and ultrasound for instrument repair. But the aim is reproduction, not innovation, and
the model is a constant one.

To make such an instrument today would be to scale the heights
of achievement; to equal that old mastery is the best that can be
wished. Composers make new music, sculptors new sculpture, and

carriage makers new cars, but a Stradivarius in a private home or concert hall remains the practitioner's dream. For performer and audience both, in the nature of their handling or the volume and quality of sound produced, in terms of aesthetics or acoustics, these wooden instruments have neither been improved upon nor by technology rendered obsolete.

Yet an instrument unplayed is an instrument ill served. The use to which it must be put is audible, and over centuries such usage entails stress: material fatigue. It's not like a text, which, printed, remains constant, or a painting, which, once framed, needs only to be seen. Fingers press on it; flesh brushes it; jewelry and liquor hover nearby, poised to scratch or spill; humidity alters from venue to venue and from day to day. The cellist who performs in Rio de Janeiro on Monday, in Seoul next week, and in London next month subjects his instrument as well as himself to continuous wear and tear. The glue will dry, the joinings split, the wood itself will splinter or the ornamental strips of purfling crack and the varnish fade. Inattentive or ignorant handling, a car crash or a train wreck or water or fire: such threats are omnipresent and everything's at risk. Strings, bridges, end pins, sound posts — each sooner or later requires attention and must be replaced.

Morel is a born raconteur, and he likes to tell stories of contests of skill; the style includes rodomontade. "I never had to work on commercial instruments. I had been trained in France, where my very first teacher was Marius Didier. He was seventy-two years old, and I was twelve years old, starting to make violins after school. Later, in Mirecourt, I studied with Maître Amédée Dieudonne. So I developed skill for making violins in the old school of violin making, and in order to earn a living I had to make them at the rate of two violins — in the white, without varnish — per week. We had no machinery, not even an electric motor. And when I came to Wurlitzer I brought along my tools, and they came with the band saw, and I said, 'Well, you take your band saw and I'll take my hand saw and we'll see who finishes first.' Also, who comes closer to the line, to the pattern. We didn't bet any money, but I won. I won out over the band saw. In my life as a luthier I seldom saw anybody else who could manage that way. It sounds as if I'm bragging, but I'm not. It's a true fact.

"When I arrived at Mr. Wurlitzer and presented myself to Maestro Sacconi — this I will never forget — he gave me a bridge to cut, for a violin, a Lupot. Maestro Sacconi spoke French, and he said, 'This violin is one of your compatriots, and this is the model I want you to cut, that's the one I like.' So I gave him the new bridge maybe forty minutes later, and he said, 'Already?' And I said, 'Yes, why not?' So he looked at it, and I'll never forget his face. He said, 'My God!' Then he looked and looked and showed it to his right arm, D'Attili; they couldn't believe that I'd cut it with my knife, you know, and they came to look at my knife because they couldn't believe that I'd done it with no knife marks, so clean and exactly similar to the model. The next bridge he gave me was for a cello, and after I'd cut that one he said, 'Bravo!'"

The cello is, of course, neither the first nor the last wooden stringed instrument to have made its appearance in Europe; its ancestors include the lute and viol as well as the viola da gamba. Relatives include the violin, viola, and guitar. Its proper name suggests a "little violin," since "cello" in Italian is a diminutive, and the first such instrument clearly referred to in print — by Jambe de Fer in 1556 — was a "violoncello da spalla," which refers to the manner of holding the instrument in church processionals or serenades. *Spalla* means "shoulder" in Italian, and the player could perform while walking; the short-necked instrument was hung across the shoulder and fastened with a strap. By the turn of the twentieth century it had grown customary to abbreviate the name "violoncello" to " 'cello," with the apostrophe indicating the six missing letters. By now it's acceptable to use the name "cello" without the apostrophe and as a full designation; I have done so here.

This change in nomenclature suits the nature of such history; alteration inheres in the craft. Although the ideal of the instrument might lay claim to intactness, no "pure" Stradivarius violoncello exists. There are roughly sixty extant, and each differs from the cello as at first designed. No matter how earnest the performance of a practitioner of "early music," what the Maestro once heard in his workshop is not what we, listening, hear. What we look at is not what he saw.

A legend attaches to "Le Messie," the Stradivarius violin in Oxford's Ashmolean Museum, that it was rarely if ever performed upon, and there are many instruments housed elsewhere under glass. This has the virtue of preservation — of keeping an artifact out of harm's way — but the luthier's work had been, of course, intended to be played. And if form follows function, then the form must shift.

In the seventeenth century the literature was written for continuo (a bass-line repetition of the featured melody), but Boccherini and Bach and their successors wrote for solo performance. This expansion of the repertoire and shift of emphasis required an equivalent increase in acoustic volume and a heightened pitch. The neck was lengthened and bridge raised and the fingerboard and interior bass bar enlarged. In the nineteenth century traditional sheep-gut strings were wire-wrapped to augment the production of sound. The locus of recital also changed, enlarging into the concert hall, and an end pin was added to provide stability and anchor the frame to the floor. Today the violoncellist — unlike soloists on the violin, viola, or bass — must sit.

Here is Bernard Greenhouse on the first viewing of his instrument. The Countess of Stanlein was not Greenhouse's first Stradivarius; he had previously owned the "Visconti," a cello dated 1684 and in the "old pattern" (built up from the viola da gamba). That instrument — now owned by Mstislav Rostropovich — had been "decorated," festooned with the Visconti coat of arms in order to disguise its added wood. The cello's sound, however, did not project well or merge compatibly with that produced by Daniel Guilet, the founding violinist of the Beaux Arts Trio. Therefore Greenhouse had been, as he puts it, "in the market" and was in Europe on tour.

"In 1957, the instrument dealer Jacques Français said he thought there might be a cello available near Cologne, in the small city of Aachen, and that if I were ever in the neighborhood I might just take a look. It happened that I was playing a concert in Cologne, and we had a free afternoon, and so I took a train to Aachen, which the French know as Aix-la-Chapelle. I arrived at the station and looked in the telephone book for a *Geigenbauer* (the German term for a luthier), then took a taxi to his shop and told him I was an American cellist and had heard there was a Stradivarius in the area. Did he know it and had he ever worked on it? The *Geigenbauer,* Mr. Niessen, said by all means, yes. For many years it had been in the collection of a Mr. Talbot, who had died just recently, and his wife still had the instrument. "I asked him to call the daughter and find out if I might look at the cello. Soon afterward a man arrived, and I opened the cello case and fell immediately in love. I had no doubt, no doubt at all, that it was a Stradivarius. I didn't even look inside to find the label. The color of the varnish, the shape of the instrument, it was so beautiful, so very beautiful, and it seemed to me a great jewel."

How did the cello reach Aachen? Where had it been before? It's not now possible to track the object throughout its lengthy provenance: who first commissioned or played it, how much it was valued and by whom. There would be charm and drama in such telling — witness the film *The Red Violin*, in which we see a fabled instrument in various cultural contexts, from Italy to China, and passing through various hands. That film may well have been inspired by John Hersey's novel *Antonietta*, in which the writer imagines a violin made by Stradivari while courting his second wife, Antonia Zambelli.

In both cases the dramatic problem is the same: how would this token of devotion be treated by musicians and collectors in the several centuries after having been created by a great luthier in love? In the film a nameless "Cremonese" mixes his dead darling's blood into the violin's varnish, and the instrument thereafter becomes an emblem of fatal romance. Hersey's plot is also episodic and sequential. He makes Mozart admire "Antonietta"; Berlioz and Stravinsky fall, turn by turn, under its spell, till it fetches up on Martha's Vineyard; thence the auction block . . .

Our information on the Countess of Stanlein's early history is limited yet suggestive. We know, for example, that "the late Count Stanlein" purchased it in 1854 from the French instrument maker and dealer Jean-Baptiste Vuillaume, who was the foremost champion of "Cremonese" instruments in Paris at that time. Let's imagine for a moment that Count Stanlein (à la Stradivari in *Antonietta*) was courting a wife. He would have commissioned a string quartet or perhaps have been an amateur himself, so the name is his high compliment to their anticipated harmony: a nuptial gift of song. This was the period when chamber music, as the term indicates, was still a private matter; aristocrats routinely concertized at home. The Count's betrothed may well have sung or played the spinet, and he would have desired to join her in the music room as well as in the bed. It's less likely, though possible, that the lady herself played the instrument and that the "Countess of Stanlein" refers to the musician who held it between her spread legs. There's a telltale splash of brandy on the rear plate of the cello where the varnish bubbled and was — perhaps by her handkerchief or the hem of a raised silk undergarment — wiped clean. Or perhaps Count Stanlein had no wife and fondled this substitute "Countess" instead. She would have been broad-beamed, deep-throated, her color reddish gold. The instrument had previously been owned — witness the title "*ex*. Paganini" — by that notorious rakehell and virtuoso, who sold it to Vuillaume. Vuillaume himself was a celebrated copyist: his gift of imitation remains unsurpassed, and he built many cellos on the model of the Countess — her proportions having been, by the mid-nineteenth century, acknowledged as ideal.

Here's what we do know of previous ownership, summarized dismissively by the brothers Hill in their *Antonio Stradivari, His Life & Work (1644–1737)*. As historians of Stradivari, the Hill family — English dealers and instrument makers — were, for many years, authoritative, and their work remains fundamental to what is accepted today:

> The most interesting fact known to us concerning this instrument is the episode of its purchase early in the last century by Signor Merighi, a violoncellist of Milan, and Piatti's master. We have it on the authority both of Piatti and of Signor Pezze, also a pupil of Merighi, that in 1822, while the last-named was passing through the streets of Milan, he perceived a working man carrying, among other things, a violoncello on a truck or barrow. Merighi at once accosted him, and ended by becoming the owner of the instrument, which was in a dilapidated state, for a sum equivalent to 4s.! Eventually, about 1834–35, Merighi disposed of the 'cello to Paganini, who sold it to J. B. Vuillaume, who resold it in 1854 to the late Count Stanlein.

In 1999 I visited the cello at regularly spaced intervals — January, March, May, June, August, October, November. It was rather like attending a much-loved patient in a nursing home or, more precisely, a hospital: the Countess of Stanlein lay broken — shattered, albeit on purpose — and then in surgery and traction and reconstruction, until little by little she was healed. On first view —

broken down into component parts and contained in a stall in Morel's locked vault — the cello appeared as forlorn as it must have to Merighi in 1822. In the streets of Milan it had lain on a barrow; in the streets of Manhattan it stood in a bin, but only the trained witness would have thought it a thing of great value or envisioned the instrument whole.

In addition to work on the varnish, Morel has three principal tasks. The first involves a patch near the sound-post top, which has been repaired before and unsuccessfully. The glue kept bleeding through minuscule cracks in the wood, and the luthier must remove and replace what was ineptly done — most probably in the mid-nineteenth century. The second and more complicated project is repair work on the ribs, which have been both wormholed and previously buttressed — sometimes to the thickness of 2.5 millimeters where Stradivarius himself had carved to the thickness of 1.5. Morel must remove all the old glue and backing, then repair the damaged wood and steam the backing of the ribs into their proper contours.

On May 13, 1999, for example, Morel takes a rib from its clamp. The wood had been in the clamp for five days, protected by padding and stretched to its original contour and its proper shape. There had been a doubling (a previous repair, with a second piece of wood glued on the inside), which Morel removes. The original width of the maple was 1.5 millimeters, and .3 millimeter of intact maple remains. Morel takes a new piece of unblemished wood and shapes it to the Stanlein rib, following the contour of the original exactly and attaching the two with glue. He lets the glue dry inside an airtight mold for two weeks. Then, removing it again, he reduces the width of the newly buttressed rib from 1.7 to 1.5 millimeters — thinning it down with a very sharp scraper to the desired thickness; smilingly he tells me, "You have to give it time."

An equivalent procedure holds true for the spruce top, which has bellied up and flattened out under the stress of the sound post and strings; this warp from "true" contour might seem infinitesimal, but it is redressed. For this purpose the luthier constructs a plaster cast in order to determine where there are, as he puts it, "bumps." The Stanlein top — delicately moistened in order to prove more malleable — is placed in a mold. All during the summer it lies encased in protective bindings beneath a sheet of brown paper so that the wood itself will not be touched, and then a sheet of wax paper, and then a sack of hot sand.

At the same time, Morel had been refashioning the neck. The block into which the neck fits is a combination of three or four previous repairs, and where the neck joins the scroll someone has shaved a segment off the peg box. This is a delicate job indeed, since, in order to repair it, the "original" wood at this junction must be worn paper-thin. It's not cracked but certainly at risk. "I could have raised it with a bottom piece like it used to be at the turn of the century," Morel explains. Instead he puts a piece coming through from the inside out. A patch would have taken him two hours; this takes him two days.

"If you look here at the scroll" — Morel points to its bottom edge — "originally, when Strad made the scroll, this part was not flat like this. There would have been a little step from the fingerboard, but by the time they changed the neck and fingerboard for modern playing, you increase the angle. So they have been planing here. The curve should look more like *this*, not flat" — he finds a pencil stub and draws the curve's arc on a piece of scrap paper — "so if I angle it this way, it will be slightly below, which is how it was done originally. It has been unscrupulously restored before, but now we have respect for its value. So the original mortise will start like this. I'm going to leave four millimeters behind it, and here will come the fingerboard. If I did it the other way, I would have to cut back some of the original, and that I refuse to do."

From 1707 to 1822, there's no formal record of the Countess of Stanlein's ownership, and we can only guess at who played and disposed of it and how. The notion of a cello "on a truck or barrow," broken apart and ready for the municipal dump, then at the last minute rescued by Merighi, has operatic flair. More probably the thing was being trundled from one owner or shop to another; most likely it wasn't at risk. But this did happen at a time, in the wake of the Napoleonic Wars, when instruments were subject to rough handling. The "violin hunter" Luigi Tarisio — himself in large part responsible for the rediscovery of the "Cremonese" masters — was said to have walked into Paris with his collection in a sack. He had acquired his treasures in the north of Italy by just such wayward and wayside encounter, finding instruments in attics and church basements and the backs of barns. So the Hill brothers' anecdote should be taken with a grain, if not a fistful, of salt. By contrast, the certificate of authenticity issued by the firm of Hamma & Co., Stuttgart, on June 19, 1949, rings with unstinting praise. From the Stanlein family the cello would appear to have been sold to Paul Grümmer of the Busch Quartet, who sold it to the Talbots, from whom in turn Greenhouse acquired it in 1958. The certificate has photographs of the top, the back, the scroll, and then a description extolling the virtues of the "*echt und zusammen gehörend*" instrument, the "*Violincello mit Originalzettel: Antonius Stradiuarius Cremona 1707.*" That "dilapidated state" of which the Hills complain is gainsaid by the German firm, which writes: "In all its essential parts a very impressive work of this master; it is authentic and belongs together . . ."

Still, not all Stradivari's creations are equally achieved. They were fashioned by hand and piece by piece and with slight variations in wood and color and shape. Little adjustments of size and proportion loom large in terms of acoustics; some instruments are forgiving and mellow, others harsh and stern. From 1680 to 1700 the luthier produced at least thirty violoncellos, of which twenty-one survive, and they are without exception built of a large size (nearly 32 inches long, of an average, as opposed to 29½). Acoustically these instruments are an uneasy cross between bass viol and viola da gamba, and for seven years the workshop produced no documented cellos. Then emerged the "great period" — a designation commonly attested to — from 1707 to 1720.

The Stanlein comes from the first year of this resumed production, and thereafter the pattern stayed fixed. The interval between 1700 and 1707 is therefore a telling time, and what we think of as the *ne plus ultra* of violoncello production lasted thirteen years. By 1720 the master's hand began to shake or at any rate tremble a little, and — with some exceptions — the work thereafter registers decline. His masterpieces of the "great period" include such other violoncellos as the Batta, the Castelbarco, the Davidoff, the Duport, the Gore-Booth, and the Piatti. Often these were named for the aristocrats who commissioned them or the musicians who performed on them. At other times they were named for distinguishing characteristics — as in instruments called the "blonde" (referring to varnish color, since the characteristic Strad varnish of the period is a deep reddish brown) and (his last violin) the "Swan."

Here again is Bernard Greenhouse speaking of his instrument: "The changes in the color of sound cannot be equaled. Color of sound is produced on an instrument in three manners; there are three elements to this, just as there are three primary colors in the painter's palette. We have the ability to place the bow closer to the bridge or to the fingerboard, and that produces a particular sound. In addition we have the speed of the bow, and the speed of the bow produces more sound without added pressure. That's the second primary color, and the third is the amount of effort we put into the bow. With those three primary colors we can produce an enormous variety of sound — analogous, again, to what a painter does with the palette."

And this is the heart of the matter, the core of the restorer's challenge. Since Greenhouse is completely pleased with the "palette" of the cello, any change in color must be by definition for the worse. It's not so much a question of leaving well enough alone as of separating out and protecting what cannot be improved.

The luthier is conscious of this issue and the exacting intensity of his client, and the two of them consult on what can and cannot be done. At some point, for instance (most probably in the late eighteenth century), a workman cut away a rear section of the scroll so as to gain easy access to the peg-wound strings. Morel could plausibly have filled in the wood and reconstructed the scroll — but this has become a "signature" feature of the cello, and the two men opted for consistency. Too, the brandy spill that marred the varnish of the back has been reduced but retained; it's part of the Stanlein lore, and traces of that bubbling indiscretion — an admirer of Paganini perhaps, a hovering lover of the Countess? — have been kept.

The neck itself has been replaced since Stradivari's time, and therefore, though exact, the act of substitution need not be exacting. The fingerboard glued to the neck is fashioned out of ebony; the wood of the neck is maple and — rubbed with oil rather than varnished — must be contrasted to the color of the instrument as such. At his country property Morel keeps a barn full of wood, and with barely concealed excitement he shows me a segment of old maple purchased in France some thirty years before. "Last weekend in the country I looked for pieces I might use and I found — discovered again, in my attic — a piece of wood from the workshop of Vuillaume. It was cut quite thick and came from the stock of my grandfather's shop; my grandfather, at the turn of the century, was dealing in wood for all the violin makers of France. This piece is definitely from Vuillaume, because my grandfather stamped his wood with the initials PM. This was cut with a circular saw — you can see it on the grain, the *maille* — because they used hydraulic power and electricity had not yet been invented."

So the reconstructed neck brings this wheel full circle: in the mid-1800s Paganini sells the instrument to Jean-Baptiste Vuillaume, and at the turn of the millennium a French luthier restores it with wood from Vuillaume's private stock. What we have here — sent south from Paris to Marseilles, then shipped to New York and stored in an upstate barn until retrieved by Morel — is a piece of maple trimmed to shape and conjoined to an instrument built in Cremona: a constancy in change.

To restore the Stanlein so that it might seem brand new would be to deny its history, and this has been the operational dynamic from the start. It's not unlike the problem posed by restoration of a famed work of visual art. Michelangelo's Sistine ceiling — to take just one example — aroused disapproval when cleaned too thoroughly. A principal measure of any such instrument's value, indeed, is how much original varnish remains intact; there's a quasi-pietistic faith in the properties of Stradivari's "secret" formula as an ingredient of sound. Greenhouse remembers the excitement with which Fernando Sacconi informed him, upon first encounter with the instrument, "There's enough varnish on this cello, original varnish, to have made three or four violins!"

So where Morel replaces the wood he imitates antiquity, replicating the grain of the spruce by brushstroke (having copied the "original" on tracing paper and transferring every capillary to the patch), then adding microscopic black spots as though the recent surface had darkened over time. He has tried to match the colors of the top and back, since the latter is almost unsullied and the former much retouched. To my eye — admittedly an amateur's — the finished product eradicates distinction and evades detection; only when he holds the wood to the light and at a particular refractive angle, only when he points to it — "Here, here!" — can I see where the "original" ends and its "imitation" begins.

The question of value is a complicated one; it, too, is subject to change. These instruments are rare enough to have no benchmark price, and this is more true of the cello — since there are so relatively few of them — than the violin. When an important Van Gogh or Cézanne routinely fetches tens of millions at auction, it's hard to escape the suspicion that a fine Strad remains undervalued. The 1727 Kreutzer Stradivarius (once owned by Rodolphe Kreutzer, for whom Beethoven wrote his violin sonata) was sold at auction in London for $1.6 million in 1998; much more expensive purchases are prearranged and private. Experts agree or disagree; prices fluctuate from year to year and instrument to instrument — two, four, six million are being bruited now as sums — while the graph's curve points constantly up.

Consider this trajectory of purchase recorded by the Hills:

A violoncello dated 1730, the property of the Hon. Mr. Greaves, was offered for sale by auction at Messrs. Phillips'. It was brought in, and subsequently sold in 1866 to W. E. Hill, who resold it for £230 to Mr. Frederick Pawle. Purchased back in 1877 for £380, and resold to Mr. Edward Hennell in 1878 for £500. Again repurchased in 1880 for £475, and sold a few months later to Mr. C. G. Meier for £525. The instrument now migrated to Paris, and was there bought in 1882 from MM. Gand & Bernardel *frères* for £600 by Mr. David Johnson, and brought back to England, to be once again purchased by our firm in 1885 for £650.

Although these amounts now seem laughably small, it's important to note the regularity with which the instrument was purchased; only once did it register a small decline — of twenty-five pounds — and in the course of nineteen years its value nearly trebled. That exponential pattern of increase remains the case today. Stradivari produced only two known guitars, twelve violas, and a few dozen cellos but hundreds of violins, and value is of course proportionate to scarcity. While the law of supply and demand still obtains, the price will continue to grow.

The restoration has been estimated to take six months, but by March 1999 it's clear that all hope of completion by summer will have been wishful thinking. As the months wear on, Morel begins to allocate his Saturdays and Sundays to the project; no phone rings in the weekend office, no customer approaches. When employed by Wurlitzer or Jacques Français the luthier could ignore matters of administration and a balance sheet; now, as his own proprietor, he has to pay attention. Where once the work could be uninterrupted, there now are the issues of getting and spending, and his profit margin as a dealer is far larger than as a restorer. In the former instance the sums can reach hundreds of thousands of dollars, in the latter tens, so his concentration is divided and his energy reduced.

"It may surprise you," he says, "but when I wake up at night I ask myself what I'm going to do, and then I make my plan. When I was young I'd make my plan, I'd tell myself I'm going to do this, this, *this*, and no matter how long it would take I would finish it. Today, if I do two thirds of what I've planned I'm very pleased with myself, because my head is getting ahead of my physique. When I come home at the end of the day my eyes tear. I try to watch a little bit of the news, and I can't even do that, because it's very tiring. When you work all day with a magnifying glass it's very very tiring, because the focus shifts. For instance, when I paint these grains here, I work very close, sometimes so close that I cut the end of my brush because it touches my magnifying glass, but my hands are still steady, thank God. I keep saying if my eyes were as good as my hands I would still work like when I was thirty. But in this class of restoration it's the last one I can do."

At eighty-four, Greenhouse has grown sleepless also. "During many hours awake in the night," he says, "and even in my dreams I've thought about the instrument; when I first saw it in its dismantled form — lying on the bench in pieces — I stroked the ribs, almost as though it was a body, a living thing. I've traveled the world with that instrument; it's been my companion for forty years. It was my career, my friend.

"Of course I did have moments when I thought that, in this last period of my life, I could simply have had the pleasure of playing the instrument, of keeping it at hand. I have to fight to keep away from the telephone; my instinct is to call René every day and say, 'Hey, did you do anything, has anything happened today?' But each time, I remind myself that things should be done to the instrument, they should have been done before my time, and I thought I owed a debt to the cello. I thought that it had done its service for me, I owed a service to it."

In fairy tales all things may be restored. That which disappeared is found and that which was hidden is revealed. The crone transforms herself into a princess when kissed by a sufficient prince; the old grow young and fair and unblemished and supple once more. To imagine the Countess of Stanlein first played is to people the candlelit hall with an audience: stiff-backed gentlemen bewigged and bright-eyed ladies whispering behind their fluttered fans. The shade of Niccolò Paganini hovers nearby somewhere, elongated, passionate, and bent above the bow. Or earlier — Merighi, and those who came to visit the maker himself in Cremona — the ones who came to purchase or lodge an order or perhaps apprentice to the trade. Who knows what Greenhouse dreamed the day he shut his eyes and saw himself a youth once more, agile, in the Pyrenees and learning from Casals?

In such a dream a cello floats upon the perfumed air. Ethereal, corporeal, it is the shape and very contour of encapsulated sound. Its archings are perfectly rounded and smooth; its varnish gleams; the purfling lends a definition and a darkness to the edge. From volute scroll to seamless rib, the pattern of the wood itself is intrinsicate with melody, suggestive of a promised plenitude: yet resonant, yet mute.

On Tuesday, May 23, 2000, Greenhouse travels once more to New York. Morel has spent the weekend readying the cello for delivery — returning the strings he removed in 1998, making adjustments to the sound post and to his newly cut bridge. He has prepared for this transfer carefully, stage-managing it to the last detail: an impresario. It is eleven o'clock. The musician, arriving, palpably nervous, says, "I have dreamed of this moment. I can't wait to see it. First I want to see it and then hold it and then touch the bow to the strings. But before that I have to warm up."

Morel conducts him to a secondary office and produces a Stradivarius that was built with a flat back. "It's one of two Stradivari built where he tried out a flat back," he says. "But this one is cut down, its back is not original. You can buy it if you wish . . ." The sound of this cello is muted and nasal, but Greenhouse plays it nevertheless, tentative at first: he is wondering, he tells me, if his own Strad's tone will have changed. "My fingers feel like sausages," he says.

After some time Morel reappears. "Are we ready, Maestro?"

In the large room at the atelier's rear there are signed photographs of Pablo Casals and Mischa Elman and Isaac Stern and photographs of Albert Einstein and Fritz Kreisler. Cello cases range like sentries at attention down the wall. Morel has placed a solid chair for the performer to sit on and, at the room's far end — some twenty feet distant, his back to the window — a second chair where he himself will listen in order to gauge projection. "All I did," he tells me, smiling, "was change the strings. It has taken me two years because I am very slow."

We laugh. Greenhouse is wearing glasses. Like a father with a newborn child or a husband with a long-lost bride, he receives the cello, embracing it, cradling it tenderly. He stares at the ribs, the front, the back, then turns the instrument upside down and reverses it again. He traces the edging, the purfling, the scroll. "Oh, René," he breathes. "It's beautiful. Bravo!"

At length he starts to play. He tries the open strings, tries fingerings, tries scales, and then searches for "wolf" notes — those places where the cello's vibrations might clash and make the sound wobble and go flat. Instead, in the echoing space of this room, the sound is pure, powerful, bright. "The voice," says the musician, "it's just what I remember — what I've been hearing in my head. Exactly how she sang before."

In a week or a month or a year, perhaps, Morel will make adjustments — but not now, not today. "There's nothing to adjust," the men agree.

Then there is lunch. This is a celebration, and we walk to a French restaurant in the neighborhood. Emmanuel Gradoux-Matt joins the party, and the four of us order champagne. "*Auf die Musik*," I offer, and Morel and Gradoux-Matt, clicking glasses, say, "*Santé*," and Greenhouse says, "*Tchin-Tchin*." Close attention is paid to the menu and then to the prospect of food. "But the red wine with the entrée," cautions Morel. "They serve it too cold here. We should have the waiter bring it already. In this matter they are not quite correct. It has to be *chambrée*."

I ask my father-in-law what he plans to do now.

"I'm going to put my cello in its case and take a taxi to the airport and buy it a ticket and carry it home." Greenhouse raises his glass. "And we will never ever be separated again."

At two-thirty in the morning of Thursday, June 1, 2000, three cellists are fondling a scroll. The cello beneath it stands mute. "Sensuous," says Yo-Yo Ma; "Sensational," says Ko Iwasaki, and Bernard Greenhouse, its owner, traces the instrument's neck. "Sensuous," says Ma again, and smiles and shuts his eyes.

This has been a long day. The weeklong World Cello Congress III is taking place in Baltimore, and more than five hundred cellists flock to master classes and panels and recitals both exhaustive and exhausting. Wednesday's program, for example, has included a symposium on the Influence of Folk Music on Cello Literature, a discussion of Cello Music from China, Music on Jewish Themes, a workshop on Jazz Improvisation, a film, a master class taught collectively by Janos Starker, the honorary president of the Congress, and Greenhouse, its artistic adviser.

The evening's concert, in Joseph Meyerhoff Symphony Hall, has featured two young musicians, Wendy Warner — in her twenties — and the teenage Han-Na Chang. After intermission, and to thunderous applause, Yo-Yo Ma and the Baltimore Symphony Orchestra perform a new composition, *The Six Realms* by Peter Lieberson, and Tchaikovsky's Andante Cantabile, op. 11. Then comes the usual postconcert line of well-wishers and a bus trip for invited guests to a reception on a cruise ship in the harbor. The bus driver, however, gets lost; the ship proves difficult to find, tucked into a dark corner of the marina, and by the time the cruise begins it is well past midnight. Dutifully, drinking jug wine and decaffeinated coffee, the cellists and their sponsors make slow circles in the harbor while the engines thrum and mutter and the lights over Baltimore dim.

On the bus trip back to Towson University, where the artists have been lodged, Greenhouse invites Ma to look at the cello. Ma is gracious and respectful and, it seems, indefatigable. The night before, he had been visiting late with Starker; in a few hours he must leave for New York. But this cello commands his attention, and he and Ko Iwasaki appear in Greenhouse's suite. Ma carries his tailcoat over his arm; his dress shirt and black tie seem casual now, and he's sweating lightly in the late-spring heat. With a flourish, unlocking its case, the elder man produces his reclaimed "Paganini Strad."

"Beautiful," says Ma.

"Sensational," Iwasaki repeats.

"Here." Greenhouse proffers a bow. The virtuoso demurs. Shaking his head, eyes narrowed behind wire-rimmed glasses, Ma studies the cello front and back, then plucks the strings and commences to play pizzicato. Iwasaki claps. After some time Ma takes the bow and — "Noodle a little," Greenhouse urges — plays a few notes lightly, dreamily, so as not to wake the sleeping guests. I ask him what he's hunting, what he listens for, and he says: The things it's easy to do, the things that are hard. It is three o'clock by now, and the men forget their resolution to be circumspect. "You should hear it," Greenhouse says. "Full-throated, down by the bridge."

Iwasaki excuses himself and collects his own cello, then returns to the room. He too possesses a Strad, dated 1727, but this is a copy of the one he left at home — one of six made by a luthier up in Michigan — and the men measure proportion, dimension, comparing instruments. They talk of other cellos, other makers, other performers. What they do not talk about is price. Yo-Yo Ma keeps caressing the Stanlein's scroll, and when I ask him what's the word for what this instrument possesses, he says, "Gravitas."

At the conference on Thursday morning René Morel gives a speech, discussing the technique of instrument making and repair, its challenges, its history. "I believe a lecture should be like a woman's skirt," he jokes. "Long enough to cover the subject, short enough to keep it interesting." The audience laughs. Then he discourses on the physics of sound, the general problems of restoration, and "Cello Making for Today's Virtuoso."

Each day in the hotel suite he and Greenhouse have been "fiddling" with the Stanlein's sound post, shifting its position so as to apply greater or less pressure to the top. Since he wants a setup with which he is familiar, Greenhouse shifts bridges as well, first trying the original Sacconi bridge, then the one Marten Cornelissen cut for his own copy of the instrument. "It doesn't fit," protests the luthier. "You can put a dime under its feet. It's a good bridge, I'm not saying anything against the bridge — but not for this cello," he says.

Greenhouse is unconvinced. "The strings sit too high with the one that you cut for me. You listen to it in this room, your ears are excellent, of course, I trust them absolutely, but I'm the one who plays. And it's too hard with this bridge."

"But that will change," Morel repeats. "The top has been lying alone for a year and a half; it will need to be adjusted. A month from now, Maître, you bring it back to the shop. And then" — he spreads his hands — "we will see what we hear."

What they see and hear in Meyerhoff Symphony Hall, on the Congress's final afternoon, is the refurbished instrument, its sound resplendent now. As Greenhouse comes onstage, two hundred cellists stamp their feet in a drumroll of appreciation for their "artistic adviser." This will be his first appearance in the full space of the concert hall, the first time the cello "sounds out." He plays the solo in "Song of the Birds" — a Catalan folk song transcribed for the cello by Pablo Casals. "'I have performed it,'" Greenhouse says his teacher told him, "'hundreds, hundreds of times.'"

It's a simple melody, an evocation of bird calls and flight, an easy line to play and difficult to master. This is mastery. Greenhouse has his eyes half shut, his old head bending heavily, his feet and hands and body engaged, his cello in his arms. Behind him rank upon rank of cellists listen and respond. "There were tears in our eyes," says Lluís Claret, himself a Catalan. "There were many of us crying."

The audience erupts. Greenhouse rises, bows, accepts flowers. "He has moved beyond music," the man beside me says, standing.

BARBARA EHRENREICH

Welcome to Cancerland

FROM HARPER'S MAGAZINE

I WAS THINKING of it as one of those drive-by mammograms, one stop in a series of mundane missions including post office, supermarket, and gym, but I began to lose my nerve in the changing room, and not only because of the kinky necessity of baring my breasts and affixing tiny x-ray opaque stars to the tip of each nipple. I had been in this place only four months earlier, but that visit was just part of the routine cancer surveillance all good citizens of HMOs or health plans are expected to submit to once they reach the age of fifty, and I hadn't really been paying attention then. The results of that earlier session had aroused some "concern" on the part of the radiologist and her confederate, the gynecologist, so I am back now in the role of a suspect, eager to clear my name, alert to medical missteps and unfair allegations. But the changing room, really just a closet off the stark windowless space that houses the mammogram machine, contains something far worse, I notice for the first time now — an assumption about who I am, where I am going, and what I will need when I get there. Almost all of the eye-level space has been filled with photocopied bits of cuteness and sentimentality: pink ribbons, a cartoon about a woman with iatrogenically flattened breasts, an "Ode to a Mammogram," a list of the "Top Ten Things Only Women Understand" ("Fat Clothes" and "Eyelash Curlers" among them), and, inescapably, right next to the door, the poem "I Said a Prayer for You Today," illustrated with pink roses.

It goes on and on, this mother of all mammograms, cutting into gym time, dinnertime, and lifetime generally. Sometimes the machine doesn't work, and I get squished into position to no purpose at all. More often, the x-ray is successful but apparently alarming to the invisible radiologist, off in some remote office, who calls the shots and never has the courtesy to show her face with an apology or an explanation. I try pleading with the technician: I have no known risk factors, no breast cancer in the family, had my babies relatively young and nursed them both. I eat right, drink sparingly, work out, and doesn't that count for something? But she just gets this tight little professional smile on her face, either out of guilt for the torture she's inflicting or because she already knows something that I am going to be sorry to find out for myself. For an hour and a half the procedure is repeated: the squishing, the snapshot, the technician bustling off to consult the radiologist and returning with a demand for new angles and more definitive images. In the intervals while she's off with the doctor I read the *New York Times* right down to the personally irrelevant sections like theater and real estate, eschewing the stack of women's magazines provided for me, much as I ordinarily enjoy a quick read about sweatproof eyeliners and "fabulous sex tonight," because I have picked up this warning vibe in the changing room, which, in my increasingly anxious state, translates into: femininity is death. Finally there is nothing left to read but one of the free local weekly newspapers, where I find, buried deep in the classifieds, something even more unsettling than the growing prospect of major disease — a classified ad for a "breast cancer teddy bear" with a pink ribbon stitched to its chest.

Yes, atheists pray in their foxholes — in this case, with a yearning new to me and sharp as lust, for a clean and honorable death by shark bite, lightning strike, sniper fire, car crash. Let me be hacked to death by a madman, is my silent supplication — anything but suffocation by the pink sticky sentiment embodied in that bear and oozing from the walls of the changing room.

My official induction into breast cancer comes about ten days later with the biopsy, which, for reasons I cannot ferret out of the surgeon, has to be a surgical one, performed on an outpatient basis but under general anesthesia, from which I awake to find him standing perpendicular to me, at the far end of the gurney, down near my feet, stating gravely, "Unfortunately, there is a cancer." It takes me all the rest of that drug-addled day to decide that the

most heinous thing about that sentence is not the presence of cancer but the absence of me — for I, Barbara, do not enter into it
even as a location, a geographical reference point. Where I once
was — not a commanding presence perhaps, but nonetheless a
standard assemblage of flesh and words and gesture — "there is a
cancer." I have been replaced by it, is the surgeon's implication.
This is what I am now, medically speaking.

In my last act of dignified self-assertion, I request to see the pathology slides myself. This is not difficult to arrange in our small-
town hospital, where the pathologist turns out to be a friend of a
friend, and my rusty Ph.D. in cell biology (Rockefeller University,
1968) probably helps. He's a jolly fellow, the pathologist, who calls
me "hon" and sits me down at one end of the dual-head microscope while he mans the other and moves a pointer through the
field. These are the cancer cells, he says, showing up blue because
of their overactive DNA. Most of them are arranged in staid semi-
circular arrays, like suburban houses squeezed into a cul-de-sac,
but I also see what I know enough to know I do not want to see: the
characteristic "Indian files" of cells on the march. The "enemy," I
am supposed to think — an image to save up for future exercises
in "visualization" of their violent deaths at the hands of the body's
killer cells, the lymphocytes and macrophages. But I am impressed,
against all rational self-interest, by the energy of these cellular
conga lines, their determination to move on out from the back-
water of the breast to colonize lymph nodes, bone marrow, lungs,
and brain. These are, after all, the fanatics of Barbaraness, the rebel cells that have realized that the genome they carry, the genetic
essence of me, has no further chance of normal reproduction in
the postmenopausal body we share, so why not just start multiplying like bunnies and hope for a chance to break out?

It has happened, after all; some genomes have achieved immor-
tality through cancer. When I was a graduate student, I once asked
about the strain of tissue-culture cells labeled "HeLa" in the heavy-
doored room maintained at body temperature. "HeLa," it turns
out, refers to one Henrietta Lacks, whose tumor was the progeni-
tor of all HeLa cells. She died; they live, and will go on living until
someone gets tired of them or forgets to change their tissue-culture medium and leaves them to starve. Maybe this is what my rebel cells have in mind, and I try beaming them a solemn warning:

The chances of your surviving me in tissue culture are nil. Keep up this selfish rampage and you go down, every last one of you, along with the entire Barbara enterprise. But what kind of a role model am I, or are multicellular human organisms generally, for putting the common good above mad anarchistic individual ambition? There is a reason, it occurs to me, why cancer is our metaphor for so many runaway social processes, like corruption and "moral decay": we are no less out of control ourselves.

After the visit to the pathologist, my biological curiosity drops to a lifetime nadir. I know women who followed up their diagnoses with weeks or months of self-study, mastering their options, interviewing doctor after doctor, assessing the damage to be expected from the available treatments. But I can tell from a few hours of investigation that the career of a breast-cancer patient has been pretty well mapped out in advance for me: You may get to negotiate the choice between lumpectomy and mastectomy, but lumpectomy is commonly followed by weeks of radiation, and in either case if the lymph nodes turn out, upon dissection, to be invaded — or "involved," as it's less threateningly put — you're doomed to chemotherapy, meaning baldness, nausea, mouth sores, immunosuppression, and possible anemia. These interventions do not constitute a "cure" or anything close, which is why the death rate from breast cancer has changed very little since the 1930s, when mastectomy was the only treatment available. Chemotherapy, which became a routine part of breast-cancer treatment in the eighties, does not confer anywhere near as decisive an advantage as patients are often led to believe, especially in postmenopausal women like myself — a two or three percentage point difference in ten-year survival rates,* according to America's best-known breast-cancer surgeon, Dr. Susan Love.

I know these bleak facts, or sort of know them, but in the fog of anesthesia that hangs over those first few weeks, I seem to lose my capacity for self-defense. The pressure is on, from doctors and loved ones, to do something right away — kill it, get it out now. The endless exams, the bone scan to check for metastases, the

*In the United States, one in eight women will be diagnosed with breast cancer at some point. The chances of her surviving for five years are 86.8 percent. For a black woman this falls to 72 percent; and for a woman of any race whose cancer has spread to the lymph nodes, to 77.7 percent.

high-tech heart test to see if I'm strong enough to withstand chemotherapy — all these blur the line between selfhood and thing-
hood anyway, organic and inorganic, me and it. As my cancer career unfolds, I will, the helpful pamphlets explain, become a com-
posite of the living and the dead — an implant to replace the
breast, a wig to replace the hair. And then what will I mean when I
use the word "I"? I fall into a state of unreasoning passive aggres-
sivity: They diagnosed this, so it's their baby. They found it, let
them fix it.

I could take my chances with "alternative" treatments, of course,
like punk novelist Kathy Acker, who succumbed to breast cancer in
1997 after a course of alternative therapies in Mexico, or actress
and ThighMaster promoter Suzanne Somers, who made tabloid
headlines last spring by injecting herself with mistletoe brew. Or I
could choose to do nothing at all beyond mentally exhorting my
immune system to exterminate the traitorous cellular faction. But I
have never admired the "natural" or believed in the "wisdom of the
body." Death is as "natural" as anything gets, and the body has always seemed to me like a retarded Siamese twin dragging along behind me, a hysteric really, dangerously overreacting, in my case, to
everyday allergens and minute ingestions of sugar. I will put my
faith in science, even if this means that the dumb old body is about
to be transmogrified into an evil clown — puking, trembling, swelling, surrendering significant parts, and oozing postsurgical fluids.
The surgeon — a more genial and forthcoming one this time —
can fit me in; the oncologist will see me. Welcome to Cancerland.

Fortunately, no one has to go through this alone. Thirty years ago,
before Betty Ford, Rose Kushner, Betty Rollin, and other pioneer
patients spoke out, breast cancer was a dread secret, endured in silence and euphemized in obituaries as a "long illness." Something
about the conjuncture of "breast," signifying sexuality and nurtur-
ance, and that other word, suggesting the claws of a devouring
crustacean, spooked almost everyone. Today, however, it's the biggest disease on the cultural map, bigger than AIDS, cystic fibro-
sis, or spinal injury, bigger even than those more prolific killers
of women — heart disease, lung cancer, and stroke. There are
roughly hundreds of Web sites devoted to it, not to mention news-
letters, support groups, a whole genre of first-person breast-cancer

books, even a glossy, upper-middle-brow monthly magazine, *Mamm*. There are four major national breast-cancer organizations, of which the mightiest, in financial terms, is the Susan G. Komen Foundation, headed by breast-cancer veteran and Bush's nominee for ambassador to Hungary Nancy Brinker. Komen organizes the annual Race for the Cure©, which attracts about a million people — mostly survivors, friends, and family members. Its Web site provides a microcosm of the new breast-cancer culture, offering news of the races, message boards for accounts of individuals' struggles with the disease, and a "marketplace" of breast-cancer-related products to buy.

More so than in the case of any other disease, breast-cancer organizations and events feed on a generous flow of corporate support. Nancy Brinker relates how her early attempts to attract corporate interest in promoting breast-cancer "awareness" were met with rebuff. A bra manufacturer, importuned to affix a mammogram-reminder tag to his product, more or less wrinkled his nose. Now breast cancer has blossomed from wallflower to the most popular girl at the corporate charity prom. While AIDS goes begging and low-rent diseases like tuberculosis have no friends at all, breast cancer has been able to count on Revlon, Avon, Ford, Tiffany, Pier 1, Estée Lauder, Ralph Lauren, Lee Jeans, Saks Fifth Avenue, JC Penney, Boston Market, Wilson athletic gear — and I apologize to those I've omitted. You can "shop for the cure" during the week when Saks donates 2 percent of sales to a breast-cancer fund; "wear denim for the cure" during Lee National Denim Day, when for a five-dollar donation you get to wear bluejeans to work. You can even "invest for the cure," in the Kinetics Assets Management's new no-load Medical Fund, which specializes entirely in businesses involved in cancer research.

If you can't run, bike, or climb a mountain for the cure — all of which endeavors are routine beneficiaries of corporate sponsorship — you can always purchase one of the many products with a breast-cancer theme. There are 2.2 million American women in various stages of their breast-cancer careers, who, along with anxious relatives, make up a significant market for all things breast-cancer-related. Bears, for example: I have identified four distinct lines, or species, of these creatures, including "Carol," the Remembrance Bear; "Hope," the Breast Cancer Research Bear, which wears a pink turban as if to conceal chemotherapy-induced baldness; the "Susan Bear," named for Nancy Brinker's deceased sister, Susan; and the new Nick & Nora Wish Upon a Star Bear, available, along with the Susan Bear, at the Komen Foundation Web site's "marketplace."

And bears are only the tip, so to speak, of the cornucopia of pink-ribbon-themed breast-cancer products. You can dress in pink-beribboned sweatshirts, denim shirts, pajamas, lingerie, aprons, loungewear, shoelaces, and socks; accessorize with pink rhinestone brooches, angel pins, scarves, caps, earrings, and bracelets; brighten up your home with breast-cancer candles, stained-glass pink-ribbon candleholders, coffee mugs, pendants, wind chimes, and night-lights; pay your bills with special BreastChecks or a separate line of Checks for the Cure. "Awareness" beats secrecy and stigma, of course, but I can't help noticing that the existential space in which a friend has earnestly advised me to "confront [my] mortality" bears a striking resemblance to the mall.

This is not, I should point out, a case of cynical merchants exploiting the sick. Some of the breast-cancer tchotchkes and accessories are made by breast-cancer survivors themselves, such as "Janice," creator of the "Daisy Awareness Necklace," among other things, and in most cases a portion of the sales goes to breast-cancer research. Virginia Davis of Aurora, Colorado, was inspired to create the "Remembrance Bear" by a friend's double mastectomy and sees her work as more of a "crusade" than a business. This year she expects to ship ten thousand of these teddies, which are manufactured in China, and send part of the money to the Race for the Cure. If the bears are infantilizing — as I try ever so tactfully to suggest is how they may, in rare cases, be perceived — so far no one has complained. "I just get love letters," she tells me, "from people who say, 'God bless you for thinking of us.'"

The ultrafeminine theme of the breast-cancer "marketplace" — the prominence, for example, of cosmetics and jewelry — could be understood as a response to the treatments' disastrous effects on one's looks. But the infantilizing trope is a little harder to account for, and teddy bears are not its only manifestation. A tote bag distributed to breast-cancer patients by the Libby Ross Foundation (through places such as the Columbia Presbyterian Medical Center) contains, among other items, a tube of Estée Lauder

Perfumed Body Crème, a hot-pink satin pillowcase, an audio-tape "Meditation to Help You with Chemotherapy," a small tin of peppermint pastilles, a set of three small inexpensive rhinestone bracelets, a pink-striped "journal and sketch book," and — somewhat jarringly — a small box of crayons. Maria Willner, one of the founders of the Libby Ross Foundation, told me that the crayons "go with the journal for people to express different moods, different thoughts," though she admitted she has never tried to write with crayons herself. Possibly the idea is that regression to a state of childlike dependency puts one in the best frame of mind with which to endure the prolonged and toxic treatments. Or it may be that, in some versions of the prevailing gender ideology, femininity is by its nature incompatible with full adulthood — a state of arrested development. Certainly men diagnosed with prostate cancer do not receive gifts of Matchbox cars.

But I, no less than the bear huggers, need whatever help I can get, and start wading out into the Web in search of practical tips on hair loss, lumpectomy versus mastectomy, how to select a chemotherapy regimen, what to wear after surgery and eat when the scent of food sucks. There is, I soon find, far more than I can usefully absorb, for thousands of the afflicted have posted their stories, beginning with the lump or bad mammogram, proceeding through the agony of the treatments; pausing to mention the sustaining forces of family, humor, and religion; and ending, in almost all cases, with warm words of encouragement for the neophyte. Some of these are no more than a paragraph long — brief waves from sister sufferers; others offer almost hour-by-hour logs of breast-deprived, chemotherapized lives:

> Tuesday, August 15, 2000: Well, I survived my 4th chemo. Very, very dizzy today. Very nauseated, but no barfing! It's a first . . . I break out in a cold sweat and my heart pounds if I stay up longer than 5 minutes.

> Friday, August 18, 2000: . . . By dinner time, I was full out nauseated. I took some meds and ate a rice and vegetable bowl from Trader Joe's. It smelled and tasted awful to me, but I ate it anyway . . . Rick brought home some Kern's nectars and I'm drinking that. Seems to have settled my stomach a little bit.

I can't seem to get enough of these tales, reading on with panicky fascination about everything that can go wrong — septicemia, ruptured implants, startling recurrences a few years after the completion of treatments, "mets" (metastases) to vital organs, and — what scares me most in the short term — "chemo-brain," or the cognitive deterioration that sometimes accompanies chemotherapy. I compare myself with everyone, selfishly impatient with those whose conditions are less menacing, shivering over those who have reached Stage IV ("There is no Stage V," as the main character in *Wit,* who has ovarian cancer, explains), constantly assessing my chances.

Feminism helped make the spreading breast-cancer sisterhood possible, and this realization gives me a faint feeling of belonging. Thirty years ago, when the disease went hidden behind euphemism and prostheses, medicine was a solid patriarchy, women's bodies its passive objects of labor. The Women's Health Movement, in which I was an activist in the seventies and eighties, legitimized self-help and mutual support and encouraged women to network directly, sharing their stories, questioning the doctors, banding together. It is hard now to recall how revolutionary these activities once seemed, and probably few participants in breast-cancer chat rooms and message boards realize that when postmastectomy patients first proposed meeting in support groups in the mid-1970s, the American Cancer Society responded with a firm and fatherly "no." Now no one leaves the hospital without a brochure directing her to local support groups and, at least in my case, a follow-up call from a social worker to see whether I am safely ensconced in one. This cheers me briefly, until I realize that if support groups have won the stamp of medical approval, this may be because they are no longer perceived as seditious.

In fact, aside from the dilute sisterhood of the cyber (and actual) support groups, there is nothing very feminist — in an ideological or activist sense — about the mainstream of breast-cancer culture today. Let me pause to qualify: you can, if you look hard enough, find plenty of genuine, self-identified feminists within the vast pink sea of the breast-cancer crusade, women who are militantly determined to "beat the epidemic" and insistent on more user-friendly approaches to treatment. It was feminist health activists who led the campaign, in the seventies and eighties, against the most savage form of breast-cancer surgery — the Halsted radical mastectomy, which removed chest muscle and lymph nodes as well as breast tissue and left women permanently disabled. It was the Women's Health Movement that put a halt to the surgical practice, common in the seventies, of proceeding directly from biopsy to mastectomy without ever rousing the patient from anesthesia. More recently, feminist advocacy groups such as the San Francisco–based Breast Cancer Action and the Cambridge-based Women's Community Cancer Project helped blow the whistle on "high-dose chemotherapy," in which the bone marrow was removed prior to otherwise lethal doses of chemotherapy and later replaced — to no good effect, as it turned out.

Like everyone else in the breast-cancer world, the feminists want a cure, but they even more ardently demand to know the cause or causes of the disease without which we will never have any means of prevention. "Bad" genes of the inherited variety are thought to account for fewer than 10 percent of breast cancers, and only 30 percent of women diagnosed with breast cancer have any known risk factor (such as delaying childbearing or the late onset of menopause) at all. Bad lifestyle choices like a fatty diet have, after brief popularity with the medical profession, been largely ruled out. Hence suspicion should focus on environmental carcinogens, the feminists argue, such as plastics, pesticides (DDT and PCBs, for example, though banned in this country, are still used in many Third World sources of the produce we eat), and the industrial runoff in our ground water. No carcinogen has been linked definitely to human breast cancer yet, but many have been found to cause the disease in mice, and the inexorable increase of the disease in industrialized nations — about 1 percent a year between the 1950s and the 1990s — further hints at environmental factors, as does the fact that women migrants to industrialized countries quickly develop the same breast-cancer rates as those who are native born. Their emphasis on possible ecological factors, which is not shared by groups such as Komen and the American Cancer Society, puts the feminist breast-cancer activists in league with other, frequently rambunctious, social movements — environmental and anti-corporate.

But today theirs are discordant voices in a general chorus of sentimentality and good cheer; after all, breast cancer would hardly be the darling of corporate America if its complexion changed from pink to green. It is the very blandness of breast cancer, at least in mainstream perceptions, that makes it an attractive object of corporate charity and a way for companies to brand themselves friends of the middle-aged female market. With breast cancer, "there was no concern that you might actually turn off your audience because of the life style or sexual connotations that AIDS has," Amy Langer, director of the National Alliance of Breast Cancer Organizations, told the *New York Times* in 1996. "That gives corporations a certain freedom and a certain relief in supporting the cause." Or as Cindy Pearson, director of the National Women's Health Network, the organizational progeny of the Women's Health Movement, puts it more caustically: "Breast cancer provides a way of doing something for women, without being feminist."

In the mainstream of breast-cancer culture, one finds very little anger, no mention of possible environmental causes, few complaints about the fact that, in all but the more advanced, metastasized cases, it is the "treatments," not the disease, that cause illness and pain. The stance toward existing treatments is occasionally critical — in *Mamm*, for example — but more commonly grateful; the overall tone almost universally upbeat. The Breast Friends Web site, for example, features a series of inspirational quotes: "Don't Cry Over Anything that Can't Cry Over You," "I Can't Stop the Birds of Sorrow from Circling My Head, but I Can Stop Them from Building a Nest in My Hair," "When Life Hands Out Lemons, Squeeze Out a Smile," "Don't wait for your ship to come in . . . Swim out to meet it," and much more of that ilk. Even in the relatively sophisticated *Mamm*, a columnist bemoans not cancer or chemotherapy but the end of chemotherapy, and humorously proposes to deal with her separation anxiety by pitching a tent outside her oncologist's office. So pervasive is the perkiness of the breast-cancer world that unhappiness requires a kind of apology, as when "Lucy," whose "long term prognosis is not good," starts her personal narrative on breastcancertalk.org by telling us that her story "is not the usual one, full of sweetness and hope, but true nevertheless."

There is, I discover, no single noun to describe a woman with breast cancer. As in the AIDS movement, upon which breast-cancer activism is partly modeled, the words "patient" and "victim," with their aura of self-pity and passivity, have been ruled un-PC. In-

stead, we get verbs: those who are in the midst of their treatments
are described as "battling" or "fighting," sometimes intensified
with "bravely" or "fiercely" — language suggestive of Katharine
Hepburn with her face to the wind. Once the treatments are over,
one achieves the status of "survivor," which is how the women in
my local support group identify themselves, AA style, as we convene to share war stories and rejoice in our "survivorhood": "Hi,
I'm Kathy and I'm a three-year survivor." For those who cease to be
survivors and join the more than forty thousand American women
who succumb to breast cancer each year — again, no noun applies. They are said to have "lost their battle" and may be memori-
alized by photographs carried at races for the cure — our lost,
brave sisters, our fallen soldiers. But in the overwhelmingly Dar-
winian culture that has grown up around breast cancer, martyrs
count for little; it is the "survivors" who merit constant honor and
acclaim. They, after all, offer living proof that expensive and painful treatments may in some cases actually work.

Scared and medically weakened women can hardly be expected
to transform their support groups into bands of activists and rush
out into the streets, but the equanimity of breast-cancer culture
goes beyond mere absence of anger to what looks, all too often,
like a positive embrace of the disease. As "Mary" reports, on the
Bosom Buds message board:

> I really believe I am a much more sensitive and thoughtful person now.
> It might sound funny but I was a real worrier before. Now I don't want
> to waste my energy on worrying. I enjoy life so much more now and in a
> lot of aspects I am much happier now.

Or this from "Andee":

> This was the hardest year of my life but also in many ways the most re-
> warding. I got rid of the baggage, made peace with my family, met many
> amazing people, learned to take very good care of my body so it will
> take care of me, and reprioritized my life.

Cindy Cherry, quoted in the *Washington Post*, goes further:

> If I had to do it over, would I want breast cancer? Absolutely. I'm not the
> same person I was, and I'm glad I'm not. Money doesn't matter any-
> more. I've met the most phenomenal people in my life through this.
> Your friends and family are what matter now.

The First Year of the Rest of Your Life, a collection of brief narratives with a foreword by Nancy Brinker and a share of the royalties going to the Komen Foundation, is filled with such testimonies to the redemptive powers of the disease: "I can honestly say I am happier now than I have ever been in my life — even before the breast cancer." "For me, breast cancer has provided a good kick in the rear to get me started rethinking my life." "I have come out stronger, with a new sense of priorities." Never a complaint about lost time, shattered sexual confidence, or the long-term weakening of the arms caused by lymph-node dissection and radiation. What does not destroy you, to paraphrase Nietzsche, makes you a spunkier, more evolved sort of person.

The effect of this relentless brightsiding is to transform breast cancer into a rite of passage — not an injustice or a tragedy to rail against, but a normal marker in the life cycle, like menopause or graying hair. Everything in mainstream breast-cancer culture serves, no doubt inadvertently, to tame and normalize the disease: the diagnosis may be disastrous, but there are those cunning pink rhinestone angel pins to buy and races to train for. Even the heavy traffic in personal narratives and practical tips, which I found so useful, bears an implicit acceptance of the disease and the current barbarous approaches to its treatment: you can get so busy comparing attractive head scarves that you forget to question a form of treatment that temporarily renders you both bald and immuno-incompetent. Understood as a rite of passage, breast cancer resembles the initiation rites so exhaustively studied by Mircea Eliade: First there is the selection of the initiates — by age in the tribal situation, by mammogram or palpation here. Then come the requisite ordeals — scarification or circumcision within traditional cultures, surgery and chemotherapy for the cancer patient. Finally, the initiate emerges into a new and higher status — an adult and a warrior — or in the case of breast cancer, a "survivor."

And in our implacably optimistic breast-cancer culture, the disease offers more than the intangible benefits of spiritual upward mobility. You can defy the inevitable disfigurements and come out, on the survivor side, actually prettier, sexier, more femme. In the lore of the disease — shared with me by oncology nurses as well as by survivors — chemotherapy smoothes and tightens the skin, helps you lose weight; and, when your hair comes back, it will be fuller, softer, easier to control, and perhaps a surprising new color. These may be myths, but for those willing to get with the prevailing program, opportunities for self-improvement abound. The American Cancer Society offers the "Look Good . . . Feel Better" program, "dedicated to teaching women cancer patients beauty techniques to help restore their appearance and self-image during cancer treatment." Thirty thousand women participate a year, each copping a free makeover and bag of makeup donated by the Cosmetic, Toiletry, and Fragrance Association, the trade association of the cosmetics industry. As for that lost breast: after reconstruction, why not bring the other one up to speed? Of the more than fifty thousand mastectomy patients who opt for reconstruction each year, 17 percent go on, often at the urging of their plastic surgeons, to get additional surgery so that the remaining breast will "match" the more erect and perhaps larger new structure on the other side.

Not everyone goes for cosmetic deceptions, and the question of wigs versus baldness, reconstruction versus undisguised scar, defines one of the few real disagreements in breast-cancer culture. On the more avant-garde, upper-middle-class side, *Mamm* magazine — which features literary critic Eve Kosofsky Sedgwick as a columnist — tends to favor the "natural" look. Here, mastectomy scars can be "sexy" and baldness something to celebrate. The January 2001 cover story features women who "looked upon their baldness not just as a loss, but also as an opportunity: to indulge their playful sides . . . to come in contact, in new ways, with their truest selves." One decorates her scalp with temporary tattoos of peace signs, panthers, and frogs; another expresses herself with a shocking purple wig; a third reports that unadorned baldness makes her feel "sensual, powerful, able to recreate myself with every new day." But no hard feelings toward those who choose to hide their condition under wigs or scarves; it's just a matter, *Mamm* tells us, of "different aesthetics." Some go for pink ribbons; others will prefer the Ralph Lauren Pink Pony breast-cancer motif. But everyone agrees that breast cancer is a chance for creative self-transformation — a makeover opportunity, in fact.

Now, cheerfulness, up to and including delusion and false hope, has a recognized place in medicine. There is plenty of evidence that depressed and socially isolated people are more prone to succumb to diseases, cancer included, and a diagnosis of cancer is probably capable of precipitating serious depression all by itself. To be told by authoritative figures that you have a deadly disease, for which no real cure exists, is to enter a liminal state fraught with perils that go well beyond the disease itself. Consider the phenomenon of "voodoo death" — described by ethnographers among, for example, Australian aborigines — in which a person who has been condemned by a suitably potent curse obligingly shuts down and dies within a day or two. Cancer diagnoses could, and in some cases probably do, have the same kind of fatally dispiriting effect. So, it could be argued, the collectively pumped-up optimism of breast-cancer culture may be just what the doctor ordered. Shop for the Cure, dress in pink-ribbon regalia, organize a run or hike — whatever gets you through the night.

But in the seamless world of breast-cancer culture, where one Web site links to another — from personal narratives and grassroots endeavors to the glitzy level of corporate sponsors and celebrity spokespeople — cheerfulness is more or less mandatory, dissent a kind of treason. Within this tightly knit world, attitudes are subtly adjusted, doubters gently brought back to the fold. In *The First Year of the Rest of Your Life*, for example, each personal narrative is followed by a study question or tip designed to counter the slightest hint of negativity — and they are very slight hints indeed, since the collection includes no harridans, whiners, or feminist militants:

> Have you given yourself permission to acknowledge you have some anxiety or "blues" and to ask for help for your emotional well-being?

> Is there an area in your life of unresolved internal conflict? Is there an area where you think you might want to do some "healthy mourning"?

> Try keeping a list of the things you find "good about today."

As an experiment, I post a statement on the Komen.org message board, under the subject line "angry," briefly listing my own heartfelt complaints about debilitating treatments, recalcitrant insurance companies, environmental carcinogens, and, most daringly, "sappy pink ribbons." I receive a few words of encouragement in my fight with the insurance company, which has taken the position that my biopsy was a kind of optional indulgence, but mostly a chorus of rebukes. "Suzy" writes to say, "I really dislike saying you have a bad attitude towards all of this, but you do, and it's not going to help you in the least." "Mary" is a bit more tolerant, writing, "Barb, at this time in your life, it's so important to put all your energies toward a peaceful, if not happy, existence. Cancer is a rotten thing to have happen and there are no answers for any of us as to why. But to live your life, whether you have one more year or 51, in anger and bitterness is such a waste . . . I hope you can find some peace. You deserve it. We all do. God bless you and keep you in His loving care. Your sister, Mary."

"Kitty," however, thinks I've gone around the bend: "You need to run, not walk, to some counseling . . . Please, get yourself some help and I ask everyone on this site to pray for you so you can enjoy life to the fullest."

I do get some reinforcement from "Gerri," who has been through all the treatments and now finds herself in terminal condition: "I am also angry. All the money that is raised, all the smiling faces of survivors who make it sound like it is o.k. to have breast cancer. IT IS NOT O.K.!" But Gerri's message, like the others on the message board, is posted under the mocking heading "What does it mean to be a breast cancer survivor?"

"Culture" is too weak a word to describe all this. What has grown up around breast cancer in just the past fifteen years more nearly resembles a cult — or, given that it numbers more than two million women, their families, and friends — perhaps we should say a full-fledged religion. The products — teddy bears, pink-ribbon brooches, and so forth — serve as amulets and talismans, comforting the sufferer and providing visible evidence of faith. The personal narratives serve as testimonials and follow the same general arc as the confessional autobiographies required of seventeenth-century Puritans: first there is a crisis, often involving a sudden apprehension of mortality (the diagnosis or, in the old Puritan case, a stern word from on high); then comes a prolonged ordeal (the treatment or, in the religious case, internal struggle with the devil); and finally, the blessed certainty of salvation, or its breast-cancer equivalent, survivorhood. And like most recognized religions, breast cancer has its great epideictic events, its pilgrimages and mass gatherings where the faithful convene and draw strength from their numbers. These are the annual races for a cure, attracting a total of about a million people at more than eighty sites — seventy thousand of them at the largest event, in Washington, D.C., which in recent years has been attended by Dan and Marilyn Quayle and Al and Tipper Gore. Everything comes together at the races: celebrities and corporate sponsors are showcased; products are hawked; talents, like those of the "Swinging, Singing Survivors" from Syracuse, New York, are displayed. It is at the races, too, that the elect confirm their special status. As one participant wrote in the *Washington Post:*

> I have taken my "battle scarred" breasts to the Mall, donned the pink shirt, visor, pink shoelaces, etc. and walked proudly among my fellow veterans of the breast cancer war. In 1995, at the age of 44, I was diagnosed and treated for Stage II breast cancer. The experience continues to redefine my life.

Feminist breast-cancer activists, who in the early nineties were organizing their own mass outdoor events — demonstrations, not races — to demand increased federal funding for research, tend to keep their distance from these huge, corporate-sponsored, pink gatherings. Ellen Leopold, for example — a member of the Women's Community Cancer Project in Cambridge and author of *A Darker Ribbon: Breast Cancer, Women, and Their Doctors in the Twentieth Century* — has criticized the races as an inefficient way of raising money. She points out that the Avon Breast Cancer Crusade, which sponsors three-day, sixty-mile walks, spends more than a third of the money raised on overhead and advertising, and Komen may similarly fritter away up to 25 percent of its gross. At least one corporate-charity insider agrees. "It would be much easier and more productive," says Rob Wilson, an organizer of charitable races for corporate clients, "if people, instead of running or riding, would write out a check to the charity."

To true believers, such criticisms miss the point, which is always, ultimately, "awareness." Whatever you do to publicize the disease — wear a pink ribbon, buy a teddy, attend a race — reminds other women to come forward for their mammograms. Hence, too, they would argue, the cult of the "survivor": if women neglect their annual screenings, it must be because they are afraid that a diagnosis amounts to a death sentence. Beaming survivors, proudly displaying their athletic prowess, are the best possible advertisement for routine screening mammograms, early detection, and the ensuing round of treatments. Yes, miscellaneous businesses — from tiny distributors of breast-cancer wind chimes and note cards to major corporations seeking a woman-friendly image — benefit in the process, not to mention the breast-cancer industry itself, the estimated $12-billion- to $16-billion-a-year business in surgery, "breast health centers," chemotherapy "infusion suites," radiation treatment centers, mammograms, and drugs ranging from anti-emetics (to help you survive the nausea of chemotherapy) to tamoxifen (the hormonal treatment for women with estrogen-sensitive tumors). But what's to complain about? Seen through pink-tinted lenses, the entire breast-cancer enterprise — from grassroots support groups and Web sites to the corporate providers of therapies and sponsors of races — looks like a beautiful example of synergy at work: cult activities, paraphernalia, and testimonies encourage women to undergo the diagnostic procedures, and since a fraction of these diagnoses will be positive, this means more members for the cult as well as more customers for the corporations, both those that provide medical products and services and those that offer charitable sponsorships.

But this view of a life-giving synergy is only as sound as the science of current detection and treatment modalities, and, tragically, that science is fraught with doubt, dissension, and what sometimes looks very much like denial. Routine screening mammograms, for example, are the major goal of "awareness," as when Rosie O'Donnell exhorts us to go out and "get squished." But not all breast-cancer experts are as enthusiastic. At best the evidence for the salutary effects of routine mammograms — as opposed to breast self-examination — is equivocal, with many respectable large-scale studies showing a vanishingly small impact on overall breast-cancer mortality. For one thing, there are an estimated two to four false positives for every cancer detected, leading thousands of healthy women to go through unnecessary biopsies and anxiety. And even if mammograms were 100 percent accurate, the admirable goal of "early" detection is more elusive than the current breast-cancer dogma admits. A small tumor, detectable only by mammogram, is not necessarily young and innocuous; if it has not spread to the lymph nodes, which is the only form of spreading detected in the common surgical procedure of lymph-node dissection, it may have already moved on to colonize other organs via the bloodstream. David Plotkin, director of the Memorial Cancer Research Foundation of Southern California, concludes that the benefits of routine mammography "are not well established; if they do exist, they are not as great as many women hope." Alan Spievack, a surgeon recently retired from the Harvard Medical School, goes further, concluding from his analysis of dozens of studies that routine screening mammography is, in the words of famous British surgeon Dr. Michael Baum, "one of the greatest deceptions perpetrated on the women of the Western world."

Even if foolproof methods for early detection existed,* they would, at the present time, serve only as portals to treatments offering dubious protection and considerable collateral damage. Some women diagnosed with breast cancer will live long enough to die of something else, and some of these lucky ones will indeed owe their longevity to a combination of surgery, chemotherapy, radiation, and/or anti-estrogen drugs such as tamoxifen. Others, though, would have lived untreated or with surgical excision alone, either because their cancers were slow-growing or because their bodies' own defenses were successful. Still others will die of the disease no matter what heroic, cell-destroying therapies are applied. The trouble is, we do not have the means to distinguish between these three groups. So for many of the thousands of women who are diagnosed each year, Plotkin notes, "the sole effect of early detection has been to stretch out the time in which the woman bears the knowledge of her condition." These women do not live longer than they might have without any medical intervention, but more of the time they do live is overshadowed with the threat of death and wasted in debilitating treatments.

To the extent that current methods of detection and treatment fail or fall short, America's breast-cancer cult can be judged as an outbreak of mass delusion, celebrating survivorhood by downplaying mortality and promoting obedience to medical protocols known to have limited efficacy. And although we may imagine ourselves to be well past the era of patriarchal medicine, obedience is

---

*Some improved prognostic tools, involving measuring a tumor's growth rate and the extent to which it is supplied with blood vessels, are being developed but are not yet in use.

the message behind the infantilizing theme in breast-cancer culture, as represented by the teddy bears, the crayons, and the prevailing pinkness. You are encouraged to regress to a little-girl state, to suspend critical judgment, and to accept whatever measures the doctors, as parent surrogates, choose to impose.

Worse, by ignoring or underemphasizing the vexing issue of environmental causes, the breast-cancer cult turns women into dupes of what could be called the Cancer Industrial Complex: the multinational corporate enterprise that with the one hand doles out carcinogens and disease and, with the other, offers expensive, semitoxic pharmaceutical treatments. Breast Cancer Awareness Month, for example, is sponsored by AstraZeneca (the manufacturer of tamoxifen), which, until a corporate reorganization in 2000, was a leading producer of pesticides, including acetochlor, classified by the EPA as a "probable human carcinogen." This particularly nasty conjuncture of interests led the environmentally oriented Cancer Prevention Coalition (CPC) to condemn Breast Cancer Awareness Month as "a public relations invention by a major polluter which puts women in the position of being unwitting allies of the very people who make them sick." Although AstraZeneca no longer manufactures pesticides, CPC has continued to criticize the breast-cancer crusade — and the American Cancer Society — for its unquestioning faith in screening mammograms and careful avoidance of environmental issues. In a June 12, 2001, press release, CPC chairman Samuel S. Epstein, M.D., and the well-known physician activist Quentin Young castigated the American Cancer Society for its "longstanding track record of indifference and even hostility to cancer prevention . . . Recent examples include issuing a joint statement with the Chlorine Institute justifying the continued global use of persistent organochlorine pesticides, and also supporting the industry in trivializing dietary pesticide residues as avoidable risks of childhood cancer. ACS policies are further exemplified by allocating under 0.1 percent of its $700 million annual budget to environmental and occupational causes of cancer."

In the harshest judgment, the breast-cancer cult serves as an accomplice in global poisoning — normalizing cancer, prettying it up, even presenting it, perversely, as a positive and enviable experience.

*

When, my three months of chemotherapy completed, the oncology nurse calls to congratulate me on my "excellent blood work results," I modestly demur. I didn't do anything, I tell her, anything but endure — marking the days off on the calendar, living on Protein Revolution canned vanilla health shakes, escaping into novels and work. Courtesy restrains me from mentioning the fact that the tumor markers she's tested for have little prognostic value, that there's no way to know how many rebel cells survived chemotherapy and may be carving out new colonies right now. She insists I should be proud; I'm a survivor now and entitled to recognition at the Relay for Life being held that very evening in town.

So I show up at the middle school track where the relay's going on just in time for the Survivors' March: about a hundred people, including a few men, since the funds raised will go to cancer research in general, are marching around the track eight to twelve abreast while a loudspeaker announces their names and survival times and a thin line of observers, mostly people staffing the raffle and food booths, applauds. It could be almost any kind of festivity, except for the distinctive stacks of cellophane-wrapped pink Hope Bears for sale in some of the booths. I cannot help but like the funky small-town gemütlichkeit of the event, especially when the audio system strikes up that universal anthem of solidarity, "We Are Family," and a few people of various ages start twisting to the music on the jury-rigged stage. But the money raised is going far away, to the American Cancer Society, which will not be asking us for our advice on how to spend it.

I approach a woman I know from other settings, one of our local intellectuals, as it happens, decked out here in a pink-and-yellow survivor T-shirt and with an American Cancer Society "survivor medal" suspended on a purple ribbon around her neck. "When do you date your survivorship from?" I ask her, since the announced time, five and a half years, seems longer than I recall. "From diagnosis or the completion of your treatments?" The question seems to annoy or confuse her, so I do not press on to what I really want to ask: at what point, in a downwardly sloping breast-cancer career, does one put aside one's survivor regalia and admit to being in fact a die-er? For the dead are with us even here, though in much diminished form. A series of paper bags, each about the right size for a junior burger and fries, lines the track. On them are the names of the dead, and inside each is a candle that will be lit later, after dark, when the actual relay race begins.

My friend introduces me to a knot of other women in survivor gear, breast-cancer victims all, I learn, though of course I would not use the V-word here. "Does anyone else have trouble with the term 'survivor'?" I ask, and, surprisingly, two or three speak up. It could be "unlucky," one tells me; it "tempts fate," says another, shuddering slightly. After all, the cancer can recur at any time, either in the breast or in some more strategic site. No one brings up my own objection to the term, though: that the mindless triumphalism of "survivorhood" denigrates the dead and the dying. Did we who live "fight" harder than those who've died? Can we claim to be "braver," better people than the dead? And why is there no room in this cult for some gracious acceptance of death, when the time comes, which it surely will, through cancer or some other misfortune?

No, this is not my sisterhood. For me at least, breast cancer will never be a source of identity or pride. As my dying correspondent Gerri wrote: "IT IS NOT O.K.!" What it is, along with cancer generally or any slow and painful way of dying, is an abomination, and, to the extent that it's manmade, also a crime. This is the one great truth that I bring out of the breast-cancer experience, which did not, I can now report, make me prettier or stronger, more feminine or spiritual — only more deeply angry. What sustained me through the "treatments" is a purifying rage, a resolve, framed in the sleepless nights of chemotherapy, to see the last polluter, along with, say, the last smug health-insurance operative, strangled with the last pink ribbon. Cancer or no cancer, I will not live that long, of course. But I know this much right now for sure: I will not go into that last good night with a teddy bear tucked under my arm.

JONATHAN FRANZEN

My Father's Brain

FROM THE NEW YORKER

HERE'S A MEMORY. On an overcast morning in February 1996, I received in the mail from my mother, in St. Louis, a Valentine's package containing one pinkly romantic greeting card, two four-ounce Mr. Goodbars, one hollow red filigree heart on a loop of thread, and one copy of a neuropathologist's report on my father's brain autopsy.

I remember the bright gray winter light that morning. I remember leaving the candy, the card, and the ornament in my living room, taking the autopsy report into my bedroom, and sitting down to read it. *The brain* (it began) *weighed 1,255 gm and showed parasagittal atrophy with sulcal widening.* I remember translating grams into pounds and pounds into the familiar shrink-wrapped equivalents in a supermarket meat case. I remember putting the report back into its envelope without reading any further.

Some years before he died, my father had participated in a study of memory and aging sponsored by Washington University, and one of the perks for participants was a postmortem brain autopsy, free of charge. I suspect that the study offered other perks of monitoring and treatment which had led my mother, who loved freebies of all kinds, to insist that my father volunteer for it. Thrift was also probably her only conscious motive for including the autopsy report in my Valentine's package. She was saving thirty-two cents' postage.

My clearest memories of that February morning are visual and spatial: the yellow Mr. Goodbar, my shift from living room to bedroom, the late-morning light of a season as far from the winter solstice as from spring. I'm aware, however, that even these memories aren't to be trusted. According to the latest theories, which are based on a wealth of neurological and psychological research in the last few decades, the brain is not an album in which memories are stored discretely like unchanging photographs. A memory is, instead, in the phrase of the psychologist Daniel L. Schachter, a "temporary constellation" of activity — a necessarily approximate excitation of neural circuits that bind a set of sensory images and semantic data into the momentary sensation of a remembered whole. These images and data are seldom the exclusive property of one particular memory. Indeed, even as my experience on that Valentine's morning was unfolding, my brain was relying on preexisting categories of "red" and "heart" and "Mr. Goodbar"; the gray sky in my windows was familiar from a thousand other winter mornings; and I already had millions of neurons devoted to a picture of my mother — her stinginess with postage, her romantic attachments to her children, her lingering anger toward my father, her weird lack of tact, and so on. What my memory of that morning therefore consists of, according to the latest models, is a set of hardwired neuronal connections among the pertinent regions of the brain, and a predisposition for the entire constellation to light up — chemically, electrically — when any one part of the circuit is stimulated. Speak the words "Mr. Goodbar" and ask me to free-associate, and if I don't say "Diane Keaton" I will surely say "brain autopsy."

My Valentine's memory would work this way even if I were dredging it up now for the first time ever. But the fact is that I've re-remembered that February morning countless times since then. I've told the story to my brothers. I've offered it as an Outrageous Mother Incident to friends of mine who enjoy that kind of thing. I've even, shameful to report, told people I hardly know at all. Each succeeding recollection and retelling reinforces the constellation of images and knowledge that constitute the memory. At the cellular level, according to neuroscientists, I'm burning the memory in a little deeper each time, strengthening the dendritic connections among its components, further encouraging the firing of that specific set of synapses. One of the great adaptive virtues of our brains, the feature that makes our gray matter so much smarter than any machine yet devised (my laptop's cluttered hard drive or a World Wide Web that insists on recalling, in pellucid detail, a *Beverly Hills 90210* fan site last updated on 11/20/98), is our ability to forget almost everything that has ever happened to us. I retain general, largely categorical memories of the past (a year spent in Spain; various visits to Indian restaurants on East Sixth Street) but relatively few specific episodic memories. Those memories that I do retain I tend to revisit and, thereby, strengthen. They become literally — morphologically, electrochemically — part of the architecture of my brain.

This model of memory, which I've presented here in a rather loose layperson's summary, excites the amateur scientist in me. It feels true to the twinned fuzziness and richness of my own memories, and it inspires awe with its image of neural networks effortlessly self-coordinating, in a massively parallel way, to create my ghostly consciousness and my remarkably sturdy sense of self. It seems to me lovely and postmodern. The human brain is a web of a hundred billion neurons, maybe as many as two hundred billion, with trillions of axons and dendrites exchanging quadrillions of messages by way of at least fifty different chemical transmitters. The organ with which we observe and make sense of the universe is, by a comfortable margin, the most complex object we know of in that universe.

And yet it's also a lump of meat. At some point, maybe later on that same Valentine's Day, I forced myself to read the entire pathology report. It included a "Microscopic Description" of my father's brain:

> Sections of the frontal, parietal, occipital, and temporal cerebral cortices showed numerous senile plaques, prominently diffuse type, with minimal numbers of neurofibrillary tangles. Cortical Lewy bodies were easily detected in H&E stained material. The amygdala demonstrated plaques, occasional tangles and mild neuron loss.

In the notice that we had run in local newspapers nine months earlier, my mother insisted that we say my father had died "after long illness." She liked the phrase's formality and reticence, but it was hard not to hear her grievance in it as well, her emphasis on "long." The pathologist's identification of senile plaques in my father's brain served to confirm, as only an autopsy could, the fact with which she'd struggled daily for many years: like millions of other Americans, my father had had Alzheimer's disease.

This was his disease. It was also, you could argue, his story. But you have to let me tell it.

Alzheimer's is a disease of classically "insidious onset." Since even healthy people become more forgetful as they age, there's no way to pinpoint the first memory to fall victim to it. The problem was especially vexed in the case of my father, who not only was depressive and reserved and slightly deaf but also was taking strong medicines for other ailments. For a long time it was possible to chalk up his non sequiturs to his hearing impairment, his forgetfulness to his depression, his hallucinations to his medicines; and chalk them up we did.

My memories of the years of my father's initial decline are vividly about things other than him. Indeed, I'm somewhat appalled by how large I loom in my own memories, how peripheral my parents are. But I was living far from home in those years. My information came mainly from my mother's complaints about my father, and these complaints I took with a grain of salt; she'd been complaining to me pretty much all my life.

My parents' marriage was, it's safe to say, less than happy. They stayed together for the sake of their children and for want of hope that divorce would make them any happier. As long as my father was working, they enjoyed autonomy in their respective fiefdoms of home and workplace, but after he retired, in 1981, they commenced a round-the-clock performance of *No Exit* in their comfortably furnished suburban house. I arrived for brief visits like a U.N. peacekeeping force to which each side passionately presented its case against the other.

In contrast to my mother, who was hospitalized nearly thirty times in her life, my father had perfect health until he retired. His parents and uncles had lived into their eighties and nineties, and he, Earl Franzen, fully expected himself to be around at ninety "to see," as he liked to say, "how things turn out." (His anagrammatic namesake Lear imagined his last years in similar terms: listening to "court news," with Cordelia, to see "who loses and who wins, who's in, who's out.") My father had no hobbies and few pleasures besides eating meals, seeing his children, and playing bridge, but he did take a *narrative* interest in life. He watched a staggering amount of TV news. His ambition for old age was to follow the unfolding histories of the nation and his children for as long as he could.

The passivity of this ambition, the sameness of his days, tended to make him invisible to me. From the early years of his mental decline I can dredge up exactly one direct memory: watching him, toward the end of the eighties, struggle and fail to calculate the tip on a restaurant bill.

Fortunately, my mother was a great writer of letters. My father's passivity, which I regarded as regrettable but not really any of my business, was a source of bitter disappointment to her. As late as the fall of 1989 — a season in which, according to her letters, my father was still playing golf and undertaking major home repairs — the terms of her complaints remained strictly personal:

> It is extremely difficult living with a very unhappy person when you know you must be the major cause of the unhappiness. *Decades* ago when Dad told me he didn't believe there is such a thing as love (that sex is a "trap") and that he was not cut out to be a "happy" person I should have been smart enough to realize there was no hope for a relationship satisfactory to *me.*

This letter dates from a period during which the theater of my parents' war had shifted to the issue of my father's hearing impairment. My mother maintained that it was inconsiderate not to wear a hearing aid; my father complained that other people lacked the consideration to "speak up." The battle culminated Pyrrhically in his purchase of a hearing aid that he then declined to wear. Here again, my mother constructed a moral story of his "stubbornness" and "vanity" and "defeatism"; but it's hard not to suspect, in hindsight, that his faulty ears were already serving to camouflage more serious trouble.

A letter from January 1990 contains my mother's first written reference to this trouble:

> Last week one day he had to skip his breakfasttime medication in order to take some motor skills tests at Wash U. where he is in the Memory & Ageing study. That night I awakened to the sound of his electric razor, looked at the clock & he was in the bathroom shaving at 2:30 A.M.

Within a few months my father was making so many mistakes that my mother was forced to entertain other explanations:

> Either he's stressed or not concentrating or having some mental deterioration but there have been quite a few incidents recently that really worry me. He keeps leaving the car door open or the lights on & twice

in one week we had to call triple A & have them come out & charge the
battery (now I've posted signs in the garage & that seems to have
helped) . . . I really don't like the idea of leaving him in the house alone
for more than a short while.

My mother's fear of leaving him alone assumed greater urgency
as the year wore on. Her right knee was worn out, and, because she
already had a steel plate in her leg from an earlier fracture, she was
facing complicated surgery followed by prolonged recovery and
rehab. Her letters from late 1990 and early 1991 are marked by
paragraphs of agonizing over whether to have surgery and how to
manage my father if she did.

> Were he in the house alone more than overnight with me in the hos-
> pital I would be an absolute basket case as he leaves the water running,
> the stove on at times, lights on everywhere, etc. . . . I check & recheck as
> much as I can on most things lately but even so many of our affairs are
> in a state of confusion & what really is hardest is his resentment of my in-
> trusion — "stay out of my affairs!!!" He does not accept or realize my
> *wanting* to be *helpful* & that is the hardest thing of all for me.

At the time, I'd recently finished my second novel, and so I offered to stay with my father while my mother had her operation.
To steer clear of his pride, she and I agreed to pretend that I was
coming for her sake, not his. What's odd, though, is that I was only
half pretending. My mother's characterization of my father's incapacity was compelling, but so was my father's portrayal of my
mother as an alarmist nag. I went to St. Louis because, for her, his
incapacity was absolutely real; once there, I behaved as if, for me, it
absolutely wasn't.

My mother was in the hospital for nearly five weeks. Strangely, although I'd never lived alone with my father for so long and never
would again, I can now remember almost nothing specific about
my stay with him; I have a general impression that he was somewhat quiet, maybe, but otherwise completely normal. Here, you
might think, was a direct contradiction of my mother's earlier reports. And yet I have no memory of being bothered by the contradiction. What I do have is a copy of a letter that I wrote to a friend
while in St. Louis. In the letter, I mention that my father has had
his medication adjusted and now everything is fine.

Wishful thinking? Yes, to some extent. But one of the basic features of the mind is its keenness to construct wholes out of frag-

mentary parts. We all have a literal blind spot in our vision where the optic nerve attaches to the retina, but our brain unfailingly registers a seamless world around us. We catch part of a word and hear the whole. We see expressive faces in floral-pattern upholstery; we constantly fill in blanks. In a similar way, I think I was inclined to interpolate across my father's silences and mental absences and to persist in seeing him as the same old wholly whole Earl Franzen. I still needed him to be an actor in my story of myself. In my letter to my friend, I describe a morning practice session of the St. Louis Symphony that my mother insisted that my father and I attend so as not to waste her free tickets to it. After the first half of the session, in which the very young Midori *nailed* the Sibelius violin concerto, my father sprang from his seat with miserable geriatric agitation. "So," he said, "we'll go now." I knew better than to ask him to sit through the Charles Ives symphony that was coming, but I hated him for what I took to be his philistinism. On the drive home, he had one comment about Midori and Sibelius. "I don't understand that music," he said. "What do they do — memorize it?"

Later that spring, my father was diagnosed with a small, slow-growing cancer in his prostate. His doctors recommended that he not bother treating it, but he insisted on a course of radiation. With a kind of referred wisdom about his own mental state, he became terrified that something was dreadfully wrong with him: that he would not, after all, survive into his nineties. My mother, whose knee continued to bleed internally six months after her operation, had little patience with what she considered his hypochondria. In September 1991 she wrote:

> I'm relieved to have Dad started on his radiation therapy & it forces him to get out of the house *every day* [inserted here a smiley face] — a big plus . . . Actually, being so sedentary now (content to do nothing), he has had too much time to worry & think about himself — he NEEDS distractions! . . . More & more I feel the greatest attributes anyone can have are (1), a positive attitude & (2), a sense of humor — wish Dad had them.

There ensued some months of relative optimism. The cancer was eradicated, my mother's knee finally improved, and her native hopefulness returned to her letters. She reported that my father had taken first place in a game of bridge: "With his confusion cleared up & his less conservative approach to the game he is doing remarkably well & it's about the only thing he enjoys (& can stay awake for!)." But my father's anxiety about his health did not abate; he had stomach pains that he was convinced were caused by cancer. Gradually, the import of the story my mother was telling me migrated from the personal and the moral toward the psychiatric. "The past six months we have lost so many friends it is very unsettling — part of Dad's nervousness & depression I'm sure," she wrote in February 1992. The letter continued:

> Dad's internist, Dr. Rouse, has about concluded what I have felt all along regarding Dad's stomach discomfort (he's ruled out all clinical possibilities). Dad is (1) terribly nervous, (2) terribly depressed & I hope Dr. Rouse will put him on an anti-depressant. I *know* there has to be help for this . . . If he won't go for counseling (suggested by Dr. Weiss) perhaps he now will accept pills or whatever it takes for nervousness & depression.

For a while, the phrase "nervousness & depression" was a fixture of her letters. Prozac briefly seemed to lift my father's spirits, but the effects were short-lived. Finally, in July 1992, to my surprise, my father agreed to see a psychiatrist.

My father had always been supremely suspicious of psychiatry. He viewed therapy as an invasion of privacy, mental health as a matter of self-discipline, and my mother's increasingly pointed suggestions that he "talk to someone" as acts of aggression — little lobbed grenades of blame for their unhappiness as a couple. It was a measure of his desperation that he had voluntarily set foot in a psychiatrist's office.

In October, when I stopped in St. Louis on my way to Italy, I asked him about his sessions with the doctor. He made a hopeless gesture with his hands. "He's extremely able," he said. "But I'm afraid he's written me off."

The idea of anybody writing my father off was more than I could stand. From Italy I sent the psychiatrist a three-page appeal for reconsideration, but even as I was writing it the roof was caving in at home. "Much as I dislike telling you," my mother wrote in a letter faxed to Italy, "Dad has regressed terribly. Medicine for the urinary problem a urologist is treating in combination with medication for depression and nervousness blew his mind again and the hallucinating, etc., was terrible. " There had been a weekend with my Uncle Erv in Indiana, where my father, removed from his familiar surroundings, unleashed a night of madness that culminated in my uncle's shouting into his face, "Earl, my God, it's your brother, Erv, we slept in the same bed!" Back in St. Louis, my father had begun to rage against the retired lady, Mrs. Pryble, whom my mother had engaged to sit with him two mornings a week while she ran errands. He didn't see why he needed sitting, and, even assuming that he did need sitting, he didn't see why a stranger, rather than his wife, should be doing it. He'd become a classic "sundowner," dozing through the day and rampaging in the wee hours.

There followed a dismal holiday visit during which my wife and I finally intervened on my mother's behalf and put her in touch with a geriatric social worker, and my mother urged my wife and me to tire my father out so that he would sleep through the night without psychotic incident, and my father sat stone-faced by the fireplace or told grim stories of his childhood while my mother fretted about the expense, the prohibitive expense, of sessions with a social worker. But even then, as far as I can remember, nobody ever said "dementia." In all my mother's letters to me, the word "Alzheimer's" appears exactly once, in reference to an old German woman I worked for as a teenager.

I remember my suspicion and annoyance, fifteen years ago, when the term "Alzheimer's disease" was first achieving currency. It seemed to me another instance of the medicalization of human experience, the latest entry in the ever-expanding nomenclature of victimhood. To my mother's news about my old employer I replied, "What you describe sounds like the same old Erika, only quite a bit worse, and that's not how Alzheimer's is supposed to work, is it? I spend a few minutes every month fretting about ordinary mental illness being trendily misdiagnosed as Alzheimer's."

From my current vantage, where I spend a few minutes every month fretting about what a self-righteous thirty-year-old I was, I can see my reluctance to apply the term "Alzheimer's" to my father as a way of protecting the specificity of Earl Franzen from the generality of a namable condition. Conditions have symptoms; symptoms point to the organic basis of everything we are. They point to the brain as meat. And, where I ought to recognize that, yes, the brain is meat, I seem instead to maintain a blind spot across which I then interpolate stories that emphasize the more soul-like aspects of the self. Seeing my afflicted father as a set of organic symptoms would invite me to understand the *healthy* Earl Franzen (and the healthy me) in symptomatic terms as well — to reduce our beloved personalities to finite sets of neurochemical coordinates. Who wants a story of life like that?

Even now, I feel uneasy when I gather facts about Alzheimer's. Reading, for example, David Shenk's *The Forgetting: Alzheimer's: Portrait of an Epidemic,* I'm reminded that when my father got lost in his own neighborhood or forgot to flush the toilet, he was exhibiting symptoms identical to those of millions of other afflicted people. There can be comfort in having company like this, but I'm sorry to see the personal significance drained from certain mistakes of my father's, like his confusion of my mother with her mother, which struck me at the time as singular and orphic and from which I gleaned all manner of important new insights into my parents' marriage. My sense of private selfhood turns out to have been illusory.

Senile dementia has been around for as long as people have had the means of recording it. While the average human life span remained low and old age was a comparative rarity, senility was considered a natural byproduct of aging — perhaps the result of sclerotic cerebral arteries. The German neuropathologist Alois Alzheimer believed he was witnessing an entirely new variety of mental illness when, in 1901, he admitted to his clinic a fifty-one-year-old woman, Auguste D., who was suffering from bizarre mood swings and severe memory loss and who, in Alzheimer's initial examination of her, gave problematic answers to his questions:

"What is your name?"
"Auguste."
"Last name?"
"Auguste."
"What is your husband's name?"
"Auguste, I think."

When Auguste D. died in an institution, four years later, Alzheimer availed himself of recent advances in microscopy and tissue staining and was able to discern, in slides of her brain tissue, the striking dual pathology of her disease: countless sticky-looking globs of "plaque" and countless neurons engulfed by "tangles" of neuronal fibrils. Alzheimer's findings greatly interested his patron Emil Kraepelin, then the dean of German psychiatry, who was engaged in a fierce scientific battle with Sigmund Freud and Freud's psycho-literary theories of mental illness. To Kraepelin, Alzheimer's plaques and tangles provided welcome clinical support for his contention that mental illness was fundamentally organic. In his *Handbook of Psychiatry* he dubbed Auguste D.'s condition *Morbus Alzheimer.*

For six decades after Alois Alzheimer's autopsy of Auguste D., even as breakthroughs in disease prevention and treatment were adding fifteen years to life expectancy in developed nations, Alzheimer's continued to be viewed as a medical rarity à la Huntington's disease. David Shenk tells the story of an American neuropathologist named Meta Neumann, who in the early fifties autopsied the brains of 210 victims of senile dementia and found sclerotic arteries in few of them, plaques and tangles in the majority. Here was ironclad evidence that Alzheimer's was far more common than anyone had guessed; but Neumann's work appears to have persuaded no one. "They felt that Meta was talking nonsense," her husband recalled.

The scientific community simply wasn't ready to consider that senile dementia might be more than a natural consequence of aging. In the early fifties there was no self-conscious category of "seniors," no explosion of Sun Belt retirement developments, no AARP, no Early Bird tradition at low-end restaurants; and scientific thinking reflected these social realities. Not until the seventies did conditions become ripe for a reinterpretation of senile dementia. By then, as Shenk says, "so many people were living so long that senility didn't feel so normal or acceptable anymore." Congress passed the Research on Aging Act in 1974 and established the National Institute on Aging, for which funding soon mushroomed. By the end of the eighties, at the crest of my annoyance with the clinical term and its sudden ubiquity, Alzheimer's had achieved the same social and medical standing as heart disease or cancer — and had the research-funding levels to show for it.

What happened with Alzheimer's in the seventies and eighties wasn't simply a diagnostic paradigm shift. The number of new cases really is soaring. As fewer and fewer people drop dead of heart attacks or die of infections, more and more survive to become demented. Alzheimer's patients in nursing homes live much longer than other patients, at a cost of at least forty thousand dollars annually per patient; until they're institutionalized, they increasingly derange the lives of family members charged with caring for them. Already, five million Americans have the disease, and the number could rise to fifteen million by 2050.

Because there's so much money in chronic illness, drug companies are investing feverishly in proprietary Alzheimer's research while publicly funded scientists file for patents on the side. But because the science of the disease remains cloudy (a functioning brain is not a lot more accessible than the center of the earth or the edge of the universe) nobody can be sure which avenues of research will lead to effective treatments. Early-onset Alzheimer's is usually linked to specific genes, but the vastly more common late-onset variety cannot be traced to a single factor. And the disease's etiology is like the proverbial elephant — it looks like an inflammation of the brain but also like a neurochemical imbalance but also like a disease of abnormal-protein deposition of the kind that occasionally strikes the heart and kidneys.

Treatments currently under study target each of these aspects. People taking cholesterol-reducing drugs or nonsteroidal anti-inflammatory drugs (like aspirin or Celebrex) may enjoy a lower risk of Alzheimer's. Those who already have the disease can sometimes be helped for a while with acetylcholine-boosting medications or antioxidants like vitamin E. There is intense competition among drug companies to develop enzyme inhibitors that zero in on the abnormal proteins. On the immunological front, researchers at Elan Pharmaceuticals recently came up with the seemingly outlandish idea of a vaccine for Alzheimer's — of teaching the immune system to produce antibodies that attack and destroy amyloid plaques in the brain — and found that the vaccine not only prevented plaque formation in transgenic mice but actually reversed the mental deterioration of mice already addled by it. Overall, the feeling in the field seems to be that if you're under fifty you can reasonably expect to be offered effective drugs for Alzheimer's by the time you need them. Then again, twenty years ago many cancer researchers were predicting a cure within twenty years.

David Shenk, who is comfortably under fifty, makes the case in

The Forgetting that a cure for senile dementia might not be an un-
mitigated blessing. He notes, for example, that one striking pecu-
liarity of the disease is that its sufferers often suffer less and less as
it progresses. Caring for an Alzheimer's patient is gruelingly repeti-
tious precisely because the patient himself has lost the cerebral
equipment to experience anything as a repetition. Shenk quotes
patients who speak of "something delicious in oblivion" and who
report an enhancement of their sensory pleasures as they come to
dwell in an eternal, pastless Now. If your short-term memory is
shot, you don't remember, as you stoop to smell a rose, that you've
been stooping to smell the same rose all morning.

As the psychiatrist Barry Reisberg first observed twenty years
ago, the decline of an Alzheimer's patient mirrors in reverse the
neurological development of a child. The earliest capacities a child
develops — raising the head (at one to three months), smiling
(two to four months), sitting up unassisted (six to ten months) —
are the last capacities an Alzheimer's patient loses. Brain development in a growing child is consolidated through a process called
myelinization, wherein the axonal connections among neurons
are gradually strengthened by sheathings of the fatty substance
myelin. Apparently, since the last regions of the child's brain to
mature remain the least myelinated, they're the regions most vulnerable to the insult of Alzheimer's. The hippocampus, which
processes short-term memories into long-term, is very slow to
myelinize. This is why we're unable to form permanent episodic
memories before the age of three or four, and why the hippocampus is where the plaques and tangles of Alzheimer's first appear.
Hence the ghostly apparition of the middle-stage patient who continues to be able to walk and feed herself even as she remembers
nothing from hour to hour. The inner child isn't inner anymore.
Neurologically speaking, we're looking at a one-year-old.

Although Shenk tries valiantly to see a boon in the Alzheimer's
patient's childish relief from responsibility and childlike focus on
the Now, I'm mindful that becoming a baby again was the last
thing my father wanted. The stories he told from his childhood, in
northern Minnesota, were mainly (as befits a depressive's recollections) horrible: brutal father, unfair mother, endless chores, back-
woods poverty, family betrayals, hideous accidents. He told me
more than once, after his retirement, that his greatest pleasure in

life had been going to work as an adult in the company of other men who valued his abilities. My father was an intensely private person, and privacy for him had the connotation of keeping the shameful content of one's interior life out of public sight. Could there have been a worse disease for him than Alzheimer's? In its early stages, it worked to dissolve the personal connections that had saved him from the worst of his depressive isolation. In its later stages it robbed him of the sheathing of adulthood, the means to hide the child inside him. I wish he'd had a heart attack instead.

Still, shaky though Shenk's arguments for the brighter side of Alzheimer's may be, his core contention is harder to dismiss: senility is not merely an erasure of meaning but a source of meaning. For my mother, the losses of Alzheimer's both amplified and reversed long-standing patterns in her marriage. My father had always refused to open himself to her, and now, increasingly, he *couldn't* open himself. To my mother, he remained the same Earl Franzen napping in the den and failing to hear. She, paradoxically, was the one who slowly and surely lost her self, living with a man who mistook her for her mother, forgot every fact he'd ever known about her, and finally ceased to speak her name. He, who had always insisted on being the boss in the marriage, the maker of decisions, the adult protector of the childlike wife, couldn't help behaving like the child. Now the unseemly outbursts were his, not my mother's. Now she ferried him around town the way she'd once ferried me and my brothers. Task by task, she took charge of their life. And so, although my father's "long illness" was a crushing strain and disappointment to her, it was also an opportunity to grow slowly into an autonomy she'd never been allowed: to settle some very old scores.

As for me, once I accepted the scope of the disaster, the sheer duration of Alzheimer's forced me into unexpectedly welcome closer contact with my mother. I learned, as I might not have otherwise, that I could seriously rely on my brothers and that they could rely on me. And, strangely, although I'd always prized my intelligence and sanity and self-consciousness, I found that watching my father lose all three made me less afraid of losing them myself. I became a little less afraid in general. A bad door opened, and I found I was able to walk through it.

*

The door in question was on the fourth floor of Barnes Hospital in St. Louis. About six weeks after my wife and I had put my mother in touch with the social worker and gone back east, my oldest brother and my father's doctors persuaded him to enter the hospital for testing. The idea was to get all the medications out of his bloodstream and see what we were dealing with underneath. My mother helped him check in and spent the afternoon settling him into his room. He was still his usual semipresent self when she left for dinner, but that evening, at home, she began to get calls from the hospital, first from my father, who demanded that she come and remove him from "this hotel," and then from nurses who reported that he'd become belligerent. When she returned to the hospital in the morning, she found him altogether gone — raving mad, profoundly disoriented.

I flew back to St. Louis a week later. My mother took me straight from the airport to the hospital. While she spoke to the nurses, I went to my father's room and found him in bed, wide awake. I said hello. He made frantic shushing gestures and beckoned me to his pillow. I leaned over him and he asked me, in a husky whisper, to keep my voice down because "they" were "listening." I asked him who "they" were. He couldn't tell me, but his eyes rolled fearfully to scan the room, as if he'd lately seen "them" everywhere and were puzzled by "their" disappearance. When my mother appeared in the doorway, he confided to me, in an even lower whisper, "I think they've gotten to your mother."

My memories of the week that followed are mainly a blur, punctuated by a couple of life-changing scenes. I went to the hospital every day and sat with my father for as many hours as I could stand. At no point did he string together two coherent sentences. The memory that appears to me most significant in hindsight is a very peculiar one. It's lit by a dreamlike indoor twilight, it's set in a hospital room whose orientation and cramped layout are unfamiliar from any of my other memories, and it returns to me now without any of the chronological markers that usually characterize my memories. I'm not sure it even dates from that first week I saw my father in the hospital. And yet I'm sure that I'm not remembering a dream. All memories, the neuroscientists say, are actually memories of memory, but usually they don't feel that way. Here's one that does. I remember remembering: my father in bed, my mother sitting beside it, me standing near the door. We've been having an anguished family conversation, possibly about where to move my father after his discharge from the hospital. It's a conversation that my father, to the slight extent that he can follow it, is hating. Finally he cries out with passionate emphasis, as if he's had enough of all the nonsense, "I have *always* loved your mother. *Always.*" And my mother buries her face in her hands and sobs.

This was the only time I ever heard my father say he loved her. I'm certain the memory is legitimate because the scene seemed to me immensely significant even at the time, and I then described it to my wife and brothers and incorporated it into the story I was telling myself about my parents. In later years, when my mother insisted that my father had never said he loved her, not even once, I asked if she remembered that time in the hospital. I repeated what he'd said, and she shook her head uncertainly. "Maybe," she said. "Maybe he did. I don't remember that."

My brothers and I took turns going to St. Louis every few months. My father never failed to recognize me as someone he was happy to see. His life in a nursing home appeared to be an endless troubled dream populated by figments from his past and by his deformed and brain-damaged fellow inmates; his nurses were less like actors in the dream than like unwelcome intruders on it. Unlike many of the female inmates, who at one moment were wailing like babies and at the next moment glowing with pleasure while someone fed them ice cream, I never saw my father cry, and the pleasure he took in ice cream never ceased to look like an adult's. He gave me significant nods and wistful smiles as he confided to me fragments of nonsense to which I nodded as if I understood. His most consistently near-coherent theme was his wish to be removed from "this hotel" and his inability to understand why he couldn't live in a little apartment and let my mother take care of him.

For Thanksgiving that year, my mother and my wife and I checked him out of the nursing home and brought him home with a wheelchair in my Volvo station wagon. He hadn't been in the house since he'd last been living there, ten months earlier. If my mother had been hoping for a gratifying show of pleasure from him, she was disappointed; by then, a change of venue no more impressed my father than it does a one-year-old. We sat by the fireplace and, out of unthinking, wretched habit, took pictures of a man who, if he knew nothing else, seemed full of unhappy knowledge of how dismal a subject for photographs he was. The images are awful to me now: my father listing in his wheelchair like an unstrung marionette, eyes mad and staring, mouth sagging, glasses smeared with strobe light and nearly falling off his nose; my mother's face a mask of reasonably well-contained despair; and my wife and I flashing grotesquely strained smiles as we reach to touch my father. At the dinner table my mother spread a bath towel over my father and cut his turkey into little bites. She kept asking him if he was happy to be having Thanksgiving dinner at home. He responded with silence, shifting eyes, sometimes a faint shrug. My brothers called to wish him a happy holiday; and here, out of the blue, he mustered a smile and a hearty voice; he was able to answer simple questions and thanked them both for calling.

This much of the evening was typically Alzheimer's. Because children learn social skills very early, a capacity for gestures of courtesy and phrases of vague graciousness survives in many Alzheimer's patients long after their memories are shot. It wasn't so remarkable that my father was able to handle (sort of) my brothers' holiday calls. But consider what happened next, after dinner, outside the nursing home. While my wife ran inside for a geri chair, my father sat beside me and studied the institutional portal that he was about to reenter. "Better not to leave," he told me in a clear, strong voice, "than to have to come back." This was not a vague phrase; it pertained directly to the situation at hand, and it strongly suggested an awareness of his larger plight and his connection to the past and future. He was requesting that he be spared the pain of being dragged back toward consciousness and memory. And, sure enough, on the morning after Thanksgiving, and for the remainder of our visit, he was as crazy as I ever saw him, his words a hash of random syllables, his body a big flail of agitation.

For David Shenk, the most important of the "windows onto meaning" afforded by Alzheimer's is its slowing down of death. Shenk likens the disease to a prism that refracts death into a spectrum of its otherwise tightly conjoined parts — death of autonomy, death of memory, death of self-consciousness, death of personality, death of body — and he subscribes to the most common trope of

Alzheimer's: that its particular sadness and horror stem from the sufferer's loss of his or her "self" long before the body dies.

This seems mostly right to me. By the time my father's heart stopped, I'd been mourning him for years. And yet, when I consider his story, I wonder whether the various deaths can ever really be so separated, and whether memory and consciousness have such secure title, after all, to the seat of selfhood. I can't stop looking for meaning in the two years that followed his loss of his supposed "self," and I can't stop finding it.

I'm struck, above all, by the apparent persistence of his *will.* I'm powerless not to believe that he was exerting some bodily remnant of his self-discipline, some reserve of strength in the sinews beneath both consciousness and memory, when he pulled himself together for the request he made to me outside the nursing home. I'm powerless as well not to believe that his crash on the following morning, like his crash on his first night alone in a hospital, amounted to a relinquishment of that will, a letting go, an embrace of madness in the face of unbearable emotion. Although we can fix the starting point of his decline (full consciousness and sanity) and the end point (oblivion and death), his brain wasn't simply a computational device running gradually and inexorably amok. Where the subtractive progress of Alzheimer's might predict a steady downward trend like this —

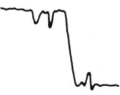

— what I saw of my father's fall looked more like this:

He held himself together longer, I suspect, than it might have seemed he had the neuronal wherewithal to do. Then he collapsed and fell lower than his pathology may have strictly dictated, and he chose to stay low, 99 percent of the time. What he *wanted* (in the early years, to stay clear; in the later years, to let go) was integral to what he *was*. And what *I* want (stories of my father's brain that are not about meat) is integral to what I choose to remember and retell.

One of the stories I've come to tell, then, as I try to forgive myself for my long blindness to his condition, is that he was bent on concealing that condition and, for a remarkably long time, retained the strength of character to pull it off. My mother used to swear that this was so. He couldn't fool the woman he lived with, no matter how he bullied her, but he could pull himself together as long as he had sons in town or guests in the house. The true solution of the conundrum of my stay with him during my mother's operation probably has less to do with my blindness than with the additional will he was exerting.

After the bad Thanksgiving, when we knew he was never coming home again, I helped my mother sort through his desk. (It's the kind of liberty you take with the desk of a child or a dead person.) In one of his drawers we found evidence of small, covert endeavors not to forget. There was a sheaf of papers on which he'd written the addresses of his children, one address per slip, the same address on several. On another slip he'd written the birth dates of his older sons — "Bob 1-13-48" and "TOM 10-15-50" — and then, in trying to recall mine (August 17, 1959), he had erased the month and day and made a guess on the basis of my brothers' dates: "JON 10-13-49."

Consider, too, what I believe are the last words he ever spoke to me, three months before he died. For a couple of days, I'd been visiting the nursing home for a dutiful ninety minutes and listening to his mutterings about my mother and to his affable speculations about certain tiny objects that he persisted in seeing on the sleeves of his sweater and the knees of his pants. He was no different when I dropped by on my last morning, no different when I wheeled him back to his room and told him I was heading back out of town. But then he raised his face toward mine and — again, out of nowhere, his voice was clear and strong — he said, "Thank you for coming. I appreciate your taking the time to see me."

Set phrases of courtesy? A window on his fundamental self? I seem to have little choice about which version to believe.

In relying on my mother's letters to reconstruct my father's disintegration, I feel the shadow of the undocumented years after 1992, when she and I talked on the phone at greater length and ceased to write all but the briefest notes. Plato's description of writing, in the *Phaedrus,* as a "crutch of memory" seems to me fully accurate: I couldn't tell a clear story of my father without those letters. But, where Plato laments the decline of the oral tradition and the atrophy of memory which writing induces, I at the other end of the Age of the Written Word am impressed by the sturdiness and reliability of words on paper. My mother's letters are truer and more complete than my self-absorbed and biased memories; she's more alive to me in the written phrase "he NEEDS distractions!" than in hours of videotape or stacks of pictures of her.

The will to record indelibly, to set down stories in permanent words, seems to me akin to the conviction that we are larger than our biologies. I wonder if our current cultural susceptibility to the charms of materialism — our increasing willingness to see psychology as chemical, identity as genetic, and behavior as the product of bygone exigencies of human evolution — isn't intimately related to the postmodern resurgence of the oral and the eclipse of the written: our incessant telephoning, our ephemeral e-mailing, our steadfast devotion to the flickering tube.

Have I mentioned that my father, too, wrote letters? Usually typewritten, usually prefaced with an apology for misspellings, they came much less frequently than my mother's. One of the last is from December 1987:

> This time of the year is always difficult for me. I'm ill at ease with all the gift-giving, as I would love to get things for people but lack the imagination to get the right things. I dread the shopping for things that are the wrong size or the wrong color or something not needed, and anticipate the problems of returning or exchanging. I like to buy tools, but Bob pointed out a problem with this category, when for some occasion I gave him a nice little hammer with good balance, and his comment was that this was the second or third hammer and I don't need any more, thank you. And then there is the problem of gifts for your mother. She is so sentimental that it hurts me not to get her something nice, but she has access to my checking account with no restrictions. I have told her

to buy something for herself, and say it is from me, so she can compete with the after-Christmas comment: "See what I got from my husband!" But she won't participate in that fraud. So I suffer through the season.

In 1989, as his powers of concentration waned with his growing "nervousness & depression," my father stopped writing letters altogether. My mother and I were therefore amazed to find, in the same drawer in which he'd left those addresses and birth dates, an unsent letter dated January 22, 1993 — unimaginably late, a matter of weeks before his final breakdown. The letter was in an envelope addressed to my nephew Nick, who, at age six, had just begun to write letters himself. Possibly my father was ashamed to send a letter that he knew wasn't fully coherent; more likely, given the state of his hippocampal health, he simply forgot. The letter, which for me has become an emblem of invisibly heroic exertions of the will, is written in a tiny penciled script that keeps veering away from the horizontal:

Dear Nick,
    We got your letter a couple days ago and were pleased to see how well you were doing in school, particularly in math. It is important to write well, as the ability to exchange ideas will govern the use that one country can make of another country's ideas.
    Most of your nearest relatives are good writers, and thereby took the load off me. I should have learned better how to write, but it is so easy to say, Let Mom do it.
    I know that my writing will not be easy to read, but I have a problem with the nerves in my legs and tremors in my hands. In looking at what I have written, I expect you will have difficulty to understand, but with a little luck, I may keep up with you.
    We have had a change in the weather from cold and wet to dry with fair blue skies. I hope it stays this way. Keep up the good work.
                                                    Love, Grandpa
    P.S. Thank you for the gifts.

My father's heart and lungs were very strong, and my mother was bracing herself for two or three more years of endgame when, one day in April 1995, he stopped eating. Maybe he was having trouble swallowing, or maybe, with his remaining shreds of will, he'd resolved to put an end to his unwanted second childhood.

His blood pressure was seventy over palpable when I flew into town. Again, my mother took me straight to the nursing home from the airport. I found him curled up on his side under a thin sheet, breathing shallowly, his eyes shut loosely. His muscle had wasted away, but his face was smooth and calm and almost entirely free of wrinkles, and his hands, which had changed not at all, seemed curiously large in comparison to the rest of him. There's no way to know if he recognized my voice, but within minutes of my arrival his blood pressure climbed to 120/90. I worried then, worry even now, that I made things harder for him by arriving: that he'd reached the point of being ready to die but was ashamed to perform such a private or disappointing act in front of one of his sons.

My mother and I settled into a rhythm of watching and waiting, one of us sleeping while the other sat in vigil. Hour after hour, my father lay unmoving and worked his way toward death; but when he yawned, the yawn was *his*. And his body, wasted though it was, was likewise still radiantly *his*. Even as the surviving parts of his self grew ever smaller and more fragmented, I persisted in seeing a whole. I still loved, specifically and individually, the man who was yawning in that bed. And how could I not fashion stories out of that love — stories of a man whose will remained intact enough to avert his face when I tried to clear his mouth out with a moist foam swab? I'll go to my own grave insisting that my father was determined to die and to die, as best he could, on his own terms.

We, for our part, were determined that he not be alone when he died. Maybe this was exactly wrong — maybe all he was waiting for was to be left alone. Nevertheless, on my sixth night in town, I stayed up and read a light novel cover to cover while he lay and breathed and loosed his great yawns. A nurse came by, listened to his lungs, and told me he must never have been a smoker. She suggested that I go home to sleep, and she offered to send in a particular nurse from the floor below to visit him. Evidently, the nursing home had a resident angel of death with a special gift for persuading the nearly dead, after their relatives had left for the night, that it was OK for them to die. I declined the nurse's offer and performed this service myself. I leaned over my father, who smelled faintly of acetic acid but was otherwise clean and warm. Identifying myself, I told him that whatever he needed to do now was fine by me, he should let go and do what he needed to do.

Late that afternoon, a big early-summer St. Louis wind kicked up. I was scrambling eggs when my mother called from the nursing home and told me to hurry over. I don't know why I thought I had plenty of time, but I ate the eggs with some toast before I left, and in the nursing home parking lot I sat in the car and turned up the radio, which was playing the Blues Traveler song that was all the rage that season. No song has ever made me happier. The great white oaks all around the nursing home were swaying and turning pale in the big wind. I felt as though I might fly away with happiness.

And still he didn't die. The storm hit the nursing home in the middle of the evening, knocking out all but the emergency lighting, and my mother and I sat in the dark. I don't like to remember how impatient I was for my father's breathing to stop, how ready to be free of him I was. I don't like to imagine what he was feeling as he lay there, what dim or vivid sensory or emotional forms his struggle took inside his head. But I also don't like to believe that there was nothing.

Toward ten o'clock, my mother and I were conferring with a nurse in the doorway of his room, not long after the lights came back on, when I noticed that he was drawing his hands up toward his throat. I said, "I think something is happening." It was agonal breathing: his chin rising to draw air into his lungs after his heart had stopped beating. He seemed to be nodding very slowly and deeply in the affirmative. And then nothing.

After we'd kissed him goodbye and signed the forms that authorized the brain autopsy, after we'd driven through flooding streets, my mother sat down in our kitchen and uncharacteristically accepted my offer of undiluted Jack Daniel's. "I see now," she said, "that when you're dead you're really dead." This was true enough. But, in the slow-motion way of Alzheimer's, my father wasn't much deader now than he'd been two hours or two weeks or two months ago. We'd simply lost the last of the parts out of which we could fashion a living whole. There would be no new memories of him. The only stories we could tell now were the ones we already had.

ATUL GAWANDE

Final Cut

FROM THE NEW YORKER

YOUR PATIENT is dead; the family is gathered. And there is one last thing that you must ask about: the autopsy. How should you go about it? You could do it offhandedly, as if it were the most ordinary thing in the world: "Shall we do an autopsy, then?" Or you could be firm, use your Sergeant Joe Friday voice: "Unless you have strong objections, we will need to do an autopsy, ma'am." Or you could take yourself out of it: "I am sorry, but they require me to ask, Do you want an autopsy done?"

What you can't be these days is mealy-mouthed about it. I once took care of a woman in her eighties who had given up her driver's license only to get hit by a car — driven by someone even older — while she was walking to a bus stop. She sustained a depressed skull fracture and cerebral bleeding, and, despite surgery, she died a few days later. So, on the spring afternoon after the patient took her last breath, I stood beside her and bowed my head with the tearful family. Then, as delicately as I could — not even using the awful word — I said, "If it's all right, we'd like to do an examination to confirm the cause of death."

"An *autopsy?*" a nephew said, horrified. He looked at me as if I were a buzzard circling his aunt's body. "Hasn't she been through enough?"

The autopsy is in a precarious state. A generation ago, it was routine; now it has become a rarity. Human beings have never quite become comfortable with the idea of having their bodies cut open after they die. Even for a surgeon, the sense of violation is inescapable.

Not long ago, I went to observe the dissection of a thirty-eight-year-old woman I had taken care of who had died after a long struggle with heart disease. The dissecting room was in the sub-basement, past the laundry and a loading dock, behind an unmarked metal door. It had high ceilings, peeling paint, and a brown tiled floor that sloped down to a central drain. There was a Bunsen burner on a countertop and an old-style grocer's hanging scale, with a big clockface red-arrow gauge and a pan underneath, for weighing organs. On shelves all around the room there were gray portions of brain, bowel, and other organs soaking in formalin in Tupperware-like containers. The facility seemed rundown, chintzy, low-tech. On a rickety gurney in the corner was my patient, sprawled out, completely naked. The autopsy team was just beginning its work.

Surgical procedures can be grisly, but dissections are somehow worse. In even the most gruesome operations — skin-grafting, amputations — surgeons maintain an attitude of tenderness and aestheticism toward their work. We know that the bodies we cut still pulse with life, and that these are people who will wake again. But in the dissecting room, where the person is gone and only the carcass remains, you find little of this delicacy, and the difference is visible in the smallest details. There is, for example, the simple matter of how a body is moved from gurney to table. In the operating room, we follow a careful, elaborate procedure for the unconscious patient, involving a canvas-sleeved rolling board and several gentle movements. We don't want so much as a bruise. Down here, by contrast, someone grabbed my patient's arm, another person a leg, and they just yanked. When her skin stuck to the stainless-steel dissecting table, they had to wet her and the table down with a hose before they could jerk her the rest of the way.

The young pathologist for the case stood on the sidelines and let a pathology assistant take the knife. Like many of her colleagues, the pathologist had not been drawn to her field by autopsies but by the high-tech detective work that she got to do on tissue from living patients. She was happy to leave the dissection to the PA, who had more experience at it anyway.

The PA was a tall, slender woman of around thirty with straight, sandy brown hair. She was wearing the full protective garb of mask, face shield, gloves, and blue plastic gown. Once the body was on the table, she placed a six-inch metal block under the back, between the shoulder blades, so that the head fell back and the chest arched up. Then she took a scalpel in her hand, a big number 6 blade, and made a huge Y-shaped incision that came down diagonally from each shoulder, curving slightly around each breast before reaching the midline, and then continued down the abdomen to the pubis.

Surgeons get used to the opening of bodies. It is easy to detach yourself from the person on the table and become absorbed by the details of method and anatomy. Nevertheless, I couldn't help wincing as she did her work: she was holding the scalpel like a pen, which forced her to cut slowly and jaggedly with the tip of the blade. Surgeons are taught to stand straight and parallel to their incision, hold the knife between the thumb and four fingers, like a violin bow, and draw the belly of the blade through the skin in a single, smooth slice to the exact depth desired. The PA was practically sawing her way through my patient.

From there, the evisceration was swift. The PA flayed back the skin flaps. With an electric saw, she cut through the exposed ribs along both sides. Then she lifted the rib cage as if it were the hood of a car, opened the abdomen, and removed all the major organs — including the heart, the lungs, the liver, the bowels, and the kidneys. Then the skull was sawed open, and the brain, too, was removed. Meanwhile, the pathologist was at a back table, weighing and examining everything, and preparing samples for microscopy and thorough testing.

Despite all this, the patient came out looking surprisingly undisturbed. The PA had followed the usual procedure and kept the skull incision behind the woman's ears, where it was completely hidden by her hair. She had also taken care to close the chest and abdomen neatly, sewing the incision tightly with weaved seven-cord thread. My patient actually looked much the same as before, except now a little collapsed in the middle. (The standard consent allows the hospital to keep the organs for testing and research. This common and long-established practice is now causing huge controversy in Britain — the media have branded it "organ stripping" — but in America it remains generally accepted.) Families can still have an open-casket funeral, and most do. Morticians employ fillers to restore a corpse's shape, and when they're done you cannot tell that an autopsy has been performed.

Still, when it is time to ask for a family's permission to do such a thing, the images weigh on everyone's mind — not least the doctor's. You strive to achieve a cool, dispassionate attitude toward these matters. But doubts nevertheless creep in.

One of the first patients for whom I was expected to request an autopsy was a seventy-five-year-old retired New England doctor who died one winter night while I was with him. Herodotus Sykes (not his real name, but not unlike it, either) had been rushed to the hospital with an infected, rupturing abdominal aortic aneurysm and taken to emergency surgery. He survived it, and recovered steadily until, eighteen days later, his blood pressure dropped alarmingly and blood began to pour from a drainage tube in his abdomen. "The aortic stump must have blown out," his surgeon said. Residual infection must have weakened the suture line. We could have operated again, but the patient's chances were poor, and his surgeon didn't think he would be willing to take any more. He was right. No more surgery, Sykes told me. He'd been through enough. We called Mrs. Sykes, who was staying with a friend, about two hours away, and she set out for the hospital.

It was about midnight. I sat with him as he lay silent and bleeding, his arms slack at his sides, his eyes without fear. I imagined his wife out on the Mass Pike, frantic, helpless, with six lanes, virtually empty at that hour, stretching far ahead.

Sykes held on, and at two-fifteen A.M. his wife arrived. She turned ashen at the sight of him, but she steadied herself. She gently took his hand in hers. She squeezed, and he squeezed back. I left them to themselves.

At two-forty-five, the nurse called me in. I listened with my stethoscope, then turned to Mrs. Sykes and told her that he was gone. She had her husband's Yankee reserve, but she broke into quiet tears, weeping into her hands, and seemed suddenly frail and small. A friend who had come with her soon appeared, took her by the arm, and led her out of the room.

We are instructed to request an autopsy on everyone as a means of confirming the cause of death and catching our mistakes. And this was the moment I was supposed to ask — with the wife despondent and reeling with shock. But surely, I began to think, here was a case in which an autopsy would be pointless. We knew what had happened — a persistent infection, a rupture. We were sure of it. What would cutting the man apart accomplish?

And so I let Mrs. Sykes go. I could have caught her as she walked through the ICU's double doors. Or even called her on the phone later. But I never did.

Such reasoning, it appears, has become commonplace in medicine. Doctors are seeking so few autopsies that in recent years the *Journal of the American Medical Association* has twice felt the need to declare "war on the nonautopsy." According to the most recent statistics available, autopsies have been done in less than 10 percent of deaths; many hospitals do none. This is a dramatic turnabout. Through much of the twentieth century, doctors diligently obtained autopsies in the majority of all deaths — and it had taken centuries to reach this point. As Kenneth Iserson recounts in his fascinating almanac, *Death to Dust,* physicians have performed autopsies for more than two thousand years. But for most of history they were rarely performed, and only for legal purposes (if religions permitted them at all — Islam, Shinto, and the Greek Orthodox Church still frown on them). The Roman physician Antistius performed one of the earliest forensic examinations on record, in 44 B.C., on Julius Caesar, documenting twenty-three wounds, including a final, fatal stab to the chest. In 1410, the Catholic Church itself ordered an autopsy — on Pope Alexander V, to determine whether his successor had poisoned him. No evidence of this was found.

Even in the nineteenth century, long after church strictures had loosened, people in the West rarely allowed doctors to autopsy their family members for medical purposes. As a result, the practice was largely clandestine. Some doctors went ahead and autopsied hospital patients immediately after death, before relatives could turn up to object. Others waited until burial and then robbed the graves, either personally or through accomplices, an activity that continued into the twentieth century. To deter such autopsies, some families would post nighttime guards at the gravesite — hence the term "graveyard shift." Others placed heavy stones on the coffins. In 1878, one company in Columbus, Ohio, even sold "torpedo coffins," equipped with pipe bombs rigged to blow up if they were tampered with. Yet doctors remained undeterred. Ambrose Bierce's *The Devil's Dictionary,* published in 1906, defined "grave" as "a place in which the dead are laid to await the coming of the medical student."

By the turn of the century, however, prominent physicians such as Rudolf Virchow, in Berlin, Karl Rokitansky, in Vienna, and William Osler, in Baltimore, began to win popular support for the practice. They defended it as a tool of discovery, one that was used to identify the cause of tuberculosis, reveal how to treat appendicitis, and establish the existence of Alzheimer's disease. They showed that autopsies prevented errors — that without them doctors could not know when their diagnoses were incorrect. Most deaths were a mystery then, and perhaps what clinched the argument was the notion that autopsies could provide families with answers — give the story of a loved one's life a comprehensible ending. Once doctors had ensured a dignified and respectful dissection at the hospital, public opinion turned. With time, doctors who did *not* obtain autopsies were viewed with suspicion. By the end of the Second World War, the autopsy was firmly established as a routine part of death in Europe and North America.

So what accounts for its decline? It's not because families refuse — to judge from recent studies, they still grant that permission up to 80 percent of the time. Doctors, once so eager to perform autopsies that they stole bodies, have simply stopped asking. Some people ascribe this to shady motives. It has been said that hospitals are trying to save money by avoiding autopsies, since insurers don't pay for them, or that doctors avoid them in order to cover up evidence of malpractice. And yet autopsies lost money and uncovered malpractice when they were popular, too.

Instead, I suspect, what discourages autopsies is medicine's twenty-first-century, tall-in-the-saddle confidence. When I failed to ask Mrs. Sykes whether we could autopsy her husband, it was not because of the expense or because I feared that the autopsy would uncover an error. It was the opposite: I didn't see much likelihood that an error would be found. Today, we have MRI scans, ultrasound, nuclear medicine, molecular testing, and much more. When somebody dies, we already know why. We don't need an autopsy to find out.

Or so I thought. Then I had a patient who changed my mind.

He was in his sixties, whiskered and cheerful, a former engineer who had found success in retirement as an artist. I will call him Mr. Jolly, because that's what he was. He was also what we call a vasculopath — he did not seem to have an undiseased artery in him. Whether because of his diet or his genes or the fact that he used to smoke, he had had, in the previous decade, one heart attack, two abdominal aortic-aneurysm repairs, four bypass operations to keep blood flowing past blockages in his leg arteries, and several balloon procedures to keep hardened arteries open. Still, I never knew him to take a dark view of his lot. "Well, you can't get miserable about it," he'd say. He had wonderful children. He had beautiful grandchildren. "But, aargh, the wife," he'd go on. She would be sitting right there at the bedside, and would roll her eyes, and he'd break into a grin.

Mr. Jolly had come into the hospital for treatment of a wound infection in his legs. But he soon developed congestive heart failure, causing fluid to back up into his lungs. Breathing became steadily harder for him, until we had to put him in the ICU, intubate him, and place him on a ventilator. A two-day admission turned into two weeks. With a regimen of diuretics and a change in heart medications, however, his heart failure reversed, and his lungs recovered. And one bright Sunday morning he was reclining in bed, breathing on his own, watching the morning shows on the TV set that hung from the ceiling. "You're doing marvelously," I said. I told him we would transfer him out of intensive care by the afternoon. He would probably be home in a couple of days.

Two hours later, a code-blue call went out on the overhead speakers. When I got to the ICU and saw the nurse hunched over Mr. Jolly, doing chest compressions, I blurted out an angry curse. He'd been fine, the nurse explained, just watching TV, when suddenly he sat upright with a look of shock and then fell back, unresponsive. At first, he was asystolic — no heart rhythm on the monitor — and then the rhythm came back, but he had no pulse. A crowd of staffers set to work. I had him intubated, gave him fluids and epinephrine, had someone call the attending surgeon at home, someone else check the morning lab-test results. An x-ray technician shot a portable chest film.

I mentally ran through possible causes. There were not many. A collapsed lung, but I heard good breath sounds with my stethoscope, and when his x-ray came back the lungs looked fine. A massive blood loss, but his abdomen wasn't swelling, and his decline happened so quickly that bleeding just didn't make sense. Extreme acidity of the blood could do it, but his lab tests were fine. Then there was cardiac tamponade — bleeding into the sac that contains the heart. I took a six-inch spinal needle on a syringe, pushed it through the skin below the breastbone, and advanced it to the heart sac. I found no bleeding. That left only one possibility: a pulmonary embolism — a blood clot that flips into the lung and instantly wedges off all blood flow. And nothing could be done about that.

I went out and spoke to the attending surgeon by phone and then to the chief resident, who had just arrived. An embolism was the only logical explanation, they agreed. I went back into the room and stopped the code. "Time of death: ten-twenty-three A.M.," I announced. I phoned his wife at home, told her that things had taken a turn for the worse, and asked her to come in.

This shouldn't have happened; I was sure of it. I scanned the records for clues. Then I found one. In a lab test done the day before, the patient's clotting had seemed slow, which wasn't serious, but an ICU physician had decided to correct it with vitamin K. A frequent complication with vitamin K is blood clots. I was furious. Giving the vitamin was completely unnecessary — just fixing a number on a lab test. Both the chief resident and I lit into the physician. We all but accused him of killing the patient.

When Mrs. Jolly arrived, we took her to a family room where it was quiet and calm, with table lamps instead of fluorescent lights and soft, plump chairs. I could see from her face that she'd already surmised the worst. His heart had stopped suddenly, we told her, because of a pulmonary embolism. We said the medicines we gave him may have contributed to it. I took her in to see him and left her with him. After a while, she came out, her hands trembling and her face stained with tears. Then, remarkably, she thanked us. We had kept him for her all these years, she said. Maybe so, but neither of us felt any pride about what had just happened. I asked her the required question. I told her that we wanted to perform an autopsy and needed her permission. We thought we already knew what had happened, but an autopsy would confirm it, I said. She considered my request for a moment. If an autopsy would help us, she finally said, then we could do it. I said, as I was supposed to, that it would. I wasn't sure I believed it.

*

I wasn't assigned to the operating room the following morning, so I went down to observe the autopsy. When I arrived, Mr. Jolly was already laid out on the dissecting table, his arms splayed, skin flayed back, chest exposed, abdomen open. I put on a gown, gloves, and a mask, and went up close. The PA began buzzing through the ribs on the left side with the electric saw, and immediately blood started seeping out, as dark and viscous as crankcase oil. Puzzled, I helped him lift open the rib cage. The left side of the chest was full of blood. I felt along the pulmonary arteries for a hardened, embolized clot, but there was none. He hadn't had an embolism after all. We suctioned out three liters of blood, lifted the left lung, and the answer appeared before our eyes. The thoracic aorta was almost three times larger than it should have been, and there was a half-inch hole in it. The man had ruptured an aortic aneurysm and had bled to death almost instantly.

In the days afterward, I apologized to the physician I'd reamed out over the vitamin, and pondered how we had managed to miss the diagnosis. I looked back through the patient's old x-rays and now saw a shadowy outline of what must have been his aneurysm. But none of us, not even the radiologists, had caught it. Even if we had caught it, we wouldn't have dared to do anything about it until weeks after treating his infection and heart failure, and that would have been too late. It disturbed me, however, to have felt so confident about what had happened that day and to have been so wrong.

The most perplexing thing was his final chest x-ray, the one we had taken during the code blue. With all that blood filling the chest, I should have seen at least a haze over the left side. But when I pulled the film out to look again there was nothing.

How often do autopsies turn up a major misdiagnosis in the cause of death? I would have guessed this happened rarely, in 1 or 2 percent of cases at most. According to three studies done in 1998 and 1999, however, the figure is about 40 percent. A large review of autopsy studies concluded that in about a third of the misdiagnoses the patients would have been expected to live if proper treatment had been administered. George Lundberg, a pathologist and former editor of the *Journal of the American Medical Association* who has done more than anyone to call attention to these figures, points out the most surprising fact of all: the rates at which misdiagnosis is detected have not improved in autopsy studies since at least 1938. With all the recent advances in imaging and diagnostics, it's hard to accept that we not only get the diagnosis wrong in two out of five of our patients who die but that we have also failed to improve over time. To see if this could really be true, doctors at Harvard put together a simple study. They went back into their hospital records to see how often autopsies picked up missed diagnoses in 1960 and 1970, before the advent of CT, ultrasound, nuclear scanning, and other technologies, and then in 1980, after they became widely used. The researchers found no improvement. Regardless of the decade, physicians missed a quarter of fatal infections, a third of heart attacks, and almost two thirds of pulmonary emboli in their patients who died.

In most cases, it wasn't technology that failed. Rather, the physicians did not consider the correct diagnosis in the first place. The perfect test or scan may have been available, but the physicians never ordered it.

In a 1976 essay, the philosophers Samuel Gorovitz and Alasdair MacIntyre explored the nature of fallibility. Why would a meteorologist, say, fail to correctly predict where a hurricane was going to make landfall? They saw three possible reasons. One was ignorance: perhaps science affords only a limited understanding of how hurricanes behave. A second reason was ineptitude: the knowledge is available, but the weatherman fails to apply it correctly. Both of these are surmountable sources of error. We believe that science will overcome ignorance, and that training and technology will overcome ineptitude. The third possible cause of error the philosophers posited, however, was an insurmountable kind, one they termed "necessary fallibility."

There may be some kinds of knowledge that science and technology will never deliver, Gorovitz and MacIntyre argued. When we ask science to move beyond explaining how things (say, hurricanes) generally behave to predicting exactly how a particular thing (say, Thursday's storm off the South Carolina coast) will behave, we may be asking it to do more than it can. No hurricane is quite like any other hurricane. Although all hurricanes follow predictable laws of behavior, each one is continuously shaped by myriad uncontrollable, accidental factors in the environment. To say precisely how one specific hurricane will behave would require a complete understanding of the world in all its particulars — in other words, omniscience.

It's not that it's impossible to predict anything; plenty of things are completely predictable. Gorovitz and MacIntyre give the example of a random ice cube in a fire. Ice cubes are so simple and so alike that you can predict with complete assurance that an ice cube will melt. But when it comes to inferring exactly what is going on in a particular person, are people more like ice cubes or like hurricanes?

Right now, at about midnight, I am seeing a patient in the emergency room, and I want to say that she is an ice cube. That is, I believe I can understand what's going on with her, that I can discern all her relevant properties. I believe I can help her.

Charlotte Duveen, as we will call her, is forty-nine years old, and for two days she has had abdominal pain. I began observing her from the moment I walked through the curtains into her room. She was sitting cross-legged in the chair next to her stretcher and greeted me with a cheerful, tobacco-beaten voice. She did not look sick. No clutching the belly. No gasping for words. Her color was good — neither flushed nor pale. Her shoulder-length brown hair had been brushed, her red lipstick neatly applied.

She told me the pain had started out crampy, like a gas pain. But then, during the course of the day, it had become sharp and focused, and as she said this she pointed to a spot on the lower right side of her abdomen. She had developed diarrhea. She constantly felt as if she had to urinate. She didn't have a fever. She was not nauseated. Actually, she was hungry. She told me that she had eaten a hot dog at Fenway Park two days ago, and she asked if that might have anything to do with this. She had also seen the birds at the zoo a few days earlier. She has two grown children. Her last period was three months ago. She smokes half a pack a day. She used to use heroin but said she's clean now. She once had hepatitis. She has never had surgery.

I felt her abdomen. It could be anything, I thought: food poisoning, a virus, appendicitis, a urinary tract infection, an ovarian cyst, a pregnancy. Her abdomen was soft, without distension, and there was an area of particular tenderness in the lower right quadrant.

When I pressed there, I felt her muscles harden reflexively beneath my fingers. On the pelvic exam, her ovaries felt normal. I ordered some lab tests. Her white-blood-cell count came back elevated. Her urinalysis was normal. A pregnancy test was negative. I ordered an abdominal CT scan.

I am sure I can figure out what's wrong with her, but, if you think about it, that's a curious faith. I have never seen this woman before in my life, and yet I presume that she is like the others I've examined. Is it true? None of my other patients, admittedly, were forty-nine-year-old women who had had hepatitis and a drug habit, had recently been to the zoo and eaten a Fenway frank, and had come in with two days of mild lower-right-quadrant pain. Yet I still believe. Every day, we take people to surgery and open their abdomens, and, broadly speaking, we know what we will find: not eels or tiny chattering machines or a pool of blue liquid but coils of bowel, a liver to one side, a stomach to the other, a bladder down below. There are, of course, differences — an adhesion in one patient, an infection in another — but we have catalogued and sorted them by the thousands, making a statistical profile of mankind.

I am leaning toward appendicitis. The pain is in the right place. The timing of her symptoms, her exam, and her white-blood-cell count all fit with what I've seen before. She's hungry, however; she's walking around, not looking sick, and this seems unusual. I go to the radiology reading room and stand in the dark, looking over the radiologist's shoulder at the images of Duveen's abdomen flashing up on the monitor. He points to the appendix, wormlike, thick, surrounded by gray, streaky fat. It's appendicitis, he says confidently. I call the attending surgeon on duty and tell him what we've found. "Book the OR," he says. We're going to do an appendectomy.

This one is as sure as we get. Yet I've worked on similar cases — with identical results from the CT scan — in which we opened the patient up and found a normal appendix. Surgery itself is a kind of autopsy. "Autopsy" literally means "to see for oneself," and, despite our knowledge and technology, when we look we're often unprepared for what we find. I want to think that my patient's condition is as predictable as the sun's rising, as the melting of an ice cube, and maybe I have to. But I've been around long enough to know that in human beings the simplest certainties can be dashed.

Whether with living patients or dead, however, we cannot know until we look. Even in the case of Mr. Sykes's, I now wonder whether we put our stitches in correctly, or whether the bleeding had come from somewhere else entirely. Doctors are no longer asking such questions. Equally troubling, people seem happy to let us off the hook. In 1995, the National Center for Health Statistics stopped collecting autopsy statistics altogether. We can no longer even say how rare autopsies have become.

From what I've learned looking inside people, I've decided human beings are somewhere between a hurricane and an ice cube: in some respects, permanently mysterious, but in others — with enough science and careful probing — entirely scrutable. It would be as foolish to think we have reached the limits of human knowledge as it is to think we could ever know everything. There is still room enough to get better, to ask questions of even the dead, to learn from knowing when our simple certainties are wrong.

DAVID HALBERSTAM

Who We Are

FROM VANITY FAIR

THE NIGHT BEFORE the world changed completely I was driving
back to New York late, after lecturing at Drew University in exur-
ban New Jersey. The sky was relatively clear, and I did what I often
do on such occasions — I looked up at the Twin Towers as a kind
of beacon for my approach, the first sign that Manhattan was close
and that I was almost home. The next morning, when I got up to
walk the dogs, I was still in a somewhat churlish mood because the
New York Giants, whose fortunes I took very seriously, had opened
their season the night before by playing terribly. At the moment I
was about to go out the door, eight A.M., that game still seemed ex-
ceptionally important to me.

After I got back, at a few minutes before nine, a telephone call
came from my friend the writer John Gregory Dunne, who told me
to turn on the television set — a plane had struck the World Trade
Center and one of the towers was in flames. By then the world had
already changed, mine and virtually everyone else's. Perhaps only
once before in our history, with the attack on Pearl Harbor, has
there been such a difference between yesterday and today, between then and now. Looking now at the newspaper headlines of
Tuesday morning, September 11, 2001, I find them distant and removed from our reality — like museum pieces, relics from another
time, aged memorabilia from another city, another country.

We are left with the rubble at Ground Zero, a term that was not
much in our vocabulary a few weeks ago. The rubble is even worse
than it appears to be on television. In some ways it is reminiscent of
Berlin in April 1945, because the two World Trade Center build-

ings were so grand; in truth, they were self-contained little cities, and so the rubble is that of small cities. When the attack happened, we who live here were shocked — but in some ways not surprised — that that which we had always feared had finally happened. Slowly in the days afterward we began to come to terms with the complexity of our emotions, first with the sheer horror of the event itself, destructive and violent, and then with the more terrible knowledge of the magnitude of the long-range implications of it: that it is a threat *in continuum,* the abrupt start of a new chapter in our lives, a deadly struggle that is all too familiar in other parts of the world but absolutely new to us here.

Yet the threat was always there. And New York was always uniquely vulnerable to it — despite the cinematic versions, in which protection was offered by Schwarzenegger, Stallone, and Willis, who always got the bad guy in the last sequence of any movie that deigned to address terrorism. We dealt with terrorism in the past, it seems, by turning to Hollywood; we believed that we were protected by our fantasies. But when the unthinkable happened, there was no action hero to rescue us at the end.

Anyone who paid any attention to the way the world was going knew deep down before the attack that America was no longer immune; on the last page of a book that I was in the process of publishing in mid-September, there is a sentence about the missile shield, which has always struck me as a kind of high-tech Maginot Line. I wrote that the real threat to this country would come not from some rogue state vulnerable to our power, but from terrorists who could walk into any American city with a crude atomic bomb in a suitcase. That sentence was born not of any great prophetic sense on my part but, regrettably, of mere common sense.

Our very strength makes us a target, and the symbols of that strength — the tallest edifices of capitalism, and the center of our military command — are targets in particular. We have had a good deal of time — some twenty-five years, perhaps more — to understand two things. First, that the great threat to our country is not from another developed nation with a nuclear-strike force, against which our immense military power is so readily deployed, but from terrorists who do not offer an easy target, and who hate the United States for what it represents (a pervasive, in their eyes, corrupting, decadent culture) and for its alliances (not just with Israel but, equally important, with moderate Arab states). These terrorists were at war with us before we were at war with them. Second, that these groups are increasingly well financed, and that the level of their craft was bound to improve; they have allies, overt and covert, who are helping them bridge the vast gap between the primitive conditions that have given birth to their hatreds and the modern sophistication that enables them to pull off violent acts like this.

We have witnessed a turning point in American history, the beginning of what I think is going to be the most challenging of our geopolitical struggles — because the enemy is so difficult to do battle with, because he offers so poor a target for our high-technology weaponry, and because no small part of his strength is his patience, which he matches against our innate impatience, an inevitable byproduct of a dynamic society constantly in some sort of overdrive. If we are wise, strong, and patient, and if the fates smile upon us, we will be able to say years from now that the people who launched this attack succeeded beyond their own best interests, in that they finally got on our radar screen, thereby forcing us to focus our national attention on something so elemental as our survival as a free society. We have dealt with the issue only sporadically and haphazardly in the past, precisely because we were so free, so strong, and so eager to enjoy the benefits of our great freedom and affluence.

Rarely have our previous concerns and agendas, that which seemed so important and galvanizing — Connie Chung's semi-famous get of Congressman Gary Condit, the trials and tribulations of Lizzie Grubman, the ever-absorbing saga of movie-star romances and divorces — come to seem so inconsequential so fast. Even before the bombing of Pearl Harbor occurred, in December 1941, there had been all kinds of evidence that the rest of the civilized world was already deeply involved in a titanic struggle that would surely determine the future of civilization as we knew it.

I was seven at the time of Pearl Harbor, and I have very clear memories of that critical day. We lived in the Bronx, where my father, who had served in World War I, was a doctor. I can remember that we were in the family car, and we got the news from the radio, as almost everyone did that Sunday — in a stream of interruptions by announcers with stentorian, doomsday voices. My brother, who was two years older, and I had never heard of Pearl Harbor, and we had little idea where Hawaii was, but hearing the radio, hearing the hushed serious tones with which our parents discussed the news, tones that we had never heard them use before, we knew in some instinctive way that our lives had changed fatefully. Which they had.

It was not just that the next morning when we got to school we performed air-raid drills, and then repeated them almost daily for two weeks. Within a few months my father went back into the service — he was forty-six at the time — and we gave up our apartment in the Bronx, moving first to my uncle's house in Winsted, Connecticut, and then to El Paso, and Austin, and Rochester, Minnesota, as my father was posted to different, domestic army bases before going overseas. But I remember that we, and I use the word "we" in the larger sense — not just my family but everyone around us — were not fearful. There seemed at the moment an odd steadiness and confidence — perhaps it was fatalism about what was going to happen next and the fact that it was not going to be easy. All we wanted to know was what we were supposed to do from that moment on.

Looking back at those days and reading books about that time, most Americans will be struck by that sense of immediate unity and lack of panic, how everyone seemed to understand and accept what his or her role was supposed to be. The challenge before us then, though very difficult at the time, seems easier than the one before us now, because it so readily fitted our strengths — even if we did not yet know it — and because we had no alternative to the singular focus of our energies. Hearing that the Japanese had bombed us at Pearl Harbor, Winston Churchill, vastly relieved, immediately understood the changed equation of the war, and wrote that the deed was done, that the Allies would win, that the colossus of America (he knew we were a colossus before we knew we were a colossus) would rise to the occasion. Japan, in his phrase, would be "ground to powder." He understood that our vast industrial resources — the arsenal of democracy — operated outside the reach of enemy planes and would become the determining factor in the war.

That enemy back in 1941 was more easily definable, the definition of the war more traditional, and our power more readily applicable against the Axis than against the elusive enemy we now face, working in the shadows, often at so great a distance and often, it turns out, right among us. Never has there been an enemy less visible to our intelligence operations and so invulnerable to any military strike.

This is a brand-new era, and war has come home to us as it never has before. At Pearl Harbor we were attacked, but it was a distant attack. By contrast, this is an attack against two of our best-known and most symbolic edifices; as such it has ended a unique historical span for us as a great, untouchable power, a span that I would place at eighty-seven years, to be exact. In that period the immense carnage of the modern era was always somewhere else. Because of that we were permitted many illusions. We became somewhat schizophrenic, isolationist — due to our geography, our size, our power, our wealth, and our self-sufficiency — but still the guardian and shield, in a shrewd kind of enlightened self-interest, of like-minded democratic regimes. Yet true internationalism has always been an uneasy role for America.

For our geography has always dominated our psyche; we are apart from Europe and we *like* being apart from Europe. Our modern history confirms our love/hate relationship with internationalism. Even as America was beginning to surge forward as a major industrial player, when the First World War began, we came in three years after the other major powers. With most of Europe already bled white and exhausted, we eventually played the decisive role. Then, still protected by our two oceans, we went back to our old ways and rejected President Wilson's attempt at internationalism. During World War II, we once again came in later than most of the other players — two years later if you mark the calendar from the war's beginnings in Europe, longer if you count Asian events.

That war ended with us emerging as a new superpower, one dramatically more internationalist than when we had entered. We were brought into close connection with the rest of the world by the generation of men who had actually fought and who had witnessed firsthand the calamity caused by the previous generation's isolationism. They understood the importance and synergy of the new weaponry unsheathed at the very end of the war, the atomic bomb and the German V-2 rockets. All this made isolationism no longer viable. Thus for the first time did we begin to deal with the knowledge that the immunities and protections that had been ours no longer existed.

Still, we remained very different from the rest of the world. Unlike almost any other nation that had been part of World War II, we felt better about ourselves when it was over than we had before it began. The devastation inflicted on others — some 20 million people dead in Russia, 6 million in Germany, 6 million in Poland — was on a different scale from our losses. We sacrificed, to be sure, some 400,000 men and women on both fronts, but our soil was essentially untouched. Europe was shattered; the British, exhausted emotionally, physically, and financially, could no longer sustain their role as the leader of the West.

Thus did we begin the ascent to superpower status. That the ascent has been not much desired, and is probably even unwanted, is critically important to understanding how America responds to crises in foreign policy, why it does so more slowly and more awkwardly, but, when finally aroused, does so with a certain finality. Our instinct is to be apart. We are a vast country, with all kinds of different regions and people; we do not unite lightly or quickly for any single purpose. It is, I think, in the long run, a source of strength and tolerance.

The period that followed World War II was a new and chilling one, a hot war followed by a cold one. In Eastern Europe lines were drawn, and we quickly found ourselves facing the challenge of the formidable new Soviet empire. The lessons of World War II were applied to the new demands of the Cold War. That which had always protected us in the past — our geographical isolation — no longer existed; the oceans had become ponds.

There were still powerful pockets of isolationism in this country, especially in the Midwest. It is easy to underestimate today the resistance to much of the policy of containing communism in the late forties, and the number of Americans who wanted to never again become involved in Europe, who did not want to help support and strengthen our fragile European allies, and who in some cases believed that our old alliances were a source of vulnerability. (In the Midwest the fear that it was the old eastern establishment doing the work of the British was powerful. The least Secretary of State Dean Acheson — he of a certain generational Anglophilia, with his fancy old-boy manners and British tailoring — could do to help a politically embattled President Truman, Averell Harriman once said, was to shave off his British guard's mustache.) Resistance to Soviet imperialism could not be sold in too low-key and abstract a way, as Senator Arthur Vandenberg of Michigan, a last-minute convert to internationalism, understood. If Truman wanted his containment policy to go through the Congress, Vandenberg said, he could have it, but he would have to go and scare the hell out of the American people.

Still, through all the paranoia in both societies, and the terror of the Cold War, there was an equilibrium of power, a mutuality of terror. There were certain fears of a nuclear attack earlier in the struggle, but they gradually receded. Once again our scientific-industrial base was more than adequate — indeed, by the end of the Cold War we were, because of our vast technological superiority, systematically widening the gap on the Soviet Union, something of which Mikhail Gorbachev, with his extensive ties to the KGB, was all too aware.

Then the Soviet empire collapsed. The threat that had hung over this country for some forty years disappeared. The oceans, which had become ponds, were, in the minds of far too many people here, oceans once again. John F. Kennedy, taking as his topic the period before England rallied itself against the threat posed by Hitler, wrote a college thesis that was turned into a short book called *Why England Slept*. If someone were to write a book about America from the collapse of the Berlin Wall in 1989 to September 11, 2001, it might be called *Why America Napped*.

When social historians come to measure us in the future, they may look at the decade that just passed with unusual distaste, as a time of trivial pursuits and debate in the public sector and singular greed in the private one, where the heads of our biggest corporations were given unacceptably large rewards. A poem which W. H. Auden wrote at the time of the start of World War II seems particularly apropos at this moment. It is called "September 1, 1939." The first five lines go: "I sit in one of the dives / On Fifty-second Street / Uncertain and afraid / As the clever hopes expire / Of a low dishonest decade." With luck, and I say this very carefully, with luck, that era is past.

What is at stake here is something elemental to what we are as a people and a nation: the survival of the open and free society. Our very openness makes us unusually vulnerable to enemies. When we show up at hotels or airports, we do not have to lug with us all kinds of documentation to prove that we are who we say we are; that has been a curious kind of privilege, and it is going to be more difficult to preserve in the future. But our freedom in a larger sense is much more than that.

Those of us, I suspect, who have over the years worked in societies that are not free have treasured, more than most, freedom in America, not just the freedom to move about but the freedom to be who and what you want to be, to be different from those who went before you in your own family, to if necessary reinvent yourself and become the person of your own imagination. I believe as a matter of political faith not merely that freedom represents an easier, more pleasurable life in the simplest sense for the individual, but also that all our great strengths — industrial, scientific, military, and artistic — flow from it. The freer we are, the more we are able to use the talents of all our people. We waste less human potential than any other society that I know of.

What an irony that we, who have always depended on this scientific excellence and industrial might to protect us, are threatened not by a First World or even Second or Third World country, but by a terrorist guerrilla group, rootless in terms of nationhood and with a medieval vision for the future. Yet this group has managed to find exceptional financing and to adapt itself to a shrewd if minimalist application of borrowed or stolen modern technology. Even as we reel from this assault, our enemies are trying to buy the most modern weapons of mass destruction, and they have shown a remarkable ability to move money around the world to finance such operations.

This, then, is the ultimate challenge to us as a society, far more difficult and complicated than the one that followed Pearl Harbor; Pearl Harbor had the ability not merely to unify the country — as this attack has — but also to *sustain* that unity for as long as was required. The phrase we used in those days, lest we forget, was "for the duration." The September 11 assault is infinitely more insidious, and it strikes a nation that after a half century of relentless affluence is quite different — much more materialistic, with a significantly more abbreviated and fragmented attention span. The responses the attack inspired at different levels of our society are quite complicated and in some ways terribly revealing: contrast, if you will, the selfless behavior of those magnificent New York firefighters, rushing into the inferno of the Twin Towers to save strangers, with that of the stock-market players, architects of the greatest one-week drop in the stock market since the Depression. Both the firefighters and the Wall Street operators were, I suppose, merely doing their jobs.

The America of 1941 was poorer, and expectations were much, much lower, much closer to a certain kind of Calvinist root. There was a greater sense, I believe, on the part of ordinary citizens of what they *owed* back. That is very different from today. We have been quite differently conditioned than our parents and grandparents were in what to expect out of life. This is a much more self-absorbed society, one that demands ever quicker results; it is accustomed to being secure — and *entertained*. When things go wrong it is likely to be thought of as someone else's fault, and therefore merely a mistake that ought to be rectified. And quickly. What is especially difficult about this new challenge is that it challenges our attention span.

Of the many results of the end of the Cold War — the amazing surge in the American economy, the rise of nationalism and tribalism in certain parts of the world — the most surprising and distressing was the trivialization of the American political agenda. This was reflected in the media, most especially in the decline in foreign reporting among the three main networks. Any serious look at the larger world was presumed to be boring. Fifty-six years after World War II ended I can still tell you the names of the great CBS radio reporters of that era: Edward R. Murrow, Eric Sevareid, Charles Collingwood, David Schoenbrun, Winston Burdett. Who can name five foreign correspondents for the networks today? Sadly, the people who make the biggest salaries, our new specialists in instant, artificial empathy, have, with some exceptions, by and large produced the most frivolous work — the sum of which has seemed to say that America was unthreatened, that there was no challenge to us, and that we need not know anything about the rest of the world. Not surprisingly, our national debates on important issues atrophied. During the last election, allegedly serious political commentators would sit around telling us which of the candidates seemed more likable, as if they were judging a campaign for high school class president. We have been bingeing for a decade, all of us in different degrees. (I include in this myself, and this magazine as well.) For many in the rest of the world, especially people who wish us well, it has been inexplicable, a nation of so much power and responsibility paying so little attention to the world around it. It was as if the old isolationist impulse had been restored and magnified.

We have gone from having a serious agenda, worthy of a monopoly superpower, to an ever more trivial one of scandal and celebrity. When we have wanted (or needed) in the last decade or so to exercise our power in certain foreign policy crises, the disconnect between our complex international role and the lack of public knowledge and interest — and our government's innate caution about taking any risks — has mandated what is virtually a zero-casualties approach, especially after the events in Somalia in 1993. Whatever else, that era ended on September 11.

I have always thought the concept, so fashionable in the last few years, of a "greatest generation" as exceptional historical foolishness. I say that with the most profound admiration for those who survived the Depression and fought in World War II. They bore an uncommonly heavy burden; my father — the man I revere more than anyone else, an immigrants' son who put himself through college and medical school and finished his medical training just in time for the Great Depression — was a member of it. But the idea that he belonged to a better generation than that of his father, who had helped bring our family here from the Old Country, would have surely appalled him. Generations aren't greater or lesser, weaker, noisier, or more silent. (Mine was supposedly the silent generation.) They are composed of human beings who respond to different circumstances and different challenges in different ways. Challenged in the right way and properly led, in a free society, they will almost invariably do the right thing. A world of easy security and easy affluence, with an elite, all-volunteer, professional army, will inevitably bring out lesser qualities. Responding together to a genuine threat to national security, especially in a time of economic reversals, will surely bring out other, better ones.

What is important about generations are the challenges before them, and how well those challenges are explained by their leaders. We talk now about the need for leadership as though it were George Bush's responsibility alone. But leadership during World War II came from all parts of the society. Today there must be within the private sector a parallel sense of obligation. If this country is to enter a new era — "a long twilight struggle," to use John Kennedy's extremely apt phrase — with a very difficult adversary, then it needs patient, thoughtful leadership in all walks of life. For we are being brought back into contact with a part of the world that is hard for us to understand and where it is extremely difficult to exercise power. We will not do well by simply lashing out at a supple, elusive adversary in a way that makes us feel better but does little to change his modus operandi.

One of the advantages of being older and having some degree of historical knowledge is the faith in the free society that eventually comes with it. The terrible thing about the Communists, the poet Allen Ginsberg once told me years ago, when we were in Eastern Europe and he had had a difficult little struggle with the Czech and Polish authorities, is that all the clichés about them were true. I would add to that a corollary: that one of the good things about our democracy is that many of the clichés about it are also true — you just have to stick around long enough to bear witness. In my lifetime I have seen the resilience of American democracy time and again — in those months after World War II, when we moved so quickly from being a sleeping isolationist nation to becoming an awesome new international power. And post-*Sputnik*, when we showed our capacity to go all out in space, with the pledge of John Kennedy in 1961 to put a man on the moon, which resulted, only eight years later, in our doing exactly that. Over the years, I have come to admire in our society the loyalty and energies and resolve of free men and women freely summoned.

What I have also learned is that opponents of a free society — whether it was the Nazis and the leaders of imperial Japan, or the Soviets during the Cold War, or even more recently Slobodan Milosevic, who kept telling America's diplomats that he could out-bluff us because he could accept death and we could not — tend to underestimate our strengths and even see them as weaknesses. The most recent example of that kind of thinking comes from

Osama bin Laden, who was quoted in a 1996 interview as saying that his battle with America was easier than the one with the Russians, who were more courageous and above all more patient. Men such as bin Laden believe that what I consider to be our strengths — the slowness of our political responses, the complexity and diversity of our social fabric — reflect a certain kind of decadence. Getting America to change directions and attitudes from one era to another sometimes must seem like trying to change the direction of an aircraft carrier by trailing your hand behind it in the water. But our strengths, when summoned and focused, when the body politic is aroused and connects to the top of the political process, are never to be underestimated.

In some ways this inevitably comes back to the personal. I am a New Yorker. What was bombed was the city in which I live. It is an assault upon so many things that I cherish: the way I live — that is, the love of the constant possibilities in a free society — and the place where I live as well. Among those killed were eleven firefighters at Engine Company 40, Ladder Company 35, whose station house is only two blocks from our apartment, men who have protected me and my family for years.

Being a New Yorker is as much a condition as it is a description of where I reside. Not that many of us are born here; one becomes a New Yorker in most instances by choice. I happen to have been born in one of the boroughs, but I did not grow up here, and I came back quite warily in my thirties, twenty-five years after World War II had driven us from the city. Then I was not at all sure whether I wanted to stay. But I did, tentatively at first and then, in time, lovingly. I came to love New York's grittiness and excitement, even coming to accept its edgier, harsher, often angrier side; Rudy Giuliani in that sense is the perfect New York mayor, reflecting all of our best and, on occasion, a good many of our lesser qualities. I came to understand that that very edginess was a critical part of the New York condition, and sometimes I have surely made my own contributions to it. I understand that being a true New Yorker is not necessarily a warm and fuzzy role. True New Yorkers celebrate the flaws of their city as much as they do its virtues.

I have lived here almost thirty-five years now. My wife and I were married here, our daughter was born here and grew up here. I al-

ways start my day by walking our dogs through Central Park, and I
thrill every morning to the vista in front of me as I look south, over
the bucolic Sheep Meadow, then down to the skyscrapers that begin on Central Park South. There are constant changes and grada-
tions of light, according to the time of day and year. For me, it still
remains, for all its flaws, an alabaster city, always gleaming. Living
here now seems more important than ever before. There are many
things worth cherishing in life, and I have found all of them here
— above all, the human pulse of the city itself, which has always
seemed to me so regenerative, perhaps now more than ever.

CHRISTOPHER HITCHENS

For Patriot Dreams

FROM VANITY FAIR

O, what a fall was there, my countrymen!
Then I, and you, and all of us fell down.

— *Julius Caesar,* act 3, scene 2

I COMMENCED to dream about the Manhattan skyline when I was
in my early teens and an ocean away. It remains the only fantasy-
dream that I have ever had that's come true or, perhaps, the only
one that hasn't been some kind of a disappointment. (And I am
going to stay with "I" for now, because I haven't yet earned the
right to say "we," and "we" is what I want to come to.)

The World Trade Center wasn't yet finished when I first got my
wish and disembarked in New York. In the summer of 1970, you
could see two *Titanic*-sized hulls and keels being constructed, at
the southern extremity of the island, but you could not yet imagine
what the great vessels would resemble when they were triumphantly launched. Some locals bitched and moaned about how the
towers were too grandiose in design, and about the nice little
neighborhood that had been doomed by development. Even then
I understood that no New York argument would be complete without this refrain.

Once I had found the magnetic compass point of my life, which
is a piece of good fortune that doesn't occur for everyone, it was an
easy matter to follow it. That skyline had pull. And so did the
southern part of the island. I know people who never go above
Fourteenth Street, and I know people who seldom venture below
it, and while I was never that dogmatic, I became a southerner
from the start. It was the East and West "villages" that drew me, and

the idea of a skyscraper-free zone is essential to their charm. Still, it would have seemed provincial and lowly to ignore the big shiny twins. I conducted a tempestuous romance in the Windows on the World restaurant, with its oddly erotic view of New Jersey. I once got engaged there, in a moment of folly and euphoria for which I have since been forgiven. When I decided to become an immigrant, it was to the Social Security office in the South Tower that I went, to get in line for the first digits of my American identity.

The place I stayed first, before I got my own address, was with patient friends on Bank Street — the green thoroughfare of that lovely fretwork of little streets around Greenwich and Bleecker. Later, over on Tompkins Square in the early 1980s, the WTC was my city view at sundown as I sat writing. I wasn't exactly bewitched by it, as I was by the Chrysler Building, but it was a good part of my sky. With the light refracting through the twins, I would pause and have a cocktail break and play some music. Then I'd generally go out to St. Marks Place and eat in the neighborhood where W. H. Auden had become, if not the first Englishman to become an American, the first Englishman to become an accepted New Yorker. He was actually uptown, in a bar on Fifty-second Street, when he wrote one of the most reproachful and haunting poems of the twentieth century. It consists of ninety-nine perfectly incised lines. Its title is a date. The date is "September 1, 1939." It shudders with premonitions of a coming cataclysm, and it contains the early-warning couplet "The unmentionable odour of death / Offends the September night."

Now I'm just back from walking through my old neighborhoods. As with every scene of calamity, it is the stench that makes the difference between seeing it on TV and seeing it for yourself. The unmentionable odor this September was a compound of a refugee camp and a blitzed town. So I'm confronting the inescapable fact that others, too, dreamed from far away about the Manhattan skyscape. But dreamed yearningly of bringing it down, didn't see it from Ellis Island or the Statue of Liberty, thought only of maiming and disfiguring and poisoning it. "Let it come down," says Banquo's murderer in *Macbeth*, expressing so much, and in so few thuggish words, by this brutish fatalism. There's a cadence for you: "Let it come down." What am I to do with a thought like this?

> Into this neutral air [wrote Auden]
> Where blind skyscrapers use
> Their full height to proclaim
> The strength of Collective Man,
> Each language pours its vain
> Competitive excuse . . .

There are no excuses. Many people missed this evident point when they began, in their aching search for an appropriate poetry, to circulate that same Auden poem via e-mail. What is the poet saying? He is saying that the great towers of New York may be "capitalist" (the lines come from the end of his Marxist phase) but that they also represent the combined labor and skill and hope of untold numbers of tough and dignified workers. Much the same applies to the lines on languages. The coded suggestion is that of Babel, but the Twin Towers actually looked down quite benignly on a neighborhood, a district, a quarter, where each language had a chance. My Palestinian tobacconist, my cheap all-you-can-eat Ukrainian joint, my Italian grocery . . . everybody knows the mosaic. The college where I teach, the New School for Social Research, became the lighthouse for the anti-Nazi scholars of the 1930s. (Our downtown dorm had to be closed and evacuated "that week.") The numberless cafés and bars and chess hangouts where the fugitive spirit of bohemia found a home, and where there were bookstores to spare. The offices of the indispensable "little magazines," which helped keep the culture going on a shoestring. The Cedar Tavern, the White Horse, the old Lion's Head, where exiles could be safe to curse their own governments and locals could excel at cursing the American one. What can I say? I was happy there. The work and the conversation were worthwhile. And there was something more: the crucial four words in the greatest of all documents. The pursuit of happiness. Just to name that is to summarize and encapsulate all that is detested by the glacial malice of fundamentalism and tribalism. That's what they can't stand. They confuse it with hedonism and selfishness and profanity, and they have no idea. No idea at all.

The word "village" sounds provincial in its way, and no less so if you put "East" or "West" in front of it. The time came when, having been mugged in New York (a rite of passage in those days) and

married in New York, and otherwise infected with its multifarious
fevers, I had to move away. I went to live in Washington, D.C., the
nation's capital. As it happens, I took the train on the day I left and
twisted round in my seat, like a child leaving a seaside holiday, until
I could see the Twin Towers no more. But I couldn't have lived in
D.C. without an umbilical cord to New York, and every time I came
back on a train or plane or by car, it was the big friendly commercial twins that signaled my return. Now each of them has met its
own evil twin. As you know, my new hometown was also gravely injured that week. But Washington has always seemed to me more
parochial than New York. You may feel patriotic about the United
States, but you can't quite feel patriotic about Washington, D.C.
(Not even the blitzing of the Pentagon could accomplish this transformation; it's a sad subject for another time, but it's true. New
York and Pennsylvania are the only shrines of the national heart in
this extremity.)

Mark Antony, speaking to the movable crowd in the lines with
which I began, was addressing his fellow Romans as his "countrymen." And Mr. Bush and the networks, for the first few days, addressed their fellow Americans. But it didn't take very long before
that rhetoric was being qualified and modified. For a moment, indeed, it looked as if there were too many nationalities to be mentioned in any one speech. Turks, Filipinos, Yemenis, Pakistanis,
Icelanders. At a certain point, I was asked if I wanted to attend the
midtown memorial service for the hundreds of my immolated fellow Englishmen. I can't say that it was exactly at this moment that
my thoughts crystallized, but it was at about that time. No, I don't
want to go to anybody's gender-specific or national or ethnic-iden-
tity ceremony. I have found the patch of soil on which I will take
my own stand, and the people with whom I'll stand, and it's the
only place in history where patriotism can be divorced from its evil
twins of chauvinism and xenophobia. Patriotism is not local; it's
universal. (No, finally — and what a relief! — all together now: All
politics are *not* local.) I checked carefully every day with my friend
Hussein Ibish, a Lebanese Kurd who speaks for the American-Arab
Anti-Discrimination Committee, and who had a lot of monitoring
to do. There were not all that many nuts and dolts that week who
were so shameless and idiotic as to bully or insult a Sikh or a Sri
Lankan. But of the incidents of vandalism and barbarity reported

and recorded, barely a one took place in the epicenter of Manhattan. If patriotism can be democratic and internationalist — and this remains to be fought for — then that's good enough for me; perhaps there's a better chance now than anyone could have envisioned. In this microcosm, there was the code for a macrocosm. Call it a rooted cosmopolitanism.

I told newly enrolled New School students, some of whose parents wanted them back in the heartland, that they'd be sorry forever if they abandoned the city at such a time. I told the same to some nervous students who had arrived from countries with far more gruesome problems. I went at night to Union Square and Washington Square Park, and though the herbivorous ethos was a bit too much Strawberry Fields and even "Candle in the Wind" for my taste, I recognized that the atmosphere was serious and reflective. Auden, whose emotions lay in the direction of religious pacifism, would have felt at home. But he would also have registered some feeling, I think (and I don't mean to be flippant about his famous tastes), for the burly, uncomplaining, stoic proletarian defenders, busting their sinews in the intractable and nameless wreckage and carnage of downtown. I took the groaning subway underneath Chambers Street, as it slowed to the pace of a funeral cortège (whether out of respect for the dead or out of respect to the mountain of hell above, I don't know). I got out at the Broadway-Nassau station and paced the streets until my clothes reeked and until another evacuation was called because of the toxic material in the hideous core. And I swore a small oath. One has to be capable of knowing when something is worth fighting for. One has to be capable of knowing an enemy when one sees one.

That enemy, let us never forget, had hoped to do far, far worse. Limited only by the schedules and booking of civilian aviation, the airborne death squads could have counted on packed planes and, with a slight flight delay, on much more densely crowded towers. They could also have hoped to bring the towers down sideways — each of them a quarter of a mile high — across the streets. A toll of more than 50,000 was possible, and — as was doubtless fantasized at many a sniggering and giggling secret meeting — a body count of 100,000 could have been seriously aimed at. This would not have been — in the stalest phrase of the crisis — a "Pearl Harbor." It would have been the Dresden of the Taliban.

In the fall of 1940 (and the once beautifully combined words

"New York" and "the fall" will never again have quite the same
sound to me), George Orwell wrote of a certain human quality
that attaches itself to particular horrors. He was looking back to his
boyhood, through the prisms of a frightful war that had just begun
and a frightful war that had clouded his youth. As he put it:

> I must admit that nothing in the whole war moved me so deeply as
> the loss of the *Titanic* had done a few years earlier. This comparatively
> petty disaster shocked the whole world, and the shock has not quite
> died away even yet. I remember the terrible, detailed accounts read out
> at the breakfast table (in those days it was a common habit to read the
> newspaper aloud), and I remember that in all the long list of horrors
> the one that most impressed me was that at the last the *Titanic* suddenly
> up-ended and sank bow foremost, so that the people clinging to the
> stern were lifted no less than three hundred feet into the air before they
> plunged into the abyss. It gave me a sinking sensation in the belly which
> I can still all but feel. Nothing in the war ever gave me quite that sen-
> sation.

"Look, teacher," a child cried during a school evacuation as the
towers were becoming pyres. "The birds are on fire." The infant
was rationalizing the sight of human beings making a public
choice between incineration and suicide, and often suffering the
most extreme pangs of both fates. Yes, we will look. And yes, we will
remember it long after other miseries have intervened. The title of
Orwell's 1940 essay, incidentally, was "My Country Right or Left."
Confronted in this manner, and affronted too, one has to be able
to say, My country after all.

And one may have to say it without waving or displaying any flag.
My reservations about this are not just the usual ones. More than I
worry about flag-waving I worry about what will happen when flag-
waving has to stop. All these ceremonies of emotion, from children's drawings to fund drives, are prone to diminishing returns. A
time will come when fewer taxis fly the Stars and Stripes, and it
could be just at that point that another awful wound is inflicted by
covert and nefarious enemies. What then? What encore? One
should probably start now to practice the virtues of stoicism and
solidarity — and also of silence. No more brave and vague military
briefings; no more bluff boosterism by local politicians. Just a set,
private determination, as the French once resolved when they lost

Alsace and Lorraine to foreign conquest: "Always think of it. Never speak of it."
As Auden too pessimistically phrased it in the closing lines of the greatest poem ever written in the city:

> Defenceless under the night
> Our world in stupor lies;
> Yet, dotted everywhere,
> Ironic points of light
> Flash out . . .

I don't know so much about "defenceless." Some of us will vow to defend it, or help the defenders. As for the flashes of light, imagine the nuance of genius that made Auden term them "ironic." It would be a holy fool who mistook this for weakness or sentimentality. Shall I take out the papers of citizenship? Wrong question. In every essential way, I already have.

SEBASTIAN JUNGER

The Lion in Winter

FROM NATIONAL GEOGRAPHIC ADVENTURE

THE FIGHTERS were down by the river, getting ready to cross over, and we drove out there in the late afternoon to see them off. We parked our truck behind a mud wall, where it was out of sight, and then walked one by one down to the position. In an hour or so it would be dark, and they'd go over. Some were loading up an old Soviet truck with crates of ammunition, and some were cleaning their rifles, and some were just standing in loose bunches behind the trees, where the enemy couldn't see them. They were wearing old snow parkas and blankets thrown over their shoulders, and some had old Soviet Army pants, and others didn't have any shoes. They drew themselves into an uneven line when we walked up, and they stood there with their Kalashnikovs and their RPGs cradled in their arms, smiling shyly.

Across the floodplain, low, grassy hills turned purple as the sun sank behind them, and those were the hills these men were going to attack. They were fighting for Ahmad Shah Massoud — genius guerrilla leader, last hope of the shattered Afghan government — and all along those hills were trenches filled with Taliban soldiers. The Taliban had grown out of the *madrasahs,* or religious schools, that had sprung up in Pakistan during the Soviet invasion, and they had emerged in 1994 as Afghanistan sank into anarchy following the Soviet withdrawal. Armed and trained by Pakistan and driven by moral principles so extreme that many Muslims feel they can only be described as a perversion of Islam, the Taliban quickly overran most of the country and imposed their ironfisted version of Koranic law. Adulterers faced stoning; women's rights became nonexistent. Only Pakistan, Saudi Arabia, and the United Arab Emirates recognize their government as legitimate, but it is generally thought that the rest of the world will have to follow suit if the Taliban complete their takeover of the country. The only thing that still stands in their way are the last-ditch defenses of Ahmad Shah Massoud.

The sun set, and the valley edged into darkness. It was a clear, cold November night, and we could see artillery rounds flashing against the ridgeline in the distance. Hundreds of Taliban soldiers were dug in up there, waiting to be attacked, and hundreds of Massoud's soldiers were down here along the Kowkcheh River, waiting to attack them. In a few hours, they would cross the river by truck and make their way through the fields and destroyed villages of no man's land. Then it would begin.

We wished Massoud's men well and walked back to the truck. The stars had come out, and the only sound was of dogs baying in the distance. Then the whole front line, from the Tajik border to Farkhar Gorge, rumbled to life.

I'd wanted to meet Massoud for years, ever since I'd first heard of his remarkable defense of Afghanistan against the Soviets in the 1980s. A brilliant strategist and an uncompromising fighter, Massoud had been the bane of the Soviet Army's existence and had been largely responsible for finally driving them out of the country. He was fiercely independent, accepting little, if any, direction from Pakistan, which controlled the flow of American arms to the mujahidin. His independence made it impossible for the CIA to trust him, but agency officials grudgingly admitted that he was an almost mythological figure among many Afghans. He was a native of the Panjshir Valley, north of Kabul, the third of six sons born to an ethnic Tajik army officer. In 1974, he went to college to study engineering, but he dropped out in his first year to join a student resistance movement. After a crackdown on dissidents, Massoud fled to Pakistan, where he underwent military training. By 1979, when the Soviet Union invaded Afghanistan to prop up the teetering Communist government, Massoud had already collected a small band of resistance fighters in the Panjshir Valley.

As a guerrilla base the Panjshir couldn't have been better. Protected by the mountain ranges of the Hindu Kush and blocked at the entrance by a narrow gorge named Dalan Sang, the seventy-mile-long valley was the perfect staging area for raids against a highway that supplied the Soviet bases around Kabul, Afghanistan's capital. Massoud quickly organized his Panjshiri fighters, rumored to number as few as three thousand men, into defense groups comprising four or five villages each. The groups were self-sufficient and could call in mobile units if they were threatened with being overrun. Whenever a Soviet convoy rumbled up the highway, the mujahidin would mine the road, then wait in ambush. Most of the fighters would provide covering fire while a few insanely brave men worked their way in close to the convoy and tried to take out the first and last vehicles with rocket-propelled grenades. With the convoy pinned down, the rest of the unit would pepper it with gunfire and then retreat. They rarely stood and fought, and the Soviets rarely pursued them beyond the protection of their armored vehicles. It was classic guerrilla warfare, and if anything, Massoud was amazed at how easy it was. For his defense of the valley, Massoud became known as the Lion of Panjshir.

Very quickly, the Soviets understood that there was no way to control Afghanistan without controlling the Panjshir Valley, and they started attacking it with forces of up to fifteen thousand men, backed by tanks, artillery, and massive air support. Massoud knew that he couldn't stop them, and he didn't even try. He would evacuate as many civilians as possible and then retreat to the surrounding peaks of the Hindu Kush; when the Soviets entered the Panjshir, they would find it completely deserted. That was when the real fighting began. Massoud and his men slept in caves and prayed to Allah and lived on nothing but bread and dried mulberries; they killed Russians with guns taken from other dead Russians and they fought and fought and fought, until the Soviets simply couldn't afford to fight anymore. Then the Soviets would pull back, and the whole cycle would start all over again.

Between 1979 and their withdrawal ten years later, the Soviets launched nine major offensives into the Panjshir Valley. They never took it. They tried assassinating Massoud, but his intelligence network always warned him in time. They made local peace deals, but he used the respite to organize resistance elsewhere in the country. The ultimate Soviet humiliation came in the mid-eighties, after the Red Army had lost hundreds of soldiers trying to take the Panjshir. The mujahidin had shot down a Soviet helicopter, and some resourceful Panjshiri mechanic patched it up, put a truck engine in it, and started running it up and down the valley as a bus. The Soviets got wind of this, and the next time their troops invaded, the commanders decided to inspect the helicopter. The last thing they must have seen was a flash; Massoud's men had booby-trapped it with explosives.

The night attack on the Taliban positions began with waves of Katyusha rockets streaming from Massoud's positions and arcing across the valley. The rockets were fired in volleys of ten or twelve, and we could see the red glare of their engines wobble through the darkness and then wink out one by one as they found their trajectories and headed for their targets. Occasionally an incoming round would explode somewhere down the line with a sound like a huge oak door slamming shut. The artillery exchange lasted an hour, and then the ground assault started, Massoud's men moving under the cover of darkness through minefields and machine-gun fire toward the Taliban trenches. The fighting was three or four miles away and came to us only as a soft, frantic *pap-pap-pap* across the valley.

We had driven to a hilltop command post to watch the attack. The position had a code name, Darya, which means "river" in Dari, the Persian dialect that's Afghanistan's lingua franca, and on the radio we could hear field commanders yelling, "Darya! Darya! Darya!" as they called in reports or shouted for artillery. The commander of the position, a gentle-looking man in his thirties named Harun, was dressed for war in corduroy pants and a cardigan. He was responsible for all the artillery on the front line; we found him in a bunker, studying maps by the light of a kerosene lantern. He was using a schoolboy's plastic protractor to figure out trajectory angles for his tanks.

Harun was working three radios and consulting the map continually. After a while a soldier brought in tea, and we sat cross-legged on the floor and drank it. Calls kept streaming in on the radios. "We've just captured another position; it's got a big ammo depot," one commander shouted. Another reported, "The enemy has no morale at all; they're just running away. We've just taken ten more prisoners."

Harun showed us on the map what was happening. As we spoke,

Massoud's men were taking small positions around the ridgeline and moving into the hills on either side of a town called Khvajeh Ghar, which was at a critical part of the frontline. Khvajeh Ghar was held by Pakistani and Arab volunteers, part of an odd assortment of foreigners — Burmese, Chinese, Chechens, Algerians — who are fighting alongside the Taliban to spread fundamentalist Islam throughout Central Asia. Their presence here is partly due to Saudi extremist Osama bin Laden, who has been harbored by the Taliban since 1997 and is said to repay his hosts with millions of dollars and thousands of holy warriors. The biggest supporter of the Taliban, however, is Pakistan, which has sent commandos, military advisers, and regular army troops. More than a hundred Pakistani prisoners of war sit in Massoud's jails; most of them — like the Taliban — are ethnic Pashtuns who trained in the *madrasahs*.

None of the help was doing the Taliban fighters much good at the moment, though. Harun switched his radio to a Taliban frequency and tilted it toward us. They were being overrun, and the panic in their voices was unmistakable. One commander screamed that he was almost out of ammunition; another started insulting the fighters at a neighboring position. "Are you crazy are you crazy are you crazy?" he demanded. "They've already taken a hundred prisoners! Do you want to be taken prisoner as well?" He went on to accuse them all of sodomy.

Harun shook his head incredulously. "They are supposed to represent true Islam," he said. "Do you see how they talk?"

I went into Afghanistan with Iranian-born photographer Reza Deghati, who knew Massoud well from several long trips he'd taken into the country during the Soviet occupation. Back then, the only way in was to take a one- to three-month trek over the Hindu Kush on foot, avoiding minefields and Russian helicopters, and every time Reza did it he lost twenty or thirty pounds. The conditions are vastly easier now but still unpredictable. Last summer, in a desperate effort to force international recognition for their regime, the Taliban launched a six-month offensive that was supposed to be the coup de grâce for Massoud. Some fifteen thousand Taliban fighters — heavily reinforced, according to Massoud's intelligence network, by Pakistani Army units — bypassed the impregnable Panjshir Valley and drove straight north toward the border of Tajikistan. Their goal was to move eastward along the border until Massoud was completely surrounded and then starve him out. They almost succeeded. Waiting to go into Afghanistan that September and October, Reza and I watched one town after another fall into Taliban hands, until even Massoud's old friends began to wonder if he wasn't through. "It may be his last season hunting," as one journalist put it.

Massoud finally stopped the Taliban at the Kowkcheh River, but by then the season was so far advanced that the mountain roads were snowbound, and the only way for Reza and me to get in was by helicopter from the Tajik capital of Dushanbe. Massoud's forces owned half a dozen aging Russian military helicopters, and the Afghan embassy in Dushanbe could put you on a flight that left at a moment's notice, whenever the weather cleared over the mountains. On November 15, late in the afternoon, Reza and I got the word. We raced to the airfield, and two hours later we were in Afghanistan.

The helicopters flew to a small town just across the border called Khvajeh Baha od Din, and we were provided a floor to sleep on in the home of a former mujahidin commander who was now a local judge. Each night, anywhere from ten to twenty fighters stayed there, sleeping in rows on the floor next to us. The electricity was supplied by a homemade waterwheel that had been geared to a generator through an old truck transmission. Some fuel came in by truck over the mountains — a five-day trip — but farther north it all came in by donkey and cost twenty dollars a gallon. (The locals jokingly refer to donkeys as "Afghan motorcycles.") We washed at an outdoor spring and subsisted on rice and mutton and kept warm at night around a woodstove; we lived comfortably enough. The situation around us, though, was unspeakable.

Eighty thousand civilians had fled the recent fighting, adding to the hundred thousand or so who were already displaced in the north, and thousands of them were subsisting in a makeshift refugee camp along the Kowkcheh River half a mile away. They slept under tattered blue U.N. tarps and had so little food that some were reduced to eating grass. Tribal politics have long dominated Afghanistan; many observers, in fact, say that Massoud, a Tajik, will never be able to unite the country. These refugees were mostly ethnic Tajiks and Uzbeks, and they claimed that when the Taliban, who are Pashtun, took over a town, they raped the women, killed the men, and sold the young into servitude. One old man at a refugee camp pulled back his quilted coat to show me a six-inch scar on his stomach. A Taliban soldier, he said, had stabbed him with a bayonet and left him for dead.

A week or so after we arrived inside Afghanistan, Reza and I were told that Massoud was coming in — he'd been in Tajikistan, negotiating support from the government — and we rushed down to the river to meet him. A lopsided boat made of sheet metal, powered by a tractor engine that had paddle wheels instead of tires, churned across the Kowkcheh with Massoud in the bow. He wore khaki pants and Czech Army boots and a smart camouflage jacket over a V-neck sweater. He looked to be in his late forties and was as lean and spare as the photographs of him from the Soviet days. He was not tall, but he stood as if he were. The great man stepped onto the riverbank along with a dozen bodyguards and greeted us. Then we all drove off to the judge's compound in Khvajeh Baha od Din.

There he met with his commanders, listened to their preparations for the coming offensive, then hurried off. We later found out that he'd been forced to return to Tajikistan because of a chronically bad back; apparently the problem was so severe that it had put him in the hospital.

Finding ourselves once again waiting for Massoud, Reza and I decided to go out to the frontline to see a position that had just been taken from the Taliban. We drove south along the Kowkcheh, past miles of trenches and bunkers, and stopped at an old Soviet base that had been gutted by artillery fire. The local commander was there, housed in the shell of the building. The wind whistled through the gaping windows, and his soldiers crouched in the shadows, preparing their weapons. The commander said that the position they'd taken was code-named Joy and that the bodies of the dead Taliban were still lying in the trenches.

He made a call on his radio and arranged for some men and packhorses to meet us on the other side of the river. Then he directed us to the crossing point; it was in a canyon a few miles away, just below a town called Laleh Meydan. When we stopped there to sort our gear, a Taliban MiG jet appeared and made a pass over the town, completely ignoring the antiaircraft fire that was directed at it. The townsmen scattered but drifted back within minutes to help us carry our gear down to the river. The raft that was to ferry us across was made from a design that must have been around since Alexander the Great: eight cowhides sewn shut and inflated like tires, each stoppered by a wood plug in one leg and lashed to a frame made of tree limbs. Four old men paddled it across the river and then tied our gear to some horses. Three soldiers with Kalashnikovs were waiting to take us to the front.

It took us all afternoon to get there, walking and riding through mud hills, bare and smooth as velvet, that undulated south toward the Hindu Kush. There was no sound but the wind — not even any fighting — and nothing to look at but the hills and the great, empty sky. When we turned the last ridgeline, we saw Massoud's men silhouetted on a hilltop, waving us on.

Maybe the Taliban spotted our horses, or maybe they'd overheard the radio communications, but we were halfway up the last slope when I found myself facedown in the dirt as a Taliban rocket slammed into the hillside behind us. Then we were up and running, and the next rocket hit just as we got to the top, and they continued to come in, slightly off target, as we crouched in the safety of the trenches.

There was nothing exciting about it, nothing even abstractly interesting. It was purely, exclusively bad. Whenever the Taliban fired off another salvo, a spotter on a nearby hilltop would radio our position to say that more were on the way. The commander would shout a warning, and the fighters would pull us down into the foxholes, and then we'd wait five or ten seconds until we heard the last, awful whistling sound right before they hit. In a foxhole you're safe unless the shell drops right in there with you, in which case you'd never know it; you'd simply cease to exist. No matter how small the odds were, the idea that I could go straight from life to nonexistence was almost unbearable; it turned each ten-second wait into a bizarre exercise in existentialism. Bravery — the usual alternative to fear — also held no appeal, because bravery could get you killed. It had become very simple: it was their war, their problem, and I didn't want any part of it. I just wanted off the hill.

The problem was, "off" meant rising out of this good Afghan dirt we'd become part of and running back the way we'd come. Four hundred yards away was a hilltop that they weren't shelling; over there it was just another normal, sunny day. After we'd spent half an hour ducking the shells, the commander said he'd just received word that Taliban troops were preparing to attack the position, and it might be better if we weren't around for it. Like it or not, we had to leave. Reza and I waited for a quiet spell and then climbed out of the trenches, took a deep breath, and started off down the hill.

Mainly there was the sound of my breathing: a deep, desperate rasp that ruled out any chance of hearing the rockets come in. The commander stood on the hilltop as we left, shouting goodbye and waving us away from a minefield that lay on one side of the slope. Ten minutes later it was over: we sat behind the next ridge and watched Taliban rockets continue to pound the hill, each one raising a little puff of smoke, followed by a muffled explosion. From that distance, they didn't look like much; they almost looked like the kind of explosions you could imagine yourself acting bravely in.

The Taliban kept up the shelling for the next twelve hours and then attacked at dawn. Massoud's men fought them off with no casualties.

Massoud returned one week later, flying in by helicopter to Harun's command post to start planning a heavy offensive across the entire northern front. The post was at the top of a steep, grassy hill in some broken country south of a frontline town called Dasht-e Qaleh. It was late afternoon by the time we arrived, and Massoud was studying the Taliban positions through a pair of massive military binoculars on a tripod. The deposed Afghan government's foreign minister, a slight, serious man named Dr. Abdullah, walked up to greet us as we got out of the truck. Reza wished him a good evening.

"Good morning," Dr. Abdullah corrected, nodding toward the Taliban positions across the valley. "Our day is just beginning."

The shelling had started again, an arrhythmic thumping in the distance that suggested nothing of the terror it can produce up close. That morning, I'd awakened from a dream in which an airplane was dropping bombs on me, and in the dream I'd thrown myself on the ground and watched one of the bombs bounce past me toward a picnicking family. "Good," I'd thought, "it will kill them and not me." It was an ugly, ungenerous dream that left me unsettled all day.

Massoud knew where the Taliban positions were, and they obviously knew where his were, and the upshot was that you were never entirely safe. A guy in town had just had both legs torn off by a single, random shell. You couldn't let yourself start thinking about it or you'd never stop.

Massoud was still at the binoculars. He had a face like a hatchet. Four deep lines cut across his forehead, and his almond-shaped eyes were so thickly lashed that it almost looked as if he were wearing eyeliner. When someone spoke, he swiveled his head around and affixed the speaker with a gaze so penetrating it occasionally made the recipient stutter. When he asked a question, it was very specific, and he listened to every word of the answer. He stood out not so much because he was handsome but simply because he was hard to stop looking at.

I asked Dr. Abdullah how Massoud's back was doing. Dr. Abdullah spoke low so that Massoud couldn't hear him. "He says it's better, but I know it's not," he said. "I can see by the way he walks. He needs at least a month's rest . . . but, of course, that won't be possible."

The shelling got heavier, and the sun set, and Massoud and his bodyguards and generals lined up on top of the bunker to pray. The prayer went on for a long time, the men standing, kneeling, prostrating themselves, standing again, their hands spread toward the sky to accept Allah. Islam is an extraordinarily tolerant religion — more so than Christianity in some ways — but it is also strangely pragmatic. Turning the other cheek is not a virtue. The prophet Muhammad, after receiving the first revelations of the Koran in A.D. 610, was forced into war against the corrupt Quraysh rulers of Mecca, who persecuted him for trying to make Arab society more egalitarian and to unite it under one god. Outnumbered three to one, his fighters defeated the Quraysh in 627 at the Battle of the Trench, outside Medina. Three years later he marched ten thousand men into Mecca and established the reign of Islam. Muhammad was born during an era of brutal tribal warfare, and he would have been useless to humanity as a visionary and a man of peace if he had not also known how to fight.

It was cold and almost completely dark when the prayers were finished. Massoud abruptly stood, folded his prayer cloth, and strode into the bunker, attended by Dr. Abdullah and a few commanders. We followed and joined them on the floor. A soldier brought in a pot for us to wash our hands, then spread platters of rice and mutton on a blanket. Massoud asked Dr. Abdullah for a pen, and Dr. Abdullah drew one out of his tailored cashmere jacket.

"I recognize that pen, it's mine," Massoud said. He was joking. "Well, in a sense everything we have is yours," Dr. Abdullah replied.

"Don't change the topic. Right now I'm talking about this pen." Massoud wagged his finger at Dr. Abdullah, then turned to the serious business of preparing the offensive.

Massoud's strategy was simple and exploited the fact that no matter how one looked at it, he was losing the war. After five years of fighting, the Taliban had fractured his alliance and cut its territory in half. Massoud was confined to the mountainous northeast, which, although easily defensible, depended on long, tortuous supply lines to Tajikistan. The Russians, ironically, had begun supplying Massoud with arms — with the Taliban near their borders, they couldn't afford to hold a grudge — and India and Iran were helping as well. It all had to go through Tajikistan. The most serious threat to Massoud's supply lines came last fall, when he lost a strategically important town called Taloqan, just west of the Kowkcheh River. The Taliban, convinced that recapturing Taloqan was of supreme importance to Massoud, shipped the bulk of their forces over to the Taloqan front. Massoud arrayed his forces in a huge V around the town and began a series of focused, stabbing attacks, usually at night, that guaranteed that the Taliban would remain convinced that he would do anything to retake the town.

In the meantime he was thinking on a completely different scale. Massoud had been fighting for twenty-one years, longer than most of the Taliban conscripts had been alive. In that context, Taloqan didn't matter, the next six months didn't matter. All that mattered was that the Afghan resistance survive long enough for the Taliban to implode on their own. The trump card of any resistance movement is that it doesn't have to win; the guerrillas just have to stay in the hills until the invaders lose their will to fight. The Afghans fought off the British three times and the Soviets once, and now Massoud was five years into a war that Pakistan could not support forever. Moreover, the civilian population in Taliban-controlled areas had started to bridle under the conscription of soldiers and the harshness of Taliban law. Last summer, in fact, a full-fledged revolt boiled over in a town called Musa Qaleh, and the Taliban had to send in six hundred troops to crush it. "Every day, I bathe in the river without my pistol," the local Taliban governor later told a reporter, with no apparent irony. "What better proof is there that the people love us?" The end of the Taliban, it seemed, was only a matter of time.

The Dari word for war is *jang*, and as Massoud ate his mutton, he explained to his commanders that within weeks he would start a *jang-e-gerilla-yee*. Here in the north he was locked into a frontline war that neither side could win, but he had groups of fighters everywhere — even deep in areas the Taliban thought they controlled. "In the coming days, we will engage the Taliban all over Afghanistan," he announced. "Pakistan brought us conventional war; I'm preparing a guerrilla war. It will start in a few weeks from now, even a few days."

Massoud had done the same thing to the Soviets. In 1985 he had disappeared into the mountains for three months to train 120 commandos and had sent each of them out across Afghanistan to train 100 more. These 12,000 men would attack the vital supply routes of the cumbersome Soviet Army. They used an operations map that had been found in a downed Soviet helicopter, and they took their orders from Massoud, who had informers throughout the Soviet military, even up to staff general. All across Afghanistan, Russian soldiers traded their weapons for drugs and food. Morale was so bad that there were gun battles breaking out among the Soviet soldiers themselves.

Dinner finished, Massoud spread the map out on the floor and bent over it, plotting routes and firing questions at his commanders. He wanted to know how many tanks they had, how many missile launchers, how much artillery. He wanted to know where the weapons were and whether their positions had been changed according to his orders. He occasionally interrupted his planning to deliver impromptu lectures, his elegant hands slicing the air for emphasis or a single finger shaking in the harsh light of the kerosene lantern. His commanders — many of them older than he, most veterans of the Soviet war — listened in slightly chastised silence, like schoolboys who hadn't done their homework.

"The type of operation you have planned for tonight might not be so successful, but that's OK; it should continue," he said. "This is not our main target. We're just trying to get them to bring reinforcements so they take casualties. The main thrust will be elsewhere."

Massoud was so far ahead of his commanders that at times he seemed unable to decide whether to explain his thinking or to just give them orders and hope for the best. The Soviets, having lost as many as fifteen thousand men in Afghanistan, reportedly now study his tactics in the military academies. And here he was, two decades later, still waging war from some bunker, still trying to get his commanders to grasp the logic of what he was doing.

It was getting late, but Massoud wasn't even close to being finished. He has been known to work for thirty-six hours straight, sleeping for two or three minutes at a time. There was work to do, and his men might die if it wasn't done well, and so he sat poring over an old Soviet map, coaxing secrets from it that the Taliban might have missed. At one point he turned to one of the young commanders and asked him whether he could fix the hulk of a tank that sat rusting on a nearby hill.

"I have already been up there to see it," the young man said. "I have fixed tanks much worse than that."

There were a total of three destroyed tanks; Massoud thought they all could be salvaged. One was stuck in an alleyway between two houses, and the young commander said the passageway was too narrow for them to drag it out. "Buy the houses, destroy them, and get it out," Massoud said. "Get two more tanks from Rostaq; that's five. Paint them like new and show them on the streets so people will see them. Then the Taliban will think we're getting help from another country."

On and on it went, commander by commander, detail by detail. *Don't shell from Ay Khanom Hill; you're just wasting your ammunition. Don't shell any positions near houses or towns; the Taliban are too deeply dug in in those spots and you'll just hurt civilians. Send your men forward in jeeps to save the heavy machinery and shell heavily beforehand to raise a lot of dust. That way, the Taliban won't see the attack.*

When Massoud was growing up in Kabul, he was part of a neighborhood gang that had regular battles with other gangs. One particularly large gang would occupy a hilltop near his house, and he and his friends would go out and challenge them. Naturally enough, Massoud was the leader. He would split his force, sending one half straight up the hill while the other half circled and attacked from the rear. It always worked. It still worked. Massoud sat cross-legged on the floor, bent forward at the waist, methodically opening and eating pistachios. His head hung low and swung from side to side as he spoke. He had a slight tic that ran like a shiver up his back and into his shoulders. "Get me your best guys," he said, looking around. "I don't want hundreds. I want sixty of your best. Sixty from each commander. Tomorrow I want to launch the best possible war."

Like so many fundamentalist movements, the Taliban were born of war. After the Soviet Union invaded Afghanistan on December 27, 1979, it ultimately sent in eight armored divisions, two enhanced parachute battalions, hundreds of attack helicopters, and well over a hundred thousand men. What should have been the quick crushing of a backward country, however, turned into the worst Soviet defeat of the Cold War. The very weaknesses of the fledgling resistance movement — its lack of military bases, its paucity of weapons, its utterly fractured command structure — meant that the Soviets had no fixed military objectives to destroy. Fighting Afghans was like nailing jelly to a wall; in the end there was just a wall full of bent nails. Initially using nothing but old shotguns, flintlock rifles, and Lee-Enfield .303s left over from British colonial days, the mujahidin started attacking Soviet convoys and military bases all across Afghanistan. According to a CIA report at the time, the typical life span of a mujahidin RPG operator — rocket-propelled grenades were the antitank weapon of choice — was three weeks. It's not unreasonable to assume that every Afghan who took up arms against the Soviets fully expected to die.

Without the support of the villagers, however, the mujahidin would never have been able to defeat the Soviets. They would have had nothing to eat, nowhere to hide, no information network — none of the things a guerrilla army depends on. The Soviets knew this, of course, and by the end of the first year — increasingly frustrated by the stubborn mujahidin resistance — they turned the dim Cyclops eye of their military on the people themselves. They destroyed any village the mujahidin were spotted in. They carpetbombed the Panjshir Valley. They cut down fruit trees, disrupted harvests, tortured villagers. They did whatever they could to drive a wedge between the people and the resistance. Still, it didn't work. After ten years of war, the Soviets finally pulled out of Afghanistan, leaving behind a country full of land mines and more than one million Afghans dead.

A country can't sustain that kind of damage and return to normal overnight. The same fierce tribalism that had defeated the Soviets — "radical local democracy," the CIA termed it — made it extremely hard for the various mujahidin factions to get along. (It would be three years before they would be able to take Kabul from the Communist regime that the Soviets had left.) Moreover, the mujahidin were armed to the teeth, thanks to a CIA program that had pumped three billion dollars' worth of weapons into the country during the war. Had the United States continued its support — building roads, repatriating the refugees, clearing the minefields — Afghanistan might have stood a chance of overcoming its natural ethnic factionalism. But the United States didn't. No sooner had the Soviet-backed government crumbled away than America's Cold War–born interest in Afghanistan virtually ceased. Inevitably, the Afghans fell out among themselves. And when they did, it was almost worse than the war that had just ended.

The weapons supplied by the United States to fight the Soviets had been distributed through Pakistan's infamous Inter-Services Intelligence branch. The ISI, as it is known, had chosen a rabidly anti-Western ideologue named Gulbuddin Hekmatyar to protect its strategic interests in Afghanistan, so of course the bulk of the weapons went to him. Now, using Hekmatyar to reach deep into Afghan politics, Pakistan systematically crippled any chance of a successful coalition government. As fighting flared around Kabul, Hekmatyar positioned himself in the hills south of the city and started raining rockets down on the rooftops. His strategy was to pound the various mujahidin factions into submission and gain control of the capital, but he succeeded merely in killing tens of thousands of civilians. Finally, in exchange for peace, he was given the post of prime minister. But his troops remained where they were, the barrels of their tanks still pointed down at the city they had largely destroyed.

While the commanders fought on, life in Afghanistan sank into a lawless hell. Warlords controlled the highways; opium and weapons smuggling became the mainstay of the economy; private armies battled one another for control of a completely ruined land. This was one of the few times that Massoud's forces are thought to have committed outright atrocities, massacring several hundred to several thousand people in the Afshar district of Kabul. There is no evidence, however, that Massoud gave the orders or knew about it beforehand. As early as 1994 Pakistan, dismayed by the fighting and increasingly convinced that Hekmatyar was a losing proposition, began to look elsewhere for allies. Its attention fell on the Taliban, who had been slowly gaining power in the *madrasahs* while Afghanistan tore itself apart. The Taliban were religious students, many of them Afghan refugees in Pakistan, who were trained in an extremely conservative interpretation of the Koran called Deobandism. Here, in the tens of thousands of teenage boys who had been orphaned or displaced by the war, Pakistan found its new champions.

Armed and directed by Pakistan and facing a completely fractured alliance, the Taliban rapidly fought their way across western Afghanistan. The population was sick of war and looked to the Taliban as saviors, which, in a sense, they were, but their brand of salvation came at a tremendous price. They quickly imposed a form of Islam that was so archaic and cruel that it shocked even the ultratraditional Muslims of the countryside. With the Taliban closing in on Kabul, Massoud found himself forced into alliances with men — such as Hekmatyar and former Communist Abdul Rashid Dostum — who until recently had been his mortal enemies. The coalition was a shaky one and didn't stand a chance against the highly motivated Taliban forces. After heavy fighting, Kabul finally fell to the Taliban in early September 1996, and Massoud pulled his forces back to the Panjshir Valley. With him were Burhanuddin Rabbani, who was the acting president of the coalition government, and a shifty assortment of mujahidin commanders who became known as the Northern Alliance. Technically, Rabbani and his ministers were the recognized government of Afghanistan — they still held a seat at the U.N. — but in reality, all they controlled was the northern third of one of the poorest countries in the world.

Worse still, there was a growing movement from a variety of Western countries — particularly the United States — to overlook

the Taliban's flaws and recognize them as the legitimate government of the country. There was thought to be as much as two hundred billion barrels of untapped oil reserves in Central Asia and
similar amounts of natural gas. That made it one of the largest fos-
sil fuel reserves in the world, and the easiest way to get it out was to
build a pipeline across Afghanistan to Pakistan. However appalling
Taliban rule might be, their cooperation was needed to build the
pipeline. Within days of the Taliban takeover of Kabul, a U.S. State
Department spokesman said that he could see "nothing objection-
able" about the Taliban's version of Islamic law.

While Massoud and the Taliban fought each other to a standstill
at the mouth of the Panjshir Valley, the American oil company
Unocal hosted a Taliban delegation to explore the possibility of an
oil deal.

The day before the offensive, Massoud decided to go to the frontline for a close look at the Taliban. He couldn't tell if the attack, as
planned, would succeed in taking their ridgetop positions; he was
worried that his men would die in a frontal assault when they could
just as easily slip around back. He had been watching the Taliban
supply trucks through the binoculars and had determined that
there was only one road leading to their forward positions. If his
men could take that, the Taliban would have to withdraw.

Massoud goes everywhere quickly, and this time was no exception. He jumped up from a morning meeting with his commanders, stormed out to his white Land Cruiser, and drove off. His
commanders and bodyguards scrambled into their own trucks to
follow him.

The convoy drove through town, raising great plumes of dust,
and then turned down toward the river and plowed through the
braiding channels, muddy water up to their door handles. One
truck stalled in midstream, but they got it going again and tore
through no man's land while their tanks on Ay Khanom Hill
shelled the Taliban to provide cover. They drove up to the forward
positions and then got out of the trucks and continued on foot,
creeping to within five hundred yards of the Taliban frontline.
This was the dead zone: anything that moves gets shot. Dead zones
are invariably quiet; there's no fighting, no human noise, just an
absolute stillness that can be more frightening than the heaviest

gunfire. Into this stillness, as Massoud studied the Taliban positions, a single gunshot rang out.

The bullet barely missed one of his commanders — he felt its wind as it passed — and came to a stop in the dirt between Massoud's feet. Massoud called in more artillery fire, and then he and his men quickly retraced their route to the trucks. The trip had served its purpose, though. Massoud had identified two dirt roads that split in front of the Taliban positions and circled behind them. And he had let himself be seen on the frontline, reinforcing the Taliban assumption that this was the focus of his attack.

Late that afternoon Massoud and his commanders went back up to the command post. The artillery exchanges had started up again, and a new Ramadan moon hung delicately in the sunset over the Taliban positions. That night, in the bunker, Massoud gave his commanders their final instructions. The offensive was to be carried out by eight groups of sixty men each, in successive waves. They must not be married or have children; they must not be their families' only sons. They were to take the two roads Massoud had spotted and encircle the Taliban positions on the hill. He told them to cut the supply road and hold their positions while offering the Taliban a way to escape. The idea was not to force the Taliban to fight to the last man. The idea was just to overtake their positions with as few casualties as possible.

The commanders filed out, and Reza and Dr. Abdullah were left alone with Massoud. He was exhausted, and he lay down on his side with his coat over him and his hands folded under his cheek. He fell asleep, woke up, asked Reza a question, then fell asleep, over and over again for the next hour. Occasionally a commander would walk in, and Massoud would ask if he'd repositioned those mortars or distributed the fifty thousand rounds of ammunition to the front. At one point, he asked Reza which country he liked best of all the ones he'd worked in.

"Afghanistan, of course," Reza said.

"Have you been to Africa?"

"Yes."

"Have you been to Rwanda?"

"Yes."

"What happened there? Why those massacres?"

Reza tried to explain. After a few minutes, Massoud sat up. "A few years ago in Kabul, I thought the war was finished, and I started building a home in Panjshir," he said. "A room for my children, a room for me and my wife, and a big library for all my books. I've kept all my books. I've put them in boxes, hoping one day I'll be able to put them on the shelves and I'll be able to read them. But the house is still unfinished, and the books are still in their boxes. I don't know when I'll be able to read my books."

Finally Massoud bade Reza and Dr. Abdullah good night and then lay back down and went to sleep for good. Though he holds the post of vice president in Rabbani's deposed government, Massoud is a man with few aspirations as a political leader, no apparent desire for power. Over and over he has rejected appeals from his friends and allies to take a more active role in the politics of his country. The Koran says that war is such a catastrophe it must be brought to an end as quickly as possible and by any means necessary. That, perhaps, is why Massoud has devoted himself exclusively to waging war.

I woke up at dawn. The sky was pale blue and promised a warm, clear day, which meant that the offensive was on. Reza and I ate some bread and drank tea and then went outside with the fighters. There seemed to be more of them milling around, and they were talking less than usual. They stood in tense little groups in the morning sun, waiting for Commander Massoud to emerge from his quarters.

The artillery fire started up in late morning, a dull smattering of explosions on the frontline and the occasional heavy boom of a nearby tank. The plan was for Massoud's forces to attack at dusk along the ridge, drawing attention to that part of the front, and then around midnight other attacks would be launched farther south. That was where the front passed close to Taloqan. As the afternoon went by, the artillery fire became more and more regular, and then suddenly at five-fifteen a spate of radio calls came into the bunker. Massoud stood up and went outside.

It had begun. Explosions flashed continually against the Taliban positions on the ridge, and rockets started streaking back and forth across the dark valley. We could see the lights from three Taliban tanks that were making their way along the ridgeline to reinforce positions that were getting overrun. A local cameraman named Yusuf had shown me footage of seasoned mujahidin attacking a hill, and I was surprised by how calm and purposeful the process was. In his video the men moved forward at a crouch, stopping to shoot from time to time and then moving forward again until they had reached the top of the hill. They never stopped advancing, and they never went faster than a walk.

Unfortunately, I doubted that the battle I was watching was being conducted with such grace. They were just kids up there, mostly, on the hill in the dark with the land mines and the machine-gun fire and the Taliban tanks. Massoud was yelling on the radio a lot, long bursts of Dari and then short silences while whomever he was talking to tried to explain himself. Things were not going well, it seemed. Some of the commanders weren't on the frontline where they belonged, and their men had gone straight up the hill instead of circling. As a result, they had attacked through a minefield. Massoud was in a cold fury.

"I never told you to attack from below. I knew it would be mined," he told one commander in the bunker. The man's head tipped backward with the force of Massoud's words. "The plan was not to attack directly. That's why you hit the mines. You made the same mistake last time."

The commander suggested that the mistake might have been made by the fighters on the ground.

"I don't care. These are my children, your children," Massoud shot back. "When I look at these fighters, they are like lions. The real problem is the commanders. You attacked from below and lost men to land mines. For me, even if you took the position, you lost the war."

The offensive was supposed to continue all night. Reza and I ate dinner with Massoud, then packed up our truck and set out on the long drive back to Khvajeh Baha od Din. We were leaving the front for good, and on the way out of town we decided to check in at the field hospital. It was just a big canvas tent set up in a mud-walled courtyard, lit inside by kerosene lanterns that glowed softly through the fabric. We stopped the truck and walked inside, and we were just wrapping up our conversation with the doctor when an old Soviet flatbed pulled up.

It was the first truckload of wounded, the guys who had stepped on mines. They were stunned and quiet, each face blackened by the force of a land mine blast, and their eyes cast around in confusion at the sudden activity surrounding them. The medics lifted the men off the back of the truck, carried them inside, and laid them on metal cots. A soldier standing next to me clucked his disapproval when he saw the wounds. The effect of a land mine on a person is so devastating that it is almost disorienting. It takes several minutes to understand that the sack of bones and blood and shredded cloth that you're looking at used to be a man's leg. One man lost a leg at the ankle; another man lost a leg at the shin; a third lost an entire leg to the waist. This man didn't seem to be in pain, and he didn't seem to have any understanding of what had happened to him. Both would come later. "My back hurts," he kept saying. "There's something wrong with my back."

The medics worked quickly and wordlessly in the lamplight, wrapping the stumps of the legs with gauze. The wounded men would be flown out by helicopter the next day and would eventually wind up in a hospital in Tajikistan. "*This* is the war," Reza hissed over and over again as he shot photos. "*This* is what war means."

Reza had covered a lot of wars and seen plenty of this in his life, but I hadn't. I ducked out of the tent and stood in the cold darkness, leaning against a wall. Dogs were barking in the distance, and a soldier shouted into his radio that the wounded were coming in and they needed more medicine, *now.* I thought about what Reza had said, and after a while I went back inside. This is the war too, and you have to look straight at it, I told myself. You have to look straight at all of it or you have no business being here at all.

AMY KOLEN

Fire

FROM THE MASSACHUSETTS REVIEW

1

THE NIGHT AFTER I read about the deadly Triangle factory fire of March 25, 1911, I saw flames as I slept, and heard the screams of young women trapped in rooms nine stories above the street — piercing screams distinct from the noise of fire engines and police patrol wagons clanging toward the corner of Washington Place and Greene Street. I imagined Celia Walker — poised on the ledge of a ninth-floor window of the Asch Building wondering whether or not to jump — and Yetta Lubitz and Ethel Monick, and Celia Weintraub, from Henry Street, who lay buried under a pile of bodies for two hours before she was discovered, barely alive. I saw the young man who, as flames flirted with their skirts, helped the girls out of the inferno and into space, dropping them to the pavement one hundred feet below before he himself leaped to his death. And I watched as firefighters rushed toward my father's mother — fifteen-year-old Rose Alter — who escaped to the roof of the building of which Triangle Shirtwaist Company occupied the top three floors.

We were on the tenth floor and escaped through the roof, she said in one of the last letters she wrote to me (before she died at age eighty-two in 1978) after I asked for information about her and her family. *It's a long, long story and I don't care to go into details. I'll never forget it.*

My grandmother was among those lucky enough to have been led to the roof and safety, lucky because her connection to the fire and the factory was far different from that of Yetta Lubitz, Celia Weintraub, or Ethel Monick — a connection that's disturbing for me to consider, even now, twenty-two years after having received her letters: the quintessential sweatshop of the early 1900s — the Triangle Shirtwaist Company — was owned by two men. One of them, Isaac Harris, was my grandmother's cousin.

My father was given a job as head of the shipping department in my cousin Isaac Harris's firm, The Triangle Waist Co. At that time they were the largest in the industry. So, we were luckier than most immigrants who struggled to find jobs and to make a dollar. My dad received a nice salary, more than enough to take care of our family. My brother-in-law also got a job at Triangle. So did my sister Mary, and eventually so did I. Our whole family worked for my cousin and life was an easy one.

My grandmother's letters place her in the Triangle Shirtwaist Factory near the year 1909, when two hundred Triangle workers went on strike, prompting a general walkout of twenty thousand garment workers from New York to Philadelphia. It was Grandma's cousin Isaac Harris who brought in the thugs who beat the women on the picket line outside his sweatshop, Harris who bribed the police to haul the women off to jail: "The hoodlums hired by the company could do their work without interference," the historian Leon Stein reported a cashier at Triangle as saying. "You could get a man on the beat to look away by giving him a box of cigars with a $100.00 bill in it." It was Isaac Harris who helped ensure that some of the progress other strikers gained after the walkout — a shorter work week, an end to the subcontracting system, a wage increase, adequate fire escapes, and open doors from the factories to the streets — would not affect his employees at Triangle.

And my grandmother's letters place her at her desk in Triangle's tenth-floor administrative offices on March 25, 1911, when, on the eighth floor where the cutters worked, a cigarette butt supposedly tossed into a rag bin ignited the fire that raged through the sweatshop and left 146 people, mostly young women, dead in less than twenty minutes. "On the 25th of March," said one writer at the time, "it was the same policemen who had clubbed [the girls] back into submission [during the strike] who kept the thousands in Washington Square from trampling upon their dead bodies, sent for ambulances to carry them away and lifted them one by one into the receiving coffins."

I worked at Triangle as a factory bookkeeper until March 25, 1911. That was a day to remember. It was a nice cool day on a Saturday afternoon about 4 P.M. We heard the word FIRE and within ten minutes, we were surrounded on all four sides by flames. Triangle occupied the 8th, 9th, and 10th floors of the safest building at that time and all three floors were in flames. 146 people died. It was the worst fire in the history of New York. We were on the 10th floor and escaped through the roof. It's a long, long story and I don't care to go into details. I'll never forget it.

I'll never forget it. But my grandmother never told me much about the fire in her letters. Though I understand her inevitable loyalty to the relatives who provided so well for her and her family, the pride she sustained in being connected to one of the most exploitative manufacturers in the women's garment industry is more difficult for me to comprehend.

When Triangle went out of business several years after the fire, Grandma became personnel manager at another factory. *I also took charge of payroll,* she writes.

It was a very good position with excellent pay. Then all of a sudden, the unions interfered. Our shop was non-union and I took over for management and had to arbitrate.

If she felt outrage over the tyrannical conditions at Triangle, she didn't evidence it in her letters to me. Yet the knowledge I've acquired researching my own family's part in the tragedy has compelled me to look at what my grandmother didn't allow herself to see, to pose questions she didn't ask.

What allowed people to look the other way before and after the fire? While the ashes were still warm, many ignited questions: What had happened here and why? What's to keep it from happening again? Who is to blame? So many others demanded answers, and laws to ensure that such horror would not be forgotten. Because of so many other voices, from the ashes came reforms. From the ashes also came my private search for detail. For answers Grandma never revealed.

On my desk I see the photo of Grandma Rose at age twenty, her thick dark hair wound into two loose braids that fall below her shoulders, her small, bright blue eyes so darkly circled they disappear into apostrophes with her smile. In the photo she's gazing over eight decades into the future while I'm gazing back to a time I'm struggling to understand. What did it feel like to know that security was tenuous in a world where signs reading "No Jews or Dogs Allowed" infected roadsides along the East Coast for at least the first four decades she called this country home? What drove people like Isaac Harris to exploit their fellow immigrants, fellow Jews who, like themselves, had fled from tyranny in their homeland to a life that promised, as Grandma said in her letters, *streets paved with gold*?

I look at the photograph of my grandmother, hold her in my hands, try to find my place in a continuum of which I know so little. What would you say, Grandma, if you knew that my niece, your twenty-year-old great-granddaughter born two months before your death, feels that she now must make "reparations" and has focused her energies on eliminating the sweatshop system that your cousin helped flourish? What would you say if you knew that my questions were what first pushed her to make connections? And while I raise certain questions of others, I must ask myself too, Grandma, what have I done to further social change in this arena? I've never spoken out on sweatshop labor issues, or in any way helped ensure the removal of contemporary sweatshops. Is it fair for me to demand from others in the past what I'm not demanding from myself now, while I try to make connections of my own, gain entry into history, to bring what I can of the unknown from the shadows?

2

I never lived close to any of my grandparents, who remained in New York while my parents chose an academic life in Iowa, where I was born. Though distant in miles, Grandma Rose and I corresponded regularly by letter from the time I was eight until her death the year I turned twenty-seven. My grandmother was not only a true epistolary companion, she was also the only adult in my life who offered unconditional and consistent support. The letters we exchanged were filled with details that kept us in touch with each other's lives: how much she'd lost at her last mahjong game; what boys filled out my dance card at my first box social and the grades on my most recent report cards; updates on Grandpa's health and the new teeth he got courtesy of the hospital after his physicians misplaced the original set; and birthday cards emblazoned with prepubescent girls (no matter what my age), their silky hair fixed into smooth pageboys, and wearing white gloves and flouncy dresses with pink pumps and satin bows cinching their waists, opening screechingly turquoise doors to gay birthday verses: "May every candle on your cake shine with the love this brings, and may your special day be filled with fun and happy things!"

Just as Grandma Rose was the only grandparent with whom I communicated regularly, she was my only entry into extended family I otherwise would not have known. During my family's biannual visit, she hosted late-night card games including every relative within fifty miles, my cousins and I raiding her cherry-wood hutch for the fancy marzipan, sugared fruit slices, and chocolates that she stocked in seemingly endless supplies. To me, she was the emblematic GRANDMA who served soft-boiled eggs in elegant porcelain heart-shaped egg cups, yolks cooked just the right consistency to coat the toast; who, whenever I used words like "magenta" or "irresistible," praised me for having "such a strong vocabulary."

Though mining the past suggested in her letters was, at times, like coaxing water from rock, Grandma Rose was also an entry into Jewish history — from the pogroms in Russia, to immigration to America, to employment at the Triangle Shirtwaist Company — which, no matter how appalling I may find it, is a story that is mine, to shape and hold on to.

The biggest excitement in my life came when my folks decided to go to America due to all the pogroms in Russia. Jews were being killed right and left and the police and government did nothing about it, just laughed. It's all too gruesome to write about. We were given protection by a countess. She took us into her home and the murderers dared not touch us. They wouldn't enter her place because she was royalty.

Grandma described herself as a young child in 1903 — in the little town of Bender, about thirty miles south of Kishinev, in

Bessarabia province — running through the countess's estate and playing tag with the countess's children among the walnut and fruit trees and peacocks that strolled through the yard. The children had to stay in the front yard. *Too many gypsies around to grab a child,* Grandma wrote that her mother, Dina, often warned her. Evenings Grandma played lotto with her family. Perhaps letters from her eldest sister, Dora, studying in France, were piled on the table near the sofa, along with papers regarding her father Louis's wheat business. Grandma's aqua school uniform and her older sister Mary's brown one draped across the back of the sofa where their mother left them after pressing them for school the next day. Both girls attended Catholic school after they refused to continue in the local *cheder* (Hebrew school). *There were only a few Jewish girls in this parochial school,* Grandma wrote. *It cost a lot of money to get us in.* It also cost a lot to bribe the police — to bribe a countess too? — to keep a Jewish family from being murdered, to keep home and business intact during the spring and the coming of Passover and Easter — "pogrom season" — in Eastern Europe and Russia.

Four months after the massacre of Jews in Kishinev and eight months before a mob attacked the Jewish quarter of their hometown, the Alter family arrived in America. While they planned their move to a country where *we believed,* wrote Grandma, *that the streets were paved with gold,* thousands of Jews wound their way through the streets of Kishinev behind the velvet-draped caskets containing the Torah scrolls desecrated in the pogrom of April 6 and 7, 1903, to a gravesite marked with plain wooden posts. A few months before Grandma's seventh birthday, while the Alters collected their feather pillows and comforters, brass candlesticks and lace, across the ocean in New York, tens of thousands of mourners filled the streets of the Lower East Side, marching for the living and the dead in Russia.

We began preparations for our trip to our dream world. Personally, I'm surprised this information would interest you. None of my relatives were celebrities, just everyday people. So far, not much interesting for your family tree, I'll bet. We took a boat to Liverpool and boarded the ship, Fatherland, and settled in for a long ride in third class. We were on that ship a week before we landed at Ellis Island on August 20, 1903.

A multistoried brick structure with minaret-capped towers and decorative cornices, the immigration center is set on an island that once housed explosives for the navy. Over twelve million immigrants who came through its Great Hall saw America as "an adventure, a beacon of hope." Over two hundred thousand were sent back to the homelands they had fled, often because of physical disabilities or other so-called medical reasons. There are photographs of medical inspections immigrants who'd traveled in third class or steerage were forced to endure after embarkation — like the photo of a young child, her eyes red from crying, having her upper eyelid flipped back with a hook to determine whether or not she has trachoma — pictures that prefigure the photographs and instruments behind glass at the United States Holocaust Memorial Museum — instruments that developed as eugenics was born: the metal ruler with prongs used by the Nazis to examine nose width, the stethoscope-shaped object used to examine skull width, the photo of the young girl, nude to the waist, head tipped to one side, as an inspector compares the color of her dark brown eyes to the eye colors on a chart developed in Germany to identify non-Aryans.

In the Great Hall my grandmother's cousin, Isaac Harris, vouched that she and her family would not be a burden on this country. Then he transported her family to the apartment he'd set up for them at Ninety-ninth Street and Lexington Avenue — a place complete with gaslights, steam heat, toilet, and running water, the latter so amazing Grandma, she wrote that she *ran from room to room and back to the kitchen opening faucets, just letting the water run . . .*

For my grandmother, from a little Russian town not far from Kishinev, who was accustomed to water sold by the barrel, outdoor toilets, no electricity or gas, and rooms lit by kerosene lamps, walking into this apartment was, she wrote, *like a magic story*. Unlike so many immigrants who fled to America at the turn of the century, Grandma wasn't forced to battle an unsympathetic landlord demanding rent. She didn't have to wait in long lines for a nonexistent job in a sweatshop, vie for sleeping space in a filthy, bug-infested room with seven other relatives, without even a toothbrush or towel of her own. She didn't have to haggle for dry goods from the pushcart vendors that lined Manhattan's Lower East Side.

From the minute her cousin Isaac Harris met her family on Ellis Island, Grandma's position in the New World was secured.

3

Two years ago, having reread my grandmother's letters and studied various accounts of the fire and subsequent court case in which Triangle's owners were tried for manslaughter, I stood at the northwest corner of Greene Street and Washington Place reading the plaque commemorating the workers who died in the fire. I stood at this spot, in what is now at the edge of SoHo, and projected myself back to the early 1900s and the Washington Square Park area as it may have looked when my grandmother arrived. It was not as fashionable as it had been fifty years earlier when wealthy New Yorkers started building "country homes" here. But in 1911, it was a peaceful residential area. Horses, their hooves clopping along the streets, pulled covered landaus with women inside, elegantly dressed under French serge coats in Empire dinner gowns of lace and apricot velvet, their large hats trimmed with sprigs of wisteria or plumes. Stanford White's Washington Arch graced the eight-acre park to the north, at the foot of Fifth Avenue. Along Washington Square North were the Greek Revival townhouses that made up "The Row." Facing the park to the east were the buildings of New York University and the American Book Company, on the same block as the Asch Building. And inside the Asch Building, more than five hundred people, mainly girls and young women, toiled at their sewing machines fashioning thin cotton fabric into shirtwaists.

These sheer, high-necked blouses were less expensive than dresses. Typically, they were worn with tailored skirts and featured masculine collars and bouffant sleeves and tapered to a tightly fitted waistline. Artist and illustrator Charles Gibson became famous at the turn of the century for his "Gibson girl," the ideal young American woman, ready to compete with any man in the workplace, dressed in her efficient yet feminine shirtwaist and skirt.

In 1911, Triangle was among several of the major firms that dominated the shirtwaist industry, and owners Isaac Harris and Max Blanck, known as "the shirtwaist kings," epitomized the sweatshop boss. Both owned large cars and used chauffeurs. Both were competitive and ambitious. Within six years after they moved Triangle into the ninth floor of the Asch Building, they had taken over the eighth and tenth floors. Each had separate responsibilities in the firm. Harris, a "frail man and slight," was, according to historian Leon Stein, the "inside man [who] knew all about garment production, machinery, how to keep the work flow going through the plant. His daily task was to patrol the factory, moving impressively down its aisles, checking, questioning, directing." Themselves refugees from Russia, Harris and Blanck exploited the immigrants who worked for them through a subcontracting system common in the industry at the time: they dealt only with their "master craftsman" machine operators — actually men they'd hired as contractors for the factory. In turn, the contractor hired, and had the power to fire, the young immigrant workers whom he taught to make the separate shirtwaist pieces, which he eventually joined together. At Triangle, there were between five and ten contractors per floor. The firm's owners felt no responsibility for the workers, and never knew exactly how many employees they had because only the contractors' names were listed on the payroll. It was the contractor who, on Saturdays, paid the workers. (Other, similar shops were closed on Saturday afternoons, but Harris and Blanck had managed to ignore the union's demand for a five-and-a-half-day work week.) There was no starting salary — though the pay was reportedly no lower than at other shops — and little chance of a raise. "The girls . . . got whatever the contractor wanted to pay as a start," recalled a cashier at Triangle. "In two or three weeks they knew how to sew very well. Never mind. For a long time they still got the same low pay. Triangle and the inside contractor got the difference." Contemporaries of my grandmother's called the subcontracting system "an admitted evil . . . [that] the best manufacturers condemn."

Triangle workers were charged for supplies and for the electricity they needed to run the sewing machines. They were also charged "rent" for the chairs they sat in eight to thirteen hours a day, six days a week, in overcrowded rooms — chokingly hot in the summer — where on the ninth floor, 240 sewing machine operators were packed together elbow to elbow at tables seventy-five feet long that almost filled the entire floor in a room of about ten thousand square feet. There was no belonging to unions. Most doors, even the one to the inadequate fire escape, were usually locked during business hours to keep union organizers out and to prevent theft.

To further ensure that their property was protected, Harris and Blanck had watchmen stand guard at each exit at closing time, rifling through the girls' pocketbooks and poking at their upswept pompadours, hunting for pieces of shirtwaists that might have been stolen, or bits of fabric that a working girl might use to turn her simple straw hat into a treasure. "If one of the Triangle girls was caught filching a ten-cent bit of shirtwaist material," wrote Samuel Gompers two months after the fire, "she would have been liable to arrest and sentenced to a term in prison." Harris even admitted under cross-examination during the trial after the fire that he'd had six girls arrested in 1908 after the detectives he'd sent to their homes found shirtwaists the girls had supposedly stolen from his shop. More recently, though, there had been no arrests. A few girls who were accused of stealing had sued the firm for damages, and, Harris said, "We found the best way to deal with the girls was to discharge them on the spot and not bother with them anymore."

Grandma must have visited the eighth and ninth floors during her time at Triangle and seen the sewers packed together on nine. Hunched over their machines, they breathed in smells of human sweat and dust and machine oil, the silent pounding in their temples a metronome to keep their pace allegro, to ensure they'd each bring home at least twelve dollars that week. She must have heard the roar of the 240 new electric Singers — powerful machines, which operated with a foot pedal rather than a hand-turned crank wheel — as vibrating needles zipped across flimsy material so quickly, novice sewers' fingers were easily mangled: "I didn't know how to sew on an electric sewing machine," eighty-six-year-old Bertha Lanxner admitted during an interview sixty-eight years after she'd quit Triangle. "The needle went into my finger and I have yet a cut . . . so my future husband told me, don't tell that. I'll tell them you have a sore finger so maybe they'll excuse you so you'll have a chance to learn."

As part of the administrative staff, my grandmother, like everyone else in her family who worked for the firm, was allowed to enter Triangle through the front entrance on the Washington Place side, "beautiful with marble floors," and take the front elevator up to the spacious tenth floor, where she had her own desk near her cousin's office. Because she was family, after stepping off the elevator, she didn't have to confront a partition with an opening through which she had to squeeze — an opening wide enough for only one person at a time, to enable the watchman to easily detain workers and search them at closing time. Unlike my grandmother on the tenth floor, the hundreds of girls on the floors below had to step into enormous rooms filled almost entirely with long wooden tables and sewing machines. On the ninth floor, where most of the fire victims worked, passage from aisle to aisle was difficult. If a girl worked at the end of the room far from the entrance, she was forced to wind her way around the seventy-five-foot-long lead table — one of eight such continuous tables arranged in rows parallel to one another — before she could worm her way to her seat, trying not to bang into the wooden chairs, the backs of which, even when they were shoved under the table, almost touched each other, "like the 'double two' in dominoes." A savvy worker quickly learned to arrive at the shop early to avoid the crush of bodies that rushed from the cloakroom to assigned seats before the six-o'clock bell announced the beginning of a workday.

If Grandma let her eyes roam around the eighth and ninth floors for a few moments, she'd have seen the wicker baskets on the floor to the right of each girl overflowing with bundles of fabric. She couldn't have helped noticing that the machines of the girls sitting across the troughs from each other dripped oil — oil that collected on the wooden floor beneath their feet when the wooden shells above their knees became too full to hold the drippings. Did Grandma wonder what any of these hundreds of girls would do if they had to leave the room quickly, if there was a real emergency? If there was a fire?

There had been fires in the past. In 1902 two fires had broken out on the ninth floor of the Asch Building, and in 1909, there was a fire on eight when a motor supplying power for the two hundred machines there emitted a spark that ignited a pile of remnants under a table. According to her letters, Grandma could have been at work the day of that fire. Though the flames were contained on the eighth floor, there was little damage, and no lives were lost, she would have remembered how the girls panicked. Did Grandma wonder what she'd do if a fire broke out on her floor? Did she ever dream of falling from a window one hundred feet above the pavement, falling from her father and her sister who were nowhere to be seen?

In trying to look at what my grandmother did not, I must also try to envision her as she describes herself in her letters: a young woman filled with energy and plans, chattering with her older sister Mary while they wait for their father so they can travel the one hundred plus blocks home together after work. They're enjoying the view out the windows overlooking Washington Place and discussing the boy Rose had invited to Shabbat dinner that night — a smart, good-looking accountant for a well-known millinery shop on Broadway, who also attended Wadleigh High School. And though *mishegass, shaineh maidel, faidrai zich dem kop!* and many other scraps of Yiddish patterned her speech, she had heeded her cousin Isaac Harris's advice and worked hard at school, speaking only English, leaving her native Russian and Yiddish behind — just as her family was forced to leave Dora and Solomon, Rose's older sister and brother, behind when they emigrated to America, never to see them again.

I never knew my eldest sister Dora. She was always away studying in France. And just before we left for America, Solomon told my parents he was in love and couldn't leave. His clothes were already on the way to America and had to be sent back when we arrived. I never saw him again. He and his family as well as my sister and her family were no doubt killed by the Germans. When Solomon finally wanted to come to the U.S. he wasn't allowed to emigrate. After the war we tried to locate him but got nowhere.

By 1911, eight years had passed since Rose witnessed her own mother's longing for her lost son and daughter, but to a young woman, it must have seemed like decades ago that she and Mary, three years her senior, sat in Miss Müller's class, trying to learn English after school, trying to ignore the insults their classmates heaped on them for being greenhorns: *Children in class laughed at us because we couldn't understand English. Our relatives told us never to speak Russian or Yiddish. "Forget it," they said, or you'll be stoned.*

It must have seemed eons since her name and those of her sisters were changed at Ellis Island: Roza becoming Rose, Malta metamorphosing to Mary, Zina turning into Juliet. *I wish my sister's name had remained Zina, I loved it. So stupid that it was changed. At least mine stayed almost the same.* Rose was proud of her agility with English, of her ability to attract such an intelligent boy. As she, her father, and Mary rode the Sixth Avenue El north to Central Park South and then hopped the trolley for the remaining forty blocks to their apartment at 103rd Street and Madison Avenue, I see her father settling in with a copy of the *Daily Forward* while his daughters discuss which china they should use on their new Sabbath tablecloth, which dress brought out the blue of Rose's eyes — the gloxinia shift with the cream-colored collar or the wild lilac princess dress with the matching starched hair bow. The two are still in deep conversation as they reach their stop at 105th Street and Fifth Avenue, where, in comparison to the floods of people in the streets where most of Triangle's employees lived, only a handful of well-dressed men and women are out strolling. It is at this site, almost fifteen years later, that a museum will be built encapsulating New York history. And in this museum will be a painting, made shortly after the Triangle fire, depicting the fire and firefighting apparatus of that time: ladders that reach only six stories, life nets built to support the bodies of girls — but not when they link arms in twos and threes and jump from the windows of burning buildings — and high-pressure hoses that can cool those burning buildings on the outside but can't extinguish the fire cremating the bodies within.

4

My daughter Raychel has heard me talk about my excavations into the fire, and shows me a copy of this painting — in the collection of the Museum of the City of New York — illustrated in her high school American Studies text. Under the picture the caption reads: "The fire at the Triangle Shirtwaist Company in 1911, in which 147 [sic] people died, finally convinced many Americans of the need to reform the appalling working conditions that existed in many industries at the time." I'm glad the editors mentioned the fire. It wasn't even a footnote in my history books when I was in high school. Yet its depiction is too smooth, whitewashed. In the painting the building is intact and delicately rendered in what looks like tempera paint. From the sixth floor, six cartoon flames sputter from six windows as two tiny firemen standing on ladders aim their hoses at the flames. On the street below, there's the suggestion of a crowd in the foreground — fifteen static and silent figures depicted from the shoulders up — while firemen carry two shrouded figures to the side of the building where more of the mummy shapes are propped in an orderly line. That's all there is to this sanitized version of the inferno. There's no accompanying text, no witnessing of the chaos and terror of the fire and the minutes that it took for 146 people to die. There are no signs of smoke, charred flesh, crushed and mangled and headless bodies burned to crisps. No anguished pleas of the living, no crying out of pet names in Italian and Yiddish for the unrecognizable masses collecting on the street. No signs of the police officers and firefighters, bewildered, collapsed by the curb, sobbing and sick. There is no glimpse of the mob of undertakers hovering at crowd's edge, vying with each other to haul away sister, daughter, mother, wife.

Black and smudgy tiny script writhes in front of my face, and I struggle to make sense of the crammed prose on the screen. For three hours I've been twisting the knob on the microfiche machine to the left, to the right, fast, slow, to get the immediate story of the fire as it looked to someone eighty-seven years ago when it first appeared in the *New York Times:* 141 MEN AND GIRLS DIE IN WAIST FACTORY FIRE; TRAPPED HIGH UP IN WASHINGTON PLACE BUILDING; STREET STREWN WITH BODIES; PILES OF DEAD INSIDE (from March 26, 1911, page one, before the final body count). And then, on page four, under the headline PARTNERS' ACCOUNT OF THE DISASTER: "Harris took the lead in guiding people to the roof and once there, led them to safety."

> On the roof Harris took the lead and marshaled the women, pushing them toward the northeast corner of the building where it joins a factory building at Wooster St. and Waverly Pl. This building adjoins the rear of the Triangle Waist Company's factory for only about one-quarter of its length . . . The rest of the way . . . the buildings are separated from each other by a narrow wall . . . ten feet wide. This was spouting flames

and embers, which rained on the roof, and swirling eddies of hot gases added to the peril.

My grandmother's cousin managed to get the forty or fifty people who followed him to the Waverly Place building and safety, but cut his right hand severely in the process when he bashed in a skylight with his fists. During an interview with the *New York Times* reporter, he paced the room nursing his injured hand, more interested, the reporter claims, in explaining precautions that the firm took to avoid fires than in recounting his part in the escape from the building.

Someone laid a board, a very narrow plank, from the roof of the Asch building to the building next door, my grandmother once told a cousin of mine five decades after the fire. *This board was one hundred feet above the street and I had to crawl across it. I was terrified.*

Not so lucky were the three men on the eighth floor — their story on the same page as that of Isaac Harris — who made a "human bridge," swinging their bodies across an alley to the building fronting Greene Street. "As people crossing upon the human bridge crowded more and more over the men's bodies, the weight upon the center man became too great and his back broke," says Pauline Grossman, eighteen-year-old survivor. "He fell to the alley below and the other two men lost their holds upon the window sills and fell. People who were crossing upon them dropped with them."

The story unfolds as it was written over three quarters of a century ago.

As fashion writers cringe at the "pantaloon skirt" in favor of the "gown," and announce the designs that await readers in the following Sunday's "Easter and Spring Fashion" section, Isaac Harris and Max Blanck deny that their factory's doors were locked from the outside, even though the two remaining doors that hadn't burned were still locked in the ruins and had to be chopped down by firemen. As hawkers slide through the crowds of sightseers that gather near 123 Washington Place after the fire, shouting, "Souvenirs from the big fire! Get a ring from a dead girl's finger!" H.F.J. Porter, city fire prevention expert, interviews factory owners regarding their use of fire drills: "Let 'em burn," one owner says. "They're a lot of cattle anyway." While three hundred thousand mourners prepare to follow the caskets of the seven unidentified fire victims from the morgue to Mt. Zion Cemetery in Brooklyn, New York City Building Department inspectors issue Triangle a violation notice after discovering that the firm's new quarters at 9–11 University Place isn't fireproof, and that Harris and Blanck have arranged the tiers of sewing machines to block access to the fire escapes. While Jews all over the world prepare to celebrate Passover and freedom from four hundred years of slavery in Egypt, Blanck and Harris determine how to fight charges of first- and second-degree manslaughter — punishment for their contemporary tyranny of keeping factory doors locked — that are leveled against them after the fire. And as ads for automatic sprinkler systems spatter the *New York Times,* and J. M. Gidding suggests half-price after-Christmas gift-giving ideas, the jury in the case of Harris and Blanck bring in a verdict of not guilty.

The charge against Triangle's proprietors was manslaughter in the first and second degrees. The state intended to prove that the ninth-floor exit door on the Washington Place side was locked at the time of the fire, that the owners knew the door was locked, and that this violation was the direct cause of the death of Margaret Schwartz, one of the 146 victims.

For defense counsel, Harris and Blanck hired attorney Max D. Steuer, a rising star, with "that instinct for the jugular vein," says American history expert Richard B. Morris, "which was to keep him in the first rank of notable trial lawyers." According to Leon Stein, Steuer, like most of the witnesses called by the prosecution, grew up on the Lower East Side. "He knew them well, spoke their language, sensed their fears and resentments," and, says Stein, he used this understanding to his advantage as the trial progressed. In one instance, he cross-examined the state's star witness to the point where he discredited her story (in his own words after the trial, "toyed with the story"), leaving the jury with the impression that she'd been overcoached by the prosecution.

Despite the procession of witnesses for the state who all testified they'd never seen the Washington Place door open and had never seen anyone pass through it; despite all the witnesses who said they'd tried unsuccessfully to open the door during the fire, who swore that no fire drills were ever held at Triangle, and that flammable refuse was allowed to accumulate to dangerous proportions; despite irrefutable evidence that the door in question had been locked at the time of the fire, and the disclosure that a number of witnesses for the defense who had made sworn statements to the district attorney that the door was locked were given pay raises after perjuring themselves during the trial, testifying that the door was open, Harris and Blanck were found innocent. Despite the testimony from Triangle's head cutter who swore that Harris told him a few days after the fire, "The dead ones are dead and will be buried. The live ones are alive and they will have to live. Sure the doors were locked. I wouldn't let them rob my fortune"; despite the evidence against Harris and Blanck proving that they'd violated factory laws and did nothing to improve the "desperately bad" conditions in the shop and that they'd "habitually neglected necessary precautions," after three weeks of listening to testimony in the courtroom of Judge Thomas T. C. Crain, the jurors — deliberating less than two hours — returned to the courtroom with a verdict of not guilty.

This "complete miscarriage of justice," as the *New York Times* put it two days after the verdict, did not mean that "nobody was to blame for this hideous disaster . . . What it really means . . . is that . . . Harris and Blanck were not guilty as charged." Richard B. Morris points out that before the jurors considered a verdict, Judge Crain's charge to them "virtually constituted a directed verdict of acquittal." He told them to remember that the defense contended that Margaret Schwartz died as the result of the Washington Place door on the ninth floor being locked. The judge gave his interpretation of the New York penal code and explained that the accused were on trial for first- or second-degree manslaughter, which meant that the girl's "death resulted from a misdemeanor or an intention to commit one, or that her death was a direct result of the firm's negligence." Morris says that Judge Crain reminded the jury that "manslaughter was a felony and unless it could be shown that the accused were *aware* of the violations, they could not be found guilty. It must be shown '*beyond a reasonable doubt*,' Crain charged, that the door was locked *with the knowledge of the defendants,* and that the locking of the door caused the death of Margaret Schwartz."

The verdict troubled at least two jurors. Afterward, one of them told a reporter:

I believed that the Washington Place door, on which the district attorney said the whole case hinged, was locked at the time of the fire. But I could not make myself feel certain that Harris and Blanck knew that it was locked. And so, because the judge had charged us that we could not find them guilty unless we believed that they *knew* the door was locked, then, I did not know what to do. It would have been much easier for me if the state inspectors instead of Harris and Blanck had been on trial. There would have been no doubt in my mind then as to how to vote.

Harris and Blanck, threatened by mobs earlier in the month during the trial proceedings, were smuggled out of the courthouse accompanied by policemen, and again almost attacked by over one hundred relatives and friends of the victims. "Justice! Where is Justice?" Josephine Nicolosi cried, and others echoed her. "Murderers!" screamed David Weiner, whose seventeen-year-old sister died in the fire. Breaking from the throng and shaking his fist in Isaac Harris's face, he's reported to have screamed, "Murderers! You're acquitted now, but we'll get you yet. Murderers!" he yelled again, before collapsing in convulsions, before the ambulance took him to Hudson Street Hospital, where doctors pronounced him suffering from a "disordered mind."

Two years after the fire, after Triangle had moved to another location on the corner of Sixteenth Street and Fifth Avenue, Max Blanck was fined the minimum twenty dollars (the law considered this his first offense) for keeping one of Triangle's doors locked during working hours, with 150 girls inside. Three years after the fire, the families of twenty-three of the victims collected seventy-five dollars apiece from the owner of the Asch Building for each life lost.

5

"Management got a bum rap." That's what my cousin says when I ask him if he remembers anything Grandma said about the fire or the factory. Kenneth and his sister Lois lived a few blocks away from Grandma a good part of their lives. In response to my request for any information she might have on Grandma and her connection to Triangle, Lois sent me a scrap of paper she'd discovered that her brother had used to jot notes on the fire for a junior high history project, now long gone. Over thirty years have passed since I last talked to Kenneth, over thirty years since he'd worked on this project, yet when I read him the fifteen words on this scrap that has somehow survived the decades, he recalls his interview with our grandmother as if it had happened recently.

"Grandma was always anti-union," he says. "She insisted that they didn't keep doors locked in the factory. She was angry about the locked-door story that the media reported at the time, and adamant that other misinformation was reported."

Called a sweatshop but not really. I ask him what he thinks Grandma meant by that declaration he'd noted on the scrap of paper. "She said that after the fire, the media portrayed Blanck and Harris as evil, as treating their workers unfairly, even brutally, like during the strikes before 1911, but that 'they weren't that bad to the workers.' Grandma stressed that Triangle was not unlike any other factory at the time, and if people couldn't get the doors open during the fire, it was because the doors were hinged so that they opened in instead of out and were simply more difficult to open. She said Blanck and Harris were charged with manslaughter on the basis of this locked-door theory, but 'no way were those doors locked,' she'd insisted."

If only I could believe my grandmother. How do I condemn someone who'd been always generous with her love, gentle, and considerate, who never found fault with my behavior or appearance, who flattered me with attentive questions and lively discourse about her own life? I'm uneasy taking sides — management against workers — but everything I've read and heard makes me embrace, instead, the workers, the survivors from the eighth and ninth floors, whose words (recorded in interviews conducted more than forty-five years after the fire) are testimony to a reality different from the one Grandma experienced.

Survivor Max Hochfield had worked at Triangle only several months before the 1911 fire. As he recalled the horror of that day almost five decades later, his voice trembled, his emotions, after so many years, still blistering to the surface. "I can tell you this much," he says to the interviewer, "I think that if the door on the ninth floor would've been opened, most of the people would've been safe." Mr. Hochfield, whose sister was killed in the fire, wanted to kill Harris and Blanck, but couldn't raise the money necessary to buy a gun. "I can't prove it," he says, ending his interview, "but if this door on the ninth floor had been open, I'm sure that the casualties would have been much less."

Dore Maisler, who had her "teeth knocked out and was arrested three times a day" as she picketed during the strike of 1909, escaped the fire on one of the few elevators working that day. That elevator only made one trip up to the eighth floor, where she worked, before the cable broke from the weight of so many people jammed in so tightly the door wouldn't close, and it crashed into the basement of the building. "People had torn my clothes off because I was the first one there [in the elevator]. I was on the floor and they was stacked on top of me. I was black and blue. By the time I got carried out from the basement they was jumping from the windows already." She says that people were frantic because the doors to the stairway were locked, a fact corroborated by Pauline Pepe and Bertha Mandel Lanxner. Though not a survivor of the 1911 fire — Ms. Lanxner worked at Triangle only a short time before quitting in 1910 — she repeatedly stated her simple reason for quitting: "I didn't like closed doors. With doors like this, I always saw a prison . . . They shouldn't have locked doors. It was locked on the outside."

During the trial, Ms. Maisler was a witness for the state. To the interviewer she repeats the question that Max Steuer asked her: "How did you *feel* when you knew the building was burning and you couldn't save yourself?" And her voice, level and strong, spits back her answer with a venom that forty-six years hasn't dulled: "How would *you* feel if you would be trapped in a cage and I put in a match?"

After the fire, Ms. Maisler had to leave New York. She needed a job, but could no longer work in tall buildings, and left to find employment in California. At the end of his interview, Max Hochfield also admits that after the fire he was afraid to work in a factory, and that "even today [1957] when I go to the theatre, or a movie, or a banquet, I need to make sure that the building is fireproof before I can enjoy myself."

I listen to this admission and recall the fires I've been in, minor fires with minimal damage and no deaths, but alarming just the same: Two in the morning, a hotel in London, I'm nineteen. A fireman carries me on his shoulders from the fourth floor down to the curb after a dozing smoker drops a smoldering cigarette butt into an upholstered couch and sets the place on fire. Four years later, at five A.M., a cheap hotel in Hollywood where I'm visiting Grandma Rose. Again, a lit cigarette and napping smoker, but this time, as columns of dark smoke rise by pink stucco, I'm the first one at the curb.

March of 1997 was cold and windy in Manhattan, but that didn't stop schoolchildren, members of UNITE (Union of Needle-trades, Industrial and Textile Employees), and firefighters from gathering at the corner of Washington Place and Greene Street to remember the victims of the fire. Beneath the plaque dedicated by the International Ladies Garment Workers Union in 1961 to com-memorate the lives lost, students, union members, and firefighters placed 146 white carnations — each bearing the name of a worker who died — and read aloud the name of each fire victim. Brisk winds had marked the fiftieth anniversary of the fire, and it was chilly during ceremonies on the seventy-fifth anniversary too. Yet, each time, crowds number in the hundreds for the memorial ser-vice at Washington Place and Greene Street and the subsequent ceremony at the cemetery in Brooklyn where the seven unidenti-fied fire victims are buried in a common grave.

Page one of the *New York Times* from Sunday, March 26, 1961, in-cludes a large photo of David Dubinsky, then president of the ILGWU, standing on the speakers' platform during the fiftieth-an-niversary ceremonies. He's flanked by Frances Perkins, former sec-retary of labor and member of the state commission that investi-gated the Triangle fire, Eleanor Roosevelt, and two survivors. Dubinsky's expression is emotional; his plea to Governor Rocke-feller to veto a measure that would delay, by almost two years, the installation of sprinkler systems in old buildings is eloquent and ur-gent. But it's the face of one of the survivors, Isidore Wegodner, on which I focus. Sitting erect in fedora and trenchcoat, the collar of which is pulled up around his neck to block the wind, he appears dignified, quiet. When Dubinsky asks "on whose conscience will it rest if before 1962 there is another fire with loss of life in an unsprinklered building?" and appeals to those gathered to fight the "outrage" of a bill that would keep buildings unsafe and the "mockery [this bills makes] of the sacrifice of 146 garment workers," did Isidore see himself again, as he must have seen himself countless times in the fifty years since the fire, escaping down the stairs from the ninth floor, where he and his father worked as sleeve setters? He must have dreamed so often about the street — a street he probably once envisioned as being paved with gold, just as Grandma Rose had — littered with bodies after the fire. He must have felt a sharp tug in his belly each time he recalled thinking that his father was among those broken bodies in the street. The boy Isidore eventually found his father alive, stumbling from a subway car, his pants torn, his flesh bleeding. "I remember," Isidore said in an interview with historian Leon Stein, "how with my last strength I shouted to him, how I went tearing over the little bridge that connected the two platforms, how we fell into each other's arms and how the people stopped to look while sobbing he embraced me and kissed me."

6

It's late summer in 1958 and I'm kneeling on the sidewalk in front of my grandparents' house in Jamaica, New York, hunched over a magnifying glass and a maple leaf. Grandma Rose is pressed close beside me, knees apart and bent, bottom almost brushing the sidewalk, elbows balanced on her knees, hands hanging loosely from relaxed wrists. Her olive paisley-print shift gapes open at the neck, revealing bronze, ample cleavage beaded with sweat. The sun is so hot, Grandma has made me wear one of my grandfather's white V-neck undershirts over my swimming suit so my seven-year-old fair skin won't "fry like an egg on the sidewalk." As intent as I am on having this leaf catch fire, I'm aware of Grandma's smell — musky and damp, like the sweet and sour smell of earth after snow has melted and the scent of decaying plants fills the air. Outside her brick row house near one of the few trees on this busy block, Grandma is giving me my first lesson in combustion. Suddenly, the leaf catches fire, its edges magically curling up and over itself, and we're both transfixed by the exquisite flame, the brief crackling, and then the quick burning as veins and stem turn to ash.

Note: In writing this essay, the author consulted numerous sources, including the *New York Times* and other newspapers; audiotapes and transcripts at the Kheel Center for Labor-Management Documentation and Archives, Cornell University; and a variety of books and collections of articles. In some cases, the source is indicated in the essay itself. Interested readers will find a selected bibliography in the journal in which the essay originally appeared: the *Massachusetts Review,* vol. 42, no. 1, spring 2001. A list of works consulted may also be obtained from the author via e-mail: AmyKolen@aol.com.

ANDREW LEVY

The Anti-Jefferson

FROM THE AMERICAN SCHOLAR

THERE IS ONLY ONE known portrait of Robert Carter III. He
posed for it sometime around 1749 in Thomas Hudson's London
studio, and when one looks at the result two and a half centuries
later, it is easy enough to imagine what the painter was thinking.
Probably Carter was just another country gentleman — this one a
little young, with that flat American accent making him seem more
like a Scot or an Ulsterman — and Hudson knew that type, knew
its vanities. And so Carter appears to us in a billowing gold suit and
green cape, brown hair neatly tied back, smirking, a mask dangling
from the tapered fingers of his left hand. He looks as if he is on
his way to a ball, a lifetime of balls, except for a pair of huge dark
eyes that suggest something else, something open and unfinished,
something that resisted being posed as the young patriarch on
the rise.

When Carter stood for this portrait he was twenty-one, and he
seemed poised for a brilliant, perhaps even notorious, career. He
had wealth: more than seventy thousand acres of New World soil
and more than one hundred slaves. He had family: his grandfather
was Robert "King" Carter, who presided like royalty over large parcels of early-eighteenth-century Virginia. He had arrogance, perhaps something worse than arrogance: his cousin John Page, who
knew him well, called him an "inconceivable illiterate and also cor-
rupted and vicious." And he had powerful friends, and friends who
would become powerful: his neighbors were Washingtons and
Lees, and among his friends and correspondents he would also
soon count Thomas Jefferson, James Madison, George Mason, and

Patrick Henry, all of whom would eventually ascend to mythic status as founders of a new nation. The mystery of Robert Carter, however, lies in what happened to him as his neighbors, friends, and peers made that ascent. By the dawn of the American Revolution, Carter had tamed his youthful excesses and was probably the richest, most powerful, most literate man in the rich, powerful, enlightened colony of Virginia. He owned more slaves and more land than Jefferson or Washington, had a larger library than either, and was so serenely confident of his social position that he lent money at interest to the former, and was reluctant to allow his daughters to marry into the family of the latter. By 1794, however, he lived alone and monkish in a small house in Baltimore, and by 1804 he was buried in an unmarked grave in a Virginia pasture. His home plantation, Nomini Hall, sits uncommemorated less than fifteen miles from the park sites devoted to the Lee mansion and Washington's birthplace at Pope's Creek. And historians, with a few isolated exceptions, have avoided all but passing glances at his life, despite the fact that Carter left behind a vast canon of letters, diaries, and daybooks.

Taken together, these details suggest that Carter is not an important figure in American history, that we treat him rightly by ignoring him; but there is one detail that haunts that conclusion. In 1791, he wrote a "Deed of Gift" that, with schedules, lists, and tables, ran for pages, and that signaled his intent to free more than five hundred slaves. In the long history of antebellum America, no one else, while living, freed that many slaves; no one even came close. No one walked away from slaveholding and slavery with as much to lose, simply gave up the plantation and moved on. And no other Virginian of the Revolutionary era — including those, like Jefferson and Washington, who spoke out passionately against slavery — managed to reconcile freedom in theory and freedom in practice with such transparent simplicity.

The mystery of Robert Carter, then, is really two mysteries: what caused him to free his slaves, and why we couldn't care less.

By the time I saw that portrait, on a postcard reproduction that the Virginia Historical Society no longer sells, it was the summer of 1998, and I was six months deep into the what and the why, the eyes and the mask. It began for me with a handful of sentences in

Fox Butterfield's fine, vivid *All God's Children* that made glancing
reference to a slaveholder who had undertaken the largest private
manumission in American history. Butterfield's reference was so
short, so confident, that I felt abashed: this was surely something
that everyone knew, that I did not.

But I was wrong: the number of men and women who have argued that Robert Carter III and the Deed of Gift have a significant
place in American history can be counted, literally, on the fingers
of one hand. A library search turned up scarce, curious resources:
an inexplicably unpublished Duke doctoral dissertation from
1993; a 1941 out-of-print biography that made little of the Deed of
Gift, giving it fewer pages than Carter's "Agricultural Readjust-
ments"; four pages in one volume of Joy Hakim's *A History of US*, a
series for nine- to twelve-year-olds ("Emancipated!" she tells them.
"That means free! Robert Carter freed his slaves!"); and a scattering of articles, mostly local to eastern Virginia, few of which added
new facts to the case. Stranger yet was the treatment of Carter's
manumission within the enormous body of scholarship about early
American history and slavery. I went through book after book, article after article, and could find almost nothing: occasional passing
glances like Butterfield's, at most an isolated page, even when the
subject was explicitly slaveholders; even when the subject was slaveholders who freed their slaves; even when the subject was Virginian
slaveholders who freed their slaves. Most compelling, however, was
the fact that the very best historians knew who Robert Carter was,
knew the Deed of Gift, and still, somehow, hesitated. Philip D.
Morgan mentions Robert Carter III thirty-seven times in his landmark *Slave Counterpoint*, usually as an example of a progressive
Southern patriarch, and yet never mentions that Carter manumitted his slaves. Ira Berlin, in a newspaper interview in 1991, called
the Deed of Gift "an extraordinary, very, very exceptional event";
his recent, eloquent *Many Thousands Gone*, however, mentions
Carter only once, twenty pages away from the passage in the book
devoted to manumissions in the upper South. As a fact, Robert
Carter's Deed of Gift was interesting; but as an un-fact, a non-pres-
ence, it became even more interesting. Something buried that
deep must be buried for a reason, and I wanted to know what
it was.

But first I wanted to know why Carter did it, and the answer to that query lay in the dusty volumes of his correspondence, so dry, so rhetorically uncompelling, that it is easy enough to understand why so few people have had any interest in them. It is impossibly counterintuitive to imagine that a song of liberty this provocative might be cloaked in such minutiae. Why did Robert Carter free his slaves, when those around him did not? He felt the same pull toward the ideals of freedom as did his more famous peers and neighbors. He supported the Revolutionary forces, offering provisions and support whenever asked. He respected democracy in theory, but made a bad candidate for public office: he ran for the Virginia House of Burgesses twice, and each time he was crushed, polling seventh out of seven candidates the first time, and winning 7 votes out of 330 the second, losing to a Lee and a Washington. If he had been more electable, he might have ended up a founding father too, privately dreaming about freeing his slaves but unwilling to suffer the loss of goodwill from slaveholding voters and officeholders. Perhaps he was more stubborn, more aristocratic: they had called his grandfather "King," after all, and he kept that royal affect, rarely missing an opportunity to let the revolutionaries know, even after they founded a nation, that he was still better than they. Perhaps he was tired: lost amid our *Gone with the Wind* phantasms lies the fact that running a plantation was strange and numbing work, psychically debilitating, ambiguously profitable. Perhaps Robert Carter was simply quicker to the mark, not a moral man at all, but a smart man, smart enough to recognize that there were easier ways for a powerful Southern white man to make a buck.

Or perhaps this: perhaps Robert Carter was more American than the rest of them, as long as we define America as the land of the contrarians, the mad visionary individuals who spend their lives doing what everyone else doesn't do, and not doing what everyone else does. While the other great Southern men of his age married the dutiful daughters of each other's families, Carter chose a wife from urbane Baltimore society, a well-read ironworks heiress with a lacerating wit. While those men got their religion from the aristocratic, undemanding, and pure white Anglican Church (or from the pseudo-church of Enlightenment Rationalism), Carter was sure he met Jesus one May day in 1778, and asked him, "Lord, what wilt thou have me do?" While Jefferson and Washington transformed their celebrated plantations into testaments to the agrarian ideal, Carter cast iron, tried his hand at munitions manufacture, lent money (something Jefferson and most large slaveholders would never be solvent enough to do, yet another reason why Carter was able to do what they could not), and filled his house to bursting with books and musical instruments. Other Virginian peers sent their sons to William and Mary, and reared them to be slaveholders in their turn; Robert Carter sent his children north so they would learn to be anything but slaveholders.

Out of step, out of sync. Robert Carter's timing, his vision, were so maladroit as to be marvelous. In the summer of 1776, in a letter to Richard Henry Lee (his neighbor and a prominent delegate to the Continental Congress then in session in Philadelphia), Carter ignored all civic matters and instead asked Lee to bring "two sets of curls for my daughters Priscilla + Nancy" back from Philadelphia, and enclosed "Sample(s) of hair and measure" — as if Lee, who had recently introduced the motion to declare independence, had nothing more pressing to do. In October of that same year, shortly after Thomas Jefferson came home to Virginia after composing the Declaration of Independence and fighting for its passage, Carter sent his collection agent with a bill for an unpaid loan. The loan was repaid, the message, no doubt, delivered: you may think you are independent of the king of England, Tom, but you are still dependent on me. And when Carter discovered, in the spring of 1792, that his lost copy of the *Complete Works of John Locke* had been recovered, he told his agent to donate all three volumes to the Richmond Public Library. It is a small bit of business, but suggestive: I am done with Locke, Carter seemed to be saying, done with the Age of Reason. Truthfully, however, he had never been there.

Throughout the 1770s, Robert Carter proved time and again that he and his country — at least, the elite fraction constituted by his peers — were moving in different directions. He ignored the American Revolution with an intensity that bordered on the self-destructive, refusing to move even as the British Army roamed dangerously close to Nomini. He joined the radical, fledgling Baptist Church and found himself the wealthiest man in the revival tent, the wealthiest man on his knees as mobs (supported by other wealthy men) violently dispersed the congregation, the wealthiest man taking communion alongside his slaves. His religious daybook for March 15, 1778, reads, "RC & his servant Negro Sam — received Tokens and they did both Comune," a selection of detail strongly suggesting that what Carter found extraordinary about church that day was the company he was keeping.

It was only in the 1780s, however, that slavery became the wedge. Carter's letters began to blossom with open antipathy for the institution: to John Rippon, a Baptist elder, he wrote that "tolerating Slavery indicates great depravity"; in a later letter, he observed that "the Situation of the Blacks here, is my greatest difficulty — It is a subject that our Legislature will not take up — & it appears to me Judgements will follow us so long as the Bar is held up." Such sentiments were, of course, plentiful in the papers of men like Jefferson and Washington, members of the progressive minority of plantation owners willing to speak out against slavery. And like those men, Carter spent the 1780s acknowledging that slavery was wrong, but also arguing that freeing the slaves was impracticable. At that moment in American history, however, the argument that large private emancipations were unfeasible stood on shaky ground. In 1782, the legislature of the state of Virginia passed the most liberal anti-slavery bill in its antebellum history, a law allowing private slaveholders to liberate their "tithables" under certain conditions. In the two decades that followed, while the large slaveholders flirted with plans for gradual emancipation — plans that, to them, invariably contained some flaw — many small and middle-class slaveholders began to let their slaves go. From 1780 to 1800, the number of free blacks in Virginia increased from roughly three thousand to more than twenty thousand, almost 5 percent of the black population of the state.

In this context, Robert Carter's act of private emancipation was not exemplary: he had been preceded by middle-class Quakers and Baptists on the Potomac North Shore, and he would be followed by men and women like Samuel Templeman, who, inspired by his example, freed ninety slaves, and Martha Washington, who freed her husband's slaves two years after his death, and not after her own passing, as he had specified in his will. As was often the case throughout Carter's life, what made his action unusual was that he was the most powerful and wealthiest man to repudiate the rational (and, in the case of slavery, rationalizing) republicanism practiced by his peers in the Southern gentry. What made him even more anomalous is that he did not look, act, or write like a man who possessed a single egalitarian impulse. He freed his slaves because, like Jefferson and Washington, he knew it was the right thing to do. But unlike Jefferson and Washington, he had no civic face ("we seem detached from the world," he wrote a son-in-law in 1785), no constituency he needed to satisfy by drafting an ambivalent public position toward the institution and looking like a revolutionary as he did so.

Part of what disturbed Carter was the mistreatment of his slaves: "I do forbid you," he wrote the overseer Thomas Olive on May 8, 1781, "to correct, in any manner what ever, either old or young negro belonging to me, until I my self shall hear and consider the fault or faults that may be aledged." He delivered a similar warning to Samuel Straughan, the overseer at his Forest Plantation, on July 6, 1787: "You will remember to apply to me in Case you suppose any of the people should require such Correction." What makes these letters striking is not that Carter opposed the idea that slaves could be, in his own words, "a good deal beaten and bruised." It is, rather, that he trusted the versions of events told him by his slaves. To Straughan, he wrote that "Negro Jerry of Forest Plantation informs me that you stripped him this morning, and with Switches whipped him on his bare back yet the offense you charged him with was a matter in his own house . . ." He began another letter by informing an overseer that "Negro Nanny cam here yesterday evening who informs me the Son Ben and Billy Son of Criss" were beaten with "[your] privity and knowledge." As with "Negro Nanny," many of Carter's slaves understood that they could run to Nomini to seek his intervention: "I beg leave to interfere in the present case," Carter wrote in defense of "Negro Dennis," adding that "he is not to be corrected" for running off Colespoint plantation to file his complaint.

This kind of triangle between slave, master, and overseer was common in the antebellum South: Thomas Jefferson's slaves welcomed his returns to Monticello because they understood that he would protect them from his overseers. For Carter, however, the actions of white overseers reflected, not contradicted, the carelessness and cruelty of their gentrified employers. In some instances, the differences of opinion between Carter and other wealthy landowners appear slight: in April and May of 1781, Carter sent two black servants to retrieve a supply of corn from a local granary, and Richard Henry Lee turned them away, insisting that Carter send instead "two white men and one black man." In other exchanges, however, Carter's outrage (and his condescension) are more evident, as in one case involving the Mason family and two of their escaped slaves, "Negro Winny . . . forward with Child," and a man named "Talbot" or "Tabbard." In the first letter, dated March 9, 1785, Carter told Stephen Mason that Winny had "surrendered herself up" at one of his plantations, but that Talbot had wounded two white overseers who had attempted to capture him, and "it is probable . . . he will be shot"; in veiled, gentlemanly diction, Carter then wrote, "I do advise that you give some immediate direction relative to Talbot + Winny." In a second letter, dated March 21, 1785, Carter told Mason that he had captured Talbot (who now became Tabbard) unharmed, and that Tabbard was traveling with "a Advertisement Signed by your brother Mr. G. T. Mason, which alone must be considered a full pass." Carter then added, "your people are both, almost, without shoes," and told Mason that his own black servant "Will" would deliver the two servants back home, "with provision from hence for himself + your people." If Mason missed Carter's inference that Tabbard's life was unnecessarily threatened by the failure of his masters to acknowledge that he was not an escaped slave, but was traveling with "a full pass," it would be harder to ignore the statement Carter made by returning the two slaves with new provisions, perhaps even new shoes, accompanied only by one of his own black servants.

Whatever Carter felt he shared with his fellow planters, he often felt more enthusiasm for defending poorer men and women from their trespasses. On November 10, 1777, he wrote an emotional letter to Colonel John Augustine Washington, demanding restitution on behalf of a white indentured servant who had been tied up and whipped by a patrol of American soldiers: "I do presume that a violent Trepas has been committed against a mans Person; therefore I appear on the part of the injured party." When offered an opportunity to ally himself with the Washingtons three years later, however — a proposal of marriage made to his daughter Priscilla from George Washington, the general's nephew — Carter allowed

the prospective union to languish from indifference: "I am apprehensive . . . however, if herself + mother should think otherwise, I
shall not refuse to let Priscilla marry." Throughout the period, in
fact, Carter seemed to construct dramatic set pieces in which the
crime of one propertied person was placed in relief against the
constancy of one servant, who was often given the honor (or the
burden) of receiving restitution. "I am informed," Carter wrote a
fellow slaveowner in August 1777, "that an iron pot in the house of
Negroe George Carpenter at my plantation now called Aries, was
taken and carried to your house yesterday." Not questioning the
word of "Negroe George," and not waiting to hear from the slaveholder, Carter seemed to assume that his social peer would not
find humbling the prospect of acknowledging his guilt to the slave
himself: "I hope you will deliver it [the pot] to the Bearer George."

Increasingly, as the Revolution ended and a new nation was
called into being, Robert Carter felt himself surrounded by whites
he could not trust and blacks he could trust — or at least control.
Only gradually, in fact, does the reader of Carter's massive, languid
correspondence begin to realize that, for every time he wrote
something like "these outlying negroes are too unruly," there
were a hundred complaints about the inconstancy of his white tenants, business associates, and neighbors. In strange, symbolic ways,
Carter even began to construct systems out of this contrast. During
the mid-1780s, for instance, he grew furious at the failure of
the "public Post," took control of the newspaper subscriptions of
"Washington + others of my neighbors," and began correcting
badly addressed mail: "If Westmoreland County is written on said
N Paper Scratch out the word Westmoreland and write Richmond
for Mr. R Neil lives in Richmond County and not in Westmoreland." Almost simultaneously, he began to use the name of a servant and his address as a kind of postmark to verify that a given
communication had taken place, as if he had discovered a form of
human communication upon which he could rely: "I send by Negro Dick Dr. Gill on Practical Divinity." He even began to assume
that his slaves could undertake business transactions with complete disinterestedness, an assumption grounded upon absolute
faith either in their narrative of events or in their passivity: "Negro
Harry . . . says, that theives broke into your Mill last Night, and
took three of his best bags . . . Harry now waits on you for . . . 24
Pecks of Meal he Harry to receive three good meal bags."

Whether all of these small dramas increased Robert Carter's estrangement from his peers and neighbors, or were themselves signs of that estrangement, is impossible to say. By the late 1780s, however, Carter's alienation had grown into something deeper, something that might provide the foundation for a radical act. He had watched his wife die, watched many of his favorite children die, and was sick himself, falling suddenly unconscious for minutes at a time. He had drifted away from even the radical Baptists, and was looking for smaller, wilder churches. And while he often responded with sympathy to slaves who sought to keep their families together, he tried to keep his own children from making attachments in Virginia, sending three daughters to Baltimore and two sons to the Baptist Theological Seminary in Providence, citing his "only . . . consideration . . . the most abject State of Slavery in this Commonwealth."

What Carter learned from hearing black preachers and receiving communion alongside his own slaves, what he learned from a thousand small exchanges with his slaves, must surely have catalyzed the Deed of Gift. But Robert Carter was not that simple. He spent much of the decade, for instance, complaining about his children, especially his sons and sons-in-law, sometimes viciously. Perhaps he felt that he had no heir he could trust, a circumstance that would make the Deed of Gift, which gave away $100,000 (in 1790 terms) of inheritable property, a less ambivalent project. Or perhaps he wanted to free his slaves first and foremost, and assuaged his paternal guilt about giving away his patrimony by arguing to himself the unworthiness of those potential heirs. Or perhaps he had suffered the ultimate alienation and no longer felt the pull of family on his heart, in which case the same impulse that allowed him to disperse and alienate his biological children also made it possible for him to part with the black men and women that slavery had metaphorically defined as "his children" as well.

Which meant that there remained one more act to complete. As long as the slave was a kind of postmark, he also remained a passive agent, someone who could be trusted because he had no "Will" that was not Carter's possession. On June 16, 1789, though — two years before he signed the Deed of Gift — Carter wrote a letter to a black person. It was a nervous moment. While the overwhelming majority of letters in Carter's papers were written to white correspondents, and were addressed to "Sir" or "Madam," and signed

"Your Humble and Obedient Servant" or "Your Unworthy Brother in Gospel Bonds," this letter lacked a deferential salutation, as though Carter could not bring himself to offer humbling platitudes to a slave, or saw correspondence with a slave as a defeat of the system of ritual deference embodied in those phrases. Instead, he promisingly addressed "Black brother Billy," and provided him with a set of instructions for delivering several sets of papers to several addresses. "Black brother Billy" had appeared in Carter's letters to white Baptists before, as "Black Baptist brother Billy," and it seemed even more promising that Carter still called himself Billy's brother even as his allegiance to the church that had brought them closer fell away. Whatever "Black brother Billy" was assigned to do, however, he strayed from Carter's instructions. In a letter on July 14, he was linguistically demoted to "black Billy," and Carter spoke of him in a tone of equivocal heartbreak, but with words that implied that a test had taken place: "When black Billy set out with the Papers mentioned before I expected that you would have been possessed with Said Papers long e'er now — however disappointments often happen." At this point, even "black Billy" disappeared, replaced by "Negro Billy," or "bearer Billy" — yet another linguistic demotion, or perhaps another slave with the same name.

If other events had taught him that he could not enslave blacks any longer, Robert Carter seems to have let this event teach him a corollary lesson: if he treated them as "brothers," they would disappoint him as much as white people did. Given the nature of Billy's "trial," and the rapidity with which Carter registered his disappointment, it is hard to imagine that he was prepared to reach any other conclusion. Or that any other conclusion would have led him more quickly to emancipation.

If Carter is the anti-Jefferson, the man who did not lack the will to free his own slaves but who did lack the eloquence to make his love of freedom memorable, then the Deed of Gift is the anti–Declaration of Independence, a document that makes liberty look dull but that is so devoid of loopholes and contradictions that no result but liberty could prevail.

On the first page, Carter wrote: "I have for some time past been convinced that to retain them in Slavery is contrary to the true Principles of Religion and Justice, and that therefor it was my duty to manumit them," but this statement constituted the limit of his willingness to explain himself. Instead, he seemed more interested in the manumission as a legal and practical matter: "I have with great Care and Attention endeavoured to discover that Mode of Manumission from Slavery which can be effected consonant to Law and with the Least possible Disadvantage to my Fellow Citizens." His solution was a "gradual Emancipation," fifteen slaves freed every January 1, with a series of painstaking amendments: first, that "the Oldest of my Slaves be the first emancipated"; second, that all "Male and Female Slaves . . . under the Ages of 21 and 18 Years" would be automatically freed when they attained those ages; third, that all children born to his slaves during the period of the gradual emancipation would be manumitted as well, when the males turned twenty-one and the females turned eighteen. The remainder of the document, which fills an entire volume in his correspondence, was censuses and schedules, and Carter seemed to approach this particular task with real intensity: amid these cross-referenced, redundant charts, the reader begins to sense that Carter wanted to make sure there would be no slave denied his freedom, or given his freedom one day before Carter himself had designated.

At first, Carter seemed tentative, unwilling actually to see his slaves free, or uninterested in beginning the manumission until it was foolproof. He spent the autumn of 1791 debating whether the law required that manumitted slaves register in their counties of residence across Virginia, or at his own home county courthouse: his patriarchal instinct still lively, Carter ignored his lawyer, decided that "Residency of Slaves I apprehend is to be where Master wills it," and that all emancipated slaves would have to return to Westmoreland. By winter, he began a new correspondence with his lawyer, regarding whether or not a freed slave could purchase other slaves — a crucial strategy for reconstituting the families that Carter's schedule for freeing slaves by age would divide. This time, he heeded John Maund's remarkable distinction between a "free man" and a "freed man," and concluded that "an emancipated Slave cannot hold any person in Slavery unless a particular Law Should give him the ability."

By February 1792, however, the first freed slaves finally received their manumission certificates at the Westmoreland courthouse, and Carter seemed to like the prospect. He presented "Copies of Emancipation" in person to sixteen slaves in July and August of 1792. Throughout the next year, he acted frequently either to accelerate or to ease his former servants' transition from slavery to freedom. He wrote a special deed of manumission for thirty slaves over the age of forty-five, "every expence arising on their Accounts . . . to be reimbursed by Robert Carter, or his estate," and created a "common stock" of money to pay his slaves' travel expenses to the courthouse. Over the objections of his overseers, he rented land to dozens of free blacks, hired them as artisans, and allowed individual slaves anxious for their turns at emancipation to "bargain for themselves" — to hire themselves out and keep their own wages. In this manner, the largest recorded private emancipation in American history was undertaken: the court records through which John Randolph Barden (author of that Duke dissertation) sifted confirm 280 manumissions, but other evidence — legal documents, censuses, and birth records — all implies a much larger total, one possibly exceeding Carter's initial schedules.

There are many possible reasons why Carter worked so forcefully ("this business requires expedition," he wrote in 1795), despite his initial concern that he would "inconvenience" his white neighbors. As always, he seemed willing to risk the alienation of his peers in the presence of a revelatory truth that led him elsewhere. Possibly, the white community was indifferent: the manumission was greeted with almost complete silence from local and national newspapers, except for a one-sentence note in the *Virginia Gazette* and a short commendation in the *Baptist Register.* Possibly, many resisted the manumission but were stunned into silence by its executor's wealth and power. Carter saved two letters — one from an overseer who told him, "Your negroes flushed with notions of freedom particularly at this time will require some little rigour," and an anonymous letter five years later from an individual who claimed to speak for "a vast majority of the community" and argued that "the consequences of the step, are too injurious to do otherwise than complain of them" — but there is no way to say whether these messages constituted the entirety of white protest to the manumission, or the only salvaged portion. Only Carter's sons and sons-in-law registered open bitterness toward the manumission, which, of course, was reducing their inheritance year by year: John Tasker

Carter stated that he would "do all in his power to frustrate" the "scheme of emancipation," while son-in-law John Peck chased slaves off his farm before their scheduled emancipations rather than provide for them.

As his relationship to white Virginia quieted, however, Carter's relationship with his slaves, freed and unfreed, became correspondingly more complex. Some slaves chose liberty through flight rather than waiting for their turn on his schedule: in December 1792, he told captured "Jack" and "Dick" that their actions "did not comport with the expectation of men who were to become free," and sent them back to Libra plantation to wait until 1799 and 1800. For the most part, though, Carter's slaves were adepts at patience: most chose to remain in slavery until their turn arrived, or understood that direct negotiation with Carter provided the likeliest path to early liberation.

With these slaves and ex-slaves, Carter struck terms that showed how deeply he was divided between the desire to maintain his patriarchal aura and the desire to be rid of it. He rented farms to "Prince" and "Sam Harrison," allowed them to reconstitute their still enslaved families, provided them livestock, and gave them "sundry jobs" that paid off a year's rent with six weeks of light work. Simultaneously, he forced these men to "hire" their wives and children, and wrote clauses into their leases that obliged them to remain part-time slaves: "Prince also agrees to receive + deliver Grain as heretofore without any compensation." Sometime in the mid-1790s, in fact, Carter began to use the verb "dispose" to describe the emancipation of slaves, a word that suggests how unsentimental he had grown about the enterprise. By 1792, he must also have become aware of the unintended consequences of the manumissions: the likelihood that some of his tenants were working slave children harder to compensate for their emancipated parents; the rebellious and ominous sons; the slaves from other men's plantations who, if the anonymous correspondent reported truthfully, were "procuring false . . . certificates of their being Mr. Carters free men." One suspects this last circumstance troubled Carter especially, pitting his antipathy to slavery and his respect for the political astuteness of African Americans against his desire for control and his love of a good schedule. One suspects he had just enough slaveholder left in him to want his slaves to be free only when he wanted them to be free, but not enough to close the loophole through which black men and women from neighboring plantations were passing to freedom.

By the end of 1793, however, Robert Carter was done. If the emancipation of his slaves brought him some satisfaction, he must surely have wearied of constant negotiation with newly freed slaves, with angry white tenants, with lawyers, and especially with discontented children: "Thus — thus — it is with Parents in the Material World," he wrote. Surrendering Virginia (or surrendering to Virginia) once and for all, he ended the year by moving north to Baltimore and surrounding himself with members of the tiny Swedenborgian New Church. At this point, he seemed to have accepted defeat, again, "in the material world," telling his daughter Harriet in 1803 that "I do acknowledge that my plans and advice have never been pleasing to the world."

And there was, in fact, an extraordinarily solitary quality to his last decade. His daybooks are filled with a retiree's minutiae, rendered comic by the royal third person he continued to employ: "RC paid 2 pence for one Apple"; "RC received boiling coffee on the back of Left Hand." In 1796, he gave away his remaining plantations to his children, first making sure that his sons-in-law could not inherit his property and that free black tenants were given good binding leases. In November 1798, he told his son-in-law Spencer Ball that "I have relinquished all personal claim . . . save only, an annuity during my natural life." He began writing little religious daybooks, arguing such points as "a true believer may finally fall from grace," or "Against Laying on of Hands." He collected clippings that claimed the apocalypse was near. He skipped around Baltimore's churches, sometimes with his widowed daughter Julia by his side: "in the Morning attended at the Romish Chapel — Noon at the Baptist Meeting House . . . attended the Dunckard's Meeting." Sometime in the early morning of March 11, 1804, he was found dead in his bed by his son George, who described the scene to family friend Robert Berkeley in a short note that contained a postscript arranging the purchase of new slaves.

By luck or design, however, the Deed of Gift hardened like the rock of ages. Before leaving Virginia, Robert Carter appointed Benjamin Dawson, a Baptist minister he had met four years earlier, as his business agent. From 1793 to 1804, Dawson was Carter's good and bad angel. Carter gave him broad financial responsibilities, most of which he executed so incompetently that Carter spent the last few years of his life trying to retract Dawson's control of his plantations. At the same time, Dawson proved wonderfully competent at making sure the schedules on Robert Carter's Deed of Gift were strictly followed. Carter's sons, who hated the manumission, unsurprisingly hated Dawson as well, and within six months of Carter's death in 1804 sued to revoke his power of attorney and overturn the Deed of Gift. By 1808, however, Dawson defeated Carter's sons in the Virginia Court of Appeals; the court could find no legal flaw in Carter's endless schedules and censuses. By the time Dawson was through (and Barden found evidence that he was reminding farmers to free the children of Carter's slaves in 1826), the Deed of Gift had a momentum of its own: as late as 1852, nine years before the Civil War, Carter's descendants were still freeing the descendants of Carter's slaves under the terms of Carter's original document, as if he were somehow still watching.

On my first trip to Nomini Hall I passed through Monticello, in midsummer, high season, which is the way to do it: the hour wait for admission provides plenty of time to reflect on the fact that Thomas Jefferson has never been more famous. By contrast, the small parks devoted to the birthplaces of George Washington and Robert E. Lee — roughly 150 miles east of Monticello — feel like blissful quiet backwaters of history. In the eighteenth and early nineteenth centuries, the Northern Neck of Virginia yielded up two future presidents and the Lees: the Potomac River ran along its north edge like a Parisian boulevard, and sloops from Europe went door-to-door at the great plantations, creating a commerce of goods and ideas that gave the region the intellectual hum of a powerful city. In our century, however, it is one of America's forgotten places, a run of unsentimental small towns and achingly beautiful sunsets on a scenic loop between Fredericksburg and Williamsburg.

Nomini Hall is not open to the public. A signpost on the side of Route 202, just past a Virginia Department of Transportation shed, says that the original mansion, which burned down in 1850, was "not far from here," but provides no further direction. It also describes Nomini as the home of the "celebrated" Robert Carter,

but neglects to say why he was celebrated, except as the employer
of Philip Vickers Fithian, the family tutor whose diaries remain one
of the most detailed primary sources on the slaveholding house-
hold. If you want to find Nomini, you will have to ask somebody,
maybe several people, before you can get the following directions:
take a right turn just past that marker onto Beale's Mill Road, take
another right at the stop sign, go about a mile, then look for a
modest wooden gate in the vicinity of a less modest cattle guard.
Once you are standing at that gate, though, there is no mistaking
that you are at the threshold of something that was once epic. The
two rows of giant poplars still stand, although several are gone, and
the remainder are wilder, more striking, than they must have been
when they led somewhere. The avenue that runs up the bluff to
the great house is still there, too, though it is only gravel and has
been cut in two by a wash filled with hundreds of tires. And the
house is still there — it was rebuilt in 1851 — and it is still tall,
square, and white, but even from two hundred yards you can see
that it needs paint, and some new Faulkner to tell its story.

Despite outward appearances, there has been a renaissance at
Nomini Hall in the last decade. This, however, has been largely a
private matter for the people of Westmoreland County. In 1988,
the Jerusalem Baptist Church placed a small marker alongside the
old slave cemetery, across the road and a quarter mile down past
the cattle gate. It takes a good guide to find this place, buried in
deep forest, the ground covered in periwinkle, with shallow de-
pressions marking the gravesites. In 1991, an energetic local businessman named Frank Delano (of the "People's Oil Company,"
Peace Corps, and resonant Delano bloodlines) and a group of local churches and historical organizations used the field beside the
cemetery to commemorate the bicentennial of the Deed of Gift.
One thousand men and women came to the field to dance and listen to speeches. Black men and women from neighboring towns
reported moments of sweet tension as they heard the names of the
freed slaves read aloud, and recognized names familiar to them
from the stories told by their grandparents and great-grandpar-
ents. And the media turned out — from Washington, New York,
and Richmond — and for that one day, Robert Carter had his
place in history.

On the other side of the road, the old South is being revived

from an opposite angle. One of Robert Carter's daughters, either
Frances or Anna, married one Dr. John Arnest, and the house and
surrounding lands have stayed in the line ever since; but the estate
that stretched for seventy-seven thousand acres in Carter's time was
sold off in pieces for almost two centuries, until the twenty-five-
acre parcel surrounding the house was all that remained. In the
last decade, however, Nomini has risen. An archaeologist from a
small Virginia college now brings his students here, and they have
uncovered the foundations of the old schoolhouse and the mansion. The youngest living Arnest son, who married a descendant of
Thomas Jefferson, has bought back Nomini and more than one
hundred acres of the surrounding land. He and his wife have
framed that postcard reproduction of Robert Carter's portrait on a
wall in the house, which they have restored and even stretched out,
incredibly, back nearly to the seemingly lost foundation lines of the
original plantation manse.

The family cemetery has also been recovered, cleared of cow excrement, and surrounded by a low brick wall. Here lie the remains
of Robert Carter, in a grave so unmarked that the only way you can
find him is to search for the anonymous red clay brick that marks
the gravesite of his wife and, facing south, turn to her right and
look down at nothing.

For two centuries, Robert Carter has been a non-person, erased
from almost every historical account, like a Soviet commissar who
had lost favor with Stalin. If the reason why Carter freed his slaves
remains a mystery, it remains a mystery of character, the kind we
routinely face when we try to explain why anyone who should be
fully invested in the status quo instead commits an act of radical
and self-abnegating good.

The greater mystery of Robert Carter, however, has to do with
the character of his country: how does an event that should clearly
have stirred passions in its time, and inspired at least some historical interest in our own, inspire silence? Over the past three decades, numerous historians and literary scholars have written what
are known as "reception histories": explanations of how an individual, event, or document is reinvented for different generations.
What Robert Carter requires is an "evasion history": an explanation of why two centuries of historians, politicians, and citizens,

practicing a multitude of different political stances, have side-stepped around Carter and his Deed of Gift and have never constructed a narrative of American history in which his story was valuable, useful, or even worthy of a commemorative pause.

The effacement must have begun early, as early as that first year after he signed the Deed of Gift. Robert Carter made the decision to free his slaves in the 1780s and early 1790s, a period when Virginians, inspired by revolutionary democratic fervor, created a legal space in which the emancipation of African Americans would be permitted. He freed his slaves, however, during the late 1790s and 1800s, a period in which white Virginians moved to contain the flow of emancipations and to redefine a large free black population as a threat to the social order. On the grassroots level, white Virginians in the 1790s increasingly treated the manumission of slaves like a civic sin. Publicly, they kept quiet, assigning to emancipation the aura of a taboo. Privately, they derided the emancipators: Warner Mifflin, a Quaker who freed his slaves, wrote that "it was then circulated that Mifflin had set free a parcel of lazy, worthless Negroes, that he could make nothing by them, and therefore set them at liberty"; upon providing the freed slaves land and teams in exchange for half of their produce, "their tune was turned, and it was reported, that Mifflin was making more money by his Negroes now, than ever, and keeping them in more abject slavery, under the pretence of their being free."

Whether Robert Carter heard similar "tunes" might be less relevant than whether he heard anything at all. As a Quaker and an anti-slavery activist, Mifflin was an easy target. Carter, however, was a startling one: his family had built Virginia, and built it ruthlessly, and now one of its members wanted to dismantle the social order that had taken a century to construct. If Carter faced derision, even contempt, then leaving the state — and leaving Benjamin Dawson as an abolitionist time bomb ticking in its midst — must have seemed a sensible option. For his peers and neighbors, however, the early 1790s represented the high-water mark in their tolerance of emancipation: as they digested the news of disarray in France and slave revolution in Haiti, and contemplated the increasing number of free blacks among their neighbors, Robert Carter must have begun to look like a danger and a luxury. As historians have noted, the great Virginia planters responded to the slave rebellion in Haiti by maintaining a public silence while tightening the slave code in their own country. Faced with the fact that one (and only one) of the wealthiest men in Virginia showed no fear of free blacks, the remainder likely found that silence and similar legislation were also the best ways to "absorb" (to use Philip Morgan's words) the "severe contradiction" of their ethos implied by Carter's Deed of Gift.

In retrospect, it is clear that Robert Carter freed his slaves during a brief interlude in the history of the antebellum South during which voluntary emancipation seemed like a real possibility. If the institution of slavery in America had been somehow gradually and peacefully disbanded, he might be remembered as a pioneer. Instead, as Robert McColley notes, slavery in Virginia was "fixed more securely" in 1815 than in 1776, despite the manumissions. As Edmund Morgan observes in *American Slavery/American Freedom,* "Virginia's republicans had the decency to be disturbed by the apparent inconsistency of what they were doing," but "were far more disturbed by the prospect of turning 200,000 slaves loose to find a place in their free society." In order to justify the contradiction between their stated democratic ideals and their practice of slaveholding, the gentry of the early-nineteenth-century South increasingly argued that emancipation, while desirable, was impossible. Jefferson, of course, argued famously in 1819 that "we have the wolf by the ears and we can neither hold him nor let him go." In *The Constitution Construed,* one of the first three books assigned at Jefferson's University of Virginia, John Taylor wrote that "it was folly to think of emancipating them." By 1831 a representative in the Virginia legislature was capable of describing emancipation as "a daydream." In defense of this notion, another representative in that same legislature cited Jefferson's failure to provide in his will for his slaves' freedom as evidence that emancipation was impractical — "sufficient" evidence, in fact, "to put to flight all the conclusions that have been drawn from the expressions of his abstract opinions" in the Declaration of Independence. These were easy arguments for these men to make: one can almost hear the assured, disdainful pleasure in their voices. The best evidence that contradicted them, that argued that emancipation was sensible and slavery was the daydream, was buried where no one would find it.

*

Ultimately, the reasons that Robert Carter disappeared — and remains disappeared — have less to do with what he did than with what others failed to do, less to do with the narrative of American history within which his story would fit than with the narratives of American history that his story contradicts. Just as nineteenth-century Southern politicians claimed that emancipation was impractical as a keystone argument in their defense of slavery, twentieth-century historians continued to make the same argument as a keystone in the defense of the slaveholding practices of the Virginian founding fathers. This defense has two familiar parts. First, the founders should not be judged by contemporary political standards but by the standards of their day: as Andrew Burstein writes in *The Inner Jefferson,* "We should not expect his disengagement from the moral space he occupied." Second, the founders wanted to free their slaves, but no practical plan for emancipation existed: Douglas Southall Freeman, in *George Washington,* writes: "Had there been a practicable way by which he could dispossess himself of slaves, he would have done so long ago."

Robert Carter's Deed of Gift, of course, does substantial damage to these arguments. It becomes difficult to argue that the founding fathers acted liberally within their own moral universe when small slaveowners up and down the Virginia coast were freeing their slaves. It becomes impossible, however, to make the same argument when one of their peers commits the same radical act. Similarly, the argument that there existed no feasible plan for a mass emancipation makes sense only if Robert Carter's Deed of Gift is suppressed from the historical record. Richard Norton Smith writes that Washington's last will and testament represented "the most humane yet practical solution possible," ignoring not only Carter but the fact that Martha Washington incorporated the "most humane" aspects of her husband's plan — the fund he constructed for the support of freed slaves, for instance — into a faster and more efficient emancipation than he had thought possible. Joseph Ellis, in *American Sphinx,* notes that Jefferson could find "no workable answer to the unavoidable question: what happens once the slaves are freed?" In fact, Jefferson was not looking for one. If the history of the founding fathers were written in a manner that accounted for Robert Carter, they would be that much less heroic, but they could be regarded that much more fully as active agents in their own destinies, as men who made choices — who knew, as McColley writes, that "the Virginia statesman who came out publicly against slavery would be very quickly retired to private life," and who, as John Quincy Adams once said, "had not the spirit of martyrdom." Taken individually, however, none of these arguments explains an evasion this entrenched and poetic.

Robert Carter has not disappeared from the record only because he undermines certain tenets of history, or only because of a two-hundred-year-old series of strategic and partly conscious evasions by historians, politicians, and biographers. More crucially, he has disappeared from the historical record because he did something that transcends our ability to listen to our own past: we are all talking the same language about the same limits, the same possibilities, and he belongs to an America we cannot imagine.

Read through the histories of slavery, even the histories least invested in protecting the reputations of the founding fathers, and you will find certain locutions over and over, phrases that reiterate the idea of unanimous moral failure among the slaveholding elite: "slaveholders condemned emancipation as a subversive act"; "slaveholders strongly resisted emancipation"; "among the class of wealthy planters . . . not one Virginia statesman ever advanced a practical proposal for the elimination of slavery." On one level, this kind of locution seems justified: after two centuries of antebellum nostalgia, it is late in history to find new heroic slaveholders. On another level, these phrases reinforce something deep in the American grain, something that diminishes us: the belief that the powerful cannot also be radical, that the powerful never surrender that which makes them powerful. The demoniac Simon Legree helped Harriet Beecher Stowe sell millions of copies of *Uncle Tom's Cabin;* the noble, courtly Ashley Wilkes did the same for Margaret Mitchell. But Americans have made no place for the reformed slaveholder: the "master" has two parts to play in the American story, and in both he keeps his power and his privilege until someone takes it away. No one waits for Bill Gates to give away the Windows patent, or for Nike to divide its incorporated self among the Vietnamese workers who, for pennies an hour, stitch soles to uppers. If Robert Carter's story is any guide, we would be speechless if they tried.

And speechless, too, if their songs of liberty lacked the open passion we assume precedes any stunning moral act. Of all the reasons that Robert Carter has been ignored, none is more disturbing than the most subtle: that we cannot imagine a version of American history where racial progress is made by ice, not fire. When Philip Morgan writes that "if manumission rates are a barometer for gauging the level of concern for slaves, then emotional attachments between masters and bondpeople may seem extremely shallow," he encapsulates a long-standing belief that racial progress comes from enhanced attachment between blacks and whites — from more dialogue, in the parlance of our day. Robert Carter met his slaves on the common ground of the dissenting church, but we make a mistake if we think only about the kind of bond they formed. Other slaveholders prayed with their slaves; other slaveholders probably "loved" their slaves more. Robert Carter freed his slaves because his heart was colder, because he lacked the passion for racism. His Deed of Gift was an act of profound detachment from what we might now label a codependent relationship: he transcended the phase of racial self-consciousness in which whites defined themselves (and their liberty) against blacks, and in which blacks were compelled to define themselves against whites in response. The men and women he freed, one imagines, understood: they rented his land and sold him their produce, but not one single emancipated slave took his last name at the manumission ceremony. Probably that was the safe thing to do. They did not seem to love him or hate him: they were free, and that was better.

More than ever, Robert Carter is awkward evidence. Having undermined the logic of pro-slavery politicians before the Civil War, he does nothing to help heal the rift in the national story created forty years ago, when the civil rights movement and *Brown v. Board of Education* helped black Americans emerge from the virtual apartheid of Jim Crow to join their history to that of the establishment. In the interest of promoting a multicultural (or at least bicultural) vision of American history, teachers, scholars, writers, politicians, and students alike have accepted what amounts to a schizophrenic version of our nation's founding. It is only a radical tenth on one edge of the political spectrum that refuses to acknowledge that Thomas Jefferson was a significant defender of the principles of freedom, and it is only another radical tenth on the other edge that refuses to acknowledge that his practice of keeping slaves was a stunning contradiction to his articulation of those principles. The rest of us inhabit a murky middle ground where Jefferson and Washington, along with many of the other signers of the Declaration of Independence and writers of the Constitution, seem to have given us a riddle instead of a country: were they the best of men or the best of hypocrites?

Because this perspective seems evenhanded, even sophisticated, we forget that it has been out in the open for four or five decades, and we have grown complacent with it. In this new version of American history, we accept that we are a people badly divided about race. Washington and Jefferson remain our founding fathers, even as we reveal the contradictions between what they said and what they did, precisely because we now accept those contradictions as our birthright: "the paradox is American," Edmund Morgan writes. It is even taught in the schools, where it is now more canonical than the conservative view of the founders we all pretend is canonical. Joseph Ellis writes, "My own experience as a college teacher suggested that most students could be counted on to know two things about Thomas Jefferson: that he wrote the Declaration of Independence, and that he had been accused of an illicit affair with Sally Hemings, a mulatto slave."

In our current enshrinement of Thomas Jefferson — which, as Ellis suggests, does not lose momentum for being challenged — we accept that the nation's founding inherently possesses this contradiction, that the idea of America has always promised more than Americans at any given time were willing to deliver: "Thomas Jefferson," Julian Bond writes, "embodies the conundrum on race . . . this gross imbalance between national promise and execution." We hope that our awareness of this schism will drive us over and over to do the right thing, and for historical precedent we look to the Emancipation Proclamation, women's suffrage, and the civil rights movement. But we lean heavily on this single interpretation of how we can make our country a better place. We have rejected slavery, but not the incrementalism of mind and spirit that saved slavery over and over. We still are not interested in someone who failed to suffer from a "gross imbalance" between promise and execution. There's no paradox there, only more guilt for being so paradoxical ourselves.

The possibility exists, of course, that we are the most equitable generation of Americans that has ever existed, and that we have grown comfortable with this ambivalent telling of American history because it is the only fair version. But we ought to consider the possibility that we are the shapers of history now, and that we have made for ourselves the only Jefferson and the only Washington that seem at home amid the struggling and contradictory progress toward racial equality of the last four decades — an age that, like the Revolutionary epoch, was thick with political voices who knew how to say exactly what is right on matters of race, but lacked the will to implement any motion that might be perceived as extreme. It is a sorry tribute we make to Jefferson, Washington, and the other founders when we continue to insist that they were larger than life — and when we do so in order to blame our own confusion and ambivalence on the heroic power of their confused and ambivalent legacy. But we tip our hand when we continue to ignore Robert Carter, whose example is enough to remind us that there existed men and women during the Revolutionary War who knew what was right and did not lack the personal will to act on that knowledge.

The more one reads in the twenty-first century about someone like Robert Carter, the more one feels a sense of fury and frustration that there were already men and women in the 1790s prepared to surrender money and power to bring a dull end to the institution of slavery, that the whole thing — the Civil War, Jim Crow, the Ku Klux Klan, two hundred years of relentless bitterness and division — could have whimpered and died in the Potomac tidewater. It is infuriating to consider this alternate history, in which Robert Carter is the founding father of the only American Revolution we truly lost. It is even more infuriating, however, to consider that we have been unable to find a single use for him. He does not soothe us, excuse us, or help us explain ourselves. But what is most incriminating is that Robert Carter does not even interest us, because that forces us to consider whether there now exist similar men and women, whose plain solutions to our national problems we find similarly boring, and whom we gladly ignore in exchange for the livelier fantasy of our heroic ambivalence.

ADAM MAYBLUM

The Price We Pay

FROM DOUBLETAKE

MY NAME IS Adam Mayblum. I am alive today. I am committing
this to "paper" so I never forget. SO WE NEVER FORGET. I am
sure that this is one of thousands of stories that will emerge over
the next several days and weeks.

I arrived, as usual, a little before eight A.M. My office was on the
eighty-seventh floor of 1 World Trade Center, aka Tower 1, aka the
North Tower. Most of my associates were in by eight-thirty A.M. We
were standing around, joking around, eating breakfast, checking e-
mails, and getting set for the day when the first plane hit just a few
stories above us. I must stress that we did not know that it was a
plane. The building lurched violently and shook as if it were an
earthquake. People screamed. I watched out my window as the
building seemed to move ten to twenty feet in each direction. It
rumbled and shook long enough for me to get my wits about myself and grab a coworker and seek shelter under a doorway. Light
fixtures and parts of the ceiling collapsed. The kitchen was destroyed. We were certain that it was a bomb. We looked out the windows. Reams of paper were flying everywhere, like a ticker-tape pa-
rade. I looked down at the street. I could see people in Battery
Park City looking up. Smoke started billowing in through the holes
in the ceiling. I believe that there were thirteen of us.

We did not panic. I can only assume that we thought that the
worst was over. The building was standing and we were shaken but
alive. We checked the halls. The smoke was thick and white and
did not smell like I imagined smoke should smell. Not like your
BBQ or your fireplace or even a bonfire. The phones were work-

ing. My wife had taken our nine-month-old for his checkup. I called my nanny at home and told her to page my wife, tell her that a bomb went off, I was OK and on my way out. I grabbed my laptop. Took off my T-shirt and ripped it into three pieces. Soaked it in water. Gave two pieces to my friends. Tied my piece around my face to act as an air filter. And we all started moving to the staircase. One of my dearest friends said that he was staying until the police or firemen came to get him. In the halls there were tiny fires and sparks. The ceiling had collapsed in the men's bathroom. It was gone along with anyone who may have been in there. We did not go in to look. We missed the staircase on the first run and had to double back. Once in the staircase we picked up fire extinguishers just in case. On the eighty-fifth floor a brave associate of mine and I headed back up to our office to drag out my partner who stayed behind. There was no air, just white smoke. We made the rounds through the office calling his name. No response. He must have succumbed to the smoke. We left defeated in our efforts and made our way back to the stairwell. We proceeded to the seventy-eighth floor, where we had to change over to a different stairwell. Seventy-eight is the main junction to switch to the upper floors. I expected to see more people. There were some fifty to sixty more. Not enough. Wires and fires all over the place. Smoke too. A brave man was fighting a fire with the emergency hose. I stopped with friends to make sure that everyone from our office was accounted for. We ushered them and confused people into the stairwell. In retrospect, I recall seeing Harry, my head trader, doing the same several yards behind me. I am only thirty-five. I have known him for over fourteen years. I headed into the stairwell with two friends.

We were moving down very orderly in stairwell A. Very slowly. No panic. At least not overt panic. My legs could not stop shaking. My heart was pounding. Some nervous jokes and laughter. I made a crack about ruining a brand-new pair of Merrell's. Even still, they were right, my feet felt great. We all laughed. We checked our cell phones. Surprisingly, there was a very good signal, but the Sprint network was jammed. I heard that the BlackBerry two-way e-mail devices worked perfectly. On the phones, one out of twenty dial attempts got through. I knew I could not reach my wife, so I called my parents. I told them what happened and that we were all OK and on the way down. Soon, my sister-in-law reached me. I told her we were fine and moving down. I believe that was about the sixty-fifth floor. We were bored and nervous. I called my friend Angel in San Francisco. I knew he would be watching. He was amazed I was on the phone. He told me to get out, that there was another plane on its way. I did not know what he was talking about. By now the second plane had struck Tower 2. We were so deep into the middle of our building that we did not hear or feel anything. We had no idea what was really going on. We kept making way for wounded to go down ahead of us. Not many of them, just a few. No one seemed seriously wounded. Just some cuts and scrapes. Everyone cooperated. Everyone was a hero yesterday. No questions asked. I had co-workers in another office on the seventy-seventh floor. I tried dozens of times to get them on their cell phones or office lines. It was futile. Later I found that they were alive. One of the many miracles on a day of tragedy.

On the fifty-third floor we came across a very heavyset man sitting on the stairs. I asked if he needed help or was he just resting. He needed help. I knew I would have trouble carrying him because I have a very bad back. But my friend and I offered anyway. We told him he could lean on us. He hesitated, I don't know why. I said do you want to come or do you want us to send help for you. He chose for help. I told him he was on the fifty-third floor in stairwell A and that's what I would tell the rescue workers. He said OK and we left.

On the forty-fourth floor my phone rang again. It was my parents. They were hysterical. I said relax. I'm fine. My father said get out, there is a third plane coming. I still did not understand. I was kind of angry. What did my parents think? Like I needed some other reason to get going? I couldn't move the thousand people in front of me any faster. I know they love me, but no one inside understood what the situation really was. My parents did. Starting around this floor the firemen, policemen, WTC K-9 units without the dogs, anyone with a badge, started coming up as we were heading down. I stopped a lot of them and told them about the man on fifty-three and my friend on eighty-seven. I later felt terrible about this. They headed up to find those people and met death instead.

On the thirty-third floor I spoke with a man who somehow knew most of the details. He said two small planes hit the building. Now we all started talking about which terrorist group it was. Was it an internal organization or an external one? The overwhelming but uninformed opinion was Islamic fanatics. Regardless, we now knew that it was not a bomb and there were potentially more planes coming. We understood.

On the third floor the lights went out and we heard and felt this rumbling coming towards us from above. I thought the staircase was collapsing upon itself. It was ten A.M. now and that was Tower 2 collapsing next door. We did not know that. Someone had a flashlight. We passed it forward and left the stairwell and headed down a dark and cramped corridor to an exit. We could not see at all. I recommended that everyone place a hand on the shoulder of the person in front of them and call out if they hit an obstacle so others would know to avoid it. They did. It worked perfectly. We reached another stairwell and saw a female officer emerge soaking wet and covered in soot. She said we could not go that way, it was blocked. Go up to four and use the other exit. Just as we started up she said it was OK to go down instead. There was water everywhere. I called out for hands on shoulders again and she said that was a great idea. She stayed behind instructing people to do that. I do not know what happened to her.

We emerged into an enormous room. It was light but filled with smoke. I commented to a friend that it must be under construction. Then we realized where we were. It was the second floor. The one that overlooks the lobby. We were ushered out into the courtyard, the one where the fountain used to be. My first thought was of a TV movie I saw once about nuclear winter and fallout. I could not understand where all of the debris came from. There was at least five inches of this gray pasty dusty drywall soot on the ground as well as a thickness of it in the air. Twisted steel and wires. I heard there were bodies and body parts as well, but I did not look. It was bad enough. We hid under the remaining overhangs and moved out to the street. We were told to keep walking toward Houston Street. The odd thing is that there were very few rescue workers around. Less than five. They all must have been trapped under the debris when Tower 2 fell. We did not know that and could not understand where all of that debris came from. It was just my friend Kern and I now. We were hugging but sad. We felt certain that most of our friends ahead of us died and we knew no one behind us.

We came upon a post office several blocks away. We stopped and looked up. Our building, exactly where our office is (was), was engulfed in flame and smoke. A postal worker said that Tower 2 had fallen down. I looked again and sure enough it was gone. My heart was racing. We kept trying to call our families. I could not get in touch with my wife. Finally I got through to my parents. Relieved is not the word to explain their feelings. They got through to my wife, thank G-d, and let her know I was alive. We sat down. A girl on a bike offered us some water. Just as she took the cap off her bottle we heard a rumble. We looked up and our building, Tower 1, collapsed. I did not note the time, but I am told it was ten-thirty A.M. We had been out less than fifteen minutes.

We were mourning our lost friends, particularly the one who stayed in the office, as we were now sure that he had perished. We started walking towards Union Square. I was going to Beth Israel Medical Center to be looked at. We stopped to hear the president speaking on the radio. My phone rang. It was my wife. I think I fell to my knees crying when I heard her voice. Then she told me the most incredible thing. My partner who had stayed behind called her. He was alive and well. I guess we just lost him in the commotion. We started jumping and hugging and shouting. I told my wife that my brother had arranged for a hotel in midtown. He can be very resourceful in that way. I told her I would call her from there. My brother and I managed to get a gypsy cab to take us home to Westchester instead. I cried on my son and held my wife until I fell asleep. As it turns out, my partner, the one who I thought had stayed behind, was behind us with Harry Ramos, our head trader. This is now secondhand information. They came upon Victor, the heavyset man on the fifty-third floor. They helped him. He could barely move. My partner bravely/stupidly tested the elevator on the fifty-second floor. He rode it down to the sky lobby on forty-four. The doors opened, it was fine. He rode it back up and got Harry and Victor. I don't yet know if anyone else joined them. Once on forty-four they made their way back into the stairwell. Someplace around the thirty-ninth to thirty-sixth floors they felt the same rumble I felt on the third floor. It was ten A.M. and Tower 2 was coming down. They had about thirty minutes to get out. Victor said he could no longer move. They offered to have him lean on them. He said he couldn't do it. My partner hollered at him to sit on his butt and scooch down the steps. He said he was not capable of doing it. Harry told my partner to go ahead of them. Harry once had a heart attack and was worried about this man's heart. It was his nature to be this way. He was/is one of the kindest people I know. He would not leave a man behind. My partner went ahead and made it out. He said he was out maybe ten minutes before the building came down. This means that Harry had maybe twenty-five minutes to move Victor thirty-six floors. I guess they moved one floor every 1.5 minutes. Just a guess. This means Harry was around the twentieth floor when the building collapsed. As of now, twelve of thirteen people are accounted for. As of six P.M. yesterday his wife had not heard from him. I fear that Harry is lost. However, a short while ago I heard that he may be alive. Apparently there is a Web site with survivor names on it and his name appears there. Unfortunately, Ramos is not an uncommon name in New York. Pray for him and all those like him.

With regards to the firemen heading upstairs, I realize that they were going up anyway. But it hurts to know that I may have made them move quicker to find my friend. Rationally, I know this is not true and that I am not the responsible one. The responsible ones are in hiding somewhere on this planet and damn them for making me feel like this. But they should know that they failed in terrorizing us. We were calm. Those men and women that went up were heroes in the face of it all. They must have known what was going on and they did their jobs. Ordinary people were heroes, too. Today the images that people around the world equate with power and democracy are gone, but "America" is not an image, it is a concept. That concept is only strengthened by our pulling together as a team. If you want to kill us, leave us alone because we will do it by ourselves. If you want to make us stronger, attack and we unite. This is the ultimate failure of terrorism against the United States and the ultimate price we pay to be free, to decide where we want to work, what we want to eat, and when and where we want to go on vacation. The very moment the first plane was hijacked, democracy won.

LOUIS MENAND

College: The End of the Golden Age

FROM THE NEW YORK REVIEW OF BOOKS

1

EXCEPT FOR a brief contraction in the early 1990s, the higher education system in the United States has been growing steadily since the late 1970s. Roughly half of all Americans now have attended college at some point in their lives, and roughly a quarter hold a postsecondary degree. (In the United Kingdom, by contrast, less than 15 percent of the population goes to university.) There are 14.5 million students in American colleges and universities today. In 1975 there were a little over 11 million; in 1965 there were fewer than 6 million. And yet when people in higher education talk about its condition and its prospects, doom is often in their voices. There are three matters these people tend to worry about: the future of the liberal arts college; the "collapse" (as it's frequently termed) of the academic disciplines, particularly the humanities; and the seemingly intractable disparity between the supply of Ph.D.s and the demand for new faculty. There are more college students than ever. Why does the system feel to many of the people who work in it as though it is struggling?

The fate of the liberal arts college, the decay of the disciplines, and the tightening of the academic job market present, on one level, distinct issues. The problems at the liberal arts college are chiefly financial; the problems in the humanities disciplines are chiefly philosophical (what does it mean to study "English," for example); the problems with the job market are chiefly administrative — at some point, it seems, graduate schools will simply have to stop admitting more students than they can hope to place in permanent teaching positions. (Despite the consumer warnings about the job market that are now routinely issued to applicants by graduate admissions committees, between 1985 and 1997 graduate student enrollment increased by 27 percent.) The issues are related, though, and the easiest way to see why is to look at the system as a whole.

According to the Carnegie Foundation classification (the industry standard), there are 3,941 higher education institutions in the United States. Only 228 of these — 5.8 percent of the total — are four-year liberal arts colleges that are not part of universities. Even in the major research universities (the schools categorized as Doctoral/Research–Extensive in the Carnegie classification, including such schools as Harvard, Yale, and the University of Chicago), only half of the bachelor's degrees are awarded in liberal arts fields (that is, the natural sciences, social sciences, and humanities). In fact, apart from a small rise between 1955 and 1970, the number of undergraduate degrees awarded annually in the liberal arts has been declining for a century. The expansion of American higher education has been centripetal, away from the traditional liberal arts core. The biggest undergraduate major by far in the United States is business. Twenty percent of all B.A.s are awarded in that field. Ten percent are in education. Seven percent are in the health professions. There are almost twice as many undergraduate degrees conferred every year in a field that calls itself "protective services" — and is largely concerned with training social workers — as there are in all foreign languages and literatures combined.

This helps to explain the apparent anomaly of a declining job market in an expanding industry. In 1970, nearly 25,000 students received bachelor's degrees in mathematics (about 3 percent of all B.A.s), and 1,621 received bachelor's degrees in fields categorized as "parks, recreation, leisure, and fitness studies." In 1997, 12,820 students graduated with degrees in mathematics (only 1 percent of all B.A.s), and 15,401 took degrees in parks, etc. This is why math Ph.D.s who wish to teach and do work in pure mathematics cannot find tenure-track jobs. It is not that there is no demand for college math teachers; it's that there is much less demand for specialists in pure mathematics. The same thing has happened in English language and literature. In 1970, English majors took 7.6 percent of all B.A.s; by 1997, the figure was down to 4.2 percent, a drop in absolute numbers from 64,342 to 49,345. Literature courses are still taught, but the market for specialists is much smaller, since fewer undergraduates take classes beyond an introductory level.

The shrinking of the liberal arts sector (except in a few disciplines, notably psychology and the biological sciences, which produce more B.A.s now than they did twenty-five years ago) obviously has an effect on the disciplines themselves. Scholarship is, after all, largely a byproduct of the system designed to produce college teachers. People go to graduate school most often in order to acquire the credential they need to get a job teaching college students, and in order to acquire that credential, they are obliged to produce specialized scholarship under the direction of scholarly specialists. If (hypothetically) it were suddenly decided that the ability to produce specialized scholarship had no relevance to college teaching, and different requirements for the Ph.D. were instituted, academic scholarship would pretty much dry up. But that does not seem to be the anxiety that's driving the so-called "collapse of the disciplines." In order to understand the real extent of the transformation of American higher education, we have to go back fifty years.

2

The history of higher education in the United States since World War II can be divided into two periods. The first period, from 1945 to 1975, was a period of expansion. The composition of the system remained more or less the same — in certain respects, the system became more uniform — but the size of the system increased dramatically. This is the period known in the literature on American education as the Golden Age. The second period, from 1975 to the present, has not been honored with a special name. It is a period not of expansion but of diversification. Since 1975 the size of the system has grown at a much more modest pace, but the composition — who is taught, who does the teaching, and what they teach — changed dramatically. This did not happen entirely by design.

In the Golden Age, between 1945 and 1975, the number of American undergraduates increased by almost 500 percent and the number of graduate students increased by nearly 900 percent. In the 1960s alone enrollments more than doubled, from 3.5 million to just under 8 million; the number of doctorates awarded annually tripled; and more faculty were hired than had been hired in the entire 325-year history of American higher education to that point. At the height of the expansion, between 1965 and 1972, new community college campuses were opening in the United States at the rate of one every week.

Three developments account for this expansion: the baby boom, the fairly sustained high domestic economic growth rate after 1948, and the Cold War. The impact of the Cold War on the growth of the university is well known. During the Second World War, educational leaders such as James Bryant Conant, of Harvard, and Vannevar Bush, formerly of MIT, instituted the system under which the federal government contracted its scientific research out to universities — the first time it had adopted this practice. Bush's 1945 report, *Science — The Endless Frontier,* became the standard argument for government subvention of basic science in peacetime. Bush is also the godfather of the system known as contract overhead — the practice of billing granting agencies for indirect costs (plant, overhead, administrative personnel, etc.), an idea to which not only many scientists but also many humanists owe their careers. This was the start of the gravy train that produced the Golden Age.

In 1958, as a response to *Sputnik* and concerns about a possible "technology gap," Congress passed the National Defense Education Act, which put the federal government into the business of subsidizing higher education directly, rather than through government contracts for specific research. The act singled out two fields in particular as targets of public investment — science and foreign languages — thus pumping up two distinct areas of the academic balloon. The act was passed just before the baby boom kicked in. Between 1955 and 1970, the number of eighteen- to twenty-four-year-olds in America grew from fifteen million to twenty-five million. And the entire expansion got a late and unintentional boost from the military draft, which provided a deferment for college students until 1970. The result was that by 1968, 63.2 percent of male high school graduates were going on to college, a higher proportion than do today. This is the period when all those community college campuses were bursting up out of the ground. They were, among other things, government-subsidized draft havens.

Then, around 1975, the Golden Age came to a halt. The student deferment was abolished and American involvement in the war ended; the college-age population stopped growing and leveled off; the country went into a recession; and the economic value of a college degree began to fall. In the 1970s the income differential between college graduates and high school graduates dropped from 61 percent to 48 percent. The percentage of people going on to college therefore began to drop as well, and a system that had quintupled, and more, in the span of a single generation suddenly found itself with empty dormitory beds and a huge tenured faculty. This was the beginning of the long-term job crisis for American Ph.D.s, and it was also the beginning of serious economic pressures on the liberal arts college. From 1955 to 1970, the proportion of liberal arts degrees among all bachelor's degrees awarded annually had risen for the first time in this century; after 1970, it started going back down again.

The rapid expansion that took place in the 1960s helps to explain the second phase in postwar American higher education, the phase of diversification. The numbers are not complicated. In 1965, 62 percent of students were men and 94 percent were classified as white; by 1997, 45 percent of students were men and 72 percent were classified as non-Hispanic whites. In that year, 1997, 45,394 doctoral degrees were conferred; 40 percent of the recipients were women (in the arts and humanities, just under 50 percent were women), and only 63 percent were classified as white American citizens. The other 37 percent were nonwhite Americans and foreign students.

Faculty demographics changed in the same way, a reflection not so much of changes in hiring practices as of changes in the group that went to graduate school after 1975. Current full-time American faculty who were hired before 1985 are 28 percent female and about 11 percent nonwhite or Hispanic. Full-time faculty who have been hired since 1985 — that is, for the most part, faculty who entered graduate school after the Golden Age — are half again female (40 percent) and more than half again as nonwhite (18 percent).

There are a number of reasons why more women and nonwhite Americans, not to mention more non-Americans, began entering higher education in greater proportionate numbers after 1970, but one of them is purely structural. After 1970, there were fewer white American males for selective schools to choose from. The absolute number of white male American high school graduates going on to college was dropping, and, thanks to the expansion of the 1960s, the number of institutions for those who were going to college to choose from had grown. So colleges and universities sought new types of students. After 1970, virtually every nonmilitary all-male college in the United States went coed. The system had overexpanded during the Golden Age. Too many state-subsidized slots had been created, and one result was a much higher level of competition among colleges to recruit students. People had talked before 1975 about the educational desirability of coeducational and mixed-race student bodies, but as Elizabeth Duffy and Idana Goldberg demonstrate rather dramatically in *Crafting a Class,* their study of admissions policies at sixteen liberal arts colleges in Ohio and Massachusetts, in the end it was economic necessity that made them do it.

3

The appearance of these new populations in colleges and universities obviously affected the subject matter of scholarship and teaching. An academic culture that had, for the most part, never imagined that "women's history" or "Asian-American literature" might constitute a discrete field of inquiry, or serve to name a course, was suddenly confronted with the challenge of explaining why it hadn't. The challenge led to a good deal of what might be called anti-disciplinarity — work that amounted to criticism of the practices and assumptions of its own discipline. There is no doubt that this work, by feminists, students of colonialism and postcolonialism, nonwhites, gays, and so on, tended to call into question the very idea of academic disciplines as discrete and effectively autonomous fields of inquiry. But the questioning of the traditional assumptions of academic work, particularly in the social sciences and humanities, that took place after 1975 was only adding fuel to a fire started from other causes.

One of the persistent peculiarities of the debate over higher education that has been under way, off and on, since the late 1980s — the debate over multiculturalism, political correctness, affirmative action, sex and gender studies, and so on — is the assumption of many of its participants that the university of the 1950s and 1960s, the early Cold War university, represents some kind of norm against which recent developments can usefully be measured, positively or negatively. The great contribution Thomas Bender and Carl Schorske have made in the recent collection they edited, *American Academic Culture in Transformation*, is to show how exceptional, and in some ways artificial, that earlier period was. For once the funding for academic research began coming from the state, and once "science" became the magic word needed to secure that funding, the paradigms of academic work changed. Analytic rigor and disciplinary autonomy became important to an extent they had not before the war. To put it another way: scholarly tendencies that emphasized theoretical or empirical rigor were taken up and carried into the mainstream of academic practice; tendencies that reflected a generalist or "belletrist" approach were pushed to the professional margins, as were tendencies whose assumptions and aims seemed political.

As Bender suggests, many scholars eschewed political commitments because they wished not to offend their granting agencies. The idea that academics, particularly in the social sciences, could provide the state with neutral research results on which pragmatic public policies could be based was an animating idea in the early Cold War university. In the sciences, it helped establish what Talcott Parsons called the ethos of "cognitive rationality." In fields like history, it led to the consensus approach. In sociology, it produced what Robert Merton called theories of the middle range — an emphasis on the formulation of limited hypotheses subject to empirical verification. Behaviorism and rational choice theory became dominant paradigms in fields like psychology and political science. In fields like literature, even when the mindset was antiscientific, as in the case of the New Criticism and structuralism, the ethos was still scientistic: theorists aspired to analytic rigor. Boundaries were respected and methodologies were codified. Discipline reigned in the disciplines. Scholars in the 1950s who looked back on their prewar educations (some of these contribute their reflections to Bender and Schorske's volume) tended to be appalled by what they now regarded as a lack of analytic rigor and focus.

Because the public money was being pumped into the system at the high end — into the large research universities — the effect of the Golden Age was to make the research professor the type of the professor generally. This is the phenomenon Christopher Jencks and David Riesman referred to, in 1968, as "the academic revolution": for the first time in the history of American higher education, research, rather than teaching or service, defined the vocation of the professor — not just in the doctoral institutions but all down the institutional ladder. And this strengthened the grip of the disciplines on scholarly and pedagogical practice. Distinctions among different types of institutions, so far as the professoriate was concerned, began to be sanded down. This is why when the system of higher education expanded between 1945 and 1975, it also became more uniform. The Cold War homogenized the academic profession. The Cold War introduced another element into the philosophy of higher education as well. This was the principle of meritocracy. The great champion of that principle was the same man who helped set in place the new financial relationship between the university and the federal government, James Conant. Conant was only articulating a general postwar belief that opening educational opportunities to everyone, regardless of race or gender, was simply a better way to maximize the social talent pool. If your chief concern is to close a perceived "technology gap" (or to maintain technological superiority), you can't get hung up on an irrelevance like family income or skin color. The National Defense Education Act of 1958 was fairly explicit on this point. "The security of the Nation requires the fullest development of the mental resources and technical skills of its young men and women . . . We must increase our efforts to identify and educate more of the talent of our Nation. This requires programs that will give assurance that no students of ability will be denied an opportunity for higher education because of financial need." Thus Conant was a leader in the establishment of standardized testing: he essentially created the SATs. He thought of the SATs as a culturally neutral method for matching aptitude with educational opportunity.

The meritocratic philosophy was accompanied by a new emphasis on the importance of general education — that is, curricula designed for all students, regardless of their choice of specialization. In practice, general education was mostly paid lip service to after the war; relatively few colleges actually created general education curricula or required undergraduates to take specified extradepartmental courses of the kind Columbia College is famous for. But general education did get a great deal of lip service. The ideas most educators subscribed to was that the great works of the Western tradition are accessible to all students in more or less the same way; that those works constitute a more or less coherent body of thought, or, at least, a coherent debate; and that they can serve as a kind of benign cultural ideology in a nation wary of ideology. This is the argument of the famous study Conant sponsored at Harvard, *General Education in a Free Society,* published in 1945, the volume known as the Red Book. Conant himself thought that exposure to the great books could help the United States withstand the threat of what he actually referred to as the "Russian hordes."

It seems obvious now that the dispensation put into place in the first two decades of the Cold War was just waiting for the tiniest spark to blow sky-high. And the spark, when it came, wasn't so tiny. The Vietnam War exposed almost every weakness in the system Conant and his generation of educational leaders had constructed, from the dangers inherent in the university's financial dependence on the state, to the way its social role was linked to national security policy, to the degree of factitiousness in the value-neutral standard of research in fields outside the natural sciences.

And then, as the new populations began to arrive in numbers in American universities after 1970, the meritocratic rationale was exploded as well. For it turned out that cultural differences were not only not so easy to ignore as men like Conant had imagined; those differences suddenly began to seem a lot more interesting than the similarities. This trend was made irreversible by Justice Lewis Powell's decision in *Regents of the University of California v. Bakke,* handed down in 1978. Powell changed the language of college admissions by decreeing that if admissions committees wanted to stay on the safe side of the Constitution, they had to stop talking about quotas and to begin talking about diversity instead.

Powell's opinion blew a hole in meritocratic theory, because he pointed out what should have been obvious from the beginning, which is that college admissions, even at places like Harvard, have never been purely meritocratic. Colleges have always taken non-standardized and nonstandardizable attributes into account when selecting a class, from musical prodigies to football stars, alumni legacies, and the offspring of local and national bigwigs. If you admitted only students who got top scores on the SATs, you would have a very boring class. "Diversity" is the very word Powell used in the Bakke opinion, and there are probably very few college catalogs in the country today in which the word "diversity," or one of its cognates, does not appear.

As the homogeneity of the faculty and student body broke down during the period of diversification, the disciplines began their transformations. On the level of the liberal arts college, the changes were already in evidence by 1990, the year Ernest Boyer published his landmark study of them, *Scholarship Reconsidered.* The changes are visible today in a new emphasis on multiculturalism (meaning exposure to specifically ethnic perspectives and traditions) and on values (an emphasis on the ethical implications of knowledge); in a renewed interest in service (manifested in the emergence of internship and off-campus social service programs) and in the idea of community; in what is called "education for citizenship"; and in a revival of a Deweyite conception of teaching as a collaborative process of learning and inquiry.

The Golden Age vocabulary of "disinterestedness," "objectivity," "reason," and "knowledge" and talk about things like "the scientific method," the canon of great books, and "the fact-value distinction" have been replaced, in many fields, by talk about "interpretations" (rather than "facts"), "perspective" (rather than "objectivity"), and "understanding" (rather than "reason" or "analysis"). An emphasis on universalism and "greatness" has been replaced by an emphasis on diversity and difference; the scientistic norms which once prevailed in many of the "soft" disciplines are viewed with skepticism; "context" and "contingency" are continually emphasized; attention to "objects" has given way to attention to "representations."

This trend is a backlash against the scientism, and the excessive respect for the traditional academic disciplines, of the Golden Age university. It can't be attributed solely to demographic diversifica-

tion, because most of the people one would name as its theorists —
people such as Thomas Kuhn, Hayden White, Clifford Geertz,
Richard Rorty, Paul De Man, and Stanley Fish — are white men
who were working entirely within the traditions in which they had
been trained in the 1950s and 1960s. In most cases, these scholars
were simply giving the final analytic turn to work that had been going on for two decades. They were demonstrating the limits, in the
humanities disciplines, of the notion of disinterested inquiry and
"scientific advance." The seeds of the undoing of the Cold War disciplinary models were already present within the disciplines themselves. The artificiality of those Golden Age disciplinary forma-
tions is what made the implosion inevitable.

4

One way to see the breakdown of consensus in the liberal arts disciplines is by looking at college catalogs. Compare, for example,
the English departments at two otherwise quite similar schools,
Amherst and Wellesley. English majors at Wellesley are required to
take ten English department courses, eight of which must be in
subjects other than creative writing. (Nor do basic writing courses
count toward the major.) All English majors must take a core
course, called Critical Interpretation; they must take one course
on Shakespeare; and they must take at least two courses in literature written before 1900, one of which must be in literature written before 1800. With one exception, a course on "Medieval/Re-
naissance," cross-listed courses — that is, interdisciplinary courses
— are not counted toward the major. The course listing reflects attention to every traditional historical period in English and American literature.

Down the turnpike at Amherst, on the other hand, English majors have only to take ten courses "offered or approved by the department" — in other words, apparently, they may be courses in
any department. Majors have no core requirement and no period
requirements. They must simply take one lower- and one upper-
level course, and they must declare, during their senior year, a
"concentration," consisting of three courses whose relatedness
they must argue to the department. The catalog assures students
that "the choices of courses and description of the area of concen-

tration may be revised as late as the end of the add-drop period of a student's last semester." Course listings, as they are available online, are not historically comprehensive, and many upper-level offerings are on topics like African (not African-American) writers. At Amherst, in short, the English department has a highly permissive attitude toward its majors, and I'm sure if you asked why, the reason given would be that English should be understood more as an intellectual approach, a style of inquiry, a set of broad concerns than as a distinctive body of knowledge. At Wellesley, the department obviously has the opposite view. They see the field more concretely. Of course, the way a department chooses to represent itself in a catalog and what actually goes on in its classes are not necessarily identical. It's likely that Amherst and Wellesley English majors end up learning many of the same things. But their notion of English as a field of study is probably very different.

Up the food chain at the graduate level, then, there is a problem. Does training to become an English professor entail familiarity with the history of English and American literature, or does it entail a more wide-ranging eclecticism, informed by a theoretical understanding of the essential arbitrariness of disciplinary boundaries? The closer liberal arts colleges move toward the Amherst model, the more unclear it becomes what "the study of English" means. On the other hand, the closer they stick to the older models, the more it may seem, to some people, that the liberal arts make a poor "preparation for life."

Maybe the present state of uncertainty is not a portent of doom, though. Maybe it's an opportunity. In most of what is written about higher education by people who are outside the academy, and even by some who are inside, there seems to be very little recognition that "higher education" today embraces a far more diverse set of institutions, missions, and constituencies than it did even thirty years ago. Many people still think of "college" as four years spent majoring in a liberal arts field, an experience only a minority of the people who attend college today actually have. The virtue of acknowledging this new dispensation is that it may encourage us to drop the one-size-fits-all manner of pronouncing on educational issues. Young people seek higher education for different reasons and have different needs, and different opportunities are held out to them. Institutions need to be more variously equipped to meet these needs.

The word "relevance" got very tiresome back in the 1960s, when it was used to complain about the divorce between academic studies and the "real world" of civil rights and Vietnam. But the truth is that the Golden Agers thought their work was relevant. They thought that the disinterested pursuit of knowledge, conceived as a set of relatively discrete specialties, was the best way to meet the needs of the larger society. There now seems to be a general recognition that the walls between the liberal arts disciplines were too high. Maybe it is also the case that the wall between the liberal arts and the subjects many people now go to colleges and universities to study — subjects such as business, medicine, technology, social service, education, and the law — are also too high. Maybe the liberal arts and these "nonliberal" fields have something to contribute to one another. The world has changed. It's time to be relevant in a new way.

Note: Information in this essay is drawn from the following sources: Philip G. Altbach, Robert O. Berdahl, and Patricia J. Gumport, eds., *American Higher Education in the Twenty-first Century: Social, Political, and Economic Challenges* (1999); Thomas Bender and Carl E. Schorske, eds., *American Academic Culture in Transformation: Fifty Years, Four Disciplines* (1997); Ernest L. Boyer, *Scholarship Reconsidered: Priorities of the Professoriate* (1990); Elizabeth A. Duffy and Idana Goldberg, *Crafting a Class: College Admissions and Financial Aid, 1955–1994* (1998); Martin J. Finkelstein, Robert K. Seal, and Jack H. Schuster, *The New Academic Generation: A Profession in Transformation* (1998); Roger L. Geiger, *Research and Relevant Knowledge: American Research Universities Since World War II* (1993); Joan Gilbert, "The Liberal Arts College: Is It Really an Endangered Species?" *Change* 27, 5 (September/October 1995), 36–43; Hugh Davis Graham and Nancy Diamond, *The Rise of American Research Universities: Elites and Challenges in the Postwar Era* (1997); Morton Keller and Phyllis Keller, *Making Harvard Modern: The Rise of America's University* (2001); Bruce Kimball, *The Condition of American Liberal Education: Pragmatism and a Changing Tradition* (1995); and Nicholas Lemann, *The Big Test: The Secret History of the American Meritocracy* (1999). My work on higher education is supported by a grant from the Alfred P. Sloan Foundation.

CULLEN MURPHY

Out of the Ordinary

FROM THE ATLANTIC MONTHLY

NOT LONG AGO a friend called my attention to an article by the British historian Colin Jones titled "Pulling Teeth in Eighteenth-Century Paris." I was glad she did. It would be wrong to say that I am captivated by teeth, but they do leave a lasting impression. I recall seeing as a child, in a display case at a museum, a hollow false tooth used by a spy to carry secret messages during the Revolutionary War (not successfully, it would seem). The Centers for Disease Control a few years back released a state-by-state study of tooth loss, the central finding of which I retain: in West Virginia, the most severely afflicted state, almost 50 percent of those over the age of sixty-five have no teeth at all. I can still summon the image, from a book of photographs, of a collection of teeth extracted by Czar Peter the Great, "who fancied himself a dentist," each from a different person, and each carefully labeled. I remember looking twice at an obituary headline that identified its subject as a "DENTIST AND HUMANITARIAN."

The ostensible subject of Colin Jones's article is a man known as le Grand Thomas, a freelance tooth puller of formidable girth who plied his trade from a cart on the Pont-Neuf for half a century, until the 1750s. He styled himself the "pearl of charlatans" and the "massive Aesculapius" and displayed a banner bearing the legend DENTEM SINON MAXILLAM ("The tooth, and if not, the jaw"). Tooth-pulling at the time was, like executions, a form of public entertainment. Jones situates Thomas at the beginning of a process that would lead not only to the emergence of modern dentistry but also, as a consequence, to much of the oral iconography of modern advertising.

"The mouth," Jones writes, "was becoming the imaginary site around which revolved both a nascent academic industry and a new and broader commercialism." Toothbrushes, toothpowder, and false teeth came into vogue in the eighteenth century among an expanding bourgeoisie. As teeth improved, a new phenomenon took hold in the realm of art. Ever since antiquity the convention had been to depict respectable people with their mouths closed and their teeth hidden; the open-mouthed, gap-toothed look was reserved for the depraved, the demented, and the vulgar. Now, in the 1780s, for the first time, the smile was flashed in formal portraiture, celebrating full sets of even white teeth.

Colin Jones's progression from the Pont-Neuf to the Pepsodent smile exemplifies a rapidly expanding genre. Its practitioners are drawn from many fields, and their interests range from the most pedestrian aspects of popular culture to the most rarefied precincts of serious history. The genre doesn't have a single name, but its manifestations could be lumped together under the rubric "mundane studies."

Consider two paths to enlightenment. One is to take subject matter that is vast and grand (the Middle Ages, say) and slice it into thin sections for analysis ("Glazed Pottery and Social Class in Ninth-Century Thuringia"). The other path leads from the particular to the general — it takes something seemingly unremarkable (a kind of food, an article of dress, a body part) and from it derives a larger world of meaning. In the mid-1970s the historian and John Adams biographer Page Smith and the biologist Charles Daniel published *The Chicken Book*, a conceptual vivisection of *Gallus domesticus*, and a tour de force. A decade and a half later the engineer Henry Petroski devoted an entire volume to the pencil. Last year the architect Witold Rybczynski produced *One Good Turn*, a history of the screwdriver and the screw. This approach — the mundane-studies approach — continues to gather momentum. The impetus comes partly from the rise of social history, with its focus on ordinary life. The challenge of extracting significance from some unlikely object provides the further incentive of a postmodernist daredevil thrill.

No subject is too small. A few years ago I received a letter from a man named Jay W. Stein, who, as a government archivist working with original Nazi and Soviet documents, had managed to assemble a museum-quality collection of the binders, fasteners, clamps, and clips that held the bureaucracies' papers together. Now a librarian, Stein had continued to pursue his passion, and he enclosed an article of his from the *Law Library Journal* — "Something Little and Shiny on the Judicial Stage: The Paper Clip." "What I discovered," Stein wrote in the article, "was that the paper clip is more taken for granted than almost anything in the judicial process" — despite the fact that case after case has hinged on this simple device. Paper clips have figured in deciding whether pages were part of wills. The fact that a document's edge was marked by paper clips has been accepted as evidence that the document was in fact read. Paper clips sometimes turn up as weapons. Stein observed:

> Like the horseshoe nail that crippled the horse and thwarted its rider in battle, the paper clip is small compared to most things involved in litigation. Yet, how often it is mentioned suggests pausing to remind oneself how much the little things count.

The common potato seems like a little thing — ordinariness in tuber form. But I began to see potatoes differently after reading a recent essay, "The Potato in the Materialist Imagination," by Catherine Gallagher and Stephen Greenblatt. As the potato became a European staple, two hundred years ago, it also became the focus of a fierce intellectual debate. The pro-potato forces celebrated the potato's astonishing utility: it grew with little effort, and fed people and swine alike. The anti-potato forces found this repugnant — and they worried about an insidious social consequence. Bread, the traditional staple, caught people up in a complex web of interactions — growing, harvesting, threshing, milling, baking, selling. The potato required none of that. A vast rural proletariat in a state of utter isolation could feed on roots from the ground, breed, and degrade into dust.

Dust itself is the subject of a magisterial book by the historian Joseph Amato. *Dust* surveys many topics — medieval philosophy, Victorian technology, the cleanliness movement — but the central narrative concerns how dust came to lose its special status in the poetic and the scientific imagination. Only a few centuries ago, Amato writes, dust was regarded as "the finest thing the human eye could see . . . a barrier between the visible and the invisible." Those motes dancing in shafts of sunlight represented an elemental condition to which all things would return. Then along came the microscope, revealing an "infinity of the infinitesimal." Dust was consigned to the dustbin (or the allergist).

I learned about *Dust* by way of an excerpt in the *Journal of Mundane Behavior* (www.mundanebehavior.org), a new peer-reviewed publication devoted to "research, theory and method regarding the very obvious features of our existence." The first few issues offered articles about the morning shave, elevator conversation, shopping at Wal-Mart, on-field prayer by athletes, and the use of the television remote control. One essay, "'When Nothing Happened,'" made the point that days of yore consisted mostly of circumstances that rarely get attention — stability, boredom, daydreaming, business as usual. A personal Web-cam version of ancient Babylon might look very familiar.

The journal is off to a promising start, but the task ahead is enormous. If I could give out Guggenheims for mundane studies, I'd channel young scholars toward certain potentially fruitful topics. For instance, a detailed study of the interstitial conversation in wiretap transcripts is long overdue. These documents have obvious short-term utility for what they reveal about criminal mayhem, but the long-term value lies in everything else. Here's Vincent Romano talking to John "Sideburns" Cerrella about his health: "Yeah, all right, the leg feels much better, much better, much, much better. I took a couple of glasses of tomato juice, you know, for potassium." Here's a disquisition on yogurt from Frank "Frankie California" Condo: "Brown Cow with the thick crust on top and you mix the crust, that's the, the bacteria. You mix that all in there . . . Brown Cow. That's what all the health fiends eat. Brown Cow." Eating habits, folk remedies, amorous insights, movie reviews — this is a mundane-studies mother lode.

The inane use of quotation marks on menus, advertisements, and public signage — STEAKS AND BURGERS "FROM THE GRILL"; WHEN LEAVING THE BATHROOM "PLEASE TURN OFF THE LIGHT" — would be another prime focus of investigation. The development may not seem like an urgent public issue, but we would do well to assess its subtly corrosive effects. Even the cocktail napkins on *Air Force One* now bear a legend in quotation marks: "Aboard the Presidential Aircraft." What is the semiotic essence of this form of display? If nothing is being quoted, then what is "quotation" coming to mean? Finally, there is the matter of the disappearing object. This linguistic tropism takes form in sentences like "The Yankees amaze" and "The movie fails to excite" — sentences in which a transitive verb, which takes a direct object, has been casually stripped of one. The *Wall Street Journal* recently published the following headline: "STOCK NIGHTMARES? HISTORY MAY COMFORT." Does the potential activity embodied in verbs like "amaze," "excite," and "comfort" exist as an independent force, swirling atmospherically, regardless of whether actual people or things are affected? Is the detachment of verb and object one more step toward a depersonalized world?

Sherlock Holmes boasted that he could infer Niagara Falls from a drop of water. William Blake wrote of seeing the world in a grain of sand, and heaven in a wild flower. Colin Jones chose teeth. Other pioneers of mundane studies have chosen the tulip, the cod, the color mauve, longitude, phosphorus, the F word, the handshake, and the contents of garbage cans. The world is a mundane place if it is anything at all, and the possibilities ahead cannot fail to excite.

DANIELLE OFRI

Merced

FROM THE MISSOURI REVIEW

For this is the end of examinations
For this is the beginning of testing
For Death will give the final examination and everyone will pass
— John Stone, *Gaudeamus Igitur*

"THIS IS A CASE of a twenty-three-year-old Hispanic female without significant past medical history who presented to Bellevue Hospital complaining of a headache." The speaker droned on with the details of the case that I knew so well. I leaned back in my chair, anticipating the accolades that were going to come. After all, in a roundabout way I'd made the diagnosis. I was the one who had had the idea to send the Lyme test in the first place.

Mercedes had been to two other ERs before showing up at Bellevue three weeks ago. I'd only been doing sick call that day because one of the other residents had twisted his knee playing volleyball. She was a classic aseptic meningitis, the kind that you'd send home with aspirin and some chicken soup, but the ER had decided to admit her to the hospital. Her CT scan was normal, and the spinal tap just showed a few lymphocytes, but the ER always overreacts. They gave her IV antibiotics even though there was no hint of the life-threatening bacterial meningitis.

One of the emergency room docs had scrawled something about "bizarre behavior" on the chart, then given her a stat dose of acyclovir. Another ridiculous ER maneuver; this patient had no signs of herpes encephalitis.

I'll admit that I was a little cocky that day. But I was just two months short of finishing residency, and I knew a lot more medi-

cine than those ER guys. I chewed them out for admitting Mercedes and made a big show of canceling the acyclovir order.
When I met Mercedes that first day, she was sleeping on a stretcher in a corner of the ER. I had to wake her up to take the history, but after a few shakes she was completely lucid. With her plump cheeks and wide brown eyes, she didn't even look seventeen, much less twenty-three. The sleeves of her pink sweatshirt were pushed up past her elbows. A gold cross with delicate filigree was partly obscured by the folds of the sweatshirt.

"Doctor, you have to believe me," she said, pulling herself up on the stretcher. "I've never been sick a day in my life. It's only this past month that I've been getting these headaches. They come almost every day, and aspirin doesn't do anything. I came to the ER yesterday, but they said, 'You got nothin', lady,' and just gave me a couple of Tylenols." Dark, mussed curls spilled over her pink shirt. While she spoke, one hand wove itself absent-mindedly in and out of the locks.

"So, what made you come back today?" I asked.

"This headache, it didn't go away. And then my arm. It got all pins and needles for a few minutes. Just a couple of minutes, but now it's fine." Mercedes smiled slightly, and two tiny dimples flickered in her cheeks. "I guess they got tired of me complaining, so they decided to let me stay."

I did a thorough physical exam, spending extra time on the neurologic part. I checked every reflex I could think of: biceps, triceps, brachoradialis, patellar, plantar. I examined all twelve cranial nerves. Everything seemed normal. I tried to do all the obscure neurological tests I could remember from *Bates's Guide to Physical Examination and History Taking*, but nothing seemed amiss, and the patient was certainly not behaving bizarrely.

From talking to her, I learned that Mercedes was a single mother with two children, aged three and four. She lived with her own mother but still maintained a close relationship with the father of her children. She worked as a preschool teacher in upper Manhattan. She'd been born in Puerto Rico, but since moving to the United States at age two had never left the country.

I questioned her extensively about possible exposure to viruses or atypical organisms: travel to the countryside, recent illnesses, recent vaccinations, outbreaks of sickness at her preschool, HIV risk factors, contact with pets, consumption of poorly cooked fish or meat, all of which she denied.

Based on her history and physical exam, I concluded that she had garden-variety aseptic meningitis. The ER staff, with their usual sledgehammer approach to medical care, had overdone it with intravenous antibiotics and acyclovir. Mercedes didn't even need to stay in the hospital, but she'd already been officially admitted, and the administrative folks would have a conniption if I sent a patient home just two hours after checking in.

Just to show the ER docs how real academic medicine was done, I wrote up an extensive admission note for Mercedes, detailing all the rare causes of aseptic meningitis listed in *Harrison's Principles of Internal Medicine*. Paragraph after paragraph elucidated my clinical logic; it was a textbook example of orderly scientific thinking. And I printed neatly, so it would be easy for anyone perusing the chart to read.

There was an extra tube of Mercedes's cerebrospinal fluid in my pocket, so I decided to send it for a couple of rare tests, including a Lyme titre. What the heck, I thought. This is a teaching institution. We're supposed to waste some money on exotic tests in order to learn. Besides, it would really impress the attending on rounds tomorrow when I would blithely nod my head at each diagnosis he'd ask about.

Rickettsia? "Got it."

Sarcoid? "Covered."

Coxsackie virus? "Sent it."

Toxoplasmosis? "Already there."

Lupus? "Done."

The ER docs might just toss a pile of medications at anyone who walked in the door, but here in the Department of Medicine, we utilized our diagnostic acumen.

The next morning during rounds, just as I was dazzling the crowd with my erudite analysis of Mercedes's case, the nurses called me urgently to her room. Mercedes was on the floor with her clothes off, hair askew, babbling incoherently. Her IV had been pulled out, and her body was splattered with blood. Completely disoriented, she fought us vociferously as we tried to help her back to bed.

Thirty minutes later she was entirely back to normal, with no recollection of the event. I was absolutely dumbfounded. What the hell had just happened?

Immediately I repeated a CT scan and spinal tap, but the results were no different than they'd been the day before. The neurologist felt Mercedes's behavior might have represented a seizure of the temporal lobe. The herpes virus has a predilection for the temporal lobe, so this episode might have been a sign of herpes encephalitis. Regretting my earlier haughtiness toward the ER staff, I restarted the acyclovir.

Mercedes was transferred to the neurology service for management of herpes encephalitis, and I was transferred off the ward when the other resident's knee got better. I was happy to get back to my cushy dermatology elective.

A week later, still smarting from missing the herpes encephalitis diagnosis, I tracked down the intern to see how Mercedes was doing. "Hey, did you hear the news?" he asked. "That herpes encephalitis patient really had Lyme disease. The test just came back positive yesterday."

Lyme disease? The test that I had sent came back positive? I was exhilarated. This would be the most fascinating diagnosis on the medical wards. Who would have suspected that a New York City dweller would have a disease carried by deer ticks in the forest? But hey, it was a careful diagnostic evaluation of the patient, and my thoroughness had paid off.

Soon everybody was talking about the case of Lyme meningitis in our inner-city hospital. The head of my residency program became interested and suggested I plan a seminar on Lyme disease. I set about obtaining all the details of Mercedes's case and searched the medical literature for current articles on Lyme disease.

Meanwhile, Mercedes was started on the appropriate medication for Lyme. She'd been discharged home and was finishing her three-week course of antibiotics with daily shots in the clinic.

Today the case was being presented at neurology grand rounds. I wasn't a participant in this particular conference, but I didn't care. I sat back and listened to speaker after speaker comment on the "incredible diagnosis" that had been made. My bulging Mercedes/Lyme folder sat on my lap as I took mental notes, preparing for my own presentation in the Department of Medicine two weeks from now. Residency would be over at the end of next month. I had been here ten years, from the beginning of medical school through my Ph.D. and then my residency. Ten years of medical training! But now it was truly paying off. Ten years of the scientific approach to medicine had prepared me for this case. Ten years of emphasis on careful analysis of data — whether it be of receptor binding assays in the lab or signs and symptoms in a patient — had taught me how to establish a hypothesis and reach a logical conclusion. This was the academic way that ensured the highest-quality medical care.

Our attendings were always pointing out medical disasters that occurred "out in the community" when the doctors in charge were not academic physicians. Doctors who didn't keep up with the latest medical journals — doctors who, without diligent and thoughtful analysis, ordered any old test or prescribed any fancy packaged medicine marketed by the pharmaceutical companies — could seriously harm or even kill their patients. Mercedes was lucky to have come to an academic medical center rather than to a community hospital, where her diagnosis would have been missed entirely.

Mercedes's case was presented in elaborate detail. There was a sense of triumph in the air: a patient had come to us sick, exhibiting mysterious symptoms. With the combined clinical acumen of the internists, neurologists, radiologists, infectious disease specialists, lab technicians, and nursing staff of this academic medical center, we had plumbed the unknown and come up with the diagnosis.

I let the neurologists prattle on and on. I didn't need any official praise here at the neurology conference; I'd have my moment in the limelight in two weeks at my presentation. Anyway, I knew that it had been my decision to send the initial Lyme test. If it wasn't for that Lyme test, the diagnosis would never have been made, and this whole panel of esteemed experts would not be sitting in this room patting their own backs. What a fantastic case for my residency training to culminate in. Maybe I should submit this to the *New England Journal of Medicine!*

Someone had invited Mercedes to the conference, and she sat in the back listening quietly. I watched her from my vantage point in the corner. She looked wonderful — no hint of the illness that had caused that bizarre episode on her second hospital day. Her long, curly brown hair was lustrous against her olive skin. She looked perfectly healthy. I smiled proudly. What a true success story.

I went to say hello to Mercedes at the end of the conference, but she had no recollection of me or of her initial days in the hospital. Her family, however, recognized me and thanked me for her early care. I shook Mercedes's hand heartily and congratulated her on her recovery. Her hand was warm and plump and her handshake reassuringly healthy. The conference lasted all Friday afternoon. I was looking forward to a relaxing weekend, because Monday was "switch day," and I'd be going to the intensive care unit. Though I loved the ICU, I knew I'd have no free time for the entire month. I'd be working thirty-six-hour shifts every three days, which added up to only one free Saturday for the entire month. But I knew I could make it — it was the last month of my residency, and on June 30 it would all be over. In fact, the ICU was a great way to end. I'd work like a maniac and then be done with everything. Since I wasn't starting a fellowship, I'd have the whole summer ahead of me to enjoy.

Monday morning our new team gathered in the ICU. There was a crackle in the air from all the different machines breathing life into our critically ill patients. We rounded on all of our new patients as a tightly organized team, talking in easy jargon, with no need to translate for anyone. At each bedside was a computer loaded with data for each patient. We raced each other to calculate arterial alveolar gradients and oxygen extraction ratios. We reeled off ventilator management strategies, debating the relative values of positive endexpiratory pressure versus continuous positive airway pressure. I marveled at how easy it all was. For an intern, or even a second-year resident, the ICU was a terrifying place, especially the first day. But now I took it all in stride. Just another twelve sick patients on ventilators with arterial lines and Swans. Let 'em crash; let 'em code; I could handle it. That's what ten years of Bellevue training does for you.

That evening I was home alone, gathering my thoughts about my new set of patients. It was only Monday, but it was clear it was going to be an exciting month. My residency was going to end in style. Our team would get this ICU into top shape.

I ran down my list of patients. Whom could we improve? There was that lady in bed 3, on two different antibiotics for an abdominal abscess. Maybe she could use a third. But that could wait until tomorrow. And the guy in bed 12 with esophageal cancer. His family had been vacillating on the DNR. I'd call the brother first thing in the morning.

The old guy in bed 5 who'd stroked out last month — left side not moving, already demented from Alzheimer's. I wasn't sure if his ventilator settings were optimized; his peak pressures had been fluctuating. If I could get the latest blood-gas results, I could make the adjustments over the phone and then see his new numbers before rounds in the morning. Why wait until tomorrow if I could keep that patient one step ahead? I propped my feet up on my couch and tore open a bag of chile-and-lime tortilla chips. One hand dialed the phone while the other plunged into the bag.

Instead of the clerk who usually answers the phone, George, one of the other residents, happened to answer. We chatted for a while about how much fun the ICU was — what a great way to end residency. We discussed the ventilator management of bed 5 and agreed to lower flow rate but increase the tidal volume. I asked how his first night on call was going.

"What a night," George said. "We've been incredibly busy. One cardiac arrest, one septic shock. But my third admission is the most interesting."

"Really," I said. "What did you get?"

"It's a surprise. Something rare. But you'll see on tomorrow's rounds."

"C'mon, George," I said between chomps of chips. "Give me a hint."

"It's a good one. You ain't never seen this before."

"Listen, I covered for you on your anniversary last March. You owe me one." I pestered him some more, and he finally relented. In a conspiratorially low voice, to tantalize my curiosity, he said, "Read up on Lyme meningitis for rounds tomorrow."

The chips and chili turned to sawdust in my mouth. "That's strange," I said. "I just had a case of Lyme meningitis three weeks ago." I could feel the muscles in my neck tightening. My throat began to constrict. Please, God, don't let it be the same person. Don't let it be Mercedes.

"Yep, that's the one," George said.

Mercedes? In the ICU? I had just seen her on Friday, and she was fine. How could she be in the ICU on Monday? I jammed the telephone against my ear, struggling to absorb the story that was being transmitted.

On Saturday, George told me, Mercedes had experienced another headache. On Sunday her headache worsened, so she came to the ER. Nothing was found on physical exam, and she was sent home with a diagnosis of "postmeningitic headache," a frequent phenomenon.

On Monday, this afternoon, she had complained of the "worst headache of her life," accompanied by nausea and vomiting. She returned to the ER, and this time she was admitted to the hospital. The doctors who spoke with her said she was able to give a coherent history of her recent treatment and again had a perfectly normal neurological exam. Nonetheless, they sent her for a CT scan of her head.

The CT scan lasted about fifteen minutes. When the technician went to help her out of the scanner, he found her unresponsive. A code was called, but by the time the code team arrived, her pupils were already fixed and dilated, a sign of irreversible brain swelling. She was brought to the ICU, where a hole was drilled in her skull in an attempt to relieve the pressure, but it was too late.

Steroids were given to decrease the inflammation. Antibiotics of every stripe were administered. Various maneuvers to lower her intracranial pressure were attempted — artificially increasing her breathing rate, angling the bed to keep her head above her feet, infusing massive doses of osmotic diuretics — but none worked. Now she lay in bed 10 of the ICU, her breathing maintained by a ventilator . . . brain dead.

Tests for tuberculosis, lupus, syphilis, vasculitis, and other inflammatory diseases were performed, and all were negative.

"Could this all be from the Lyme?" I stammered into the phone.

"Nah," George replied. "We sent another Lyme titre, and it came back negative. This ain't Lyme. The first Lyme was a false positive." His voice faded for a minute as he told one of the nurses to suction bed 4.

How could a young woman whom we had presumably cured, who had been so alive and healthy three days ago, be brain dead now?

I could not absorb the story as it was relayed to me over the phone. How could she be brain dead? I had been there on Friday. I had touched her and felt her warm and alive skin just seventy-two hours ago. It couldn't be the same person.

I stormed back and forth in the two cramped rooms of my Manhattan apartment. Eventually I called a pulmonologist I knew and paged two of my residency colleagues, but the case didn't make any sense to them either. I called my nonmedical friends, just to calm myself, but the very act of converting all of the clinical terminology into lay language frustrated me unbearably. I tore my textbooks off the shelves, ripping through the indexes for answers. I upended the contents of my Mercedes/Lyme folder, scouring the fine print in the scientific papers, hurling them aside when they proved useless.

Lyme in the inner city? How could I have been so stupid? So what did she have? Mercedes had received treatment for everything when she'd been in the hospital the first time: acyclovir for herpes encephalitis, regular antibiotics for bacterial meningitis, full treatment for Lyme. All the other tests were negative.

This could not be happening. This Mercedes George had told me about could not be the same as the Friday Mercedes who'd smiled at me when I shook her hand. The Friday Mercedes was real. This Monday Mercedes was just a case report over the phone.

I knew that there was nothing I could do. The neurosurgeons were already there, and the head of the infectious disease unit had personally examined Mercedes. She was already receiving the best nursing and medical care available. Everything would still be the same on morning rounds a few hours from now. Also, if I went in at this late hour I might be overstepping my bounds by insinuating that George's care was inadequate. Besides, once the pupils are fixed and dilated, everyone knows that there is nothing else to do.

But it was now two A.M. I couldn't sit still, and I'd run out of friends whom I could call at that hour. I tried to convince myself that it would be for the greater good of all my patients if I just calmed down and got a good night of sleep so I could function in the morning. But my hands wouldn't stop trembling, and I had already eaten all the chocolate I could unearth in my apartment. I had to see Mercedes with my own eyes.

I pulled on an old pair of scrubs and set off on First Avenue. The street was quiet; even the homeless had gone off somewhere to sleep. The gloomy brick behemoths of the old Bellevue buildings cast spooky shadows in the moonlight. The decaying TB sanatorium and mental hospital menaced from behind the tall cast-iron gates. The dusky ivy on the brick buildings made the walls look moist and velvety. Scalloped columns in an abandoned courtyard poked eerily out of the ground, like portals into some dark nether-world. I waded through the midnight heaviness, my feet only vaguely aware of the sidewalk beneath them. By the faint lights in the garden in front of Bellevue, I could just see the dark shadows that were the birdbath and fountain.

Inside the hospital building it was brightly lit. I squinted at the shock of light as I walked down the long white hallways, past the closed coffee shop, past the darkened candy store, past the sleepy security guard. Upstairs, the wards were alive with the night shift: orderlies wheeling newly admitted patients from the ER to their rooms, night float interns replacing IVs, clerks taking coffee breaks, nurses giving late-night doses of medicines. I felt blurry from the incongruity of it all. The Mercedes I had seen on Friday had disappeared, and another patient, all but dead, had been sub-stituted. How could normal hospital life go on when such un-earthly metamorphosis was occurring in its midst?

From the ICU doorway I saw George addressing Mercedes's fam-ily and friends, who were gathered around bed 10. I edged in closer, but the bed was obscured by the people standing around it. George was trying vainly to explain the finality of the situa-tion. Mercedes's mother and two sisters were sobbing openly. Her brother stood motionless, bewildered. Some friends clustered around the sisters, hugging them and weeping. The aunt was pleading through her tears, "Isn't there another medication to try? Can't she be transferred to another hospital that has some experi-mental treatment for this? Don't you have an expert here who knows more?"

George escaped from the family when he caught sight of me and pulled me aside at the nurses' desk. He didn't seem surprised that I was standing in the ICU at two-thirty A.M. on a noncall night. "I've been trying for hours to explain her condition to them, but they just won't accept it. They know you from before. Maybe you can convince them."

I hovered by the supply cart, gathering my courage. In the surreal penumbra of the night ICU, the family appeared like a landscape: a range of backs, with shadowed peaks and dips, sur-rounded a central canyon. The fluorescent lights from the bed glinted up off their faces, creating awkward silhouettes and oddly sculpted ravines. I crept closer to the rocky-looking human formation, hoping that no one would notice me. Though queasy with nervousness, I was drawn forward by the light. I had to see what was on the other side of them. The air seemed to thin as I neared, and I had to work harder to breathe. My stomach rebelled, and I placed a hand on it to keep it down. A rivulet of yellowish green light seeped from between the mother and one of the cousins. I peered between them, into the crack of light, to see what lay in bed 10.

It was Mercedes, the one that I knew, with luminous cheeks and luxurious black hair cascading on the pillow. Her eyelids were softly closed, and the dark lashes rested in delicate parallel lines upon her olive cheeks. Her gold filigree cross floated on the plump, unblemished skin of her neck. Her respirations were calm and even, thanks to the ventilator. Apart from the breathing tube, she looked like a beautiful, healthy woman who was only sleeping.

From the electronic monitors overhead, though, a different story was evident. The red line that indicated the pressure inside Mercedes's head was undulating menacingly at the edge of the screen, nearly off the scale entirely. Despite all of the medical interventions, her brain was swelling inside the solid walls of her skull. A pressure chamber was roiling inside those unforgiving cranial bones, driving the base of her brain out the bottom of her skull. The respiratory center of her brain was already destroyed by the relentless onslaught. The cardiac center would soon follow.

Her brother noticed me standing behind the crowd, and the whole family turned to me. Nobody said anything, but I could feel their desperation. I was still trying to convince myself that this was the same Mercedes, this beautiful, sleeping woman whom we had so triumphantly diagnosed with Lyme disease. And all because I'd sent that damn test.

The intracranial pressure alarm clanged overhead, forcing me to look again at the ominous red line. It was creeping upward inexorably, mocking my ten years of training, my ludicrous Lyme test. It was all over. Mercedes's brain was slipping out, and I had no way to catch it.

I gazed at the nine people standing before me with their swollen eyes and tear-stained cheeks. How could I get them to believe that it was hopeless? I wanted to explain how brain death is different from a persistent vegetative state, where the cardiac and respiratory centers in the brain are intact. The body can breathe and pump blood for a long time, even if a person is unconscious, but brain death is different. Brain death is death. The body can no longer carry out the most basic functions. Even on a ventilator, the person cannot "live" for very long.

The family waited for words, but I could only stare at Mercedes. I wished I weren't a doctor. I wanted the freedom to hold false hope. Usually when I've had to explain to a family that a patient is dying, the patient graciously assists me by looking the part. They are pale or emaciated, or in pain, or struggling for breath: they look like death. But Mercedes refused to play along. Serenely she lay, as beautiful as she'd been three days ago: no scars from repeated IVs and blood draws, no skin ulcers from prolonged immobility, no dull coating of the skin from weeks of not seeing the sun. No, she looked steadfastly alive.

There is no gray area in brain death, though. Mercedes's apparent vitality was just an illusion, created by the ventilator and the short duration of her condition. In a day or two her body would swell up and her skin would grow dusky. The cardiac center of her brain would be smothered by the persistent intracranial swelling, and her heart would finally give out. Then she would look like the death that we know.

The hospital chaplain arrived, a rotund, balding Catholic priest whom I had seen around the hospital but never met. A Bellevue ID card and a wooden crucifix dangled from his neck. He slowly made his way around the bed, touching each family member, offering tissues, murmuring softly. I could see the family members relax ever so slightly at his touch. With his pudgy white hands, he seemed to spread soft dapples of comfort. His job looked so much more palatable than mine.

He glanced at me from across the bed, where he was standing with one of the sisters, and he must have seen a tear welling up in my eye. He circled back to where I stood and silently reached out his arm and rested it on my shoulder. My stethoscope twisted off my neck onto the floor as I leaned into his black tunic and began to cry. His arms circled around me, and my body reacted to that touch, unraveling and letting go. I collapsed deeper into his chest, sobbing and sobbing. I prayed that I would regain my composure so I could give the medical explanation that I had been dispatched to deliver. But I could not. The family stared with quiet amazement as I cried uncontrollably in the arms of a strange priest. One of the sisters left Mercedes's side and came to me. She stroked my back, her fingers running along my hair. I only bawled louder. Unable to stop, I mumbled something incoherent and dashed out of the ICU, stumbling over my stethoscope on the floor. I escaped into a deserted conference room, where I sat hunched over in the dark, crying. The sobs hacked out of me in dry, ragged spasms as I fought for breath. I couldn't understand why I was crying so hard. I did not know Mercedes or her family very well. I had only by chance cared for her on the first two days of her admission, and again only by chance happened to telephone the ICU tonight for an unrelated reason. I could so easily have missed one or both parts of her story, but fate had me present at both ends.

Only seventy-two hours ago we doctors had celebrated our prowess in saving her life. We had been so self-congratulatory about our diagnosis. Were we being punished for our hubris? I cried for Mercedes. I cried for her family and her two little children. I cried for all the patients who had died during my years at Bellevue. I cried for the death of my belief that intellect conquers all.

When I ran out of tears and stamina, I limped back to the ICU and said quiet, embarrassed goodbyes to Mercedes's family. The older sister handed me my stethoscope. She took my hand, looked me straight in the eye, and said "thank you" with such sincerity that I felt guilty. Her sister was dying, and instead of me comforting her, she was giving comfort to me.

I walked out of Bellevue in a daze. It was raining and I didn't have an umbrella. Dawn hadn't yet risen over the East River, but the air was lighter. I was exhausted, but felt strangely relieved. That uncontrollable nervous energy had finally abated, and the drenching rain felt cleansing.

I stayed up the rest of the night and wrote down as much about Mercedes as I could remember. For the first time in my ten years of medical training, sleep did not interest me.

The next day the ICU was utter chaos. Neurosurgeons, neurologists, infectious disease specialists, internists, ethicists, social workers, and nursing leaders were all packed into the ICU, intrigued and horrified by the confounding case.

Mercedes's aunt was adamant about not turning the ventilator off. She threatened a lawsuit and tried to intimidate the medical team by flaunting her close friendship with a district attorney. I doubted she really thought we were giving Mercedes substandard care, but her panicky desperation made her willing to do anything to prevent Mercedes's death.

The reality was that the family had no say in such a decision, because Mercedes was brain dead. The ventilator was merely breathing oxygen into a dead body. But the ICU staff agreed that we could delay the moment of turning it off until everyone in the family had come to accept it.

Mercedes's entire extended family was camped out in the ICU. The nurses had long since given up enforcing the two-visitors-at-a-time rule. There was a young man in the terminal throes of AIDS in bed 8. He also possessed a huge, distraught Hispanic family. In the middle of everything, the organ transplant team slipped in, coolly evaluating Mercedes for possible organ donation. They sat in the corner reviewing her chart and making endless phone calls. In the end they could find no hospital to accept her organs, because of the unknown cause of her demise.

By nine that night, we had finally convinced the aunt that there was no more to do. With everyone at the bedside, we turned the ventilator off, and the breathing stopped. Mercedes was really dead.

Three weeks later I completed my internal medicine residency. My ten years at Bellevue had finally ended. There was little pomp as I limped out of the ICU all alone on a rainy Sunday morning after my final thirty-six-hour shift. Bed 2 was coding, but somebody else was taking care of it.

My body drooped with exhaustion, and my soul felt drained, aching for rest. I couldn't think of anything except unloading these 206 bones into a soft, warm, horizontal bed. I couldn't imagine opening a newspaper tomorrow, much less starting a fellowship or a job, as most of my colleagues were doing. I needed repose.

I knew that I had to get out of Bellevue, even if for just a little while — away from residency, away from training, away from death. I didn't know exactly what I wanted to do, but I knew I had to do something different.

I signed up with a locum tenens agency that would allow me to do short-term medical jobs anywhere in the country — after a two-month summer break, of course. I planned to work only one month at a time and then travel as far as the money would take me. I wanted to go to Central America to see the native countries of so many of my patients at Bellevue. I wanted to learn the language that had prevented me from communicating with them. And I had to write down my stories from Bellevue.

I purchased a laptop computer that fit into my backpack. I stocked up on as many novels as I could carry and canceled my subscription to the *New England Journal of Medicine* for a full year.

But Mercedes continued to haunt me. For the next two years, between my travels and my locum assignments, I cornered every neuropathologist who could spare a moment to listen. I faxed her case history to experts at different medical centers and hounded them with phone calls, but no one had an answer for me. Mercedes's autopsy was performed at the New York City medical examiner's office, in the basement of the building where I'd stood as a nervous first-year medical student watching my first autopsy ten long years ago. I remembered the spacious, echoing room. I envisioned Mercedes's unblemished body stretched out on a metal table with the troughs around it to catch the blood. I wondered if the rubber-aproned pathology residents looked at her and saw a sleeping beauty. But the autopsy was "unrevealing," and every test was negative or "nondiagnostic." The medical examiner eventually signed the case out as "unknown etiology."

What will Mercedes's children think of the medical profession, I've often wondered. Their mother, of whom they'll have only dim recollections, died mysteriously, and the doctors never knew why. I wanted to go to them and apologize for our shortcomings, our limited intellect, our inadequate tools, the false pride that led us down the wrong path, our utter failure. But they are in their own world, being raised by a loving extended family.

And while I was intellectually frustrated, I felt strangely emotionally complete. That night in the ICU with Mercedes was excruciatingly painful, but it was also perhaps my most authentic experience as a doctor. Something was sad. And I cried. Simple logic, but so rarely adhered to in the high-octane world of academic medicine.

Standing in the ICU, the chaplain's arms around me, surrounded by Mercedes's family, I felt like a person. Not like a physician or a scientist or an emissary from the world of rational logic, but just a person. Like each of the other persons who were locked in that tight circle around bed 10. There was a strength in that circle that I'd never felt from my colleagues or my professors. A strength that allowed me to relinquish the tense determination for intellectual mastery that had so supported me as a doctor. After years of toning those muscles, it was a deliriously aching relief to let them go slack. And it didn't turn me away from medicine; it enticed me. I did need a break, but I knew that I would come back. I still wanted to learn more and be a smarter doctor, but I also wanted to be in this world populated with living, breathing, feeling people. I wanted to be in this sacred zone that was alive with real feelings, theirs and mine. I didn't know why I had initially entered the field of medicine ten years ago, but I now knew why I wanted to stay.

DARRYL PINCKNEY

Busted in New York

FROM THE NEW YORKER

HOW LONG had it been since I'd been out late on the Lower East Side? Back in the New Wave bohemian days of the late 1970s and early 1980s, the Lower East Side was the capital of mischief. The low life was still literary. I could be persuaded to go anywhere in search of an authentic urban experience. But then my friends grew up, and I moved far away, as Europe seemed to me at the time. Because I don't drink and run wild anymore, because I now live down a dirt track in the English countryside, a Manhattan roomful of the young and the smooth can be intimidating.

But the reggae club the summer before last was known as a chill lounge. Rona let her hair hang over the beat. We were waiting for Billie. I was telling myself not to have a hard time waiting. I was looking forward to my session with that inner-child finder, marijuana. The reggae swelled around me. My head bobbed like a duck's when there's bread on the water. I saw what looked like a ballet dancer's leg. Billie, and a Billie who knew the score. Her opening drink would not take long. We were going to step outside. We couldn't smoke pot in this reggae club. Not even in a reggae club? That's how long it had been since I'd been out late on the Lower East Side.

Street lamps threw a spotlight over pedestrians crossing Second Avenue. Killer taxis left unpleasant gusts. I leaned into the summer heat. Soon we three were alone in the dark of Sixth Street. Rona checked behind her. Then, like backup singers on the downbeat, Billie and I snapped glances over our right shoulders. Maybe some people wouldn't have bothered, but we were pros. We were veter-

ans of the streets. Rona fired one up, and passed it. We were chat-
ting. I hogged it. We were drifting toward midnight. Billie handed
it back to Rona. Three shapes in front of a doorway decided to
heckle us. "You're having a good time." They sounded like unappe-
tizing old kids. We moved to the curb. "We know what you're doing." Rona pushed her hand against the air to let them know that
the joke, whatever it was, had to stop. "Smoke it." We shook our
heads at their being so boisterous when they were maybe getting
high themselves, and in a doorway, of all places. We should have
looked ahead instead of behind.

We saw the corner and we saw the big man in white-guy plaid
shorts cutting a pigeon-toed diagonal from across the street. Everything about him was aimed toward us. His bright white sneakers
continued to rise and fall in our direction. A huge meatpacking
arm was held out to us, and a big voice was coming at us, too. His
other arm came out of his undershirt with a square of ID. We had
to keep moving toward him, like something swirling down a drain.
There now seemed to be enough light for a film crew's night
shoot. How could we have missed the blue unmarked van parked
on the other side of Sixth Street?

"Been smoking something?" No answer. "Put your hands flat on
the trunk of this car." The women, my friends, were side by side at
the back of the car. I was on the sidewalk and had to bend over.
Other undercovers quickly appeared. "We're going to empty your
pockets." A woman had taken up position behind Rona and Billie.
I felt a hand go into my pocket. My total financial assets held by a
faded money clip hit the trunk of the car. "Did you all just meet tonight?" a new voice demanded. "No." My own voice was thin and
completely lacking in the authority of outrage. The money clip was
followed by a pack of menthol cigarettes, a disposable lighter, a
case containing reading glasses, a John Coltrane–Johnny Hartman
CD — "You listen to some good music," a head of hair said — and
a mobile phone. "Where's your beeper?" He patted me down. "You
got a beeper?" "No," came the thin reply.

The detectives murmured. They'd found the smallest stub of
weed in a matchbook in Rona's pocket. The woman detective left.
The detective with the hair asked the ladies to step over to the sidewalk. Where Plaid Shorts had, like me, the beginnings of his father's stomach, this one had pecs and biceps rolling out of a ma-

genta tank top. He looked like a television actor in the role of
maverick cop. The rest of him was in the suburban version of casual: crisp bluejeans and clean sneakers.

"So you guys just met tonight?" Tank Top asked. It was my turn.
He was going to compare answers. Plaid Shorts said he was going
over to the van to check something. "How do you know each
other?" Tank Top demanded. "School." If he identified us as middle class, wouldn't he have to watch himself? Maybe I was trying to
prick some white blue-collar resentment; anything to turn the tables a little. When he asked about my beeper, I thought maybe
he hoped he'd interrupted something good, criminally speaking,
such as a black dude giving two white chicks a taste of the street
herb they were about to buy or get ripped off for. But if he saw that
we were OK, then the paperwork on the citation that they gave out
in these cases would speed up. One black guy with gray in his
beard and one and a half white girls, not two, because by that time
they must have figured out that Billie's honey skin and the Asian
cast to her eyes and her Church of England accent were some
weird Caribbean story. Yes, Officer, I wanted to explain, the one
with the henna highlights is a famous Jewish scientist, the daughter
of the British Commonwealth is a banker, and I'm a black guy who
needs two pairs of glasses and won't be on your computer lists, not
even a credit rating.

Billie and Rona had shown no emotion until Plaid Shorts
brought the handcuffs. Then they gave out soft, pastel exclama-
tions. Plaid Shorts led them, affronted and vulnerable, across the
street to the side door of the van. I thought, Rona's daughter walks
just like her. I felt my watch being removed. Tank Top put my arms
behind me and pushed my hands high up my back. I felt the metal
around my wrists. I thought of my parents and how they would
hurl themselves into this if they found out. I felt and heard the
handcuffs lock. I thought of my parents and their lawsuits. Back in
the good old days, they'd sued our hometown police department
to force it to desegregate, and when that worked they sued the fire
department — things they did in their spare time, as good citizens,
as blacks of their generation, members of the NAACP rank and
file. Injustice had only to ring their doorbell, and they were off to
the poorhouse. And here was frivolous me letting a white man put
me in handcuffs for something other than protest. I remembered

what my father had said to my tears at my sister's memorial the year before: Keep it together.

But I was in shock. "I'm going to be sick." I was starting to list from side to side. "Have you been drinking?" "No." I was going deaf. "I'm going to pass out." Tank Top gripped me just below my right armpit, and we started off, but my feet waited before they followed my legs. The world broke into silent, colorful particles. I got to the door and fell flat into the van. Rona's face floated. I began to hear her. I concentrated on finding her face in one place, something I could get up for and move toward, even if only on my knees. "Don't hurt him," Rona and Billie called. "I'm trying to help him," Tank Top countered.

Keep it together, I chanted to myself. Not because I was a black man in handcuffs in front of two white guys; not because I was powerless, which made it all the more necessary at least to imitate the examples of dignity in confrontations with police which I'd witnessed; and not because I was a grown man losing it in front of two women who, though in handcuffs, were trying to defend me. But because they were my friends. They were the ones with children at home. I crawled over to my friends in the seatless, windowless rear of the van, dripping sweat on them.

Plaid Shorts yanked the van into the street. Because we couldn't grab, and there was nothing to grab on to, we rolled into Alice-down-the-rabbit-hole positions, and rolled again when Plaid Shorts hit the gas. "This is such bullshit," Billie said to the ceiling. "This sucks," Plaid Shorts said. But he wasn't talking to us. He looked across to Tank Top. "You got that right." "A big one," Plaid Shorts added. "Hate it," Tank Top said to his window. "Total bullshit." Rona had dusted off her repertoire of apt facial expressions. This one said, "Are these guys for real?" "Five more years, man, and then I'm out," Plaid Shorts said. "I can't wait to just do my band." He did a near wheelie around a corner. We shouldered back up into sitting positions pretty expertly after two corners. Tank Top took some gum from the dashboard and said he had to keep at this bullshit until he could pay off his wife. He told Plaid Shorts that instead of alimony he was offering his wife a once-in-a-lifetime, can't-refuse lump sum. "It's like a buyout."

The acid-driven power chords of Pink Floyd took over the van. Rona's expression said, "These guys are too much." "They're wild," Billie's eyes said back as she looked for the place behind her where the music was blaring from. Maybe the detectives were trying to tell us something. Not that they were nice guys who regrettably had to do their job but that they were better than the job they'd been reduced to doing, and that they, too, had aspirations. The Rolling Stones came on next, and Plaid Shorts sang along. The music was perhaps meant to say that they weren't uncool, redneck cops having a blast at the expense of the liberal, the black, and the in-between. I was too ashamed to be sympathetic. Being addressed as "sir" by Tank Top only after I had shown weakness and fear — that was humiliating. A cop could go off at any time. I'd thought of that and had been afraid, and there was no way to take it back. And for what had I lost my self-respect? For an offense the detectives thought beneath their training. What did you do last night? Oh, I was picked up for a reefer and I fainted like a man. The van went up one street and down another. We couldn't see much, but most likely we were driving around and around as various undercover operations didn't work out. On one dark corner we waited so long in the van by ourselves that we almost slept.

The van door slid open, and in the shaft of light Tank Top was helping a Hispanic woman, maybe in her fifties, climb aboard the bummer bus. "Hey, Officer," she said when we were under way. "My hands too hot." The detectives parked and helped Rona and Billie out. Tank Top said, "I'm going to loosen these tight cuffs, like you asked." Then he turned off the lights, slammed the door, and left me with this woman who made unsavory sounds in the dark. I thought she was trying to ditch her vials of crack and the detectives would then claim that they were mine. I went over on my side, practicing the I-was-asleep defense. They put Rona and Billie back in the van, turned on the lights, drove off, stopped again, and got out by themselves. As soon as the doors closed, the Hispanic woman, who'd freed her hands, whipped out a big bag of heroin, snorted it on her knee, and deftly worked her hands back into the cuffs. Rona was laughing in disbelief. Quietly, the Hispanic woman zoned sidewise. The detectives, when they got back in, firmly looked straight ahead.

The next time the van door opened, a Hispanic man, maybe also in his fifties, climbed in. A dark Rasta youth was pushed in after him. "Ooh," the Hispanic guy said, and tried to shift himself. He nodded greetings of solidarity. What he'd been oohing about hit Rona's hygiene radar first. It made delicate Billie draw in her legs. The gleaming Rasta youth sprawled before us had matted dreadlocks that looked like what comes from the back of a furnace when its filter is changed. Maybe I should have thought harder about this being someone's son, but the stench was overpowering. Meanwhile, he kept up a stream of Babylon raas claat denunciations of the police. He shouted curses on the white man. I thought, Rasta, my brother in Garvey, you are on your own. The detectives paid him no mind. They'd made their quota for the shift.

We'd been smoking a joint right around the corner from the local precinct house, that's how hip we were. The detectives took us inside and the handcuffs came off. After three hours, it was a relief to see my fingers. Tank Top took me and the Rasta youth upstairs to a grotty corridor, and the strip search began. He made the Rasta youth wait in the shadows at the end. He ordered me to hand him my clothes item by item. I was to turn around, bend over, and drop my shorts. He said quickly that that was enough. I was to take off my socks and turn them inside out. "Get dressed." He asked if I'd ever been arrested. No. He said he would try to tell me what was going to happen. I thought I understood. He motioned to the Rasta and sent me downstairs. He and the Rasta followed moments later. Tank Top had returned my property, except for the phone and the CD. Such stuff had to go over to the lockup at Central, he explained. If that was the case, then the Rasta youth had a prayer shawl and a Torah for Central to deal with. Tank Top tried to talk when he took my fingerprints. "So what kind of things do you write?" After that, he had paperwork to finish. Now and then, he would dial a telephone number, mutter, hang up, and shrug. A clock kept vigil over a wall of "Most Wanted" leaflets.

When Plaid Shorts announced that we were moving, around five o'clock in the morning, the Hispanic man asked how much money I had on me. I'd covered the money clip with my hand when Tank Top passed it to me, but, clearly, I hadn't been quick enough. The Hispanic man said I couldn't bring in anything where we were going, because it would get taken off me. He informed Plaid Shorts, who agreed that I'd get robbed. Rona put my belongings, even my glasses, in her pocket. My property would be safer in the women's section, the Hispanic man advised as we were put back into handcuffs and then linked to one another. I was made to lead our daisy chain of handcuffs through the precinct's main room. As Plaid Shorts increased the pace, two officers by the front door erupted into grunting song. "Working on the chain gang, uh."

We hopped out of the van into a street that was still dark. A semicircle of light waited for us to approach. This was the Tombs, that place I'd heard about, read about. Two more daisy chains of prisoners joined ours as Tank Top, having rung twice, banged on the metal grating over the entrance. It rolled up. Plaid Shorts and Tank Top surrendered us in a series of rapid clipboard signatures. When I realized that they intended to abandon us at this concrete threshold, I wanted to ask them when they planned to read us our rights. I'd begun to think of them as our undercovers. They were responsible for us. But they were gone, and we were across the line, and the metal grating was coming down.

I followed a black female corrections officer's rump up some stairs. A black male corrections officer unhooked everybody. My eyes stayed on Rona and Billie when they were ordered to move to the other side of the corridor. The women went in one direction, the men in another. Green bars streamed along either side of me as I hurried both to keep up with the corrections officer who was now taking us down to the basement and to keep ahead of someone whose footsteps menaced my heels.

The Rasta youth and I were directed into the last cell of the long jail. I insinuated myself onto the narrow metal bench that went from the bars of the cell to the rear wall, where it made a right angle toward the partition that hid the toilet. Nine mute, tired faces emphasized how cramped and stuffy the tiny cell was. One man was curled up asleep under the bench.

I didn't want to look too intently at the other men in judicial storage, in case to do so meant something I could not handle the consequences of. I also didn't want to look away too quickly when my gaze happened to meet someone else's. However, no one was interested in hassling the new arrivals. Men were waking up, and their banter competed with the locker room–type noise coming from the corrections officers' oblong station desk. A short white girl with thick glasses and a rolling lectern called my name. She said the interview was to determine who was eligible for bail, but the questions also separated the wheat from the chaff, socioeconomically speaking. Some guys probably had no job, no taxable weekly income, no address, no mother's address. She lost patience with the Rasta youth's decent background. "Education? How far did you get in school?" A community college degree. Her head was tilted up toward the spectacle of his hair. "We'll say grade fifteen."

Some time later, the Rasta youth and I were summoned again. But again we were going only a few yards. A black corrections officer shooed aside someone blocking the door of the new cell, which was large and, sneaked glances told me, held some huge dudes. Fresh apprehension was bringing my body to something like exocrine parity with the Rasta youth's. I didn't know what to expect, and so tried to prepare for the worst. We were shoulder to shoulder on a metal bench, like crows shuffling on a telephone wire. The move to this restless population had to be the final, dangerous descent, the reason I'd crammed my watch into my glasses case and handed everything off to Rona.

A black youth with his hair in tight break braids called out to a new arrival, my Hispanic comrade. "Come on in." The black youth's knuckles looked as big as Mike Tyson's. "They took the murderers out early." He slapped five with a couple of his hulking neighbors and concerned himself with what he could see of his reflection in the metal bench between his thighs. He said something more. I didn't hear what it was, but it must have been wicked.

A black corrections officer reversed himself and glared through the green bars. "What?" "Nothing, Mo," the black youth said loudly, evenly. Only one of his neighbors giggled. "Say what, chump?" He was going for the keys at his hip. "You say something?" He was so agitated that he couldn't get the key in. He was as tall as a basketball power forward. Everything he said was a variation of "You want to say something?" The cell door flew open, and in a few steps the corrections officer was over the massive head of twinkling break braids. "A real man would say something now." He waited for an answer. I could see him shaking. The black youth wasn't going to feed him any lines or provocation. The corrections officer pivoted toward the door. He had a baton on his belt, but no gun. He made a satisfied noise with his keys.

It was not an impressive performance. I knew that. The corrections officer hadn't come up with any good lines. He just kept repeating himself. I could tell that all twenty-four of my cellmates were thinking how off the hook the corrections officer had been to raise up — the lingo was coming to me — on somebody like that. I was getting excited, feeling that I was on the verge of bonding with the other guys in our high and hip judgment against the corrections officer. He didn't meet our rigorous standards when it came to "reading" someone in the street manner. The black youth with the oiled, sparkling braids delivered our verdict: "Definitely bugging behind something."

The black corrections officer flung the metal door so hard it bounced against the cell bars and rode back some. Giant steps put him in a place that blocked my view of the black youth. Spit was dancing from his head, pinwheel fashion, as he roared, "If I started to kick your black ass now, where would your black ass be next week?" I couldn't remember when I'd seen such sudden rage. It stopped all other activity in the basement. The tendons in his neck were ready to explode. I couldn't begin to think what his nostrils might be doing. Maybe our survival molecules were not the only ones to have been put on alert. Some of his colleagues had come by to monitor the situation. They turned back in a way that indicated they'd respect some code not to interfere. The cell was very still as the corrections officer made his exit. The street judgment was in the silence. Nobody wanted to look at him until he'd turned the lock. He'd made his point. He'd shown how dangerous was his longing to have a reason to lose control. The corrections officer's brown skin looked glazed, as though it had been fired in a kiln. He didn't seem to know how to finish his scene and stood wheezing by the bars. I almost thought he was going to mellow into the dispersal-of-balm-and-poultice phase of tough love. The mask of the shock-tactics practitioner would drop. He'd apologize, give advice, tell the young brothers how he was once on his way to being where they were. The black corrections officer said, "Remember. I'll be going home at four o'clock. You'll still be here. You're in jail. I'm not." Maybe I should have taken into account the possibility that he had seen and had a lot of trouble doing his job. Maybe he and the black youth already had a story going and I'd missed what started it. But that didn't matter. Only what he'd said about four o'clock mattered. It wasn't even nine o'clock in the morning yet. My Hispanic comrade was looking at me. He took his eyes heavenward and clasped his hands. Then he shot me an inaudible laugh.

Jail was going to get me over my fear of saying the obvious, because there was no way to ignore all morning the fact that everyone in the cell was either black or Hispanic. The irony, for me, was that an all-black gathering usually meant a special event, a stirring occasion. I thought back to some black guys I used to know who enjoyed telling me that black guys like me ought to hang out with black groups like theirs. It flattered me to believe that I flattered them with my yearning for instruction in the art of how to be down with it. But this was not what they had in mind. The mood in the cell was like that of an emergency room in a city hospital: a mixture of squalor, panic, boredom, and resentment at the supposed randomness of bad luck.

Some guys, the Rasta youth among them, had elected to slip down onto the concrete floor. They were opting out of consciousness. Our cell had no television, no radio, no newspapers. There was a water fountain, a disgusting toilet, and two pay phones from which collect calls could be made. I don't know how those guys knew when the corrections officers had their backs turned, or how they'd held on to the contraband of drugs and matches they'd been thoroughly searched for, or how they knew who in which cell had what, but at one moment, as if by secret signal, paraphernalia went flying through green bars from cell to cell. The next thing I knew, guys were taking turns smoking crack behind the waist-high partition of the raised open toilet of our cell. Right there in the Tombs. I guess they figured there was no chance of the crack outsmelling the toilet. I'd switched seats and, as a result, was too near the burning funk. I saw my Hispanic comrade casually walk away from the hot spot, and soon I, too, got up and crossed the cell. His look of approval after I'd eased in somewhere else told me that I'd made the right move.

A black guy with broken teeth, dressed in a torn car coat, emerged from behind the toilet. He ambled around and then seized the floor. "You remember Lucky Lou Diamond? I had twenty thousand dollar over to Jersey City." I tuned in, eager for a jailhouse Richard Pryor who could turn the cell into something else. "Nineteen seventy-five? Bunny hat on my head? Your Honor. There's no mouth on the girl he touched." His free association promised much, but it gutter-balled into such incoherence that the black youth with break braids spoke for everyone when he barked, "Sit down."

It was quiet for a while, but then the Rasta youth snapped to attention. Something jerked him to his feet and set him standing squarely in front of the cell door, his right knee pounding out a steady rhythm. I thought, Just when things were manageable, my brother in Selassie has to flip out. I braced myself for his rap. But he was ready for his lunch. He was first in the line we were commanded to make; first to march out of the cell toward stacks of chalk-colored squares on long, low trolleys that looked like what bricks are transported on at a building site. We were to pick up a sandwich, turn, take a plastic cup of grape juice from another low trolley, and then march back to the cell.

A black guy in an orange jumpsuit — a trusty — called after me to let me know that I'd missed my allotted sandwich. Something about being urged to march rendered me unable to lift anything other than a cup of juice. Very soon the cell was strewn with sandwich remnants. Leaking sachets of mustard and mayonnaise found their way under the bench. A wedge of cheese crowned one of the pay phones. Lunch added to the odors of incarceration. However, there was plenty of room, because some of the men whose size so alarmed me when I first entered the cell had dived to the floor. I counted nine guys asleep in the grime, six of them in the fetal position, their wrists between their knees. Heads had to loll down some broad shoulders before they could touch concrete. A young, crack-thin guy woke and, using his palms for locomotion, crawled along on his stomach to the trash can, where he reached up to extract sandwich remains.

I overheard some of the guys say a little while later that the police had arrested so many people in the sweep of the previous evening that two special night courts had been set up to process the haul. They would start to call names at four o'clock. Waiting might have been easier had there been no clock. At the appointed hour, the only official movement came from the black corrections officer who'd flipped out that morning. I'm sorry to report that he went through all the transparent maneuvers of rubbing it in. He paraded by us on his way back to the oblong station desk, ostensibly laughing at himself for forgetting something. And, just in case the black youth with break braids was pretending to take no notice of him, the corrections officer brought over a white officer holding a clipboard and pointed at the youth. His colleague tapped him a Have-a-good-night. "I told you when you got here not to give me problems." The black youth looked toward the bars at last, his arms hugging his chest. The black corrections officer flicked a salute.

"Yo, Pops," I heard the black youth say once the air had calmed down again around us. "Pops," he called again in my direction. I couldn't believe that he was talking to me. Pops? Everybody in the cell who spoke to someone he didn't know said, "Yo, G." I pointed to myself. Who, me? "Mind my asking what you're in for?" I made a smoking gesture with two fingers of my right hand. "Uh-huh. You dress Italian. But." A neighbor of his wanted to give him five for that observation, but he just looked at him hard. It was true. The soundtrack of brotherhood in my head was nearly all Marvin Gaye. It had finally happened: I was older than a cartoon father on television. I was older than Homer Simpson.

I wasn't sure if Old Four Eyes in the Robert Hayden poem fled to "danger in the safety zones" or to "safety in the danger zones." It was important to me, sitting there in my concrete elsewhere, which seemed dirtier and dimmer the longer I had to wait.

As the cell emptied, it got eerier. The few new guys, dressed in their garrulous night selves, were out of sympathy with the general tone of exhaustion and passivity. One new guy ranted about calling his girlfriend to tell her to hook up a plane to Canada, because after he made bail he was going to step off, boy. Another, the lone white, clung to a pay phone. He suggested to a friend that they deceive his brother-in-law. "Don't tell him it's for me." He could press telephone numbers with amazing speed. He insisted to the next friend that she had to get the bail money out of her mother, because he could not, he said, shooting his eyes across us, the nonwhite, do Rikers.

My name was called, the cell door gapped open, and I floated out. Neither my Hispanic comrade nor the Rasta youth followed. I regretted that I would not have the chance to thank the man who had watched my back. Very soon I found myself upstairs in a new cell that had an iron-lattice screen. Beyond it was the outside world. I heard the voices of what I supposed were women corrections officers, and then over the walls I heard Billie and Rona in their interview cells. They heard me, we heard one another. The public defender on the free persons' side of the barrier was a heavyset white woman. She went from cubicle to cubicle, guiding us toward a plea: Adjournment in Contemplation of Dismissal, or ACD. If we didn't get picked up for the same offense within a twelve-month period, then the charge would be dropped. ACD. I told the PD that I'd used the pay phones. I knew that that afternoon a friend of mine had come zooming down with newspapers and a criminal lawyer and had been denied access. She said they were entitled to hold us for at least twenty-four hours before they had to do anything with us. I said that being in custody was the punishment. I said prosecution of so-called quality-of-life crimes was a form of harassment. She explained that under the circumstances they didn't have to read us our rights. I was about to compare such offenses to civil disobedience, but the last thing this calm and capable PD was interested in was anybody's vanity. She said that high arrest figures justified the large increase in the number of police on the streets. It was that simple.

In the courtroom, I felt as though we were guest speakers at a high school, the offenders with us behind the court recorder looked so tadpole, so young. We stood when the judge entered. "He's not that kind of judge," a black bailiff said. Maybe because I was minutes and a plea away from getting out, tenderness got the better of me. I thought of my older sister and her practice in defense of juvenile offenders valiantly conducted from files in shopping bags in the trunk of her car. Our case was called, and we sat some rows back from the attorneys' desks, where we were unable to hear the grim PD, even if we could have concentrated enough.

God bless the old-hippie souls who still believed in public life and social responsibility, I thought, but the PD had no time for effusive thanks. I'd been so hypnotized by green bars that the marble floor outside the courtroom was dazzling. The white clerks behind the counter in a payment-and-records office were accustomed to a stressed-out public and were rude back. Down in the lobby, Rona and Billie ran for the door marked "Women." I rushed over to a rickety blue booth for my fix of those former slave crops — tobacco, sugar, coffee.

*

Perhaps our elation on Rona's rooftop was unearned, but we felt like released hostages. We made jokes as soon as we had an audience of friends. Even the squalid bits, when told the right way, got laughs. Maybe we were defending ourselves against our deeper reactions to what had happened to us. Rona's husband said that now that his little boy was old enough to play in the street, he had had to tell him what to do should the police ever stop him. Don't move; do exactly what they say; take no chances; give no lip. We wondered how popular these sweeps would be after some more white people had been caught in the net.

We'd been abruptly deprived of our liberty, and that would always make for a chilling memory. And as I'd learned sitting in the cell with all those guys whose stories I didn't know and couldn't ask for: the system exists, the system — for the nonwhite young, the poor — is real. New arrest records had been created, but we were out, and friends were standing in wreaths of smoke, savoring the night view of fire escapes, water tanks, and lights in distant windows.

Six days after my release, I was back on the Lower East Side. I understood what Rona meant when she said that she fell in love with New York the day she realized that she could get a candy bar on every corner. But jail worked, it won. I thought, I'm not doing that again. The romance was over. For me, the changes in the streets went with everything else. Once upon a time, people moved to New York to become New Yorkers. Then people moved to New York and thought it perfectly OK to remain themselves. Goodbye, Frank O'Hara.

"Yo, Papi," I heard. I was astonished. It was my Hispanic comrade. They'd given him five days on Rikers Island for possession of a crack pipe. He was selling vinyl records on the sidewalk before he got moved off that bit of Second Avenue. Could I help him out? It would be my privilege. He said he remembered what the black youth with break braids had said when they took him out of that cell in the Tombs. "Kidnapped by the mayor, y'all."

RICHARD PRICE AND
ANNE HUDSON-PRICE

Word on the Street

FROM THE NEW YORK TIMES MAGAZINE

Cabby No. 1, Sept. 13

THE TAXI PULLS to the curb across the street from the Police
Academy on Twentieth and Third. Two thickly built, sandy-haired
young men emerge from the back seat.

As they exit, the driver, a Pakistani, pats his forehead with a paper towel and exhales so profoundly that it seems as if he had been
holding his breath since they entered his cab five and a half dollars
ago.

The new passenger, coming up on his blind side, slides into the
back without warning, unthinkingly slamming the door behind
him. The driver nearly levitates off his seat. "Broadway and Forty-
fourth?"

"Please, sir," he says, his voice feathery with tension. "Just give
me a moment."

Kids No. 1, Army-Navy, Sept. 18

"Dad? Do you know where I can get a pair of camouflage pants?
The whole team has to wear camo to school tomorrow."

"Why?"

"I don't know. It's a game day. Everybody has to wear the same
stuff on a game day."

"But why camo? With all that's going on right now, they have to pick camo?"

"*Dad*," her voice edged with tears, edged with the last eight days of her life. "It's *not* my *choice*."

"OK, OK," he quickly retreats. "No problem. No problem. How about an army-navy store?" he backpedals. "Let me call the one on Twenty-third Street, see if . . ."

They answer on the first ring — "Sorry, no more gas masks" — then hang up.

Cabby No. 2, Sept. 19

The driver is a heavyset man with a cropped beard. "God Is Great" is inscribed in Arabic on a Lucite placard that dangles from his rearview mirror along with a photograph of his two kids. There are more American flags fixed to the outside of his car than on a presidential motorcade.

"Thirty-third and Lex?"

"Yes," punching the meter. "So, sir. Are you having a good day?"

"Not really," the passenger says to the eyes in the rearview. "Are those your kids?"

"Yes," he answers. "My son and his sister. The boy goes to Stuyvesant, which is a problem right now; he has to take his classes at Brooklyn Tech. But the girl goes to St. John's, so there's no problem there. You have children yourself?"

"Yeah, two girls." Then, encouraged by the driver's chattiness: "Let me ask you, are people giving you a hard time out here?"

The driver's face slams down like a riot gate.

"Sir?" the passenger persists, trying to seek him out via the rearview mirror, but the driver maintains his silence, eyes on the road, all the way to Thirty-third Street, looking away even as he reaches back to accept the fare and tip.

Kids No. 2, Sept. 20

It took more than an hour to make it uptown to pick up his older daughter from her evacuated school that afternoon, another half hour to find her on the street and an hour and a half through the semi-locked-down streets of midtown to bring her back home.

"It was insane," she said. "It's like we were sitting in the cafeteria and we heard the fire alarm but really faintly, and we're looking at each other like, What bad judgment to have a fire drill now. You know, with everybody already freaked out as is. But OK, so, we leave the cafeteria, everybody's crammed into the hallways and you can't even move, I went maybe ten feet in five minutes.

"Then they say it's a false alarm, so we go back to lunch and we're all looking at each other like, That was not cool. A minute later, someone comes in, says: 'Get out. It *is* a drill. Get out *now*.'

"We're back in the hallway, packed, and because of the World Trade Center, a few people, me included, start thinking, Bomb. We get outside the building, I go up to a teacher and ask, 'Is this a fire drill or something else?'

"She says: 'I don't know, I don't know. Pretend it's not a drill and just *walk*. Walk away *now*.'

"I say, 'Should we go to our assigned evacuation spots?' She says: 'No. Just go. *Go*.' Then we see the bomb squad pull up.

"The kids who have cell phones are calling their parents and then they do something so unusual. They go up to other kids they don't even know and ask if anyone would like to call their parents, you know, offering them their phones; other kids announce that they live only two, three blocks away, and if anybody wants, they can come stay at their houses if they don't want to be out in the street. Everybody became so generous. It was almost worth the scare to see it.

"But then something happened, Dad? I don't think I'll ever get it out of my mind. There was this girl, my age, someone who I never thought of as particularly mature, kind of the opposite in fact, and, this girl, she goes up to one of the teachers and says very calmly, 'I want to get my sister from her class.' Teacher says: 'No. No way I can let you go do that.' The girl says, 'My sister is six years old, she gets scared easily, I know she wants me, and I am going to get her.' The teacher says: 'Look, she's with her own group, her own teacher, I'm sure she's fine. They probably told her it was just a fire drill.' And then, Dad, this girl, she says, 'But *I* know what's going on, and I *want* my *sister* with *me*.'"

His daughter takes a breather, her eyes glistening with unspilled tears. "I don't know, this girl, it's like in one minute flat, she went from being this flighty kind of kid to this instant adult. It's like she turned into iron. She was so strong and clear about things. I don't even really know her, but I felt so proud for her . . . But I also felt so sad."

Her tears finally ran the rims and spilled down her cheeks. "I wish I could really find the words to explain to you how I felt."

It took her three weeks, but the words finally came, showing up on her father's desk early one morning, deposited there on her way to school.

"Dad, it's like these days, there are adults, and there are children. Only two camps now, no intermediate zone for teenagers like myself. If you possess the information, if you understand what's going on in the world, you're an adult, no matter what your biological age; all others are children.

"There is nothing that traditional 'adults' know that this new breed of 'child-adult' doesn't, and the gut instinct of kids my age to go to their parents and demand comfort, answers, or whatever doesn't work now, because we are aware that we know just as much about the world as you do.

"So many of us have been forced into this new group overnight, like that girl I was telling you about and to some extent, myself.

"And along with the scariness that comes with being a member of this new group of adults without any actual adult experience is the sadness that we bear for the years we had to surrender in order to accept this mutual burden with you."

Royalty, Sept. 29

It's the night of the unification bout for the middleweight belt, Felix Trinidad versus Bernard Hopkins, and the Garden is boiling over with both the near insanity of a mass gathering so soon after the events of the eleventh and the anticipation of the state-of-the-art violence to come.

The crowd is mad for Felix Trinidad, and there are Puerto Rican flags everywhere, reproduced on T-shirts, head wraps, pennants, scarves, and, of course, flags as flags, flags so big it takes two men to display them; dozens of these tag teams work the landings between the multitiered seating sections, racing their pride around the natural oval of the building, blocking the view of hundreds of fans at a clip, although the general consensus seems to be for people to restrain themselves from shouting out something rude and to the point, because the vibes are such that anything, it feels, can lead to anything.

After two interminable hours of prelims, the fanfare that precedes a title bout finally begins. First there's the spotlighting of the usually schizophrenic mix of New York royalty in the crowd: Sharpton, Trump, Spike, Latrell, etc., followed by the calling up into the ring of past middleweight champs: Jake LaMotta, Emile Griffith, and other, less memorable title holders. The crowd doesn't really cut loose though until the spotlight falls on Roberto Duran. Looking more like a heavyweight these days, the ex-champ milks the cheers, grinning, dancing, bathing in the love . . .

But then, in the middle of his moment, there seems to be a secondary roar overtaking the first like a succeeding wave, this one a little stronger, a little more from the gut, and strangely enough, focused slightly to the side of the ring itself, people half rising now, some to cheer more loudly, others to track down the source, and there they are, maybe a dozen New York firemen in FDNY T-shirts and jeans, heading for their places of honor next to the cast of *Oz*, walking a little stiffly, some displaying awkward smiles, others giving up half-waves of acknowledgment, and one can only imagine the great sense of disorientation they must feel; heroes, grievers, survivors; the Garden really pouring it on now, the fervid cheers gradually becoming more articulate, breaking down into three distinct sounds: U.S.A. U.S.A. U.S.A.

Tentatively, as if lowering themselves into scalding water, the city's newest royalty take their seats. (P.S.: Hopkins won the fight.)

Cabby No. 3, Oct. 3

"Fifty-ninth and Madison?"

The cab heads uptown, flags fluttering, another Yankee Doodle express. "So how's it shaking out here?" the fare asks.

"Business is bad," the cabbie says. "Very bad. Come nine, ten o'clock? This city is dead."

"Are people giving you a hard time?"

"Not really." The driver turns to face his passenger at a red light. "They've been pretty good. Mostly it's kind of polite interrogations, like, 'Where are you from, what did you do back in your country before you came here, *why* did you come here?'" The light changes and he turns back to the traffic.

"Where do you come from?" the fare asks. "I'm just curious."

"Bangladesh," he says.

"So nothing ugly? Well, that's good to hear."

"I tell you," he says, making eye contact through the mirror. "Do you know what I miss the most? The small talk. I enjoyed that very much. Now they get in, say take me to such and such and then nothing. Except for, you know, like I said, the polite interrogations."

"No, I hear you," his passenger says.

"Like you," the driver says, briefly turning again. "Like now."

Kids No. 3, Oct. 9

"Dad? Can I tell you something, you promise not to get mad at me?"

"Not really."

"I dropped my cell phone in the toilet," his younger daughter says. "It's dead."

"Don't worry about it. Take mine."

"Seriously?" Then, with as much guilt as relief, "What are you going to use?"

"Not your problem. It's just, you know, with everything going on these days? It makes me breathe easier to know that I can reach you no matter what."

The kid's face went taut, not what he intended.

"Look," touching her arm. "Don't get me wrong. Right now, in this city, you need to keep your eyes open. You know, use common sense, or whatever. But it's also very important that you live your life as normally as you can." That one opened the floodgates.

"What if they bomb us?"

"Who bomb us? Nobody's going to bomb us. I don't even know who *they* are."

"What if they hijack another plane?"

"Look, here's the deal. You go to school. You work hard, no goofing off. You do your homework, you study for your tests. You go to your soccer practices. Game time rolls around? Not too many headers. Come the weekends? You hang with your friends. Saturday morning? Sunday morning? You have a contest with your sister, see who can sleep the latest, OK? You *live* your *life,* OK?"

"OK," her face lightening. A light peck and a dash for the door.

"Where you headed?"

"I'm going to hang out with Cole."

"Hey. Do me a favor?" stopping her with one foot in the street. "Don't go into any big stores tonight, OK?"

"What?" A little stutter in her step. "Why?"

"Just . . . humor me. It's nothing."

"OK."

"And stay out of Washington Square."

"What's wrong with Washington Square?"

"Well, I never like you hanging out at Washington Square."

"What's wrong with Washington Square?"

"Absolutely probably nothing. I'm just not too crazy about crowds right now, OK?"

"OK, OK," the tightness coming back into her face, but what could you do?

"And oh," he winced preemptively. "The subway? It doesn't exist for you, OK?" then, "Sorry."

By the time the kid hit the street, she looked as if someone had strapped a boulder onto her back; her father wondering if it was more dangerous for her inside the house than out.

Haven, Oct. 21

Rafiyq Abdellah, born Torrin Williams, enters the visitors' room wearing a gray Velcro-fastened jumpsuit and greets his guest with a standing hug. At first, the talk is of lawyers and postponements, but the conversation turns to the inescapable.

"Well, I'll tell you, this is not the greatest of times to have a name like mine, you know what I'm saying?"

"They breaking your back in here?"

"Yeah, well, I don't want to make too much of it, but like, OK, what was it, ten minutes ago I come in here? The, the guard who brought me up? He's like, 'Abdellah, Abdellah, were you tight with the hijackers?' And I'm like, 'Yo, look at my *face*, hear my *speech* — do you *think* I was tight with the hijackers?'

"Yeah, and then on the other end of the spectrum, the native-born Muslims in here? Sometimes they look at the African-American Muslims and they're all like, 'You ain't *pray*ing right, you don't understand the Ko*ran* right, you this, you that . . .' I mean, I'll tell you, when we all go to the *jumah* on Fridays? Man, there is like some spirited disputations in there these days, no lie . . .

"I mean, most guys in here, they feel like everybody else about what happened, you know, the horror of it . . . I mean, there's a few guys, political types, and for them, what happened, it's all about chickens coming home to roost. But I don't see how anybody could say that with an honest heart.

"And I saw it happen that morning, did I write you about that? You get a pretty good view of the skyline from in here, and when that first building went down? Man, I couldn't even close my mouth.

"I'd like to think the worst is over, but with the anthrax now and everything? Hey, you know how I feel about being incarcerated in here, right? But I have to say it, with what's going on out there on a day-to-day basis? Rikers might very well be the safest place in the city."

Not Norman Rockwell, Oct. 24

Under a cracklingly blue sky, New York is trying harder than ever to proceed with its spiritual comeback; the shops are more crowded, overheard conversation veers more often to the blissfully inane, and erratic bursts of laughter punctuate the soundtrack of the streets, although let's not kid ourselves, the people of this city still carry themselves with a certain humped tension, as if waiting for the next unthinkable.

"Did you ever hear of Lord Buckley?" she asks her friend as they cruise the ground floor of a mammoth bookstore. "Kind of a hipster monologist from the fifties? He had this bit back then about

Khrushchev and the H-bomb, and he says something like, 'In times of great uncertainty and terror, humor is the only thing that ensures us that we do not die before we're killed.'"

"Yeah, well, have you heard any good jokes lately?" her friend asks. "Because I sure haven't."

"How about this?" she responds, gesturing to a freestanding six-book display easel by the information desk. The three titles running across the top row are *Rogue Regimes, Bin Laden: The Man Who Declared War on America,* and *Terrorism: Today's Biggest Threat to Freedom.* At the far left on the lower row is *Living Terrors: What America Needs to Know to Survive the Coming Bioterrorist Catastrophe;* at the far right, *Jihad;* and dead center, surrounded by all the others, *New York Landmarks.*

"Will that do?"

Back out on the street, they wander down Broadway and notice after a few blocks that the people in front of them have come to a standstill, their eyes on the approaching uptown traffic, where a fire truck is cruising back to its house.

Some of the people break out in applause. Others wave. The firemen wave back.

"Can you believe that?" she says. "It's like the 1950s. Like Norman Rockwell."

"No way," her friend says, joining in on the applause. "There's nothing sentimental about what those guys went through." She cut loose with a piercing two-fingered whistle. "And I'll tell you something else. Right about now? This is probably the least naive city in the world."

JOE QUEENAN

Matriculation Fixation

FROM THE NEW YORK TIMES EDUCATION LIFE

TWO YEARS AGO, I was languishing in the waiting room of a Philadelphia hospital when a complete stranger unexpectedly began telling me about his daughter's college plans. As my seventy-nine-year-old mother was recovering from major surgery that afternoon, I could not give him my complete and undivided attention. But as the briefing session wore on, I did manage to garner most of the relevant details.

The girl, bright but not brilliant, had been accepted to a first-tier university without financial aid but had also been accepted to a local, second-echelon university where she was promised a free ride. Money being tight, with other college-bound children in the family queue, the man had persuaded his daughter to accept the second university's offer. Now he was worried that she would one day rue this decision. Because she would be graduating from a less prestigious institution, fewer contacts would be made and fewer doors would be opened. Her degree would put her within striking distance of the yellow brick road, but not physically on the road itself. Did this make her father the spawn of Satan?

As a man of the world accustomed to being told the most intimate details about complete strangers' marriages, careers, and hobbies, I had long ago acquired the requisite skills to mediate this crisis. I told the man that many of my high school chums had graduated from the second-tier university in question and had gone on to live rich, full lives.

I told him that I myself had graduated from a second-echelon Philadelphia university not unlike the one his daughter was entering, and had managed to carve out a nice little niche for myself. I told him that my college days had been among the happiest of my life, that the sun never set without my thanking God for the illumination and inspiration provided by my talented, dedicated professors. Pressed for biographical data, I explained that I was a freelance writer, ticked off a list of my credentials, and said I was pretty happy with the way my career had turned out. The man had never heard of me, had never read anything I'd written. Though he tried to feign interest in my pathetic curriculum vitae, I could see that he was devastated. By following an academic path similar to mine, his daughter, who was also planning a career in journalism, was going to end up as big a failure as I. I never did find out why he was visiting the hospital.

I mention this incident because it illustrates the neurotic gabbiness that afflicts parents when it comes time to send their children to college. I know whereof I speak. Next fall, my daughter goes to college. Three years later my son will follow suit. I will be sorry to see them go; over the years they have proved to be remarkably amusing. But every dark cloud has a silver lining. Once my children have left the house, I will never again have to participate in a mind-numbing discussion about where my children or my friends' children or my neighbors' children are going to college, and why. On this subject, I am completely tapped out.

This lack of interest does not stem from pure selfishness or unalloyed contempt for other people's offspring. Rather, I feel this way because I find almost all conversations about the college selection process to be banal, self-aggrandizing, self-flagellatory, or punitive. I'd rather talk about cribbage.

The most infuriating conversation is the one where the parent clearly seeks a decisive, career-validating moment of emotional closure. Such individuals believe that securing admission to a topflight university provides a child with an irrevocable passport to success, guaranteeing a life of uninterrupted economic mirth. Parents such as these upwardly mobile chuckleheads exude an almost Prussian belligerence when announcing their children's destinations, congratulating themselves on a job well done, while issuing a sotto voce taunt to parents of the less gifted. For them, the hard part of child rearing is now over. Junior went to the right prep school, made the right friends, signed up for the right activities, and is now headed for the right school. Now we can get the heck out of here and move to Tuscany. But in reality, life doesn't end at age seventeen. Or twenty-one. In real life, some children get the finest educations but still become first-class screwups. My own profession is filled with people who went to the right school but ended up in the wrong career. (They should have been flacks; the phone ringing in the next room is not and never will be the Pulitzer committee.) Some of those boys and girls most likely to succeed are going to end up on welfare or skid row. At which point they'll need parental input. Or cash. A parent's responsibility doesn't end once the kids leave. A parent's responsibility never ends. That's why Nature gives you the job.

A second, far more numerous class of obsessives consists of people who suddenly realize that their Brand X children aren't going to make the cut. Seventeen years of unread textbooks, unvisited museums, and untaken AP courses are now finally taking their toll, and those grandiose delivery-room dreams of Amherst, Bard, and Duke are suddenly going up in smoke. Bashfully, shamefacedly, miserably, these parents now mumble the names of the glamourless institutions their progeny are skulking off to. Invariably, they are colleges you never heard of in towns no one wants to visit in states whose capitals only repeat winners on *Jeopardy!* can name. The market has spoken, the glum parental expressions seem to say. My child is an idiot.

But once again, reality has a way of upsetting the worst-laid plans of mice and Mensa. Some kids are late bloomers. Some kids are better off in a less competitive environment. Lots of people achieve huge success in this society without a degree from a prestigious university. Just because your child has failed to clear the first, or even the twentieth, hurdle doesn't mean you should disown him. Matisse didn't get rolling until he was in his forties. Bill Gates, David Geffen, Michael Dell, Graydon Carter, and Madonna are all college dropouts. Ronald Reagan attended tiny Eureka College, while Warren Buffet went to Football U in Lincoln, Nebraska. Despite what you may have read in F. Scott Fitzgerald (who dropped out of Princeton in 1917), life doesn't have just one act. There is often act two. And act five. Not to mention the sequels.

Matriculation fixation reaches its dottiest form during the obligatory campus visit. Here it is never entirely clear what parents are looking for, particularly in high-profile institutions whose renown has in some way preceded them. During a recent visit to MIT, I watched the first thirty seconds of an admissions office video poking fun at the university's reputation as a nerd factory. While my wife and daughter watched the rest of the video, which assured applicants that MIT nerds were hard to find, I took a stroll around the campus. I saw a lot of nerds. And I do not mean this as a criticism. Later that morning, a guide showed a bunch of us around campus. At one juncture, she pointed out a restaurant where students could grab a fast, inexpensive meal. "How much?" asked one highstrung mother. "About eight bucks," she was told. The woman shuddered, noting that forking over eight dollars for dinner every night could get pretty darned expensive.

"It's going to cost you forty grand to send your kid to school here," I interjected. "Don't start worrying about dinner prices."

Since that visit this fall, this incident has become an invaluable part of my repertory. Now, whenever I am dragooned into the 30,000th interminable conversation about the college selection process, I indicate that sedulous monitoring of on-campus restaurant prices should be a vital component of the winnowing procedure, particularly vis-à-vis panini. People who hear me say things like this can't decide whether I am insensitive or ornery or flat-out dumb. Well, let's just put it this way: I was never MIT material.

JOHN SACK

Inside the Bunker

FROM ESQUIRE

THE PEOPLE who say the Holocaust didn't happen asked me to speak at their recent international conference. The invitation surprised me, for I am a Jew who's written about the Holocaust and (for chrissakes, I feel like adding) certainly hasn't denied it. To my eyes, however, the invitation, which came from the Institute for Historical Review in Orange County, California, the central asylum for the delusion that the Germans didn't kill any Jews and that the Holocaust is, quote unquote, the Hoax of the Twentieth Century, was not just a wonderment; it was also a golden opportunity, a golden-engraved temptation. We journalists usually sit at the outer edge of occasions: behind the bar in courtrooms, far off the floor of Congress, well out of passing or pitching range at football or baseball games. We are the beggars at banquet halls, waiting for the brass bell and the two-second bite, and the institute offered me what every journalist hungers for: the feast of unhampered access. Its letter was a safe-conduct pass to a country so fogbound that you and I can't discern it. Who are the Holocaust deniers? What are they like behind closed doors? And why are they motionless stones as avalanches of evidence crash onto them, roaring, *You're wrong, you're wrong*? I'd been invited to mingle with them like a mole in Hitler's Eagle's Nest and then ascend to a lectern to tell them off, and I wrote the institute saying that, yes, I'd come.

I flew on a Friday to John Wayne Airport in Orange County and called up the institute, asking, "Where will the conference be?" Until then I hadn't known, for the institute feared that I might divulge it to the Jewish Defense League, a group the FBI has called active terrorists, and that the league might initiate violence. It had done so at other conferences to other speakers. One had been punched, punched by a fist also holding a cherry pie, one had been beaten up, and one had been beaten up in Paris, Vichy, Lyon, and Stockholm. A man who's older than me — I'm seventy — this last man had been maced, thrown to the ground, and kicked in the head because of his imprudent belief that the Holocaust didn't take place. For six weeks his jaw had been wired and he'd eaten through a soda straw. All three men, the leading lights of denial, would speak at this weekend's conference, and the institute didn't want to see their freedom of speech or their bodies imperiled by Jews who conducted chants of "Nazis!" "Neo-Nazis!" or "Anti-Semites!" or by Jews who threw punches. On the phone, an institute employee told me where the conference was but said, "Don't tell anyone."

Knowing where to go, I took a courtesy van to a palm-filled hotel with a Japanese footbridge over a rambling pool, the sun glinting off its rippling water. A few deniers (who'd also called up the institute and been told, "Don't tell") were down in the open-air lobby, making hollow jokes about the threat, possibly imminent, possibly not, of the Jewish Defense League. "I'm checking everything out," a man from Adelaide, Australia, laughed to me.

"Should I have concerns about my security here?" a tall and broad-shouldered man from New York, an Italian, asked me.

"Are you concerned about it?"

"Now that I'm out of the closet, yes. The people around me say I should be. Do you think my life's in jeopardy here?"

"We'll soon find out," I said. "The Jewish Defense League is right here in California and, I'm sure, know we're around."

"Heh," said the man from New York.

By six o'clock the lobby was full. The deniers (by Saturday there'd be 140) were about three-quarters men and one-quarter women. Most were white, but one was African American. One was bald, but none were razor-shaved skinheads. Many wore beards, one a white bushy one like Santa Claus's. Most wore slacks and short-sleeved shirts, but a few wore jackets, blazers, or business suits, one a safari suit, and one a white suit like Mark Twain's. Two wore T-shirts that said, NO HOLES? NO HOLOCAUST!, a text whose exegesis I'd get on Saturday. The conversations I heard were

about nutrition ("I was raised on raw milk") and about paddle
wheelers ("You know, like in *Show Boat*. You haven't seen it? I suggest you rent it"). All in all, the deniers that day and that weekend
seemed the most middling of Middle Americans. Or better: despite their take on the Holocaust, they were affable, open-minded,
intelligent, intellectual. Their eyes weren't fires of unapproachable
certitude, and their lips weren't lemon twists of astringent hate.
Nazis and neo-Nazis they didn't seem to be.

Nor did they seem anti-Semites. I'm sure many anti-Semites say
the Holocaust didn't happen (even as they take delight that it really did), but I don't believe I met any that weekend. The only de-
batably anti-Semitic comment that I heard was on Friday night,
when I dined in the downstairs restaurant with a prominent denier
in a NO HOLES? NO HOLOCAUST! shirt, an Alabama man whose
name is Dr. Robert Countess. A gangling scholar of classical Greek
and classical Hebrew, he had taught history at the University of Alabama and had retired to a farm outside Huntsville, where he plays
major league Ping-Pong and collects old Peugeots; he has twenty-
two, some dating back to the Crash. While scarcely cranky, he had
a cranky-sounding voice, and in the open-air restaurant he was
practically grinding gears as he discoursed on the Septuagint and
as I, not Countess, brought up the Jewish sacred scrolls, the Talmud. "What's called the Talmud," Countess lectured — "*talmud*
being the participle form of *lamad*, in Hebrew *learn* — developed
in Babylonia as rabbis reflected on certain passages in the Torah.
Some of these rabbis engaged in a syncretism, a bringing together,
of Babylonian paganism with the religion of Abraham, Isaac, and
Jacob. So if you read much of the Talmud, and Elda will tell you
her favorite story —"

"No," said Elda, Countess's wife, who was dining with us.

"It's unbelievable, but it's in the Talmud," said Countess.

"No, no. I don't want to tell it," said Elda, embarrassed.

"Go ahead and tell it," Countess entreated.

"Well," said Elda, blushing, "it's in the Talmud that if a Jewish
man's repairing the roof, and if his sister-in-law is down below, and
if he falls onto her and she becomes pregnant —"

"He falls off the roof in such a way —" Countess said, laughing.

"Can you picture it? Then the child won't be a bastard," said
Elda. The tale would be anti-Semitic rubbish if it weren't indeed in

the Talmud (in Yevamot, and again in Bava Kamma) and if the Countesses were just amused and not also appalled. "You and I laugh about this," said Countess, "but I sit in stark amazement saying, Jews aren't stupid people! How can they go along with this?" "The answer is, We don't," I explained. By bedtime on Friday, my impression of the Countesses was like my impression of UFO devotees. Everyone in America believes in one or another ridiculous thing. Me, I belong to the International Society for Cryptozoology, and I firmly believe that in Lake Tele, in the heart of the Congo, there is a living, breathing dinosaur. Admittedly, this is trivial compared with Holocaust denial, but fifteen years ago I even went to the Congo to photograph it. I didn't — I didn't even see it — but I still believe in it. Other people believe more momentous things, and the Countesses and the other deniers believe that the Holocaust didn't happen. Like me in the Congo, they're wrong, wrong, wrong, but to say that emphatically isn't to say (as some people do) that they're odious, contemptible, despicable. To say that they're rats (as does Deborah Lipstadt, the author of *Denying the Holocaust*) is no more correct than to say it of people who, in their ignorance, believe the less pernicious fallacy that Oswald didn't kill Kennedy. Oh, did I hit a soft spot there?

The conference started on Saturday. In the center of the lobby stood a Kentia palm and in concentric circles around it were peace lilies, crotons, bird-of-paradise flowers, and happy conferencegoers. Young and old, they talked like any Americans at any professional conference: they talked of the weather, their homes, their children ("One is a lawyer, another a businessman. For their sake I'm still in the closet"). On the hour, more and more were wearing the NO HOLES? NO HOLOCAUST! shirts in red, green, and gray as they seated themselves on bridge chairs to listen to speakers in the shuttered darkness of the garden ballroom. "It's one heck of a nice conference," I heard someone say.

Now about "No holes? No Holocaust!" The first thing to know is that no one at that palm-filled hotel would deny that Hitler hated the Jews, that Hitler sent them to concentration camps, and that Hitler said, "I want to annihilate the Jews" as hundreds of thousands died in (as one denier called them) godforsaken hell-holes like Auschwitz. It may surprise you, but no one at that hotel would deny that hundreds of thousands of Jews died of typhus, dysentery, starvation, and exhaustion at Auschwitz or that their corpses went to the constant flames of five crematoriums night and day. These deniers even call this the Holocaust, and what they deny is that some of the Jews died of something other than natural causes, that some went to rooms that the Germans poured cyanide (or at four other camps, carbon monoxide) into. The Jews, say the Holocaust deniers, weren't *murdered*, and the Germans didn't deliberately murder them.

Tens of thousands of witnesses disagree. Jews who once stood at the railroad depot at Auschwitz say that the Germans told them, "Go right," and told their mothers, fathers, and children, "Go left," and say that they never saw those mothers, fathers, and children again. I and the rest of the world believe that the Jews who went left went to cyanide chambers, but the deniers believe they went to other parts of Auschwitz or, by train, to other concentration camps. "Part of the Jews remained in Auschwitz," a speaker (another scholar, a man who speaks seventeen languages, including Chinese) said at the ballroom lectern one day. "The rest were transported farther. Many opted to stay in the Soviet Union." Tens of thousands of witnesses saw the cyanide chambers, too, saw the lilac-colored cyanide pellets cascade onto the Jews, but almost all of these witnesses died in five minutes, without being able to testify to it. A few indeed testified, among them two Auschwitz commandants. One said that children under twelve and people over fifty-five were cyanided daily, and one said, "At least 2,500,000 victims were executed by gassing," then backed off to 1,200,000. Some doctors at Auschwitz testified. One doctor said, "When the doors were opened, bodies fell out," and one doctor said, "The *Inferno*, by Dante, is in comparison almost comedy." Some Jews who toted bodies to the crematoriums testified. One said, "We found heaps of naked bodies, doubled up. They were pinkish and in places red. Some were covered with greenish marks, and saliva ran from their mouths. Others were bleeding from the nose. There was excrement on many of them," and one said, "We were met by the sight of the dead bodies lying higgledy-piggledy. I was petrified."

To this abundant evidence the Holocaust deniers say — and they're right — that one Auschwitz commandant confessed after he was tortured and that the other reports are full of bias, rumors, exaggerations, and other preposterous matters, to quote the editor of a Jewish magazine five years after the war. The deniers say, and again they're right, that the commandants, doctors, SS, and Jews at Bergen-Belsen, Buchenwald, and a whole alphabet of camps testified after the war that there were cyanide chambers at those camps that all historians today refute.

The deniers also say that at Auschwitz the witnesses said that the Germans poured cyanide pellets through holes in the chamber roofs — even said that the Germans joked as they poured, *"Na, gib Ihnen schön zu fressen"* — Well, give them something good to eat. It's there that the NO HOLES? NO HOLOCAUST! on the T-shirts comes in. The roofs at Auschwitz still stand (or, rather, lie collapsed, for the Germans blew up the buildings in November 1944 so the world wouldn't know), and, the deniers say, you can't find holes in those former roofs for the Germans to pour the cyanide through.

Myself, I'd call this one of life's mysteries, like why there are holes in Swiss cheese and not in cheddar, but everyone in the palm-filled hotel made a tremendous deal of it. One speaker there was David Irving, the British World War II historian, a man with a statesman's bearing, a statesman's elegant pinstriped suit, and a member of Parliament's elocution, a man who strung together his clear definitions, crisp distinctions, and withering innuendos in parse-perfect sentences, like graduated pearls. He had just sued, for libel, the author and publisher of *Denying the Holocaust*. The trial was in London last year. Irving lost, but not before he invoked the "No holes? No Holocaust!" argument. On the stand, a witness for the author and publisher cited some Auschwitz witnesses, and Irving, acting as his own attorney, leaped like a crouching lion. "Professor," said Irving, a granite-featured, imposing man, "we are wasting our time, really, are we not? There were never any holes in that roof. There are no holes in that roof today. They [the Germans] cannot have poured cyanide capsules through that roof. You yourself have stood on that roof and looked for those holes and not found them. Our experts have stood on that roof and not found them. The holes were never there. What do you say to *that?*"

"The roof is a mess. The roof is absolutely a mess," said the professor lamely. "The roof is in fragments."

"You have been to Auschwitz how many times?"

"Sometimes twice or three times yearly."

"Have you frequently visited this roof?"

"Yes, I have been there, yes."

"Have you never felt the urge to go and start scraping where you know those holes would have been?"

"The last thing I'd ever have done is start scraping away."

"How much does an air ticket to Warsaw cost? One hundred pounds? Two hundred pounds?"

"I have no idea."

"If," said Irving triumphantly, "you were to go to Auschwitz with a trowel and clean away the gravel and find a reinforced concrete hole, I would abandon my action immediately. That would drive such a hole through my case that I would have no possible chance of defending it."

Not quite flying to Auschwitz, the author, the publisher, or the professor apparently called up the Auschwitz Museum, for the museum told the *Times* of London that it had started searching for the fabulous holes. A two-mile drive. A trowel. A camera. That's what the search entailed, but it's now nine months later and the museum hasn't found them.

But lo! Someone did. Not someone from the Auschwitz Museum, but Charles "Chuck" Provan, a letterhead printer in Monongahela, Pennsylvania, and another scheduled speaker here in California. A man of childlike enthusiasms, a roly-poly, red-bearded, merry man, a man with a brandy-glass-shaped face, he'd been an earnest denier until he had an epiphany in December 1990. Provan was home in Monongahela, reading from *The Confessions of Kurt Gerstein,* an SS man who confessed he was at the concentration camp in Belzec, Poland, and who said, "I see everything! The mothers, their babies at the breast, the little naked children, the men and women, naked. They enter into the death chamber, pushed by the leather whips of the SS. Pack well, that is what [the] captain ordered. Seven to eight hundred persons on twenty-five square meters. More than half are children . . ."

For forty-five years, the *Confessions* had been the laughingstock of the Holocaust deniers. What? Seven to eight hundred people on twenty-five square meters? Thirty people on one square meter, three people on one square foot? "Impossible," "Incredible,"

"Nonsensical," wrote the jeering deniers. "It is feasible if one uses a scrap press, but in that case gassing would be superfluous." Even mainstream historians fudged the *Confessions'* figures, writing at best inaccurately and at worst unscrupulously of 170 to 180 people or of a hundred square meters. For forty-five years, no one had troubled himself to see if seven to eight hundred people could fit on twenty-five square meters until Provan, in Monongahela, read these words in the *Confessions:* "More than half are children." *Well, if I've got one thing,* thought Provan, *it's children,* and he put down the book and took his five children and one big baby doll into an upstairs bedroom. "What are you doing?" asked Mrs. Provan.

"An experiment: how many kids can fit in a gas chamber."

"You shouldn't use the kids like that. It's sorta gruesome."

"Aw, it won't hurt them," said Provan in his down-home voice, and he had the kids strip to their underwear. He packed them into a corner, then with two dressers corralled them into a square of sixteen by sixteen inches. Then, setting them free, he used an electronic calculator to calculate to his astonishment that he could fit 891 children into the gas chamber at Belzec. Tears came to Provan's eyes, for he saw the *Confessions* differently now. Its author, he saw, wouldn't say something so impossible, incredible, nonsensical, something no one would believe for a half century, if he himself hadn't witnessed it. Gerstein, the SS man, had seen Jews die at Belzec ("One hears them weeping, sobbing"), and the Holocaust had indeed happened.

Provan did two more experiments even as Mrs. Provan, a sort of Cesare Cremonini — the colleague of Galileo's who wouldn't look into Galileo's telescope — told him, "You shouldn't." In one, he used five kids, three mannequins, and one doll, and in the other, five kids, three adults — a printer, a minister, and an Italian woman who said, "You're nuts, but I'll do it" — all with their clothes on, and the doll, and he calculated that seven hundred fathers, mothers, children, and babies would fit in the chamber at Belzec. And last March, he used the same scientific method on the "No holes? No Holocaust!" hypothesis, going with some of his children (he had nine by now) to one collapsed chamber at Auschwitz. The witnesses there had said the holes were alongside the central columns, and Provan used a forty-dollar metric measuring tape to find where the columns had been and found — well, whaddya know? — those celebrated holes. No longer were they twenty-five by twenty-five centimeters, as the witnesses had said. Now, with the roof blown up, they were larger, and Provan photographed them, came home to Monongahela, wrote up a monograph, printed it at his print shop, and printed a cover that, in gold letters, with the exclamation point demoted to a question mark, said, NO HOLES? NO HOLOCAUST? He then flew to Orange County and appeared at the palm-filled hotel on Saturday afternoon.

Not even washing up, he sat with childlike delight on a flowery lobby love seat by the Kentia palm, handing his two dozen spiral-bound copies to the illuminati of Holocaust denial. If he expected encomiums, he misunderstood human nature, which clings to established beliefs as though to a life preserver without which we'd sink to the jet-black depths of the Mindanao Trough. "You have a bent toward evil," the chief denier from Australia, a man of German ancestry, told Provan. "You slander the German people. You believe in the Holocaust." "But Charles, if I may call you Charles, bring me the *pudding*," said the chief denier alive, a Frenchman who coined the "No holes? No Holocaust!" motto. "Bring me the holes of twenty-five by twenty-five centimeters."

"Oh, I can't," said Provan.

"Where do you see a square of twenty-five by twenty-five?"

"Oh, not anymore. But this hole is big enough to have held it."

"But you don't have a square of twenty-five centimeters."

"I admit that."

"This cannot convince me," the Frenchman said.

The angriest denier was David Irving, the British historian who'd said in London that a photograph of a hole would drive such a metaphorical hole in his case that he couldn't defend it. Irving, who isn't allowed at Auschwitz and may have been jealous of an amateur's access, sat at the open-air downstairs restaurant in front of a caesar salad. On spotting Provan, he turned black, and his words came like chisel chips. "I'm hopping mad," Irving said. "If I were an SS man and somebody said, 'Knock some holes in that ceiling, will you? We're going to start putting cyanide in,' I'd make those holes in the middle of some empty area. I wouldn't put them — bang, bang, bang, bang — next to the load-bearing pillars. What were the load-bearing pillars for? Just cosmetic purposes?" Provan, twenty years younger, stood like a boy called down to the principal's office, looking abashed, and Irving continued, "The Germans spend God knows how many hundreds of thousands of pounds building this? And then they allow some jerk with a sledgehammer to punch holes next to the load-bearing pillars? I'm having lunch," said Irving abruptly, and he attacked his salad without a whit of his ardent convictions voided by Provan's photographs. Of course, the deniers would say it's Provan and I whose convictions weren't voided by Irving, and it may be a hundred years before we know whose views prevail. "We have won," an SS man told Primo Levi at Auschwitz. "There may be suspicions, but there will be no certainties, because we'll destroy the evidence together with you."

Provan, the only speaker (other than me) who believed that the Holocaust happened, spoke in the ballroom later on. He spoke about a Jewish coroner at Auschwitz and not about his "No holes? No Holocaust?" monograph or his one other epoch-making discovery. In the cyanide chambers at Auschwitz, there are no cyanide stains, and the deniers, though they've never worn a T-shirt saying NO CYANIDE? NOBODY DIED! call this another proof that what we call cyanide chambers were, in fact, innocuous morgues. But according to Provan, the chambers have no stains because the Germans painted their walls.

Sixteen other speakers spoke on Saturday, Sunday, and Monday, for this was a holiday weekend, and I counted six who'd run afoul of the law because of their disbelief in the Holocaust and the death apparatus at Auschwitz. To profess this in anyone's earshot is illegal not just in Germany but in Holland, Belgium, France, Spain, Switzerland, Austria, Poland, and Israel, where denying the Holocaust can get you five years while denying God can get you just one. One speaker, David Irving, had been fined $18,000 for saying aloud in Germany that one of the cyanide chambers at Auschwitz is a replica built by the Poles after the war. A replica it truly is, but truth in these matters is no defense in Germany. Another speaker, a Frenchman, had been fined in France, and another speaker, a German, had been sentenced to fourteen months in Germany but, his landlord evicting him, his wife deserting him, had fled to England. Another speaker, an Australian, had come from seven months in a German jail for writing in Australia (alas, on the Internet, which

Germans in Germany can read) that there were no cyanide chambers at Auschwitz. In his defense, he'd called an expert witness, but the man couldn't testify or he'd be jailed, too, the victim of the selfsame law. The fifth speaker was a Swiss, a man I'd once roomed with (I'd met many deniers previously) and fed the kangaroos with in South Australia. He'll go to jail for three months in Switzerland for questioning the Auschwitz cyanide chambers.

In the United States, thank God, we have the First Amendment. But even in that shuttered ballroom in California, the sixth speaker couldn't say all he wanted to — couldn't, for example, say the Germans didn't kill the Jews deliberately. A few hours earlier, he and I had debated this at a waffle breakfast, debated it in audible voices with no qualms of being arrested, indicted, or imprisoned by federal marshals. "But what about Eichmann?" I'd asked him. "He wrote that Hitler ordered the physical destruction of the Jews. He wrote about *Vergasungslager,* gassing camps."

"John. The man was in Israeli captivity."

"Well, what about *during* the war? Hans Frank, the governor general of Poland, said to exterminate all the Jews, without exception."

"He was only *quoted* as saying that, John."

"And what about Goebbels? He said a barbaric method was being employed against the Jews. And Himmler? He said the SS knew what a hundred, five hundred, one thousand corpses were like."

"John, I don't know. They might have said it," the sixth speaker told me. "But it isn't true that genocide was a German national policy." A few hours later, the speaker didn't dare repeat this up in the ballroom, for he's a Canadian citizen and his speech was carried live on the Internet in Canada, and if he said what he'd said over waffles, he'd have been prosecuted in Canada. Already he'd been tried twice as well as hit, beaten, bombed, engulfed by a $400,000 fire, and told, "We'll cut your testicles off."

The man's name is Ernst Zündel. He's round-faced and redfaced like in a Hals, he's eternally jolly, and he was born in Calmbach, Germany. If you saw the recent movie about the Holocaust deniers, *Mr. Death,* he's the man in the hard hat who says, "We Germans will not go down in history as genocidal maniacs. *We. Will. Not.*" He has become a hero to anti-Semites and, like every denier, has been called anti-Semitic himself, but it's just as honest to say that the Jews who (along with God) oversee the Jewish community are in fact anti-Zündelic, anti-Countessic, anti-Irvingic, and, in one word, anti-denieric. The normal constraints of time, temperance, and truth do not obstruct some Jewish leaders from their nonstop vituperation of Holocaust deniers. "They're morally ugly. They're morally sick," said Elie Wiesel on PBS. They bombard us with disinformation, said Abraham Foxman, the national director of the Anti-Defamation League, on the op-ed page of the *New York Times*. "Holocaust deniers," said Foxman, spreading disinformation himself, "would have [us] believe there were no concentration camps." Myself, I disagree with these Jewish leaders. Most deniers, most attendees in their slacks and shorts at the palm-filled hotel, were like Zündel: people who, as Germans, had chosen to comfort themselves with the wishful thinking that none of their countrymen in the 1940s were genocidal maniacs.

I can sympathize with the Germans, for I've seen a bit of this wishful thinking among some Jews. Seven years ago, I ruefully reported in my book *An Eye for an Eye* that thousands of Jews who'd survived the Holocaust had rounded up Germans and beaten, whipped, tortured, and murdered them — German men, women, children, and babies — in concentration camps run by Jews. This little holocaust was corroborated by *60 Minutes* and the *New York Times* but not by Jewish leaders. They, pardon the expression, denied it, writing reviews whose titles were "The Big Lie" and "False Witness" and "Do Me a Favor — Don't Read This Book." If Jews feel pressed to deny what happened to sixty thousand Germans, then Jews might forgive the Germans, like Zündel, who choose to deny what happened to six million Jews.

Instead, Jewish leaders hound them. Astronomers don't spill rivers of ink denouncing the UFO fanatics, whose theories are much less malignant but whose legions are much more numerous than the dozen dozen deniers at that international conference, their first in six slow-moving years. But for various reasons (for reparations, for the survival of Israel, or for real apprehensions that it could happen again), Jewish leaders want the Holocaust to be front and center in America's consciousness. In this they've succeeded spectacularly. Americans who aren't senior citizens think it was partly to save the Jews that we declared war on Germany, though that was no factor at all. Americans who don't know if one hundred thousand, two hundred thousand, or one million of our own soldiers died (and surely don't know that fifty million people died in China) know exactly how many Jews died in World War II. Once, said Michael Berenbaum, the former research director of the U.S. Holocaust Memorial Museum, "the Holocaust was a side story of World War II. Now one thinks of World War II as a background story [to] the Holocaust." Among many ways Jewish leaders accomplished this was to tap out an SOS, an all-points alarm, whenever in any dark corner they spotted a knavish denier.

They may have adopted this from Jakob Böhme, a German mystic of Shakespeare's time. Böhme once said, "Nothing becomes manifest without opposition, for if it has nothing to oppose it, it slowly moves away from itself and does not return." Lest the Holocaust become unmanifest, lest the Holocaust move away from itself, Jewish leaders constantly point to the opposition, the bogeyman, the bugaboo, the otherwise ineffectual squad of Holocaust deniers. But there's a double edge to Böhme's sword: by opposing, opposing, opposing them in print, on the radio, and on TV, Jewish leaders make the deniers manifest, too. The deniers survive because they are being persecuted. They survive to spread their doctrine to the true Jew haters of the world.

My own speech was on Monday afternoon. It was about *An Eye for an Eye*, which the Germans among the deniers wanted to hear about so they could share their parents' guilt with the Jews, their parents' victims. No longer did I want to tell the deniers off, but I did want to edify them (and I did) that I and the Jews in *An Eye for an Eye* devoutly believe that the Holocaust happened. But also I wanted to say something therapeutic, to say something about hate. At the hotel, I'd seen none of it, certainly less than I'd seen when Jews were speaking of Germans. No one had ever said anything remotely like Elie Wiesel, "Every Jew, somewhere in his being, should set aside a zone of hate — healthy, virile hate — for what persists in the Germans," and no one had said anything like Edgar Bronfman, the president of the World Jewish Congress. A shocked professor told Bronfman once, "You're teaching a whole generation to hate thousands of Germans," and Bronfman replied, "No, I'm teaching a whole generation to hate *millions* of Germans." Jew hatred like that German hatred, or like the German hatred on every page of *Hitler's Willing Executioners,* I saw absolutely none of, but I saw that some people, all Germans, had had to struggle to suppress it.

"The tone of the Jewish establishment," said Zündel at another breakfast in the airy downstairs restaurant, "is so strident, offensive, grating, so denigrating of Germans, there's going to be —" He stopped short.

"We are so sick of the Holocaust!" a German woman with us took up. "Gentiles have it thrown in their faces morning, noon, and night without relief. Do the Jewish people know that?"

"They convict us, imprison us, make us into outcasts," said Zündel, who is now being prosecuted in Canada for, among other things, truthfully saying that Germans didn't make soap out of Jews. "Teachers lose their jobs. Professors lose their tenure, and I say this isn't good for the Jewish community."

"I see dissatisfaction," said the German woman, "that I shudder about. I think the Jewish community has to try to lessen it. This censorship! This terrorism!" In no way did her or Zündel's jaw get twisted like a twisted rubber band into the outward contours of hate, but the woman's quivered at the edges somewhat.

So at the lectern in the grand ballroom on Monday, I spoke about hate. "There are," I said, "eighty-five thousand books about the Holocaust. And none has an honest answer to How could the *Germans* do it? The people who gave us Beethoven, the Ninth Symphony, the Ode to Joy, *Alle Menschen werden Brüder,* all men become brothers. How could the Germans perpetrate the Holocaust? This mystery, we've got to solve it, or we'll keep having genocides in Cambodia, Bosnia, Zaire. Well," I said, "what I report in *An Eye for an Eye* is Lola" — the heroine, the commandant of a terrible prison in Gleiwitz, Germany — "Lola has solved it. The Jews have solved it. Because in their agony, their despair, their insanity, if you will, they felt they became like the Germans — the Nazis — themselves. And if I'd been there," I said, "I'd have become one, too, and now I understand why. A lot of Jews, understandably, were full of hate in 1945, they were volcanoes full of red-hot hate. They thought if they spit out the hate at the Germans, then they'd be rid of it.

"No," I continued. "It doesn't work that way. Let's say I'm in love with someone. I don't tell myself, Uh-oh, I've got inside of me two pounds of love, and if I love her and *love* her, then I'll use all of my love up — I'll be all out of love. No, I understand and we all understand that love is a paradoxical thing, that the more we send out, the more we've got. So why don't we understand that about hate? If we hate, and we act on that hate, then we hate even more later on. If we spit out a drop of hate, we stimulate the saliva glands and we produce a drop and a quarter of it. If we spit that out, we produce a drop and a half, then two drops, three, a teaspoon, tablespoon, a Mount Saint Helens. The more we send out, the more we've got, until we are perpetual-motion machines, sending out hate and hate until we've created a holocaust." I then said emphatically, "You don't have to be a German to become like that. You can be a Serb, a Hutu, a Jew — you can be an American. *We* were the ones in the Philippines. *We* were the ones in Vietnam. *We* were the ones in Washington, D.C., for ten thousand years the home of the Anacostia Indians. They had one of their campgrounds at what now is the United States Holocaust Memorial Museum.

"We all have it in us to become like Nazis," I said. "Hate, as Lola discovered, is a muscle, and if we want to be monsters, all we have to do is exercise it. To hate the Germans, to hate the Arabs, to hate the Jews. The longer we exercise it, the bigger it gets, as if every day we curl forty pounds and, far from being worn out, in time we are curling fifty, sixty, we are the Mr. Universe of Hate, the Heinrich Himmler. We all can be hate-full people, hateful people. We can destroy the people we hate, *maybe,* but we surely destroy ourselves."

The people who say the Holocaust didn't happen applauded. Loud and long they applauded, and a number of German deniers stood up. Some asked questions about Auschwitz, like why did I think that Germans *meant* for Jews to die? But one from Berlin, named Wolfgang, later confessed to me, "I believe that Auschwitz became unsanitary. The Jews were worked very hard, I grant you that. They died. And they had to be gotten rid of. And after they died, the SS put them into crematoriums. I won't deny that. And maybe to scare some, the SS told them, 'You're next, you're going to go up in smoke.' And maybe . . ."

The conference ended on Monday. No one was ever attacked by the Jewish Defense League. The deniers (revisionists, they call themselves) meet next in Cincinnati, and they have invited me to be the keynote speaker there. I've said yes.

MARIO VARGAS LLOSA

Why Literature?

FROM THE NEW REPUBLIC

IT HAS OFTEN happened to me, at book fairs or in bookstores, that a gentleman approaches me and asks me for a signature. "It is for my wife, my young daughter, or my mother," he explains. "She is a great reader and loves literature." Immediately I ask: "And what about you? Don't you like to read?" The answer is almost always the same: "Of course I like to read, but I am a very busy person." I have heard this explanation dozens of times: this man and many thousands of men like him have so many important things to do, so many obligations, so many responsibilities in life, that they cannot waste their precious time buried in a novel, a book of poetry, or a literary essay for hours and hours. According to this widespread conception, literature is a dispensable activity, no doubt lofty and useful for cultivating sensitivity and good manners, but essentially an entertainment, an adornment that only people with time for recreation can afford. It is something to fit in between sports, the movies, a game of bridge or chess; and it can be sacrificed without scruple when one "prioritizes" the tasks and the duties that are indispensable in the struggle of life.

It seems clear that literature has become more and more a female activity. In bookstores, at conferences or public readings by writers, and even in university departments dedicated to the humanities, the women clearly outnumber the men. The explanation traditionally given is that middle-class women read more because they work fewer hours than men, and so many of them feel that they can justify more easily than men the time that they devote to fantasy and illusion. I am somewhat allergic to explanations that divide men and women into frozen categories and attribute to each sex its characteristic virtues and shortcomings; but there is no doubt that there are fewer and fewer readers of literature, and that among the saving remnant of readers women predominate. This is the case almost everywhere. In Spain, for example, a recent survey organized by the General Society of Spanish Writers revealed that half of that country's population has never read a book. The survey also revealed that in the minority that does read, the number of women who admitted to reading surpasses the number of men by 6.2 percent, a difference that appears to be increasing. I am happy for these women, but I feel sorry for these men, and for the millions of human beings who could read but have decided not to read.

They earn my pity not only because they are unaware of the pleasure that they are missing, but also because I am convinced that a society without literature, or a society in which literature has been relegated — like some hidden vice — to the margins of social and personal life, and transformed into something like a sectarian cult, is a society condemned to become spiritually barbaric, and even to jeopardize its freedom. I wish to offer a few arguments against the idea of literature as a luxury pastime, and in favor of viewing it as one of the most primary and necessary undertakings of the mind, an irreplaceable activity for the formation of citizens in a modern and democratic society, a society of free individuals.

We live in the era of the specialization of knowledge, thanks to the prodigious development of science and technology and to the consequent fragmentation of knowledge into innumerable parcels and compartments. This cultural trend is, if anything, likely to be accentuated in years to come. To be sure, specialization brings many benefits. It allows for deeper exploration and greater experimentation; it is the very engine of progress. Yet it also has negative consequences, for it eliminates those common intellectual and cultural traits that permit men and women to coexist, to communicate, to feel a sense of solidarity. Specialization leads to a lack of social understanding, to the division of human beings into ghettos of technicians and specialists. The specialization of knowledge requires specialized languages and increasingly arcane codes, as information becomes more and more specific and compartmentalized. This is the particularism and the division against which an old proverb warned us: do not focus too much on the branch or the leaf, lest you forget that they are part of a tree, or too much on the tree, lest you forget that it is part of a forest. Awareness of the existence of the forest creates the feeling of generality, the feeling of belonging, that binds society together and prevents it from disintegrating into a myriad of solipsistic particularities. The solipsism of nations and individuals produces paranoia and delirium, distortions of reality that generate hatred, wars, and even genocide.

In our time, science and technology cannot play an integrating role, precisely because of the infinite richness of knowledge and the speed of its evolution, which have led to specialization and its obscurities. But literature has been, and will continue to be, as long as it exists, one of the common denominators of human experience through which human beings may recognize themselves and converse with each other, no matter how different their professions, their life plans, their geographical and cultural locations, their personal circumstances. It has enabled individuals, in all the particularities of their lives, to transcend history: as readers of Cervantes, Shakespeare, Dante, and Tolstoy, we understand each other across space and time, and we feel ourselves to be members of the same species because, in the works that these writers created, we learn what we share as human beings, what remains common in all of us under the broad range of differences that separate us. Nothing better protects a human being against the stupidity of prejudice, racism, religious or political sectarianism, and exclusivist nationalism than this truth that invariably appears in great literature: that men and women of all nations and places are essentially equal, and that only injustice sows among them discrimination, fear, and exploitation.

Nothing teaches us better than literature to see, in ethnic and cultural differences, the richness of the human patrimony, and to prize those differences as a manifestation of humanity's multifaceted creativity. Reading good literature is an experience of pleasure, of course; but it is also an experience of learning what and how we are, in our human integrity and our human imperfection, with our actions, our dreams, and our ghosts, alone and in relationships that link us to others, in our public image and in the secret recesses of our consciousness.

*

This complex sum of contradictory truths — as Isaiah Berlin called them — constitutes the very substance of the human condition. In today's world, this totalizing and living knowledge of a human being may be found only in literature. Not even the other branches of the humanities — not philosophy, history, or the arts, and certainly not the social sciences — have been able to preserve this integrating vision, this universalizing discourse. The humanities, too, have succumbed to the cancerous division and subdivision of knowledge, isolating themselves in increasingly segmented and technical sectors whose ideas and vocabularies lie beyond the reach of the common woman and man. Some critics and theorists would even like to change literature into a science. But this will never happen, because fiction does not exist to investigate only a single precinct of experience. It exists to enrich through the imagination the entirety of human life, which cannot be dismembered, disarticulated, or reduced to a series of schemas or formulas without disappearing. This is the meaning of Proust's observation that "real life, at last enlightened and revealed, the only life fully lived, is literature." He was not exaggerating, nor was he expressing only his love for his own vocation. He was advancing the particular proposition that as a result of literature life is better understood and better lived; and that living life more fully necessitates living it and sharing it with others.

The brotherly link that literature establishes among human beings, compelling them to enter into dialogue and making them conscious of a common origin and a common goal, transcends all temporal barriers. Literature transports us into the past and links us to those who in bygone eras plotted, enjoyed, and dreamed through those texts that have come down to us, texts that now allow us also to enjoy and to dream. This feeling of membership in the collective human experience across time and space is the highest achievement of culture, and nothing contributes more to its renewal in every generation than literature.

It always irritated Borges when he was asked, "What is the use of literature?" It seemed to him a stupid question, to which he would reply: "No one would ask what is the use of a canary's song or a beautiful sunset." If such beautiful things exist, and if, thanks to them, life is even for an instant less ugly and less sad, is it not petty to seek practical justifications? But the question is a good one. For novels and poems are not like the sound of birdsong or the spectacle of the sun sinking into the horizon, because they were not created by chance or by nature. They are human creations, and it is therefore legitimate to ask how and why they came into the world, and what is their purpose, and why they have lasted so long.

Literary works are born, as shapeless ghosts, in the intimacy of a writer's consciousness, projected into it by the combined strength of the unconscious, and the writer's sensitivity to the world around him, and the writer's emotions; and it is these things to which the poet or the narrator, in a struggle with words, gradually gives form, body, movement, rhythm, harmony, and life. An artificial life, to be sure, a life imagined, a life made of language — yet men and women seek out this artificial life, some frequently, others sporadically, because real life falls short for them, and is incapable of offering them what they want. Literature does not begin to exist through the work of a single individual. It exists only when it is adopted by others and becomes a part of social life — when it becomes, thanks to reading, a shared experience.

One of its first beneficial effects takes place at the level of language. A community without a written literature expresses itself with less precision, with less richness of nuance, and with less clarity than a community whose principal instrument of communication, the word, has been cultivated and perfected by means of literary texts. A humanity without reading, untouched by literature, would resemble a community of deaf-mutes and aphasics, afflicted by tremendous problems of communication due to its crude and rudimentary language. This is true for individuals, too. A person who does not read, or reads little, or reads only trash, is a person with an impediment: he can speak much but he will say little, because his vocabulary is deficient in the means for self-expression.

This is not only a verbal limitation. It represents also a limitation in intellect and in imagination. It is a poverty of thought, for the simple reason that ideas, the concepts through which we grasp the secrets of our condition, do not exist apart from words. We learn how to speak correctly — and deeply, rigorously, and subtly — from good literature, and only from good literature. No other discipline or branch of the arts can substitute for literature in crafting the language that people need to communicate. To speak well, to have at one's disposal a rich and diverse language, to be able to find the appropriate expression for every idea and every emotion that we want to communicate, is to be better prepared to think, to teach, to learn, to converse, and also to fantasize, to dream, to feel. In a surreptitious way, words reverberate in all our actions, even in those actions that seem far removed from language. And as language evolved, thanks to literature, and reached high levels of refinement and manners, it increased the possibility of human enjoyment.

Literature has even served to confer upon love and desire and the sexual act itself the status of artistic creation. Without literature, eroticism would not exist. Love and pleasure would be poorer, they would lack delicacy and exquisiteness, they would fail to attain to the intensity that literary fantasy offers. It is hardly an exaggeration to say that a couple who have read Garcilaso, Petrarch, Góngora, or Baudelaire value pleasure and experience pleasure more than illiterate people who have been made into idiots by television's soap operas. In an illiterate world, love and desire would be no different from what satisfies animals, nor would they transcend the crude fulfillment of elementary instincts.

Nor are the audiovisual media equipped to replace literature in this task of teaching human beings to use with assurance and with skill the extraordinarily rich possibilities that language encompasses. On the contrary, the audiovisual media tend to relegate words to a secondary level with respect to images, which are the primordial language of these media, and to constrain language to its oral expression, to its indispensable minimum, far from its written dimension. To define a film or a television program as "literary" is an elegant way of saying that it is boring. For this reason, literary programs on the radio or on television rarely capture the public. So far as I know, the only exception to this rule was Bernard Pivot's program *Apostrophes,* in France. And this leads me to think that not only is literature indispensable for a full knowledge and a full mastery of language, but its fate is linked also and indissolubly with the fate of the book, that industrial product that many are now declaring obsolete.

This brings me to Bill Gates. He was in Madrid not long ago and visited the Royal Spanish Academy, which has embarked upon a joint venture with Microsoft. Among other things, Gates assured the members of the academy that he would personally guarantee that the letter "ñ" would never be removed from computer software — a promise that allowed four hundred million Spanish speakers on five continents to breathe a sigh of relief, since the banishment of such an essential letter from cyberspace would have created monumental problems. Immediately after making his amiable concession to the Spanish language, however, Gates, before even leaving the premises of the academy, avowed in a press conference that he expected to accomplish his highest goal before he died. That goal, he explained, is to put an end to paper and then to books.

In his judgment, books are anachronistic objects. Gates argued that computer screens are able to replace paper in all the functions that paper has heretofore assumed. He also insisted that, in addition to being less onerous, computers take up less space and are more easily transportable, and also that the transmission of news and literature by these electronic media, instead of by newspapers and books, will have the ecological advantage of stopping the destruction of forests, a cataclysm that is a consequence of the paper industry. People will continue to read, Gates assured his listeners, but they will read on computer screens, and consequently there will be more chlorophyll in the environment.

I was not present at Gates's little discourse; I learned these details from the press. Had I been there I would have booed Gates for proclaiming shamelessly his intention to send me and my colleagues, the writers of books, directly to the unemployment line. And I would have vigorously disputed his analysis. Can the screen really replace the book in all its aspects? I am not so certain. I am fully aware of the enormous revolution that new technologies such as the Internet have caused in the fields of communication and the sharing of information, and I confess that the Internet provides invaluable help to me every day in my work; but my gratitude for these extraordinary conveniences does not imply a belief that the electronic screen can replace paper, or that reading on a computer can stand in for literary reading. That is a chasm that I cannot cross. I cannot accept the idea that a nonfunctional or nonpragmatic act of reading, one that seeks neither information nor a useful and immediate communication, can integrate on a computer screen the dreams and the pleasures of words with the same sensation of intimacy, the same mental concentration and spiritual isolation, that may be achieved by the act of reading a book.

Perhaps this is a prejudice resulting from lack of practice, and from a long association of literature with books and paper. But even though I enjoy surfing the Web in search of world news, I would never go to the screen to read a poem by Góngora or a novel by Onetti or an essay by Paz, because I am certain that the effect of such a reading would not be the same. I am convinced, although I cannot prove it, that with the disappearance of the book, literature would suffer a serious blow, even a mortal one. The term "literature" would not disappear, of course. Yet it would almost certainly be used to denote a type of text as distant from what we understand as literature today as soap operas are from the tragedies of Sophocles and Shakespeare.

There is still another reason to grant literature an important place in the life of nations. Without it, the critical mind, which is the real engine of historical change and the best protector of liberty, would suffer an irreparable loss. This is because all good literature is radical, and poses radical questions about the world in which we live. In all great literary texts, often without their authors' intending it, a seditious inclination is present.

Literature says nothing to those human beings who are satisfied with their lot, who are content with life as they now live it. Literature is the food of the rebellious spirit, the promulgator of nonconformities, the refuge for those who have too much or too little in life. One seeks sanctuary in literature so as not to be unhappy and so as not to be incomplete. To ride alongside the scrawny Rocinante and the confused Knight on the fields of La Mancha, to sail the seas on the back of a whale with Captain Ahab, to drink arsenic with Emma Bovary, to become an insect with Gregor Samsa: these are all ways that we have invented to divest ourselves of the wrongs and the impositions of this unjust life, a life that forces us always to be the same person when we wish to be many different people, so as to satisfy the many desires that possess us.

Literature pacifies this vital dissatisfaction only momentarily — but in this miraculous instant, in this provisional suspension of life, literary illusion lifts and transports us outside of history, and we become citizens of a timeless land, and in this way immortal. We become more intense, richer, more complicated, happier, and more lucid than we are in the constrained routine of ordinary life. When we close the book and abandon literary fiction, we return to actual existence and compare it to the splendid land that we have just left. What a disappointment awaits us! Yet a tremendous realization also awaits us, namely, that the fantasized life of the novel is better — more beautiful and more diverse, more comprehensible and more perfect — than the life that we live while awake, a life conditioned by the limits and the tedium of our condition. In this way, good literature, genuine literature, is always subversive, unsubmissive, rebellious: a challenge to what exists.

How could we not feel cheated after reading *War and Peace* or *Remembrance of Things Past* and returning to our world of insignificant details, of boundaries and prohibitions that lie in wait everywhere and, with each step, corrupt our illusions? Even more than the need to sustain the continuity of culture and to enrich language, the greatest contribution of literature to human progress is perhaps to remind us (without intending to, in the majority of cases) that the world is badly made; and that those who pretend to the contrary, the powerful and the lucky, are lying; and that the world can be improved, and made more like the worlds that our imagination and our language are able to create. A free and democratic society must have responsible and critical citizens conscious of the need continuously to examine the world that we inhabit and to try, even though it is more and more an impossible task, to make it more closely resemble the world that we would like to inhabit. And there is no better means of fomenting dissatisfaction with existence than the reading of good literature; no better means of forming critical and independent citizens who will not be manipulated by those who govern them, and who are endowed with a permanent spiritual mobility and a vibrant imagination.

Still, to call literature seditious because it sensitizes a reader's consciousness to the imperfections of the world does not mean — as churches and governments seem to think it means when they establish censorship — that literary texts will provoke immediate social upheavals or accelerate revolutions. The social and political effects of a poem, a play, or a novel cannot be foreseen, because they are not collectively made or collectively experienced. They are created by individuals and they are read by individuals, who vary enormously in the conclusions that they draw from their writing and their reading. For this reason, it is difficult, or even impossible, to establish precise patterns. Moreover, the social consequences of a work of literature may have little to do with its aesthetic quality. A mediocre novel by Harriet Beecher Stowe seems to have played a decisive role in raising social and political consciousness of the horrors of slavery in the United States. The fact that these effects of literature are difficult to identify does not imply that they do not exist. The important point is that they are effects brought about by the actions of citizens whose personalities have been formed in part by books.

Good literature, while temporarily relieving human dissatisfaction, actually increases it, by developing a critical and nonconformist attitude toward life. It might even be said that literature makes human beings more likely to be unhappy. To live dissatisfied, and at war with existence, is to seek things that may not be there, to condemn oneself to fight futile battles, like the battles that Colonel Aureliano Buendía fought in *One Hundred Years of Solitude*, knowing full well that he would lose them all. All this may be true. Yet it is also true that without rebellion against the mediocrity and the squalor of life, we would still live in a primitive state, and history would have stopped. The autonomous individual would not have been created, science and technology would not have progressed, human rights would not have been recognized, freedom would not have existed. All these things are born of unhappiness, of acts of defiance against a life perceived as insufficient or intolerable. For this spirit that scorns life as it is — and searches with the madness of Don Quixote, whose insanity derived from the reading of chivalric novels — literature has served as a great spur.

Let us attempt a fantastic historical reconstruction. Let us imagine a world without literature, a humanity that has not read poems or novels. In this kind of atrophied civilization, with its puny lexicon in which groans and apelike gesticulations would prevail over words, certain adjectives would not exist. Those adjectives include: quixotic, Kafkaesque, Rabelaisian, Orwellian, sadistic, and masochistic, all terms of literary origin. To be sure, we would still have insane people, and victims of paranoia and persecution complexes, and people with uncommon appetites and outrageous excesses, and bipeds who enjoy inflicting or receiving pain. But we would not have learned to see, behind these extremes of behavior that are prohibited by the norms of our culture, essential characteristics of the human condition. We would not have discovered our own traits, as only the talents of Cervantes, Kafka, Rabelais, Orwell, de Sade, and Sacher-Masoch have revealed them to us.

When the novel *Don Quixote de la Mancha* appeared, its first readers made fun of this extravagant dreamer, as well as the rest of the characters in the novel. Today we know that the insistence of the *caballero de la triste figura* on seeing giants where there were windmills, and on acting in his seemingly absurd way, is really the highest form of generosity, and a means of protest against the misery of this world in the hope of changing it. Our very notions of the ideal, and of idealism, so redolent with a positive moral connotation, would not be what they are, would not be clear and respected values, had they not been incarnated in the protagonist of a novel through the persuasive force of Cervantes's genius. The same can be said of that small and pragmatic female Quixote, Emma Bovary, who fought with ardor to live the splendid life of passion and luxury that she came to know through novels. Like a butterfly, she came too close to the flame and was burned in the fire.

The inventions of all great literary creators open our eyes to unknown aspects of our own condition. They enable us to explore and to understand more fully the common human abyss. When we say "Borgesian," the word immediately conjures up the separation of our minds from the rational order of reality and the entry into a fantastic universe, a rigorous and elegant mental construction, almost always labyrinthine and arcane, and riddled with literary references and allusions, whose singularities are not foreign to us because in them we recognize hidden desires and intimate truths of our own personality that took shape only thanks to the literary creation of Jorge Luis Borges. The word "Kafkaesque" comes to mind, like the focus mechanism of those old cameras with their accordion arms, every time we feel threatened, as defenseless individuals, by the oppressive machines of power that have caused so much pain and injustice in the modern world — the authoritarian regimes, the vertical parties, the intolerant churches, the asphyxiating bureaucrats. Without the short stories and the novels of that tormented Jew from Prague who wrote in German and lived always on the lookout, we would not have been able to understand the impotent feeling of the isolated individual, or the terror of persecuted and discriminated minorities, confronted with the all-embracing powers that can smash them and eliminate them without the henchmen even showing their faces.

The adjective "Orwellian," first cousin of "Kafkaesque," gives a voice to the terrible anguish, the sensation of extreme absurdity, that was generated by totalitarian dictatorships of the twentieth century, the most sophisticated, cruel, and absolute dictatorships in history, in their control of the actions and the psyches of the members of a society. In *1984*, George Orwell described in cold and haunting shades a humanity subjugated to Big Brother, an absolute lord who, through an efficient combination of terror and technology, eliminated liberty, spontaneity, and equality, and transformed society into a beehive of automatons. In this nightmarish world, language also obeys power, and has been transformed into "newspeak," purified of all invention and all subjectivity, metamorphosed into a string of platitudes that ensure the individual's slavery to the system. It is true that the sinister prophecy of *1984* did not come to pass, and totalitarian communism in the Soviet Union went the way of totalitarian fascism in Germany and elsewhere; and soon thereafter it began to deteriorate also in China, and in anachronistic Cuba and North Korea. But the danger is never completely dispelled, and the word "Orwellian" continues to describe the danger, and to help us to understand it.

So literature's unrealities, literature's lies, are also a precious vehicle for the knowledge of the most hidden of human realities. The truths that it reveals are not always flattering, and sometimes the image of ourselves that emerges in the mirror of novels and poems is the image of a monster. This happens when we read about the horrendous sexual butchery fantasized by de Sade, or the dark lacerations and brutal sacrifices that fill the cursed books of Sacher-Masoch and Bataille. At times the spectacle is so offensive and ferocious that it becomes irresistible. Yet the worst in these pages is not the blood, the humiliation, the abject love of torture; the worst is the discovery that this violence and this excess are not foreign to us, that they are a profound part of humanity. These monsters eager for transgression are hidden in the most intimate recesses of our being; and from the shadow where they live they seek a propitious occasion to manifest themselves, to impose the rule of unbridled desire that destroys rationality, community, and even existence. And it was not science that first ventured into these tenebrous places in the human mind, and discovered the destructive and the self-destructive potential that also shapes it. It was literature that made this discovery. A world without literature would be partly blind to these terrible depths, which we urgently need to see.

Uncivilized, barbarian, devoid of sensitivity and crude of speech, ignorant and instinctual, inept at passion and crude at love, this world without literature, this nightmare that I am delineating, would have as its principal traits conformism and the universal submission of humankind to power. In this sense, it would also be a purely animalistic world. Basic instincts would determine the daily practices of a life characterized by the struggle for survival, and the fear of the unknown, and the satisfaction of physical necessities. There would be no place for the spirit. In this world, moreover, the crushing monotony of living would be accompanied by the sinister shadow of pessimism, the feeling that human life is what it had to be, and that it will always be thus, and that no one and nothing can change it.

When one imagines such a world, one is tempted to picture primitives in loincloths, the small magic-religious communities that live at the margins of modernity in Latin America, Oceania, and Africa. But I have a different failure in mind. The nightmare that I am warning about is the result not of underdevelopment but of overdevelopment. As a consequence of technology and our subservience to it, we may imagine a future society full of computer screens and speakers, and without books, or a society in which books — that is, works of literature — have become what alchemy became in the era of physics: an archaic curiosity, practiced in the catacombs of the media civilization by a neurotic minority. I am afraid that this cybernetic world, in spite of its prosperity and its power, its high standard of living and its scientific achievement would be profoundly uncivilized and utterly soulless — a resigned humanity of postliterary automatons who have abdicated freedom.

It is highly improbable, of course, that this macabre utopia will ever come about. The end of our story, the end of history, has not yet been written, and it is not predetermined. What we will become depends entirely on our vision and our will. But if we wish to avoid the impoverishment of our imagination, and the disappearance of the precious dissatisfaction that refines our sensibility and teaches us to speak with eloquence and rigor, and the weakening of our freedom, then we must act. More precisely, we must read.

GORE VIDAL

The Meaning
of Timothy McVeigh

FROM VANITY FAIR

TOWARD THE END of the last century but one, Richard Wagner
made a visit to the southern Italian town of Ravello, where he was
shown the gardens of the thousand-year-old Villa Rufolo. "Maestro," asked the head gardener, "do not these fantastic gardens
'neath yonder azure sky that blends in such perfect harmony with
yonder azure sea closely resemble those fabled gardens of Klingsor where you have set so much of your latest interminable opera,
Parsifal? Is not this vision of loveliness your inspiration for Klingsor?" Wagner muttered something in German. "He say," said a
nearby translator, "'How about that?'"

How about that indeed, I thought, as I made my way toward a
corner of those fabled gardens, where ABC-TV's *Good Morning
America* and CBS's *Early Show* had set up their cameras so that I
could appear "live" to viewers back home in God's country.

This was last May. In a week's time "the Oklahoma City Bomber,"
a decorated hero of the Gulf War, one of Nature's Eagle Scouts,
Timothy McVeigh, was due to be executed by lethal injection in
Terre Haute, Indiana, for being, as he himself insisted, the sole
maker and detonator of a bomb that blew up a federal building in
which died 168 men, women, and children. This was the greatest
massacre of Americans by an American since two years earlier,
when the federal government decided to take out the compound
of a Seventh-day Adventist cult near Waco, Texas. The Branch
Davidians, as the cultists called themselves, were a peaceful group
of men, women, and children living and praying together in antici-

pation of the end of the world, which started to come their way on February 28, 1993. The federal Bureau of Alcohol, Tobacco and Firearms, exercising its mandate to "regulate" firearms, refused all invitations from cult leader David Koresh to inspect his licensed firearms. The ATF instead opted for fun. More than one hundred ATF agents, without proper warrants, attacked the church's compound while, overhead, at least one ATF helicopter fired at the roof of the main building. Six Branch Davidians were killed that day. Four ATF agents were shot dead, by friendly fire, it was thought.

There was a standoff. Followed by a fifty-one-day siege in which loud music was played twenty-four hours a day outside the compound. Then electricity was turned off. Food was denied the children. Meanwhile, the media were briefed regularly on the evils of David Koresh. Apparently, he was making and selling crystal meth; he was also — what else in these sick times? — not a man of God but a pedophile. The new attorney general, Janet Reno, then got tough. On April 19 she ordered the FBI to finish up what the ATF had begun. In defiance of the Posse Comitatus Act (a basic bulwark of our fragile liberties that forbids the use of the military against civilians), tanks of the Texas National Guard and the army's Joint Task Force Six attacked the compound with a gas deadly to children and not too healthy for adults while ramming holes in the building. Some Davidians escaped. Others were shot by FBI snipers. In an investigation six years later, the FBI denied ever shooting off anything much more than a pyrotechnic tear-gas canister. Finally, during a six-hour assault, the building was set fire to and then bulldozed by Bradley armored vehicles. God saw to it that no FBI man was hurt while more than eighty cult members were killed, of whom twenty-seven were children. It was a great victory for Uncle Sam, as intended by the FBI, whose code name for the assault was Show Time.

It wasn't until May 14, 1995, that Janet Reno, on *60 Minutes*, confessed to second thoughts. "I saw what happened, and knowing what happened, I would not do it again." Plainly, a learning experience for the Florida daughter of a champion lady alligator rassler.

The April 19, 1993, show at Waco proved to be the largest massacre of Americans by their own government since 1890, when a number of Native Americans were slaughtered at Wounded Knee, South Dakota. Thus the ante keeps upping.

Although McVeigh was soon to indicate that he had acted in retaliation for what had happened at Waco (he had even picked the second anniversary of the slaughter, April 19, for his act of retribution), our government's secret police, together with its allies in the media, put, as it were, a heavy fist upon the scales. There was to be only one story: one man of incredible innate evil wanted to destroy innocent lives for no reason other than a spontaneous joy in evildoing. From the beginning, it was ordained that McVeigh was to have no coherent motive for what he had done other than a Shakespearean motiveless malignity. Iago is now back in town, with a bomb, not a handkerchief. More to the point, he and the prosecution agreed that he had no serious accomplices.

I sat on an uncomfortable chair, facing a camera. Generators hummed amid the delphiniums. *Good Morning America* was first. I had been told that Diane Sawyer would be questioning me from New York, but ABC has a McVeigh "expert," one Charles Gibson, and he would do the honors. Our interview would be something like four minutes. Yes, I was to be interviewed In Depth. This means that only every other question starts with "Now, tell us, briefly . . ." Dutifully, I told, briefly, how it was that McVeigh, whom I had never met, happened to invite me to be one of the five chosen witnesses to his execution.

Briefly, it all began in the November 1998 issue of *Vanity Fair.* I had written a piece about "the shredding of our Bill of Rights." I cited examples of IRS seizures of property without due process of law, warrantless raids and murders committed against innocent people by various drug-enforcement groups, government collusion with agribusiness's successful attempts to drive small farmers out of business, and so on. Then, as a coda, I discussed the illegal but unpunished murders at Ruby Ridge, Idaho (by the FBI), then, the next year, Waco.

When McVeigh, on appeal in a Colorado prison, read what I had written he wrote me a letter and . . .

But I've left you behind in the Ravello garden of Klingsor, where, live on television, I mentioned the unmentionable word "why," followed by the atomic trigger word "Waco." Charles Gibson, thirty-five hundred miles away, began to hyperventilate. "Now, wait a minute . . ." he interrupted. But I talked through him. Suddenly I heard him say, "We're having trouble with the audio." Then he pulled the plug that linked ABC and me. The soundman beside me shook his head. "Audio was working perfectly. He just cut you off." So, in addition to the governmental shredding of Amendments Four, Five, Six, Eight, and Fourteen, Mr. Gibson switched off the journalists' sacred First.

Why? Like so many of his interchangeable TV colleagues, he is in place to tell the viewers that former senator John Danforth had just concluded a fourteen-month investigation of the FBI that cleared the bureau of any wrongdoing at Waco. Danforth did admit that "it was like pulling teeth to get all this paper from the FBI."

In March 1993, McVeigh drove from Arizona to Waco, Texas, in order to observe firsthand the federal siege. Along with other protesters, he was duly photographed by the FBI. During the siege the cultists were entertained with twenty-four-hour ear-shattering tapes (Nancy Sinatra: "These boots are made for walkin' / And that's just what they'll do, / One of these days these boots are gonna walk all over you") as well as the recorded shrieks of dying rabbits, reminiscent of the first George Bush's undeclared war on Panama, which after several similar concerts outside the Vatican embassy yielded up the master drug criminal (and former CIA agent) Noriega, who had taken refuge there. Like the TV networks, once our government has a hit, it will be repeated over and over again. Oswald? Conspiracy? Studio laughter.

TV watchers have no doubt noted so often that they are no longer aware of how often the interchangeable TV hosts handle anyone who tries to explain why something happened. "Are you suggesting that there was a conspiracy?" A twinkle starts in a pair of bright contact lenses. No matter what the answer, there is a wriggling of the body, followed by a tiny snort and a significant glance into the camera to show that the guest has just been delivered to the studio by flying saucer. This is one way for the public never to understand what actual conspirators — whether in the FBI or on the Supreme Court or toiling for Big Tobacco — are up to. It is also a sure way of keeping information from the public. The function, alas, of Corporate Media.

In fact, at one point, former senator Danforth threatened the recalcitrant FBI director Louis Freeh with a search warrant. It is a pity that he did not get one. He might, in the process, have discovered a bit more about Freeh's membership in Opus Dei ("God's Work"), a secretive international Roman Catholic order dedicated to getting its membership into high political, corporate, and religious offices (and perhaps even Heaven, too) in various lands to various ends. Lately, reluctant Medialight was cast on the order when it was discovered that Robert Hanssen, an FBI agent, had been a Russian spy for twenty-two years but also that he and his director, Louis Freeh, in the words of their fellow traveler William Rusher (the *Washington Times,* March 15, 2001), "not only [were] both members of the same Roman Catholic Church in suburban Virginia but . . . also belonged to the local chapter of Opus Dei." Mr. Rusher, once of the devil-may-care *National Review,* found this "piquant." Opus Dei was founded in 1928 by José María Escrivá. Its lay godfather, in early years, was the Spanish dictator Francisco Franco. One of its latest paladins was the corrupt Peruvian president Alberto Fujimoro, still in absentia. Although Opus Dei tends to fascism, the current pope has beatified Escrivá, disregarding the caveat of the Spanish theologian Juan Martín Velasco: "We cannot portray as a model of Christian living someone who has served the power of the state [the fascist Franco] and who used that power to launch his Opus, which he ran with obscure criteria — like a Mafia shrouded in white — not accepting papal magisterium when it failed to coincide with his way of thinking."

Once, when the mysterious Mr. Freeh was asked whether or not he was a member of Opus Dei, he declined to respond, obliging an FBI special agent to reply in his stead. Special Agent John E. Collingwood said, "While I cannot answer your specific questions, I note that you have been 'informed' incorrectly."

It is most disturbing that in the secular United States, a nation whose Constitution is based upon the perpetual separation of church and state, an absolutist religious order not only has placed one of its members at the head of our secret (and largely unaccountable) police but also can now count on the good offices of at least two members of the Supreme Court.

From *Newsweek,* March 9, 2001:

[Justice Antonin] Scalia is regarded as the embodiment of the Catholic conservatives . . . While he is not a member of Opus Dei, his wife Maureen has attended Opus Dei's spiritual functions . . . [while their son], Father Paul Scalia, helped convert Clarence Thomas to Catholicism four years ago. Last month, Thomas gave a fiery speech at the American Enterprise Institute, a conservative think-tank, to an audience full of Bush Administration officials. In the speech Thomas praised Pope John Paul II for taking unpopular stands.

And to think that Thomas Jefferson and John Adams opposed the presence of the relatively benign Jesuit order in our land of laws if not of God. President Bush has said that Scalia and Thomas are the models for the sort of justices that he would like to appoint in his term of office. Lately, in atonement for his wooing during the election of the fundamentalist Protestants at Bob Jones University, Bush has been "reaching out" to the Roman Catholic far right. He is already solid with fundamentalist Protestants. In fact, his attorney general, J. D. Ashcroft, is a Pentecostal Christian who starts each day at eight with a prayer meeting attended by Justice Department employees eager to be drenched in the blood of the lamb. In 1999, Ashcroft told Bob Jones University graduates that America was founded on religious principles (news to Jefferson et al.) and "we have no king but Jesus."

I have already noted a number of conspiracies that are beginning to register as McVeigh's highly manipulated story moves toward that ghastly word "closure," which, in this case, will simply mark a new beginning. The Opus Dei conspiracy is — was? — central to the Justice Department. Then the FBI conspired to withhold documents from the McVeigh defense as well as from the department's alleged master: We the People in Congress Assembled as embodied by former senator Danforth. Finally, the ongoing spontaneous media conspiracy to demonize McVeigh, who acted alone, despite contrary evidence.

But let's return to the FBI conspiracy to cover up its crimes at Waco. Senator Danforth is an honorable man, but then, so was Chief Justice Earl Warren, and the findings of his eponymous commission on the events at Dallas did not, it is said, ever entirely convince even him. On June 1, Danforth told the *Washington Post,* "I bet that Timothy McVeigh, at some point in time, I don't know when, will be executed and after the execution there will be some box found, somewhere." You are not, Senator, just beating your gums. Also on June 1, the *New York Times* ran an AP story in which lawyers for the Branch Davidians claim that when the FBI agents fired upon the cultists they used a type of short assault rifle that was later not tested. Our friend FBI spokesman John Collingwood said that a check of the bureau's records showed that "the shorter-barreled rifle was among the weapons tested." Danforth's response was pretty much, Well, if you say so. He did note, again, that he had got "something less than total cooperation" from the FBI. As H. L. Mencken put it, "[The Department of Justice] has been engaged in sharp practices since the earliest days and remains a fecund source of oppression and corruption today. It is hard to recall an administration in which it was not the center of grave scandal."

Freeh himself seems addicted to dull sharp practices. In 1996 he was the relentless Javert who came down so hard on an Atlanta security guard, Richard Jewell, over the Olympic Games bombing. Jewell was innocent. Even as Freeh sent out for a new hair shirt (Opus Dei members mortify the flesh) and gave the order to build a new guillotine, the FBI lab was found to have routinely bungled investigations (read *Tainting Evidence*, by J. F. Kelly and P. K. Wearne). Later, Freeh led the battle to prove Wen Ho Lee a Communist spy. Freeh's deranged charges against the blameless Los Alamos scientist were thrown out of court by an enraged federal judge who felt that the FBI had "embarrassed the whole nation." Well, it's always risky, God's work.

Even so, the more one learns about the FBI, the more one realizes that it is a very dangerous place indeed. Kelly and Wearne, in their investigation of its lab work, literally a life-and-death matter for those under investigation, quote two English forensic experts on the subject of the Oklahoma City bombing. Professor Brian Caddy, after a study of the lab's findings: "If these reports are the ones to be presented to the courts as evidence then I am appalled by their structure and information content. The structure of the reports seems designed to confuse the reader rather than help him." Dr. John Lloyd noted, "The reports are purely conclusory in nature. It is impossible to determine from them the chain of custody, on precisely what work has been done on each item." Plainly, the time has come to replace this vast, inept, and largely unaccountable secret police with a more modest and more efficient bureau to be called "the United States Bureau of Investigation."

*

It is now June 11, a hot, hazy morning here in Ravello. We've just watched Son of Show Time in Terre Haute, Indiana. CNN duly reported that I had not been able to be a witness, as McVeigh had requested: the attorney general had given me too short a time to get from here to there. I felt somewhat better when I was told that, lying on the gurney in the execution chamber, he would not have been able to see any of us through the tinted glass windows all around him. But then members of the press who were present said that he had deliberately made "eye contact" with his witnesses and with them. He did see his witnesses, according to Cate McCauley, who was one. "You could tell he was gone after the first shot," she said. She had worked on his legal case for a year as one of his defense investigators.

I asked about his last hours. He had been searching for a movie on television and all he could find was *Fargo*, for which he was in no mood. Certainly he died in character; that is, in control. The first shot, of sodium pentothal, knocks you out. But he kept his eyes open. The second shot, of pancuronium bromide, collapsed his lungs. Always the survivalist, he seemed to ration his remaining breaths. When, after four minutes, he was officially dead, his eyes were still open, staring into the ceiling camera that was recording him "live" for his Oklahoma City audience.

McVeigh made no final statement, but he had copied out, it appeared from memory, "Invictus," a poem by W. E. Henley (1849–1903). Among Henley's numerous writings was a popular anthology called *Lyra Heroics* (1892), about those who had done selfless heroic deeds. I doubt if McVeigh ever came across it, but he would no doubt have identified with a group of young writers, among them Kipling, who were known as "Henley's young men," forever standing on burning decks, each a master of his fate, captain of his soul.

Characteristically, no talking head mentioned Henley's name, because no one knew who he was. Many thought this famous poem was McVeigh's work. One irritable woman described Henley as "a nineteenth-century cripple." I fiercely e-mailed her network: the one-legged Henley was "extremities challenged."

The stoic serenity of McVeigh's last days certainly qualified him as a Henley-style hero. He did not complain about his fate; took responsibility for what he was thought to have done; did not beg for mercy as our always sadistic media require. Meanwhile, conflicting details about him accumulate — a bewildering mosaic, in fact — and he seems more and more to have stumbled into the wrong American era. Plainly, he needed a self-consuming cause to define him. The abolition of slavery or the preservation of the Union would have been more worthy of his life than anger at the excesses of our corrupt secret police. But he was stuck where he was and so he declared war on a government that he felt had declared war on its own people.

One poetic moment in what was largely an orchestrated hymn of hatred. Outside the prison, a group of anti-death-penalty people prayed together in the dawn's early light. Suddenly, a bird appeared and settled on the left forearm of a woman, who continued her prayers. When at last she rose to her feet, the bird remained on her arm — consolation? *Ora pro nobis.*

CNN gave us bits and pieces of McVeigh's last morning. Asked why he had not at least said that he was sorry for the murder of innocents, he said that he could say it but he would not have meant it. He was a soldier in a war not of his making. This was Henleyesque. One biographer described him as honest to a fault. McVeigh had also noted that Harry Truman had never said that he was sorry about dropping two atomic bombs on an already defeated Japan, killing around two hundred thousand people, mostly collateral women and children. Media howled that that was wartime. But McVeigh considered himself, rightly or wrongly, at war, too. Incidentally, the inexorable beatification of Harry Truman is now an important aspect of our evolving imperial system. It is widely believed that the bombs were dropped to save American lives. This is not true. The bombs were dropped to frighten our new enemy, Stalin. To a man, our leading World War II commanders, including Eisenhower, C. W. Nimitz, and even Curtis LeMay (played so well by George C. Scott in *Dr. Strangelove*), were opposed to Truman's use of the bombs against a defeated enemy trying to surrender. A friend from live television, the late Robert Alan Aurthur, made a documentary about Truman. I asked him what he thought of him. "He just gives you all these canned answers. The only time I got a rise out of him was when I suggested that he tell us about his decision to drop the atomic bombs in the actual ruins of Hiroshima. Truman looked at me for the first time. 'OK,' he said, 'but I won't kiss their asses.'" Plainly another Henley hero, with far more collateral damage to his credit than McVeigh. Was it Chaplin's M. Verdoux who said that when it comes to calibrating liability for murder it is all, finally, a matter of scale?

After my adventures in the Ravello gardens (CBS's Bryant Gumbel was his usual low-key, courteous self and did not pull the cord), I headed for Terre Haute by way of Manhattan. I did several programs where I was cut off at the word "Waco." Only CNN's Greta Van Susteren got the point. "Two wrongs," she said, sensibly, "don't make a right." I quite agreed with her. But then, since I am against the death penalty, I noted that three wrongs are hardly an improvement.

Then came the stay of execution. I went back to Ravello. The media were now gazing at me. Time and again I would hear or read that I had written McVeigh first, congratulating him, presumably, on his killings. I kept explaining, patiently, how, after he had read me in *Vanity Fair,* it was he who wrote me, starting an off-and-on three-year correspondence. As it turned out, I could not go, so I was not able to see with my own eyes the bird of dawning alight upon the woman's arm.

The first letter to me was appreciative of what I had written. I wrote him back. To show what an eager commercialite I am — hardly school of Capote — I kept no copies of my letters to him until the last one in May.

The second letter from his Colorado prison is dated "28 Feb 99." "Mr. Vidal, thank you for your letter. I received your book United States last week and have since finished most of Part 2 — your poetical musings." I should say that spelling and grammar are perfect throughout, while the handwriting is oddly even and slants to the left, as if one were looking at it in a mirror. "I think you'd be surprised at how much of that material I agree with . . .

> As to your letter, I fully recognize that "the general rebellion against what our gov't has become is the most interesting (and I think important) story in our history this century." This is why I have been mostly disappointed at previous stories attributing the OKC bombing to a simple act of "revenge" for Waco — and why I was most pleased to read your Nov. article in Vanity Fair. In the 4 years since the bombing, your work is the first to really explore the underlying motivations for such a

strike against the U.S. Government — and for that, I thank you. I believe that such in-depth reflections are vital if one truly wishes to understand the events of April 1995.

Although I have many observations that I'd like to throw at you, I must keep this letter to a practical length — so I will mention just one: if federal agents are like "so many Jacobins at war" with the citizens of this country, and if federal agencies "daily wage war" against those citizens, then should not the OKC bombing be considered a "counter-attack" rather than a self-declared war? Would it not be more akin to Hiroshima than Pearl Harbor? (I'm sure the Japanese were just as shocked and surprised at Hiroshima — in fact, was that anticipated effect not part and parcel of the overall strategy of that bombing?)

Back to your letter, I had never considered your age as an impediment [here he riots in tact!] until I received that letter — and noted that it was typed on a *manual typewriter?* Not to worry, recent medical studies tell us that Italy's taste for canola oil, olive oil and wine helps extend the average lifespan and helps prevent heart disease in Italians — so you picked the right place to retire to.

Again, thank you for dropping me a line — and as far as any concern over what or how to write someone "in my situation," I think you'd find that many of us are still just "regular Joes" — regardless of public perception — so there need be no special consideration(s) given to whatever you wish to write. Until next time, then . . .

Under this line he has put in quotes: "'Every normal man must be tempted at times to spit on his hands, hoist the black flag, and begin slitting throats.' — H. L. Mencken. Take good care."

He signed off with scribbled initials. Needless to say, this letter did not conform to any notion that I had had of him from reading the rabid U.S. press led, as always, by the *New York Times,* with its clumsy attempts at Freudian analysis (e.g., he was a broken blossom because his mother left his father in his sixteenth year — actually he seemed relieved). Later, there was a year or so when I did not hear from him. Two reporters from a Buffalo newspaper (he was born and raised near Buffalo) were at work interviewing him for their book, *American Terrorist.* I do think I wrote him that Mencken often resorted to Swiftian hyperbole and was not to be taken too literally. Could the same be said of McVeigh? There is always the interesting possibility — prepare for the grandest conspiracy of all — that he neither made nor set off the bomb outside the Murrah Building: it was only later, when facing either death or life imprisonment, that he saw to it that he would be given sole credit for hoisting the black flag and slitting throats, to the rising fury of various "militias" across the land who are currently outraged that he is getting sole credit for a revolutionary act organized, some say, by many others. At the end, if this scenario is correct, he and the detested feds were of a single mind.

As Senator Danforth foresaw, the government would execute McVeigh as soon as possible (within ten days of Danforth's statement to the *Washington Post*) in order not to have to produce so quickly that mislaid box with documents that might suggest that others were involved in the bombing. The fact that McVeigh himself was eager to commit what he called "federally assisted suicide" simply seemed a bizarre twist to a story that no matter how one tries to straighten it out never quite conforms to the ur-plot of lone crazed killer (Oswald) killed by a second lone crazed killer (Ruby), who would die in stir with, he claimed, a tale to tell. Unlike Lee Harvey ("I'm the patsy") Oswald, our Henley hero found irresistible the role of lone warrior against a bad state. Where, in his first correspondence with me, he admits to nothing for the obvious reason his lawyers have him on appeal, in his last letter to me, April 20, 2001 — "T. McVeigh 12076-064 POB 33 Terre Haute, In. 47808 (USA)" — he writes, "Mr. Vidal, if you have read the recently published 'American Terrorist,' then you've probably realized that you hit the nail on the head with your article 'The War at Home.' Enclosed is supplemental material to add to that insight." Among the documents he sent was an ABCNews.com chat transcript of a conversation with Timothy McVeigh's psychiatrist. The interview with Dr. John Smith was conducted by a moderator on March 29 of this year. Dr. Smith had had only one session with McVeigh, six years earlier. Apparently McVeigh had released him from his medical oath of confidentiality so that he could talk to Lou Michel and Dan Herbeck, authors *of American Terrorist.*

> MODERATOR: You say that Timothy McVeigh "was not deranged" and that he has "no major mental illness." So why, in your view, would he commit such a terrible crime?
> DR. JOHN SMITH: Well, I don't think he committed it because he was deranged or misinterpreting reality . . . He was overly sensitive, to the point of being a little paranoid, about the actions of the government.

But he committed the act mostly out of revenge because of the Waco assault, but he also wanted to make a political statement about the role of the federal government and protest the use of force against the citizens. So to answer your original question, it was a conscious choice on his part, not because he was deranged, but because he was serious.

Dr. Smith then notes McVeigh's disappointment that the media had shied away from any dialogue "about the misuse of power by the federal government." Also, "his statement to me, 'I did not expect a revolution.' Although he did go on to tell me that he had had discussions with some of the militias who lived in the hills around Kingman, AZ, about how easy it would be, with certain guns in the hills there, to cut interstate 40 in two and in that sense interfere with transportation from between the eastern and western part of the United States — a rather grandiose discussion."

Grandiose but, I think, in character for those rebels who like to call themselves Patriots and see themselves as similar to the American colonists who separated from England. They are said to number from two million to four million, of whom some four hundred thousand are activists in the militias. Although McVeigh never formally joined any group, for three years he drove all around the country, networking with like-minded gun lovers and federal-government haters; he also learned, according to *American Terrorist*, "that the government was planning a massive raid on gun owners and members of the Patriot community in the spring of 1995." This was all the trigger that McVeigh needed for what he would do — shuffle the deck, as it were.

The Turner Diaries is a racist daydream by a former physics teacher writing under the pseudonym Andrew Macdonald. Although McVeigh has no hangups about blacks, Jews, and all the other enemies of the various "Aryan" white nations to be found in the Patriots' tanks, he shares the *Diaries'* obsession with guns and explosives and a final all-out war against the "System." Much has been made, rightly, of a description in the book of how to build a bomb like the one he used in Oklahoma City. When asked if McVeigh acknowledged copying this section from the novel, Dr. Smith said, "Well, sort of. Tim wanted it made clear that, unlike *The Turner Diaries,* he was not a racist. He made that very clear. He did not hate homosexuals. He made that very clear." As for the book as an influence, "he's not going to share credit with anyone." Asked to sum up, the good doctor said, simply, "I have always said to myself that if there had not been a Waco, there would not have been an Oklahoma City."

McVeigh also sent me a 1998 piece he had written for *Media Bypass*. He calls it "Essay on Hypocrisy."

> The administration has said that Iraq has no right to stockpile chemical or biological weapons . . . mainly because they have used them in the past. Well, if that's the standard by which these matters are decided, then the U.S. is the nation that set the precedent. The U.S. has stockpiled these same weapons (and more) for over 40 years. The U.S. claims that this was done for the deterrent purposes during its "Cold War" with the Soviet Union. Why, then, is it invalid for Iraq to claim the same reason (deterrence) — with respect to Iraq's (real) war with, and the continued threat of, its neighbor Iran? . . .
>
> Yet when discussion shifts to Iraq, any day-care center in a government building instantly becomes "a shield." Think about it. (Actually, there is a difference here. The administration has admitted to knowledge of the presence of children in or near Iraqi government buildings, yet they still proceed with their plans to bomb — saying that they cannot be held responsible if children die. There is no such proof, however, that knowledge of the presence of children existed in relation to the Oklahoma City bombing.)

Thus, he denies any foreknowledge of the presence of children in the Murrah Building, unlike the FBI, which knew that there were children in the Davidian compound, and managed to kill twenty-seven of them.

McVeigh quotes again from Justice Brandeis: "'Our government is the potent, the omnipresent teacher. For good or ill it teaches the whole people by its example.'" He stops there. But Brandeis goes on to write in his dissent, "Crime is contagious. If the government becomes the law breaker, it breeds contempt for laws; it invites every man to become a law unto himself." Thus the straight-arrow model soldier unleashed his terrible swift sword and the innocent died. But then a lawless government, Brandeis writes, "invites anarchy. To declare that in the administration of the criminal law the end justifies the means — to declare that the government may commit crimes in order to secure the conviction of a private criminal — would bring terrible retribution."

One wonders if the Opus Dei plurality of the present Supreme Court's five-to-four majority has ever pondered these words so different from, let us say, one of its essential thinkers, Machiavelli, who insisted that, above all, the Prince must be feared. Finally, McVeigh sent me three pages of longhand notes dated April 4, 2001, a few weeks before he was first scheduled to die. It is addressed to "C.J."(?), whose initials he has struck out.

I explain herein why I bombed the Murrah Federal Building in Oklahoma City. I explain this not for publicity, nor seeking to win an argument of right or wrong. I explain so that the record is clear as to my thinking and motivations in bombing a government installation.

I chose to bomb a Federal Building because such an action served more purposes than other options. Foremost, the bombing was a retaliatory strike: a counter-attack, for the cumulative raids (and subsequent violence and damage) that federal agents had participated in over the preceding years (including, but not limited to, Waco). From the formation of such units as the FBI's "Hostage Rescue" and other assault teams amongst federal agencies during the 80s, culminating in the Waco incident, federal actions grew increasingly militaristic and violent, to the point where at Waco, our government — like the Chinese — was deploying tanks against its own citizens.

. . . For all intents and purposes, federal agents had become "soldiers" (using military training, tactics, techniques, equipment, language, dress, organization and mindset) and they were escalating their behavior. Therefore, this bombing was also meant as a pre-emptive (or pro-active) strike against those forces and their command and control centers within the federal building. When an aggressor force continually launches attacks from a particular base of operations, it is sound military strategy to take the fight to the enemy. Additionally, borrowing a page from U.S. foreign policy, I decided to send a message to a government that was becoming increasingly hostile, by bombing a government building and the government employees within that building who represent that government. Bombing the Murrah Federal Building was morally and strategically equivalent to the U.S. hitting a government building in Serbia, Iraq, or other nations. Based on observations of the policies of my own government, I viewed this action as an acceptable option. From this perspective what occurred in Oklahoma City was no different than what Americans rain on the heads of others all the time, and, subsequently, my mindset was and is one of clinical detachment. (The bombing of the Murrah Building was not personal no more than when Air Force, Army, Navy or Marine personnel bomb or launch

cruise missiles against (foreign) government installations and their personnel.)

I hope this clarification amply addresses your question.

Sincerely,

T.M.

USP Terre Haute (In.)

There were many outraged press notes and letters when I said that
McVeigh suffered from "an exaggerated sense of justice." I did not
really need the adjective except that I knew that few Americans seriously believe that anyone is capable of doing anything except out
of personal self-interest, while anyone who deliberately risks —
and gives — his life to alert his fellow citizens to an onerous government is truly crazy. But the good Dr. Smith put that one in perspective: McVeigh was not deranged. He was serious.

It is June 16. It seems like five years rather than five days since the
execution. The day before the execution, June 10, the *New York
Times* discussed "The Future of American Terrorism." Apparently,
terrorism has a real future; hence we must beware Nazi skinheads
in the boondocks. The *Times* is, occasionally, right for the usual
wrong reasons. For instance, their current wisdom is to dispel the
illusion that "McVeigh is merely a pawn in an expansive conspiracy
led by a group of John Does that may even have had government
involvement. But only a small fringe will cling to this theory for
long." Thank God: one had feared that rumors of a greater conspiracy would linger on and Old Glory herself would turn to fringe
before our eyes. The *Times,* more in anger than in sorrow, feels
that McVeigh blew martyrdom by first pleading not guilty and then
by not using his trial to "make a political statement about Ruby
Ridge and Waco." McVeigh agreed with the *Times,* and blamed his
first lawyer, Stephen Jones, in unholy tandem with the judge, for
selling him out. During his appeal, his new attorneys claimed that
the serious sale took place when Jones, eager for publicity, met
with the *Times's* Pam Belluck. McVeigh's guilt was quietly con-
ceded, thus explaining why the defense was so feeble. (Jones
claims he did nothing improper.)

Actually, in the immediate wake of the bombing, the *Times* con-
cedes, the militia movement skyrocketed from 220 anti-govern-

ment groups in 1995 to more than 850 by the end of 1996. A factor in this growth was the belief circulating among militia groups "that government agents had planted the bomb as a way to justify anti-terrorism legislation. No less than a retired Air Force general has promoted the theory that in addition to Mr. McVeigh's truck bomb, there were bombs inside the building." Although the *Times* likes analogies to Nazi Germany, it is curiously reluctant to draw one between, let's say, the firing of the Reichstag in 1933 (Göring later took credit for this creative crime), which then allowed Hitler to invoke an Enabling Act that provided him with all sorts of dictatorial powers "for protection of the people and the state," and so on to Auschwitz.

The canny *Portland Free Press* editor, Ace Hayes, noted that the one absolutely necessary dog in every terrorism case has yet to bark. The point to any terrorist act is that credit must be claimed so that fear will spread throughout the land. But no one took credit until McVeigh did, *after* the trial, in which he was condemned to death as a result of circumstantial evidence produced by the prosecution. Ace Hayes wrote, "If the bombing was not terrorism then what was it? It was pseudo terrorism, perpetrated by compartmentalized covert operators for the purposes of state police power." Apropos Hayes's conclusion, Adam Parfrey wrote in *Cult Rapture*, "[The bombing] is not different from the bogus Viet Cong units that were sent out to rape and murder Vietnamese to discredit the National Liberation Front. It is not different from the bogus 'finds' of Commie weapons in El Salvador. It is not different from the bogus Symbionese Liberation Army created by the CIA/FBI to discredit the real revolutionaries." Evidence of a conspiracy? Edye Smith was interviewed by Gary Tuchman, May 23, 1995, on CNN. She duly noted that the ATF bureau, about seventeen people on the ninth floor, suffered no casualties. Indeed they seemed not to have come to work that day. Jim Keith gives details in *OKBOMB!*, while Smith observed on TV, "Did the ATF have a warning sign? I mean, did they think it might be a bad day to go into the office? They had an option not to go to work that day, and my kids didn't get that option." She lost two children in the bombing. ATF has a number of explanations. The latest: five employees were in the offices, unhurt.

Another lead not followed up: McVeigh's sister read a letter he wrote her to the grand jury stating that he had become a member of a "Special Forces Group involved in criminal activity."

At the end, McVeigh, already condemned to death, decided to take full credit for the bombing. Was he being a good professional soldier, covering up for others? Or did he, perhaps, now see himself in a historic role with his own private Harper's Ferry, and though his ashes molder in the grave, his spirit is marching on? We may know — one day.

As for "the purposes of state police power," after the bombing, Clinton signed into law orders allowing the police to commit all sorts of crimes against the Constitution in the interest of combating terrorism. On April 20, 1996 (Hitler's birthday of golden memory, at least for the producers of *The Producers*), President Clinton signed the Anti-Terrorism Act ("for the protection of the people and the state" — the emphasis, of course, is on the second noun), while, a month earlier, the mysterious Louis Freeh had informed Congress of his plans for expanded wiretapping by his secret police. Clinton described his Anti-Terrorism Act in familiar language (March 1, 1993, *USA Today*): "We can't be so fixated on our desire to preserve the rights of ordinary Americans." A year later (April 19, 1994, on MTV): "A lot of people say there's too much personal freedom. When personal freedom's being abused, you have to move to limit it." On that plangent note he graduated cum laude from the Newt Gingrich Academy.

In essence, Clinton's Anti-Terrorism Act would set up a national police force, over the long-dead bodies of the founders. Details are supplied by HR 97, a chimera born of Clinton, Reno, and the mysterious Mr. Freeh. A twenty-five-hundred-man Rapid Deployment Strike Force would be organized, under the attorney general, with dictatorial powers. The chief of police of Windsor, Missouri, Joe Hendricks, spoke out against this supraconstitutional police force. Under this legislation, Hendricks said, "an agent of the FBI could walk into my office and commandeer this police department. If you don't believe that, read the crime bill that Clinton signed into law . . . There is talk of the Feds taking over the Washington, D.C., police department. To me this sets a dangerous precedent." But after a half century of the Russians are coming, followed by terrorists from proliferating rogue states as well as the ongoing horrors of drug-related crime, there is little respite for a people so routinely — so fiercely — disinformed. Yet there is a native suspicion that seems to be a part of the individual American psyche — as demonstrated in polls, anyway. According to a Scripps Howard News Service poll, 40 percent of Americans think it quite likely that the FBI set the fires at Waco. Fifty-one percent believe federal officials killed Jack Kennedy. (Oh, Oliver, what hast thou wrought!) Eighty percent believe that the military is withholding evidence that Iraq used nerve gas or something as deadly in the Gulf. Unfortunately, the other side of this coin is troubling. After Oklahoma City, 58 percent of Americans, according to the *Los Angeles Times,* were willing to surrender some of their liberties to stop terrorism — including, one wonders, the sacred right to be misinformed by government?

Shortly after McVeigh's conviction, Director Freeh soothed the Senate Judiciary Committee: "Most of the militia organizations around the country are not, in our view, threatening or dangerous." But earlier, before the Senate Appropriations Committee, he had "confessed" that his bureau was troubled by "various individuals, as well as organizations, some having an ideology which suspects government of world-order conspiracies — individuals who have organized themselves against the United States." In sum, this bureaucrat who does God's Work regards as a threat those "individuals who espouse ideologies inconsistent with principles of Federal Government." Oddly, for a former judge, Freeh seems not to recognize how chilling this last phrase is.

The CIA's former director William Colby is also made nervous by the disaffected. In a chat with Nebraska state senator John Decamp (shortly before the Oklahoma City bombing), he mused, "I watched as the Anti-War movement rendered it impossible for this country to conduct or win the Viet Nam War . . . This Militia and Patriot movement . . . is far more significant and far more dangerous for Americans than the Anti-War movement ever was, if it is not intelligently dealt with . . . It is not because these people are armed that America need be concerned." Colby continues, "They are dangerous because there are so many of them. It is one thing to have a few nuts or dissidents. They can be dealt with, *justly or otherwise* [my emphasis] so that they do not pose a danger to the system. It is quite another situation when you have a true movement —

millions of citizens believing something, particularly when the movement is made up of society's average, successful citizens." Presumably one "otherwise" way of handling such a movement is when it elects a president by a half-million votes — to call in a like-minded Supreme Court majority to stop a state's recounts, create arbitrary deadlines, and invent delays until our ancient electoral system, by default, must give the presidency to the "system's" candidate as opposed to the one the people voted for.

Many an "expert" and many an expert believe that McVeigh neither built nor detonated the bomb that blew up a large part of the Murrah Federal Building on April 19, 1995. To start backward — rather the way the FBI conducted this case — if McVeigh was *not* guilty, why did he confess to the murderous deed? I am convinced from his correspondence and what one has learned about him in an ever-lengthening row of books that, once found guilty — due to what he felt was the slovenly defense of his principal lawyer, Stephen Jones, so unlike the brilliant defense of his "co-conspirator" Terry Nichols's lawyer Michael Tigar — McVeigh believed that the only alternative to death by injection was a half century or more of life in a box. There is another aspect of our prison system (considered one of the most barbaric in the First World) that was alluded to by a British writer in the *Guardian.* He quoted California's attorney general, Bill Lockyer, on the subject of the CEO of an electric utility, currently battening on California's failing energy supply. "'I would love to personally escort this CEO to an 8 by 10 cell that he could share with a tattooed dude who says — "Hi, my name is Spike, Honey."' . . . The senior law official in the state was confirming (what we all suspected) that rape is penal policy. Go to prison and serving as a Hell's Angel sex slave is judged part of your sentence." A couple of decades fending off Spike is not a Henley hero's idea of a good time. Better dead than Spiked. Hence, "I bombed the Murrah building."

Evidence, however, is overwhelming that there was a plot involving militia types and government infiltrators — who knows? — as prime movers to create panic in order to get Clinton to sign that infamous Anti-Terrorism Act. But if, as it now appears, there were many interested parties involved, a sort of unified field theory is never apt to be found, but should there be one, Joel Dyer may be its Einstein. (Einstein, of course, never got his field quite together,

either.) In 1998, I read Dyer's *Harvest of Rage.* Dyer was editor of
the *Boulder Weekly.* He writes on the crisis of rural America due to
the decline of the family farm, which also coincided with the formation of various militias and religious cults, some dangerous,
some merely sad. In *Harvest of Rage,* Dyer made the case that
McVeigh and Terry Nichols could not have acted alone in the
Oklahoma City bombing. Now he has, after long investigation,
written an epilogue to the trials of the two co-conspirators.

It will be interesting to see if the FBI is sufficiently intrigued by
what Joel Dyer has written to pursue the leads that he has so gener-
ously given them.

Thus far, David Hoffman's *The Oklahoma City Bombing and the Politics of Terror* is the most thorough of a dozen or two accounts of
what did and did not happen on that day in April. Hoffman begins
his investigation with retired air force brigadier general Benton K.
Partin's May 17, 1995, letter delivered to each member of the Senate and House of Representatives: "When I first saw the pictures of
the truck-bomb's asymmetrical damage to the Federal Building,
my immediate reaction was that the pattern of damage would have
been technically impossible without supplementing demolition
charges at some of the reinforcing concrete column bases . . . For a
simplistic blast truck-bomb, of the size and composition reported,
to be able to reach out in the order of 60 feet and collapse a reinforced column base the size of column A-7 is beyond credulity." In
separate agreement was Samuel Cohen, father of the neutron
bomb and formerly of the Manhattan Project, who wrote an Oklahoma state legislator, "It would have been absolutely impossible
and against the laws of nature for a truck full of fertilizer and fuel
oil . . . no matter how much was used . . . to bring the building
down." One would think that McVeigh's defense lawyer, restlessly
looking for a Middle East connection, could certainly have called
these acknowledged experts to testify, but a search of Jones's account of the case, *Others Unknown,* reveals neither name.

In the March 20, 1996, issue of *Strategic Investment* newsletter, it
was reported that Pentagon analysts tended to agree with General
Partin. "A classified report prepared by two independent Pentagon
experts has concluded that the destruction of the Federal building
in Oklahoma City last April was caused by five separate bombs . . .

Sources close to the study say Timothy McVeigh did play a role in the bombing but 'peripherally,' as a 'useful idiot.'" Finally, inevitably — this is wartime, after all — "the multiple bombings have a Middle Eastern 'signature,' pointing to either Iraqi or Syrian involvement."

As it turned out, Partin's and Cohen's pro bono efforts to examine the ruins were in vain. Sixteen days after the bombing, the search for victims stopped. In another letter to Congress, Partin stated that the building should not be destroyed until an independent forensic team was brought in to investigate the damage. "It is also easy to cover up crucial evidence as was apparently done in Waco . . . Why rush to destroy the evidence?" Trigger words: the feds demolished the ruins six days later. They offered the same excuse that they had used at Waco, "health hazards." Partin: "It's a classic cover-up."

Partin suspected a Communist plot. Well, nobody's perfect.

"So what's the take-away?" was the question often asked by TV producers in the so-called Golden Age of live television plays. This meant: what is the audience supposed to think when the play is over? The McVeigh story presents us with several take-aways. If McVeigh is simply a "useful idiot," a tool of what might be a very large conspiracy, involving various homegrown militias working, some think, with Middle Eastern helpers, then the FBI's refusal to follow up so many promising leads goes quite beyond its ordinary incompetence and smacks of treason. If McVeigh was the unlikely sole mover and begetter of the bombing, then his "inhumane" (the Unabomber's adjective) destruction of so many lives will have served no purpose at all unless we take it seriously as what it is, a wake-up call to a federal government deeply hated, it would seem, by millions. (Remember that the popular Ronald Reagan always ran *against* the federal government, though often for the wrong reasons.) Final far-fetched take-away: McVeigh did not make nor deliver nor detonate the bomb but, once arrested on another charge, seized all "glory" for himself and so gave up his life. That's not a story for W. E. Henley so much as for one of his young men, Rudyard Kipling, author of "The Man Who Would Be King."

Finally, the fact that the McVeigh-Nichols scenario makes no sense at all suggests that yet again we are confronted with a "perfect" crime — thus far.

GARRY WILLS

The Dramaturgy of Death

FROM THE NEW YORK REVIEW OF BOOKS

1. Capital Punishment: The Rationales

> A slight perusal of the laws by which the measures of vindictive and
> coercive justice are established will discover so many disproportions
> between crimes and punishments, such capricious distinctions of guilt,
> and such confusion of remissness and severity as can scarcely be believed
> to have been produced by public wisdom, sincerely and calmly studious
> of public happiness.
>
> — Samuel Johnson, *Rambler* 114

NIETZSCHE DENIED that capital punishment ever arose from a
single or consistent theory of its intent or effect. It erupted from a
tangle of overlapping yet conflicting urges, which would be fitted
out with later rationalizations. The only common denominator he
found in the original urges was some form of grievance (he used
the French term *ressentiment*). One can expand his own list of such
urges:

Killing as exclusion. This occurs when society does not want to admit any responsibility for persons considered outsiders. Abandon-
ment of wounded or captured people one does not want to feed or
support is an example, or exposure of unwanted children, or exil-
ing the defenseless (as the blind and old Oedipus was extruded
from Thebes), or "outlawing" — leaving people without protection to any predators on them. Outlawing was an English practice
continued in our colonies. In fact, Thomas Jefferson, when he revised the laws of Virginia for the new republic, left certain categories of offenders "out of the protection of the laws" — freed slaves

who either enter the state or refuse to leave it, a white woman bearing a black child who does not leave the state within a year. These could be killed or mistreated in any way without remedy at law. The ancient Greeks denied offenders recourse to law by the penalty of *atimia* (loss of rights). There were lesser degrees of this, but the full degree of "atimia . . . and condemnation to death are interchangeable." Nietzsche calls this "Punishment as the expulsion of a degenerate element . . . as a means of preserving the purity of a race or maintaining a social type."

Killing as cleansing. Outlawing abandons people to possible or probable death but does not directly bring it about. Other forms of extrusion require society's purification by *destruction* of a polluted person. Unless society or its agents effect this purification, the pollution continues to taint them. Lesser pollutions can be robbed of their effect by simply driving away the affected person. But deeper taints are removed only by accompanying the expulsion with something like stoning the polluter to death or throwing him off a cliff. Plato said that the murderer of anyone in his own immediate family was to be killed by judicial officers and magistrate, then "thrown down naked on a designated crossroads outside the city; whereupon every official present must throw his own stone at the head of the corpse, to cleanse the whole city, and finally must take him beyond the land's outer boundaries and cast him out, all rites of burial denied" (*Laws* 873b–c).

Killing as execration. Sometimes the community must thrust away contamination by ritual curses (*arai*), joining the punitive cry of the Furies, who are also called Arai (Aeschylus, *Eumenides* 417). When Prometheus is punished by exposure as the penalty of theft, Brute Force (Bia) tells the technician clamping him to the rock (Hephaistos) that he should curse as well as immobilize him (Aeschylus, *Prometheus* 38, 67–68). Southern lynch mobs stayed to curse with fury their hanged victim from a similar impulse.

Killing to maintain social order. Superiors dramatize their dominance by showing that it is easy for those higher in the social scale to kill those lower, but harder for the lower to kill the higher. Plato's legal code devised a penalty for a slave who kills a free man — public scourging to death before the free man's tomb and family — that had no symmetrical penalty for a free man who kills a slave (*Laws* 872b–c). In Jefferson's legal code, slaves could not testify against whites, but whites could testify against slaves. In parts of this country still, a black killing a white is far more likely to receive a death sentence than a white killing a black. Nietzsche calls this "Punishment as a means of inspiring fear of those who determine and execute the punishment."

Killing to delegitimize a former social order. Revolutionary tribunals execute officials of an overthrown regime. Even without a coup, critics of Athenian democracy claimed that mass juries were too ready to condemn their leaders. When the Turkish general Lala Mustafa Pasha captured Cyprus from the Venetians in 1570, the podestà who had held out against him, Marcantonio Bragadin, was mutilated (nose and ears cut off), dragged around the city walls, dangled from a ship's mast, tied naked to a post, skinned alive, beheaded, and "quartered" (his four limbs cut off). Then his skin, stuffed with straw, was tied to a cow and led through the streets of the Famagusta, before being returned as a victory prize to Constantinople. Venetian rule was pulverized in its representative. Nietzsche calls this "Punishment as a festival, namely as the rape and mockery of a finally defeated enemy."

Killing as posthumous delegitimation. Some inquisitors tried dead men and symbolically executed them. The leaders of the Gowrie Plot that tried to supplant King James VI of Scotland in 1600 were tried posthumously and their corpses were hanged, drawn (eviscerated), and quartered. In 897, Stephen VI had the corpse of his predecessor, Pope Formosus, exhumed, propped up in his papal garb, tried and condemned for usurpation, stripped of his vestments, his head (that had borne the tiara) cut off, along with the three fingers of his right hand used in benediction, and head, fingers, and body then thrown in the Tiber — all to declare Formosus's consecration of bishops and ordination of priests invalid.

Killing as total degradation. The previous three forms of execution punished an offender as a member of a class (lower or higher); but other humiliating deaths are contrived to deprive a person of humanity as such. Public torture before death was one means for this — scourging that makes the offender scream and writhe, losing dignity along with his composure. The Greek punishment for theft was *apotympanismos,* the beating of a naked man clamped down in a crouched position before he was left to die of exposure (it is the punishment given to Prometheus in his play, though he cannot die). The death for traitors in Elizabethan England was an elaborate piece of theater. First the offender was dragged backward on a hurdle to the place of execution — signifying, said the attorney general Sir Edward Coke, that the man was "not worthy any more to tread upon the face of the earth whereof he was made; also for that he hath been retrograde to nature, therefore is he drawn backward at a horse-tail." Then the man (it was a male punishment) was stripped, hanged, cut down living, castrated, disemboweled, his heart and viscera thrown in boiling water, decapitated, quartered, and his head exposed on Tower Bridge. When Jesuit priests were hanged, drawn, and quartered, their head, members, torso, and clothes were hidden away to prevent the taking of relics.

Killing and posthumous degradation. Refusal of burial led the ancient Greeks to let bodies be exposed for ravaging by dogs and kites (Creon's treatment of Polyneices in Sophocles' *Antigone*). Romans let crucified bodies hang to be pecked at and decompose. Florentines in the Renaissance dangled the corpses of criminals from the high windows of the Bargello till they rotted, and commissioned artists like Andrea del Sarto to depict them there, prolonging the shame after they were gone. Joan of Arc was killed by a slow fire that consumed her clothes and skin, then the flames were raked away, to expose her body as a woman's and to show that no demon had spirited her away. Then intense fire was mounted to burn her down to ashes for scattering in the Seine, to prevent any collection of relics.

Killing by ordeal. In this punishment, the innocent were supposed to be protected if subjected to ordeal by combat, ordeal by fire (walking through it, as Saint Francis is supposed to have done in Egypt), or ordeal by water. The latter was especially reserved for suspected witches, who would sink only if innocent. A less lethal form of this punishment survived in the "ducking stool" for immersing witches. Jefferson's revised code says this: "All attempts to delude the people, or to abuse their understanding by exercise of the pretended [claimed] arts of witchcraft, conjuration, enchantment, or sorcery or by pretended prophecies, shall be punished by ducking and whipping at the discretion of a jury, not exceeding 15 stripes."

Threatened killing as inducement to remorse. Refusal to undergo trial by ordeal could be taken as a confession, leading to a lesser penalty than death. Recanting could have the same effect. Joan of Arc, when first brought out to the stake with its kindling, renounced her voices as "idolatry" (devil worship), and was given life imprisonment. Only when she abjured her recantation was she actually put to the stake. Scaffold repentance could reduce the sentence to less than death — or, at the least, make officials perform a "merciful" (a swifter, not a lingering) execution — e.g., letting a man die in the noose before being cut down for disemboweling. Nietzsche calls this punishment for the "improvement" of the criminal.

Killing as repayment. The *lex talionis,* as it exacts "an eye for an eye," must exact a life for a life. We say, "You're going to *pay* for this." Jefferson followed the logic of his state's *lex talionis:*

> Whosoever shall be guilty of Rape, Polygamy, or Sodomy with man or woman shall be punished, if a man, by castration, if a woman, by cutting thro' the cartilage of her nose a hole of one half inch diameter at the least . . . Whosoever on purpose and of malice forethought shall maim another, or shall disfigure him, by cutting out or disabling the tongue, slitting or cutting off a nose, lip or ear, branding, or otherwise, shall be maimed or disfigured in like sort: or if that cannot be for want of the same part, then as nearly as may be in some other part of at least equal value and estimation in the opinion of a jury, and moreover shall forfeit one half of his lands and goods to the sufferer.

Taking a life for a life on this principle is called by Nietzsche "Punishment as recompense to the injured party for the harm done."

Killing as repayment-plus. In Athenian law, repayment was of equal value if the crime was unintentional, but of double if it was intentional. On that principle, death has not been reserved only for taking a life, but can be considered an added penalty for crimes like major theft, rape, treasonous speech, and the like.

Killing as victim therapy. The Attic orator Antiphon has the father of a son killed by accident plead that the unintentional killer must be punished; the death leaves the father aggrieved (*epithymion* — much like Nietzsche's *ressentiment*). The grievance, of course, would be even greater if the killing were intentional. Soothing this sense of grievance is now called "giving closure" to the ordeal of victims.

Killing as a form of pedagogy. We say that punishing a man will "teach him a lesson." More important, it may teach others the consequence of crime, deterring anyone who contemplates a similar offense. Kant said that the person should be treated as his own end, not as a means for others' advantage. But the person executed is, by this theory, turned into a teaching instrument for the benefit of others.

2. *Public Execution*

> Experience of past times gives us little reason to hope that any reformation will be effected by a periodical havoc of our fellow beings.
>   — Samuel Johnson, *Rambler* 114

The fourteen types of capital punishment listed above do not exhaust all the possible urges expressed in our havocking of others. And as Nietzsche said, they are not neat little separate rationales. They conflict with each other at an intellectual level, but they reinforce each other at the emotional level. They are more powerful for certain people in certain combinations. But they have one thing in common: *they all demand, in logic, maximum display and publicity.* The outlaw's status must be proclaimed for people to act on it. The other effects sought — whether cleansing, order enforcement, delegitimation, humiliation, repayment, therapy, deterrence — can only be achieved if an audience sees what is being done to satisfy, intimidate, soothe, or instruct it.

In fact, various means to dramatize the process, to make its meaning clear, to show the right way to "read" it, were invented. Those going to the scaffold often had their crimes blazoned on their backs. Joan of Arc wore a fool's cap with her four crimes printed on it. A crucified man had his crime posted on the cross. Lesser criminals were branded to sustain the memory of their crime. Ingenious means of execution were invented to express society's horror, anger, power, and the like. Any punishment that fits the crime should be *seen* to fit the crime. Indeed, the only urges that people now commonly admit to — the last four in the above list (repayment of two kinds, "closure," and deterrence) — are closely linked with publicity. The repayment is to us, to society as well as to the victims, the therapy is for the victims' contemplation, and an act meant to deter should vividly catch the attention of those who might benefit from it. How can they "learn their lesson" if it is not spelled out for them?

Our unconfessed difficulty is that we have given up whatever logic there was to the death penalty, since we have become unable to embrace most of the practices of the past. We no longer believe in a divine miasma to be purged, or divine guidance to be revealed in survival by ordeal. We have given up the desecration of corpses, killing as a reinforcement of class distinctions, torture, maiming, evisceration, and all the multiple methods used to reduce the criminal to a *corpus vile*. Even Jefferson wavered on the *lex talionis* when it came to blinding an offender (he could go as far as a nose for a nose, but not as far as an eye for an eye). Our Constitution forbids cruel and unusual punishment, and we take that to mean that there will be no gratuitous humiliation of the convict — we do not even put people in the stocks anymore, much less invite the public to see a condemned man being strapped onto a gurney. We want painless executions, so we have recurred to one of the few humane-looking methods of the Greeks — lethal injection (hemlock), though among the many deterrents to becoming a philosopher, Socrates' quiet (and self-chosen) death in his seventies has never ranked very high.

So far from stigmatizing or humiliating the inmate of death row, we now provide him with a long and costly process meant to ascertain guilt, with free legal aid if he cannot afford his own, with counseling and family visits, with reading of his choice and TV, a last meal to his specifications, a last request, religious attendance, guaranteed burial, a swift and nearly painless death. We shut up his last hours from the general public, and act as if this secret rite will deter by some magic of mere occurrence. We treat the killing as a dirty little secret, as if we are ashamed of it. Well, we should be ashamed. Having given up on most of the previous justifications for the death penalty, we cling to a mere vestige of the practice, relying most urgently on one of the least defensible defenses of it.

3. Deterrence

> The gibbet, indeed, certainly disables those who die upon it from
> infesting the community; but their death seems not to contribute more to
> the reformation of their associates than any other method of separation.
> — Samuel Johnson, *Rambler* 114

The bad faith of the process shows in the insistence on using the deterrence argument when it has been discredited by all the most reputable studies. This is an old story. In the eighteenth century, Samuel Johnson, who liked to defend any tradition he could, discovered no deterrent effect following on traditional executions, though they were far more numerous and far more public than they are now (factors, some people think, that add to deterrent effect). In the middle of the twentieth century, Arthur Koestler could refer to a strong scholarly record on the matter:

> This belief in the irreplaceable deterrent value of the death-penalty has been proved to be a superstition by the long and patient inquiries of the Parliamentary Select Committee of 1930 and the Royal Commission on Capital Punishment of 1948; yet it pops up again and again. Like all superstitions, it has the nature of a Jack-in-the-box; however often you hit it over the head with facts and statistics, it will solemnly pop up again, because the hidden spring inside it is the unconscious and irrational power of traditional beliefs.

Present and former presidents of the most prestigious criminological societies, polled in 1995, overwhelmingly said they did not think the death penalty significantly reduces the homicide rate (94 percent), and they knew of no empirical evidence that would support such a claim (94.1 percent). They held (79.2 percent) that execution causes no reduction in crime — a finding confirmed by the fact that states with the death penalty have higher murder rates than those without (the region with the highest number of homicides, the South, accounts for over 80 percent of the nation's executions). Furthermore, countries in Europe that have given up the death penalty have far lower murder rates than does the United States (since those countries *do* have gun control laws). Disbelief in the deterring power of execution is also expressed, though not so overwhelmingly, by police chiefs and sheriffs — not a far-left part of the community — surveyed by Peter D. Hart Research Associates in 1995. They did not think (67 percent) that executions significantly reduce homicides. In fact, New York's former police chief Patrick V. Murphy responded that "the flimsy notion that the death penalty is an effective law enforcement tool is being exposed as mere political puffery."

Expert criminologists said (100 percent, joined in this by 85 percent of the police chiefs) that politicians support the death penalty for symbolic reasons, to show they are tough on crime, though that distracts them (86.6 percent of the criminologists, 56 percent of the police chiefs) from addressing better methods of reducing the homicide rate. The police listed five things that would be more effective in fighting crime, including longer sentences, more police, and gun control. It takes little observation of actual politicians to confirm that politicians support the death penalty for electoral reasons. Now-Senator Dianne Feinstein, who had opposed capital punishment as a very active member of the California parole board, embraced it in 1990 when she ran for governor. When I asked her during that campaign what had made her change her position, she said that she had become convinced that executions do deter other criminals. I said that most studies I had seen denied this, but she told me she had read new and better research, though she could not name it for me. "I'll send it to you," she promised — but she never did. The only empirical evidence that mattered to her was her knowledge of the way Rose Bird had been resoundingly defeated for reelection as the chief justice of the Supreme Court of California because she opposed capital punishment.

When Andrew Young ran for governor of Georgia in 1990, he too abandoned his earlier opposition to the death penalty (though his daughter remained an activist opponent of it, because of its disproportionate rate among blacks — the NAACP Legal Defense Fund discovered that a black's chance of being executed in Georgia was eleven times that of a white). I asked Young if he too had been convinced that executions deter. He said that he had not, but that as mayor of Atlanta he had listened to police tell him that it discouraged them to catch criminals and see them escape execution — "I did it for their morale." (He did it, though, only when he was leaving the mayor's office and addressing a much whiter constituency in his race for governor.)

Other politicians obviously look to the polls, not to policy studies, when taking their stand on executions. Campaigning to become the senator from New York, Hillary Clinton knew how much support the state's former governor Mario Cuomo had lost because of his resolute stand against executions. William Weld, while he was still governor of Massachusetts, said that he relied not on studies but on "my gut": "My gut is that . . . capital punishment is deterrent." The deft use of the death penalty issue by Bob Graham

as governor of Florida and in his 1986 race for the Senate is studied in a book that Timothy McVeigh is known to have read in
prison. In 1984, Graham dismissed scholarly studies on the death
penalty by saying, "This is an issue that is inherently beyond what
empirical research can validate," making him another gut-truster
like Weld. But if we cannot know the deterrent effect, we are certainly killing one man for a hypothetical effect on others that is uncertain.

Actually, the deterrent theory of capital punishment, always weak,
is especially flimsy now, when a rash of cases — some involving
DNA evidence — has proved that some innocent men are on
death row. The evidence of incompetent defenses, faked evidence,
and negligent procedures has led to announced or informal mor-
atoria on executions. In Oklahoma alone, where Timothy Mc-
Veigh's crime was committed, the evidence in approximately three
thousand cases is now tainted by the defective lab work of one technician, Joyce Gilchrist. The execution of the innocent is not a new
issue, but widespread public awareness of it is. The British study by
the Select Committee on Capital Punishment, cited by Arthur
Koestler, found cases of mistaken executions, including "many" reported by the governor of Sing Sing in America.

Some try to separate the problem of killing the *right* person from
the question of whether we should execute *any* person at all. But
since the principal prop of the death penalty is deterrence theory,
that prop is knocked out when uncertainty of guilt enters the national consciousness. Even if we were to grant that executions deter, they may not deter people who think it is a random matter
whether the right person is caught. If they might get off while
guilty, or be killed while innocent, that fact is not a very stable basis
for forswearing a particular homicide. And executing the mentally
defective or marginally juvenile, like the disproportionate killing
of blacks, cannot much intimidate a would-be murderer who is
mentally sound, of mature age, or white.

These considerations join longer-term flaws in the deterrence
argument. Juries are readiest to convict people for crimes of passion, sexually charged rape-murders, child-abuse murders, or se-
rial killings. To see these offenders caught will not necessarily affect the person most likely to have the coolness and calculation

that deterrence requires. And obviously they do not affect other people in the grip of obsessions, mental instability, or drug- or alcohol-induced frenzy. Plato was against executing those guilty of a crime of passion (*Laws* 867c–d), but our juries reflect more the anger of society than the didactic strategies of deterrence. In doing this, the juries fail to make the calculations that we are told future murderers will make. The whole theory is senseless.

4. *"Closure"*

> [People come] in thousands to the legal massacre and look with carelessness, perhaps with triumph, on the utmost exacerbations of human misery.
>
> — Samuel Johnson, *Rambler* 114

"Closure" has become a buzzword, not only for discussing the death penalty but for addressing any kind of social discontent. When the unmarried mother of Jesse Jackson's child sued Reverend Jackson, it was not about anything so crass as money, it was to find "closure" for herself and her child. Who can deprive a grieving person of solace? This is the argument Antiphon's prosecutor made when he demanded emotional relief for the loss of his child to an accident. Attorney General John Ashcroft endorsed the argument by arranging for the families of Timothy McVeigh's victims to see him die. This conflicts with the logic of deterrence, since the families are not viewing the event to deter them from becoming mass murderers. If the real point of executions is to act *in terrorem* for other criminals, the Oklahoma families are the least appropriate audience.

Ashcroft's response to the hot pressures of the McVeigh case is just that of Dianne Feinstein or Andrew Young to less emotionally charged instances of capital punishment, where no mass murder is involved. McVeigh, the cold killer revealed in *American Terrorist*, by Lou Michel and Dan Herbeck, triggers all the upsurges of emotion Nietzsche described. We feel that the very existence of a McVeigh is an affront to society, a pollutant of our life, a thing we cannot be clean of without execration. But the politician does not want to be seen ministering to atavistic reactions in their raw state. So he invokes deterrence where it does not apply, or says that humane consideration of the victims' sympathies trumps all other considerations. Seeing the murderer die, we are told, will just help the families to "close a chapter of their lives."

But is this really likely? The aim of emotional healing is to bring inflamed emotions of loss and *ressentiment* back into a manageable relationship with other parts of one's life. Does that happen when, for many years in most cases (six years so far in McVeigh's case), a victim's survivors focus on seeing that someone pays for his or her loss? This tends to reenact the outrage in a person's mind, rather than to transcend it. It prolongs the trauma, delaying and impeding the healing process. When I asked Sister Helen Prejean, the author of *Dead Man Walking,* what she has observed, she said that families are asked by prosecutors to attend the trial of a relative's murderer, but to show no emotion lest they cause a mistrial. "They learn new details of the crime, and with each new turn of the trial and its aftermath the media call them to get a reaction." This is less like healing than like tearing scabs open again and again. Some relatives who want to escape this process are accused by their own of not loving the victim, says Sister Helen: "I have seen families torn apart over the death penalty."

What's more, the sterile, anodyne, and bureaucratic procedures of a modern execution can baffle the desire for revenge encouraged before its performance. Sister Helen recalls a man who said he wished to see more suffering, and who comes with pro-death demonstrators to all later executions. This is hardly one who has found "closure." The eeriness of the closure language was revealed when McVeigh himself, through his lawyer, Rob Nigh, expressed sympathy for the relatives' "disappointment" after his execution was delayed. He is more the manipulator of these grieving people than an offering to them.

Emotional counselors work toward reconciliation with the facts, as religious leaders recommend forgiveness. Many church bodies oppose the death penalty, drawing on rich traditions in the various faiths. Saint Augustine resisted the killing of murderers, even of two men who had murdered one of his own priests, arguing that the fate of souls is in God's hands (Letters 133, 134). It is true that Thomas Aquinas likened the killing of murderers to the amputation of a limb for the good of the whole body, but his fellow Dominican Niceto Blázquez points out how defective this argument is: Thomas was drawing an analogy with the excommunication of sinners from the Church, the body of Christ — but that is a move meant to promote reunion, to rescue a person from the death of his soul, not to impose a death on the body.

Conservative Catholics, who are aghast at fellow believers' willingness to ignore the pope on matters like contraception, blithely ignore in their turn papal pleas to renounce the death penalty (addressed most recently to the McVeigh case). And I have not seen Bible-quoting fundamentalists refer to the one place in the Gospels where Jesus deals with capital punishment. At John 8:3–11, he interrupts a legal execution (for adultery) and tells the officers of the state that their own sinfulness deprives them of jurisdiction. Jesus himself gives up any jurisdiction for this kind of killing: "Neither do I condemn you." George W. Bush said during the campaign debates of last year that Jesus is his favorite philosopher — though he did not hesitate to endorse the execution of 152 human beings in Texas, where half of the public defenders of accused murderers were sanctioned by the Texas bar for legal misbehavior or incompetence. Mr. Bush clearly needs some deeper consultation with the philosopher of his choice.

PENNY WOLFSON

Moonrise

FROM THE ATLANTIC MONTHLY

AT THE Center for Creative Photography in Tucson, Arizona, my husband, Joe, and I are looking at prints of *Moonrise, Hernandez, New Mexico,* by Ansel Adams. A slender young man in a suit has brought us, as requested, three versions of this famous photograph. He dons a pair of white gloves before removing the $14\frac{1}{20}$ x $18\frac{1}{20}$ enlargements from their Plexiglas sheaths, opens the hinged glass viewing case in front of us, and places the photographs carefully, lovingly, on a slanted white board inside. He stands there while we examine the pictures; when we are finished, he will repeat the process in reverse.

I don't know exactly where Hernandez, New Mexico, is, but it reminds me a bit of Sacaton, ninety miles northwest of here, the Pima Indian village where Joe is a government doctor and where we have lived since July of 1983. Now it's December. We have made the trip to Tucson expressly to view the Ansel Adams photos, though we did not imagine that there would be so many prints from the same negative.

In *Moonrise* two thirds of the space is usurped by a rich black sky; a gibbous moon floats like a hot-air balloon in an otherworldly — and yet absolutely southwestern — landscape. A gauzy strip of low clouds or filtered light drifts along the horizon; distant mountains are lit by waning sun or rising moon. Only in the bottom third of the photo, among scrubby earth and sparsely scattered trees, does human settlement appear: a small collection of modest adobe houses and one larger adobe church. Around the edge of the village white crosses rise from the ground at many angles; at first glance they resemble clotheslines strung with sheets or socks, but on more careful examination it is obvious that they mark graves.

The prints differ greatly in quality from the reproductions one usually sees, and also differ slightly from one another: here we see a more defined darkness, burnt in by the photographer, there a variation in exposure, a grainier texture. But that does not change the essential meaning of the photograph, a meaning one never forgets in the Southwest: Nature dominates. Human life is small, fragile, and finite. And yet, still, beautiful.

1. Falling, 1998

I am at the Grand Union in Dobbs Ferry, New York, with my son Ansel, who is thirteen years old. It's raining. He begged to come, so I brought him, not really wanting to, because I had to bring his wheelchair, too: it weighs more than two hundred pounds and isn't easy to maneuver into the minivan, even with the ramp. I have to wrestle the motorized chair until it faces forward and then, bending and squeezing into the narrow confines of the van, I have to fasten it to the floor with several clasps. By the time I have done this even once, I'm irritable. A trip to the supermarket means doing it twice and undoing it twice.

Anyway, we've finished our shopping, and we leave the supermarket. Ansel is in his chair, without his hooded yellow raincoat from L. L. Bean, because he has decided that at his age a raincoat is babyish, not cool. He's afraid people at school will laugh at him. Maybe this is true, I say, but I think it's stupid. Why get wet when you can stay dry? Needless to say, I lose this argument.

Before loading the groceries I open the van door so that Ansel can get in the front seat, where he always sits if Joe isn't with us. He parks his chair at a distance from the minivan, so that I'll have room for the ramp, and starts to rise, laboriously. No, "rise" sounds too easy, like smoke going up a flue, airy, like yeast bread rising in the oven. Ansel does not rise. He shifts sideways in the seat and pulls himself up heavily, propping his eighty pounds against the armrest for balance. He leans with his left arm, twists his right shoulder around to straighten up, and brings his hip and buttocks to a partly standing position. Actually he's sort of bent in half, with his hands still on the chair's joystick. There is a moment of imbalance. His feet are planted far apart, farther out than his hips, and he needs to bounce back and forth a few times to bring his feet together. Finally he's up. He begins walking toward the door in his waddling, tiptoe way. His spine is curved quite a bit from scoliosis, his stomach is forward, his hands are out at his sides chest-high, his fingers outstretched.

His balance is so tenuous that his five-year-old brother, Toby, can knock him down. Sometimes Ansel will bellow, "I'm tired of everyone always leaving things all over the floor! Don't they know I'll fall?" It's true that we're a little careless about this. But Ansel will trip over anything — an unevenness in the sidewalk, the dog's water dish, some bits of food on the floor, things expected and unexpected — and sometimes over nothing. Sooner or later he falls. It's part of the routine. And the older he gets, the more he falls.

Now, in the Grand Union parking lot, he falls. Who knows why — it could be the wet ground. He's in the skinny aisle of asphalt between our car and the one parked next to us. He falls, and it's pouring, and I'm still loading grocery bags into the back.

"Mom!" he calls at me, half barking, half crying. "I fell!" There's such anguish, such anger, in his voice when he falls, and such resignation. He never thinks I hear him.

And why am I suddenly so angry? Such terrible impatience rises in me now. Am I really such a witch, such a bad mother, that when I'm loading groceries and my son falls, I don't have the time or patience to cope? Why am I so angry?

"Wait a minute," I say. "I'll be there in a minute."

So he sits on the wet pavement between the cars. I know his sweatpants are at this moment soaking through. I can see that the wheelchair, waiting to be rolled up the ramp, needing to be pushed and yanked into position, is also getting wet. Its foamy nylon seat will need drying out later.

A middle-aged blond woman has wheeled her shopping cart into the lot and approaches us. "Can I help?"

No, you definitely cannot help, runs through my head. This is both true and self-righteous. Physically, the job is not meant for two; it's easier for me to do on my own. How would we two, and Ansel, even fit between the cars?

I grit my teeth and smile and say, "No, no thanks, really. I can do it." People always seem puzzled and upset when they see him fall. It's so sudden, an instant crumpling, without warning. They can't see the weakness, the steady deterioration of his pelvis. Maybe someone would fall this way if he'd been hit hard in the solar plexus; I don't know. But Ansel's feet give way for no apparent reason, and he's down.

The blond woman has heard me, but she keeps standing there, her hands clamped around the handle of her cart, her eyes moving from Ansel to the grocery bags to me. I know she means to be helpful, and in a way I do want something from her — pity? an acknowledgment that I am more noble than she? But mostly I want her to go away. *Don't look at me. Don't watch this.*

"Mom! Where *are* you?"

I turn from the blond woman; she fades away. "OK, I'm coming," I say. I try to wedge myself between the cars so that I can retrieve Ansel. There's a special way to pick him up: you have to come from behind and grab him under the arms, raise him so that his toes dangle just above the ground, and then set his feet down precisely the right distance apart.

I'm in pretty good shape, but Ansel is dead weight. Another child could help you, could put his hands around your neck. His feet would come off the ground at even the suggestion of lifting. But Ansel is pulling me down, his limp shoulders, his heavy leg braces, his sodden pants, his clumsy sneakers. I can't hold him. My own sneakers slip on the wet pavement.

2. *Chaos, 1999*

The New York Academy of Medicine, on 103rd Street and Fifth Avenue, is not exactly in the slums, but it's not really the Upper East Side either. On a dreary, drizzly morning I park at the Metropolitan Museum garage, on Eightieth Street, and walk up Madison, past Banana Republic and Ann Taylor and patisseries and fancy meat purveyors and little French children's-clothing shops that display sashed dresses with hand-embroidered yokes in their windows. But above Ninety-sixth Street, near the Mount Sinai Hospital complex, the scenery and the people change abruptly; everything's older and more rundown. Street peddlers hawk books, batteries,

Yankees caps, cheap scarves, acrylic ski caps, five-dollar handbags. I see an obese black man leaning on a cane, harried-looking workers with Mount Sinai badges, a woman exiting a hospital building through a revolving door carrying crutches.

Eleven years ago, when Ansel was three, doctors diagnosed in him a form of muscular dystrophy called Duchenne, which rapidly destroys muscle tissue, confining its victims to wheelchairs by adolescence and invariably resulting in early death. Like hemophilia, it is almost always transmitted to sons from asymptomatic "carrier" mothers. In my extended family, which produced an overwhelming number of daughters and almost no sons for two generations, the existence of the Duchenne gene — or, more correctly, the existence of an altered gene that doesn't properly code for a particular muscle protein — was unknown, a subterranean truth. My mother and sister and I, all carriers without outward signs, never guessed at this defect in our genetic heritage.

Joe and I gave our son, conceived and born in Arizona, the name of the great photographer we admired, Ansel Adams, who had died earlier that year. The name seemed apt; Ansel was, as people often told us, prettier than a picture, amber-haired and round-eyed, with a perpetually quizzical but serene countenance and the build of a slender but sturdy miniature football player. For two years he developed normally, reaching all the benchmarks on or close to schedule. He was an engaging and beautiful boy, gifted, one suspected, in some intangible way. When his teacher in nursery school began to point out Ansel's deficits in language and in gross motor skills (he couldn't master rudimentary grammar, couldn't alternate legs on the stairs), we refused to see any problem. It was impossible for us to believe that this perfectly wonderful child, our child, was not perfect at all, that he was in fact handicapped and would become progressively more handicapped.

It took a year for us to accept his differentness, to have him professionally evaluated, to reach a diagnosis. And although we have been to dozens of doctors and have dealt with every aspect of his disease, it has taken me eleven years to get up the nerve to come here, to the Academy of Medicine, and look squarely at what will happen to Ansel in a future I have not yet completely faced.

The library reading room is large and quiet, with a high ceiling and a faded tapestry on the wall behind me. At a long oak table beneath a grand chandelier, surrounded by busts of famous scientists, all men, who peer down from atop the bookshelves, I sit nervously waiting for the books I've requested. It makes sense, I suppose, that Louis Pasteur sits head and shoulders above the lesser-knowns.

But not even Pasteur, I remind myself, could have cured muscular dystrophy. Nor could any of the nineteenth-century doctors who described the disease, including the English physicians Charles Bell, Edward Meryon, and William Gowers and the French neurologist G.B.A. Duchenne, after whom the most common form of muscular dystrophy is named. And despite hundreds, perhaps thousands, of studies completed and articles written and compiled in prestigious journals such as *Muscle and Nerve* and *The Lancet* and the *Journal of the American Medical Association*, sitting right here in the bound volumes surrounding me in this rarefied room, no one, even in this century, has found a way to save my son.

A young woman arrives with my books: a general text on Duchenne muscular dystrophy from 1993 by a British geneticist named Alan E. H. Emery, and two books by Duchenne himself, one from the 1870s and crumbling with age, called *A Treatise on Localized Electrization* (*De l'électrisation Localisée*, first published in 1855), and one translated in the 1950s, *Physiology of Motion*. But I find the writings of the great doctor inscrutable and bizarre, filled with stuff about electrical impulses and pictures of strange apparatus; Duchenne devised such instruments as the "dynamometer," or strength gauge, and the harpoon biopsy needle, which he used to study muscles in his patients at different stages in their short lives (before that, muscle tissue was mostly observed at autopsy). Duchenne's books have nearly no narrative; they consist mostly of pages and pages of minute drawings and observations of every muscle in the human body, with one- and two-page sections such as "Motions of the Thumb" and "Flexion of the Forearm." One forgets that before this century medicine was largely descriptive, and that one of the main questions about muscular dystrophy was whether it was primarily neurological — affecting the spine and nerves — or truly muscular. Duchenne confirmed that the disease had no neurogenic basis. Nevertheless, there was something obsessive if not downright nutty about him — or maybe my impatient twentieth-century mother's mind fails to grasp the connections between his results and his writings.

But when I open Emery's book, *Duchenne Muscular Dystrophy*, everything else vanishes. I read between lines; I am transfixed, by turns elated and restless. For the first time in eleven years I look at pictures of boys in the advanced stages of the disease. There are obese boys and skeletal boys looking like Auschwitz victims, their spines twisted and their emaciated arms and legs dangling. There is a boy with grotesquely enlarged muscles throughout his body; he resembles a deformed child bodybuilder, a waxy muscle-bound doll, a strange, surprised balloon boy. In many cases no attempt has been made to conceal the identities of these boys; their faces are in clear view, and their misshapen bodies are naked, so one can see the deterioration clearly. There is something vulgar and vulnerable about the nakedness of these boys, their genitalia seeming in some instances particularly underdeveloped compared with the rest of their bodies and often too frankly exposed. At home I don't see my son naked, as I used to when he was little; I glimpse only the outward signs of deterioration — the thick-veined calves, the legs bruised by falls, the callused, deformed feet, the increasingly swayed back, the heels that can no longer reach the floor. I focus on his face: despite its fleshy roundness, caused by steroids, it is still beautiful to me, with its alert, quizzical eyes and arched eyebrows, its stubborn mouth (how easily it registers disgust or frustration or delight!), its straight, broad nose with a suggestion of freckles, its crown of chestnut hair.

I study an engraving from 1879 of a boy in three positions rising from the floor, in what doctors call a Gowers' maneuver, named after the physician. In the first scene the boy is on his hands and knees; in the second his rump is raised into the air and his two hands press on the ground for support; in the third he rests a hand on his thigh to balance himself. Here I experience the oddest feeling — a thrill of identification. Yes! There it is, exactly. My child. So true, so utterly Ansel. But obviously true of other boys, too, over hundreds or thousands of years. I feel less lonely, in a way, but I can't deny what's in the photographs. And there's no denying the statistics either: 90 percent of boys with Duchenne die by the age of twenty. At sixteen about half are dead. A nine-year-old we know who has Duchenne can no longer walk. Should I feel happy or sad knowing that Ansel is at the far end of the curve?

Some pages I barely glance at — I know the early symptoms, and I have already witnessed some of the decay in Ansel. I know that there is a "progressive weakness of movement, first affecting the lower limbs and then later the upper limbs" and "a gradual increase in the size of many affected muscles." I have seen that the "lumbar lordosis becomes more exaggerated and the waddling gait increases"; I see the shortening of the heel cords.

But as the disease progresses, Emery's book reminds me, the breakdown intensifies: "Muscle weakness becomes more profound, contractures develop, particularly . . . of the elbows, knees, and hips . . . movements of the shoulders and wrists also become limited. The talus bone [protrudes] prominently under the skin." Finally all hell breaks loose: "Thoracic deformity . . . restricts adequate pulmonary airflow . . . a severe kyphoscoliosis [curvature of the spine] develops . . . a gradual deterioration begins in pulmonary function with reduced maximal inspiratory and expiratory pressures. By the later stages there is a significant reduction in total lung capacity." In other words, the spine contorts, compressing the chest cavity; the respiratory and heart muscles weaken; and eventually the child can't breathe. Less commonly, the heart gives out.

In a chapter called "Management," I review the paltry fixes: knee orthoses; braces that extend from ankle to groin; stretching exercises; steroids (the author, writing in 1993, downplayed their importance); wheelchairs; standing frames; rigid body jackets; the "Luque operation," which involves inserting two rods in the spine; tenotomy, or cutting the Achilles and other tendons; finally, assisted ventilation and drainage of the lungs. Some sound radical, some gruesome; at any rate, they are only Band-Aids, short-term measures that extend life perhaps one year, perhaps two. Sooner or later, usually by their mid-twenties, all boys with Duchenne succumb. Of 144 patients Emery studied, only sixteen made it to their twenty-fifth birthdays.

Every night, hands in his pockets for balance, on tiptoe, his jaw set in a grimace, his feet hesitantly reaching and shuffling, leaning longer on the right than on the left, Ansel stumbles along the hallway between his bedroom and the living room, willing himself to walk. It is unheard of — a fifteen-year-old with Duchenne walking. "Amazing," I tell him, "amazing," as he collapses in his wheelchair. We know it can't last forever, but we keep our fingers crossed.

Sunday morning I wake up, descend the stairs, begin boiling wa-

ter for coffee. From the stove I get a glimpse of the cabinets that
Joe fixed the day before: two low storage cupboards whose doors
had been yanked off by the harsh sweep of Ansel's wheelchair. For
weeks the jumble of our kitchen had been exposed, its internal disorder revealed. On Saturday, Joe finally mended them, filling in
the holes and jimmying the hardware. The doors hung a bit askew,
leaving an empty space like a knocked-out front tooth. Still, for the
moment they stayed in place.

But now I see that one door has come loose at its hinges again; it
hangs perilously from a single screw. Inside the darkness, chaos.

3. Moonrise, 2000

Ansel and I are on 165th Street in Washington Heights, on our way
to the doctor at the Neurological Institute. I picked him up at
school, and he told me he loves me, as he does at least once a day,
and then we drove here and parked in the Kinney lot, where, because of our "handicapped" placard, the attendants let us squeeze
into a ground-level spot.

This is the neighborhood where Joe and I first lived together,
in medical-school housing in one of the huge modern buildings
making up The Towers, which overlook the George Washington
Bridge. We did not particularly get along with our multiple room-
mates, and we did not always like each other, but it was our first
home, and it holds memories: the "Man in the Pan" early-morning
lectures at which the doctors-in-training studied dissected organs;
the late Sunday nights when I searched for Joe and his friend Peter, who were studying for a Monday exam in the recesses of the
vast Health Sciences Library; the white-coated world of the medical complex, with people waiting in line for treatment, and the
marble floor of Columbia-Presbyterian Hospital, through which I
walked when coming home from the subway. I had just read
Malcolm X's great book about his life, and I was always aware of
our closeness to the Audubon Ballroom, where Malcolm was shot,
and also of the darkness and danger of the 168th Street subway station, where several rapes and murders had taken place. My sister's
boyfriend, who worked in a microbiology lab at Presbyterian, had
been stabbed in the heart on the train on his way to work. He re-

covered, because he was taken to the emergency room quickly, but he had a scary, knotty scar on his chest where the mugger's knife had gone in.

There are sweet memories, too, mostly associated with food: the French toast at the Haven coffee shop, around the corner, and the farmer's cheese from the old Daitch Dairy (a remnant of the aging Jewish community), and the old-fashioned luncheonette on Fort Washington, where a soda jerk whipped up chocolate malteds made with Breyer's ice cream. The apartment in The Towers was where I held a successful surprise party for Joe; I managed to concoct Julia Child's fanciest chocolate cake, le Marquis, without his ever noticing. It was also where I had to deliver the news to Joe that his adored stepfather had died suddenly, at forty-eight, of a heart attack.

We are supposed to see Dr. DeVivo at least once a year, but it has been a year and some months since our last visit. When Ansel and I arrive, we are told to sit in a secluded, empty waiting room, where he does his math homework and I glance at a magazine called *Healthy Kids*. Joe arrives — in a suit, because he is now the head of family practice at the Catholic Medical Centers, in Brooklyn and Queens — and a receptionist says that we are in the wrong waiting room. We go and sit for another twenty minutes in a much more crowded room. A small boy in a stroller cries, seemingly overtired and cranky; his mother, in a foreign language, tries to soothe him. He has tiny white braces on his legs, but I can't make out what his problem is. I never ask, "Why are you here?" although I always want to know. It sounds too much like "What are you in for?"

When DeVivo, a white-haired, stocky man, enters the room, I am not sure I recognize him, it's been so long. But he is wearing a white coat, and he seems to be in charge, so we follow him into his large office at the end of the hallway. I am very conscious that on our last visit Ansel walked from the waiting room to the office, and I remember the look of surprise on the doctor's face: how amazing that a fourteen-year-old with Duchenne could still walk! Now Ansel wheels his way down the long corridor, and I am the one surprised that he could have walked so far so recently.

Joe, Ansel, and I sit in three upholstered chairs facing DeVivo, who sits behind a massive desk. I remember suddenly how poorly Joe did in his neurology rotation in medical school; how he didn't like the neurologists — they were too cerebral and academic, he felt. DeVivo's manner is restrained, and when he speaks, he addresses Ansel first. He asks Ansel about school, about his clarinet lessons (the doctor plays trombone), and gets only a typical teenager's grunts. The pleasantries aside, he gets to what's important: "Tell me, Ansel, how do you feel, physically, compared with the last time I saw you?"

"Well, I use the wheelchair more," Ansel says. "I get out of the wheelchair three or four times a day and stretch, and then I walk a few steps. That's all. I can't really walk more than that."

He doesn't say it sadly, just as fact; but Joe and I and the doctor know it is sad, and it sits heavy in the air, a presence among us. I think of Ansel at five, walking into town with me because he suddenly wanted to bake cookies and we had to buy cookie cutters. He walked slowly, but he walked all the way, a quarter of a mile in each direction.

For a moment no one else can speak. There isn't anything to say, is there? He gets worse. He will die. Even if it's slow, it will happen. It's a whole life, not a half-life, divided infinitely. Sooner or later it will not be there.

But in one way it's not sad. Ansel has spoken, after all, and we have all listened. He is no longer a small child but the voice of authority. Who can know the answers but Ansel? He has a deep voice and a little trace of a mustache on his upper lip. He and the neurologist discuss the best course of therapy, his medications (would Ansel agree to take three enzyme capsules a day, rather than the one he has been taking?), and his adherence to a low-salt, low-fat diet.

Joe, DeVivo, and Ansel retreat to the examining room that adjoins the office, where the table, made for small children, is too high for Ansel to mount. I stay behind, aware that he will not want his mother present when the doctor prods private parts or asks personal questions. I also don't want to see the fat that spills over the elastic of his underpants or the angry calluses on his feet when he removes his splints and shoes and socks. I'd rather look at the stack of magazines on luxury-home renovation, at the wall of books at the back of the room, at the color photos of racing sailboats — this must be one of the doctor's hobbies. I look out the dirty window of the Neurological Institute, half a block away from our old apartment at The Towers. It is strange to be here, looking out at a past that contained not even a flicker of Ansel. Why is it unthinkable to look at a future without him?

Joe and I are on the street on a Sunday afternoon, late. The forsythia is in bloom; there is yellow everywhere, and a dark sky with just a strip of light over the Palisades. Joe wants to know what I am writing: it is about Ansel's growing up and deteriorating all at once, the "unnaturalness" of a child's beginning to die just when he is beginning to flower.

Joe rejects this, furious. "What are you saying — because it's not average, not the norm, it's unnatural? That's like saying homosexuality is unnatural." I see his eyes flash behind his glasses. "What's unnatural about it?" he says. "It is in fact the natural order of things, that mutations occur. That's who we are, who we have to be, as humans."

"So you have no feelings about Ansel's getting worse?" I demand tearfully.

He purses his lips angrily, forcing air through them. "Of course I have feelings about it. But why is it necessarily sadder for someone to die young than old? Is it sadder for Ansel to die than a ninety-year-old man who's never done anything, who has nothing to show for his life? Anyway, Ansel's not dead. I can't mourn for him. And I refuse to see my life as a tragedy!"

"Well, that's what I'm writing about," I say. "And I'm sorry if you don't think it's sad!" Then I can't speak for ten minutes. I stride along next to Joe, up the hill beside the Food Emporium, and I don't look at him. I am too stubborn and angry. How can he say that a dying child is not heartrending? How about that boy Zachy, the only child of one of Joe's colleagues, who died at eight or nine of a brain tumor? Wasn't that worse, more tragic, than, say, my father's death at seventy-three? Wasn't my father's life, in concrete and substantial ways, long *enough*, whereas Zachy's was not?

At the top of the hill, thinking back on Zachy's death and its aftermath — his stunned parents sitting shiva in the apartment; the boy's baseball card collection still visible in his bedroom — I can no longer hold on to my anger at Joe. I see him simply as a fellow sufferer: trying to construct meaning from ill fate, to find solace in the destruction of his firstborn. He is just groping for a spiritual handhold. This is Joe, used to such loss (two fathers and a mother, all young, all loved), soothing himself, explaining to himself, as a child might, why death comes. And this is just the other half of me.

In six months Ansel will be old enough to drive. In September he will be sixteen, able in New York State to take that step toward adulthood — obtaining a learner's permit. Even though we don't have the details yet, even though his father is not convinced that he can physically operate a motor vehicle, Ansel and I talk about driving as a reality — how he will take over the wheelchair van and I will buy a tiny red Miata, the car of my dreams. He is not as crazy about cars as some teenage boys are, but one day when he and I see a cab-yellow sixties Camaro idling at the corner of Cedar Street and Broadway in the town where we live, his left eyebrow lifts, he peers at me sideways, and he says, "Wow." He's ready.

In the books on muscular dystrophy one learns that there are three markers: the onset of disease, confinement to a wheelchair, death. Ansel is approaching the date of confinement. He will be there, I am sure, by his sixteenth birthday.

I have panic attacks nearly every night. Awakened by some minor provocation — for instance, my daughter, Diana, enters the room to check the time — I turn over, sit up, and quite suddenly experience dread; there is no other word. I blink my eyes, because I am sure I'm going blind, and scratch my middle fingertip with my thumbnail, to assure myself that I'm not paralyzed. I try to take the pulse in my wrist, but I'm too scared and can't count right. I am outside my body, physically detached, at the end of a long passageway, drowning — all those melodramatic scenarios of what it's like to die.

Seven years ago, when I was in labor with Toby, a nurse injected me with Stadol, a painkiller, and I became distant and paranoid like this. I held on to Joe's hand, literally for dear life. "Tell me I am not dying," I said over and over, to hear my own voice and to hear him respond. *What an irony,* I thought then, *to die giving birth!*

Now my heart seems to be racing in my head, but my blood is glacial, cold and slow. I have finally gone over the edge! The fear feeds on itself. I get dressed so that I can be ready to drive to the emergency room, if need be.

Sitting on the edge of the bed, sure of my own doom, I wonder suddenly, *Am I trying to experience my own death in place of Ansel's? Am I the sacrifice?*

It is the middle of March, and every moment pulls me two ways. In a community church in White Plains, New York, that looks like a cross between a pagoda and an airline terminal, I sit with Joe, Diana, and Toby in a fan-shaped room filled with folding chairs. It is a kind of backward room, because one enters by way of the stage and descends to seats. Ansel, who will be performing with an ensemble from his music school, can wheel onto the stage but not into the audience, so after he plays, Joe will have to carry him down the steps.

When the woodwinds come onstage and are seated, Ansel seems taller than the others, though he's actually quite short, because for the first time he is playing from his wheelchair. Usually he transfers, with difficulty, to a regular chair, but it was thought that the amount of time before the next group came on was too brief to allow for that. I can see Ansel now and then between the arms of the conductor. He is puffing out his big cheeks, like Dizzy Gillespie on the horn. He loves the clarinet, the instrument he chose when he began music lessons at school, in the fifth grade. Joe was against it. "What's the point," he asked, "when all boys with muscular dystrophy develop breathing difficulties? He won't be able to play for more than a couple of years; it will just be frustrating." As he does with nearly everything, Ansel stood firm, and got his way, and it is good that he did. Clarinet playing is his breathing therapy as well as his joy, and it may be the reason his lungs show no deterioration yet.

He progressed slowly when he took lessons at the public school, but as soon as he began at the music school, he flourished. Under the guidance of a gifted teacher Ansel has become a disciplined music student who, after many days and nights of mistakes, false starts, and practice, practice, practice, can be depended on to produce a fine sound. When he leaves his bedroom door open, I enjoy the lovely strains of the Weber clarinet concertino or of a Hindemith sonata. He is not a virtuoso; he is more of a plodder, but he plods well. He has learned to respect the difficulty of the task and the beauty of the result.

Sitting at the concert, I feel the pleasure of his playing, but seeing him in the wheelchair, I cannot shake the feeling of loss, a loss
that feels sharpest when I love him most. I know that when boys become confined to their wheelchairs, their chests and lungs become
constricted. Wind is the first thing to go. *Who knows which way the
wind blows? Who knows where my love goes, how my love grows, where the
time goes?* Despite my best efforts, despite my pride in Ansel (that
serious, stubborn, laboring face!), a tear wells up in the corner
of my eye. I shift my glasses so that Diana will not see. She does
anyway.

"Mom, why are you crying?" she asks. I shake my head. "Ansel?"
she whispers urgently. I nod, and wordlessly I put my arm around
her shoulder — her bare, cool, pubescent shoulder, upon which I
perhaps place too great a burden — and hold her close to me.
Later Ansel sits with me, and Diana sits alone all the way in back.
Joe has pulled Toby out, because he is complaining so much about
being at a concert. The Festival Orchestra, sounding very professional despite being jerkily led by a very thin, very young conductor, plays Bach. In the midst of the quite proper, cultivated audience, Ansel and I dip and bounce our heads and shoulders to the
rhythms. Near the end Ansel whispers, "Have you noticed everybody else here is completely still, no one else but you and me is
moving to the music?" I have.

I keep with me much of the time a letter from a friend of a friend
whose boy died of Duchenne at twenty-four. Even though I have
never met her, I identify with this mother, because her boy did well;
he must have been an outlier, like Ansel, to live to such a ripe old
age. My son "was the absolute center of my life," she wrote. "Now I
feel like the woman in the Hopper painting 'Cape Cod Morning,'
looking out the bay window, wondering what will come next."

Ansel has been away from the house for almost the entire weekend, attending a model U.N. at a nearby high school Friday night,
all day Saturday, and Sunday morning. We are not used to his being away, and Diana and I both feel his absence. The question
seems to be not "Is this what it will be like when he's away at college?" but "Is this what it will be like when he is dead?"

"Ansel is what makes the house happy," Diana says later that week, and I think back to the moment of his birth, when I heard a sound that reminded me of the popping of a champagne cork. I think of his name: a variation of Anschel, a diminutive of Asher, which in Hebrew means "happy."

Diana and I try to think about what makes Ansel fun. "He's just a very up person," she says, which is odd, because he is also a big complainer, a class-A kvetch. "Puns," I say. "Remember when he wrote that story about the teenage monster who wasn't frightening enough because he didn't have enough 'scaritonin'?"

"Non sequiturs," Diana offers, and it's true. I used to call Ansel the king of non sequiturs. We might all be having a conversation about, say, the fact that the Lobster Roll is the only restaurant worth going to in the Hamptons. The rest of us might consider the topic exhausted and move rapidly on to two or three unrelated topics. We might be talking about the book I am reading for my psychology class in graduate school or about how boring Toby finds the second grade. And then, maybe half an hour later, sometimes a day later, Ansel will pipe up with "There is that Mexican place in East Hampton," as though there has been not even a tiny break in the conversation. His neuroses are funny too, I say: for instance, he worries about global warming every time the temperature in winter is above average. Everyone else is enjoying the sun, but Ansel is worried! And he always worries about being worried: "Should I be worried?" He is so much like me, and like my father, that I can't help laughing at the reflection.

I am aware that having a limited future makes Ansel freer. Next year, for example, he plans to enroll in the vocational-training program offered by the school system, even though he is on an academic track. The vocational program includes culinary arts, and Ansel knows that is what he wants. Isn't food what he thinks about all the time? The taste of a blood orange or a fresh fig may be the most important, most commented-on part of his day. In English he has chosen "luxury foods" for his special project; he writes of the high cost of hunting for truffles, of the packaging of caviar, of the pleasure of watching the guys behind the counter at Zabar's slice lox. He faithfully reads the "Dining Out" section of the *New York Times* and leafs through the Penzys Spices catalog.

He doesn't care that taking culinary arts each morning at a location in northern Westchester County will seriously limit his academic program. He does not want to sit through another year of science, even though it would "look better" on his college applications. He has no time to waste. Ansel calls a meeting with me and his guidance counselor and the director of the program, the last of whom he informs, "I can't do something without being serious about it. Otherwise I just don't think it's worth doing." When the director describes the culinary-arts program, which is almost completely hands-on cooking, the corners of Ansel's mouth curve into a little smile, and the guidance counselor, who knows him well, says, "I don't often see that look in Ansel's eyes."

It is apparent that cooking is what he must do. Being a public program, the vocational-training class must accommodate him, so he will probably have an aide for lifting heavy pots off the stove and similar tasks. It seems exciting, although I am a bit concerned that Ansel may miss out on two years of science, French, and math, which are given in the morning, when he will be off school grounds. After the meeting I stay behind to speak with his counselor.

"How would it be if he just does culinary arts for one year, not two?" I ask. Ansel would like to start the program this September, his junior year, but I think it will be better for college-admission purposes if he waits until his senior year.

"Yes, I assumed one year," the counselor says, adding, "Preferably his junior year."

I am surprised. "Because . . . ?"

"Because I know culinary arts will be in the morning next year; I'm not sure about the following year. And that would be better as far as academics go. Because he has to take history and English. Also . . ."

I know the other reason. She lets me say it. "Because we don't know where he will be physically in two years. This may be the only year he can do it."

I meet an old friend in the city for lunch. We walk to the restaurant, and she rattles on about the short story she is writing. I cannot open my mouth; I am sure I will start to cry. For two weeks I have been up every night with shoulder pain: a pinched nerve, probably brought on by a slipped disc. Yesterday my kitchen was gutted in advance of a major renovation for Ansel's benefit, and there are still bent nails sticking up from the floor every few inches.

My friend tells me about her latest challenge: her therapist has asked her, "What do you want?" As in life.

"Want," I say, almost sneering, and as I open my mouth, everything spills out, and in a little Vietnamese restaurant on Third Avenue, I start weeping. "Who cares what you want?" I say accusingly, and I am frightened by my feeling, which comes out so raw and powerful and pitiless. "I want my son to live a long life. So what?" Every word is a choking effort, my tongue swollen and sore, my throat like gravel. Why bother wanting?

I have two dreams. In the first one, two cars are driving fast in the left lane of the highway, in the wrong direction. Everyone in our car can see as we approach them that this is a very dangerous thing. But it's too late to stop. The cars crash head-on into other cars just in front of us, and I can see the drivers thrown aside, into the air, the cars tin-can crushed. But we are saved. We only witness the horror and move on. We don't even stop. What can we do?

In the second dream Ansel and I come upon a red-rock canyon in the middle of a southwestern desert. We are not really surprised; we have been expecting to find the canyon. It has a lip of rock across its entrance, so we cannot see beyond, its contents are secret. But once we get inside, we are aware of water and sand, and a very beautiful light glinting off beach umbrellas. We are at the ocean. Ansel can walk. We stake out our place on the sand. We have brought our lunch and a blanket, and we sit together and eat: crusty French bread, a wedge of Parmigiano-Reggiano from Todaro Brothers, slices of ripe mango. We are happy.

When Ansel rises from the table today, his legs tremble as he transfers to the wheelchair. Our house is in complete disorder: dining table and refrigerator and microwave are all sitting in the living room, because the kitchen renovation is not complete. The shelves in the living room hold two-by-fours; a sugar bowl; strips of insulation; our good silverware in a blue felt Bloomingdale's bag; a tin candy box filled with paper clips, packing tape, nail clippers, misplaced trinkets and bits of toys, Pokémon cards, and Monopoly hotels.

After dinner Ansel is sitting at the table drinking tea and trying

to read *Treasure Island,* which he finds difficult because of the anti-
quated language and because he has been interrupted over and
over again by Diana and Toby, who are bored. I am in the next
room, also reading, when I hear a commotion: Ansel is screaming
and weeping, "Stop! Stop! I can't stand it, stop!" in a weird, high,
animal-like shriek. When I run in, I see that he has taken his empty
teacup and begun to bang it over and over again on the table;
while I watch, horrified, he puts the cup down and begins to bang
his forehead rhythmically.

"What happened?" I demand angrily of Diana. "What *happened?!*" I am stamping my foot, the rage spilling out of me. "What
did you do?"

"I didn't do anything!" she retorts. "He was burping again —
which he always does! — and I told him he was disgusting and he
went crazy! God! You blame me for everything!"

Now Ansel begins to shriek again. "I'm an idiot! I'm an idiot! I
did it because I'm an idiot!" His cheeks are big and red, and he
can't catch his breath, and he begins to whimper. Embarrassment,
comprehension, a normal sibling fight turned abnormal — a fifteen-year-old acting like a three-year-old.

"Pick him up," I say quietly to Joe, who has come in from the
next room. "Pick him up and carry him into his room."

Later I ask Ansel, "What is it like — that anger? Are you on another planet, like I used to be when I had temper tantrums when I
was a kid?" I know that anger is a locked box, but it is also freedom
— a soaring, powerful white light.

"I don't know," he says. "I don't know. I just think if I scream and
scream and scream maybe I'll stop being angry. Maybe I'll get it all
out of me."

"Is there so much anger?" I ask. "What's it about?"

"Please, Mom." He turns his head away. "Please. Let's not talk
about it anymore."

Another day he comes home from school depressed. "I'm worried
about dying," he says. I honestly don't know what to say. Since
when am I so wise anyway? I'm tired, and I worry about dying too.
Driving home fast on the Saw Mill River Parkway, I sometimes
think, *What will happen to my kids if I die?* It is always Ansel's face I
see; how could he forgive me?

So I don't respond, not really, and later, when he is putting to-gether the pieces of his clarinet, he wails melodramatically, "I'm so depressed, and no one cares!" Now I feel compelled to react, so I go into his room. He continues: "I was depressed in the first place, and then when I got to health class my teacher had written 'The Stages of Grief' up on the blackboard — we're studying death — and it just made me more depressed . . . And then we saw part of *Schindler's List,* clips of the movie . . ."

"Did you see the part with the little girl in the red coat who is wandering around the ghetto and then gets shot?" I ask, thinking this had upset him.

He looks at me. "She doesn't get shot, Mom. She hides in the building . . ."

"But she does, Ans. Eventually she does get shot."

"Nope," he says. "You're wrong, Mom. You forgot."

I don't want to contradict him again, though I know I'm right. I think of his great capacity for denial. I remember something the physician John Bach wrote in an article about boys with muscular dystrophy: "Successful adaptation does not depend upon an accu-rate perception of reality."

This morning I catch sight of Toby's torso while he is dressing. He is seven and a half, slender and small, built like a dancer. He has that nice square chest that a boy is supposed to have, with a line running down the center from breastbone to belly. Ansel would have been beautiful too, perhaps more so. I remember a photo from the summer before Ansel began taking prednisone to slow down the deterioration of his muscles, when he could still walk, ploddingly, up the unrailed front steps. A blue-purple T-shirt, a sun-tinted face: a quite handsome eleven-year-old. Before the chip-munk cheeks, puffy from steroids. That must have been the sum-mer before the wheelchair. My beautiful son.

Ansel's independent reading this month: Mark Twain's *Roughing It;* most of Phillip Lopate's *The Art of the Personal Essay;* "The Snows of Kilimanjaro" and other stories by Ernest Hemingway; M.F.K. Fisher's *A Cordiall Water; The Red Badge of Courage,* by Stephen Crane; *National Geographic;* S. J. Perelman's *Chicken Inspector no. 23.* His selection of a project for social studies, any "ism": Dadaism. Fa-

vorite music: Louis Armstrong, Thelonious Monk, show tunes, the
Buena Vista Social Club.

Ansel and I are sitting in the living room, late. Everyone else has
gone to sleep. He is doing his daily exercises: leaning with his
palms against the back of the couch, pushing his heels down toward the floor, one at a time, to lengthen the Achilles tendons, trying to stay mobile for as long as possible. He has had a tough day,
and he is very tired. Earlier he asked Joe to carry him to the bathroom (he usually walks), and when he got there he fell trying to
reach the toilet.

"I don't know why I'm having so much trouble," he says to me
later. "Do you think I'm just tired? Why should I be so tired?"

"I don't know, Ans. It may just be the disease. It's getting worse, I
guess. That's really crummy, isn't it?"

He doesn't say anything. He is cutting his toenails, concentrat-
ing on the task of keeping all the parings in one pile on the coffee
table. "Isn't it?" I repeat.

He looks up. "No. I think everything that happens has a reason."

"I guess that's because you believe in God," I say.

"I used to get depressed thinking about this stuff," he continues,
seeming to ignore my remark. "But then I realized it doesn't help.
So I don't think about it anymore."

I ask him at another time, "Do you think about the fact that you
may not have as many years as other people?"

"No, Mom. I just want to be happy."

Ansel says everything that happens has a reason. He uses the toilet
in the middle of the night and flushes it, and the flood of water in
the pipes wakes up our collie in the basement, and she begins
barking, and I wake up, and it is a quarter to four.

In a way I'm not tired, so I get up and go down to the basement,
where the dog is kenneled. She is wide awake and on her feet, waiting expectantly, as though we planned a rendezvous. She nips my
heels and tries to push through my legs as we mount the stairs.
Then she shoots outside, and I follow.

It's warm out, and completely calm; the three-quarters moon is
immense and neon yellow, hanging over the Palisades, nearly
merging with the horizon. It seems otherworldly, like — and I

know this is a ridiculous thought — an object from outer space. In other words, it appears as it is — completely apart from, oblivious of, anything human.

I don't know if it's rising or setting. Joe will be able to tell me in the morning, but right now I don't want to know, not yet. I stand there with the mystery of the moon for some time, with the thrill of knowing its beauty — having it to myself for a few rare moments — while the dog sniffs under damp leaves, looking for a place to pee.

When she is finished, I take her back to the basement and give her a full bowl of water, which she drinks thirstily. I go to sleep easily, somehow fulfilled. Ansel says everything has a reason. He is fifteen. In two hours it will be daylight.

Biographical Notes

JACQUES BARZUN is a cultural historian and critic who has written a series of works setting forth the evolution of ideas in Western civilization since the Renaissance and offering at the same time a critique of contemporary culture. His latest book is *From Dawn to Decadence: Five Hundred Years of Western Cultural Life*, which attained the bestseller lists. An anthology of his writings from 1932 to 2001, edited by Michael Murray, has also been recently published.

RUDOLPH CHELMINSKI is a freelance writer living in France. Formerly a *Life* staff correspondent in Paris and Moscow, he has written for numerous major American and French publications, including *Life, Time, Fortune, People, Money, Playboy, Geo, Town & Country, Reader's Digest, Smithsonian, Signature, Saturday Review, Wired, Reporter, France Today, Le Monde,* and others. He is the author of four books, and has never won a single prize. Except, that is, the best one of all: having managed for more than thirty years to support himself and his family as a freelancer.

BERNARD COOPER'S most recent books are *Truth Serum*, a collection of memoirs, and *Guess Again*, a collection of short stories. He received the 1991 PEN/Hemingway Award, a 1995 O. Henry Prize, and a 1999 Guggenheim fellowship. This is his fourth appearance in *The Best American Essays*. He is currently the art critic for *Los Angeles* magazine.

NICHOLAS DELBANCO is the Robert Frost Collegiate Professor of English Language and Literature at the University of Michigan, where he directs the M.F.A. program in creative writing and the Hopwood Awards program. He is the author of twenty books of fiction and nonfiction; his most recent novel is titled *What Remains* and a collection of previous essays is called *The Lost Suitcase: Reflections on the Literary Life.*

BARBARA EHRENREICH has written more than a dozen books, including *The Hearts of Men: American Dreams and the Flight from Commitment; Fear of Falling: The Inner Life of the Middle Class; The Worst Years of Our Lives: Irreverent Notes from a Decade of Greed; The Snarling Citizen: Essays; Blood Rites: Origins and History of the Passions of War;* and most recently, *Nickel and Dimed: On (Not) Getting By in America.* She is a contributing editor for *Harper's Magazine* and a columnist for *The Progressive,* and writes frequently for *Time* and other periodicals nationwide. She is currently working on a book about the politics of festivities.

JONATHAN FRANZEN'S third novel, *The Corrections,* won the National Book Award for fiction in 2001. He is the author of two other novels, *Strong Motion* and *The Twenty-Seventh City,* and a collection of essays, *How to Be Alone.* He lives in New York City and has been a contributor to *The New Yorker* since 1994.

ATUL GAWANDE is a surgical resident in Boston and, since 1998, a staff writer for *The New Yorker.* A graduate of Harvard Medical School, Oxford University, and Stanford University, he has been a laboratory researcher, a senior health policy adviser to President Bill Clinton, and a research fellow at the Harvard School of Public Health. His first book, *Complications: A Surgeon's Notes on an Imperfect Science,* was published by Metropolitan Books in April.

DAVID HALBERSTAM'S eighteen books include *The Best and the Brightest, The Powers That Be, Summer of '49,* and most recently, *Firehouse.* He won the Pulitzer Prize in 1964 for his pessimistic dispatches for the *New York Times* from Vietnam.

CHRISTOPHER HITCHENS was born in 1949 and educated at the Leys School, Cambridge, and Balliol College, Oxford. He emigrated to the United States in 1981. He is a columnist for *Vanity Fair* and *The Nation,* and a professor of liberal studies at the New School for Social Research in New York. His most recent books are *Unacknowledged Legislation: Writers in the Public Sphere* and *The Trial of Henry Kissinger.* His study of George Orwell, *Orwell's Victory,* is being published this fall. In 1992 he received the Lannan Literary Award for nonfiction. He lives in Washington, D.C.

SEBASTIAN JUNGER is the author of the international bestseller *The Perfect Storm* and, most recently, *Fire,* a collection of his reportage, which concludes with "A Lion in Winter." His writing has appeared in many national publications, including *Outside, Men's Journal, American Heri-*

tage, Vanity Fair, Harper's Magazine, and *National Geographic Adventure,* and in the *New York Times.* The recipient of a National Magazine Award and an SAIS-Novartis Prize for journalism, he lives in New York City.

AMY KOLEN's work has appeared in *The Missouri Review, The Massachusetts Review, Orion, Exchanges: Translation and Commentary,* and other publications. Her essay "Living Will" received an award from the National League of American Pen Women. A graduate of the University of Iowa's nonfiction writing program, she lives with her family in Iowa City.

ANDREW LEVY is the author of *The Culture and Commerce of the American Short Story* and the coeditor of *Postmodern American Fiction: A Norton Anthology* and *Creating Fiction: A Writer's Companion.* His essays have appeared in *Harper's Magazine, Dissent, The American Scholar,* and scholarly journals. He is the Cooper Chair in English at Butler University in Indianapolis and is currently working on a biography of Robert Carter III, forthcoming from Random House.

ADAM MAYBLUM is the managing director of the May Davis Group, a private investment firm formerly located on the eighty-seventh floor of One World Trade Center. He has been working in corporate finance for more than fifteen years. Adam graduated from the Emory University School of Business Administration in 1987 with a B.B.A. in management. His experience of the events of September 11, 2001, has been recounted in newspapers and on radio and television the world over.

LOUIS MENAND is Distinguished Professor of English at the Graduate Center of the City University of New York and a staff writer at *The New Yorker.* He is the author, most recently, of *The Metaphysical Club,* which won the Pulitzer Prize for history, the Heartland Prize for nonfiction, and the Francis Parkman Prize. A collection of his essays, *American Studies,* is being published in November 2002.

CULLEN MURPHY is the managing editor of *The Atlantic Monthly,* to which he is also a regular contributor of essays and longer reporting. He also writes the syndicated comic strip *Prince Valiant,* which appears in some 350 newspapers worldwide and which is drawn by his father, the illustrator John Cullen Murphy. And he is contributing editor of *Slate,* for which he writes the column "The Good Word," about language. He is the author, with William L. Rathje, of *Rubbish! The Archaeology of Garbage* (1992) and the author of *Just Curious* (1995), a collection of essays, and *The Word According to Eve: Women and the Bible* (1998).

DANIELLE OFRI is an attending physician at Bellevue Hospital and on the faculty of the NYU School of Medicine. She is editor in chief of *The Bellevue Literary Review* and has also edited a medical textbook, *The Belle-*

vue Guide to Outpatient Medicine (2001). Dr. Ofri's stories have appeared in both medical and literary journals as well as several anthologies. She is the recipient of the 2001 *Missouri Review* Editor's Prize for the essay "Merced." Her collection of essays, *Taking a History: A Doctor's Training at Bellevue*, is forthcoming from Beacon Press in spring 2003

DARRYL PINCKNEY, a frequent contributor to *The New York Review of Books,* is the author of a novel, *High Cotton.*

RICHARD PRICE is the author of six novels, including *The Wanderers, Clockers,* and *Freedomland.* His seventh, *Samaritan,* will be published by Knopf in February 2003. Born in 1985, ANNE HUDSON-PRICE was a high school junior in Manhattan at the time of the World Trade Center disaster. The father-daughter collaboration of "Word on the Street" evolved from their nightly efforts in the weeks following September 11 to describe to each other, both in writing and in conversation, the changes in their respective spheres of the city. This is her first published essay.

JOE QUEENAN is the author of seven books, including *If You're Talking to Me, Your Career Must Be in Trouble* and *Balsamic Dreams: A Short but Self-Important History of the Baby Boomers.* A columnist for *GQ,* he is currently working on a book investigating why men follow sports. He lives in Tarrytown, New York.

JOHN SACK is a founder of literary journalism, the one new literary form of the twentieth century. He has been a journalist for fifty-five years. He was a newspaper reporter in North and South America, Europe, Africa, and Asia; a contributor to *Harper's Magazine, The Atlantic Monthly,* and *The New Yorker;* a contributing editor for *Esquire;* a writer, producer, and special correspondent for CBS News and its bureau chief in Spain; a war correspondent in Korea, Vietnam, Iraq, Yugoslavia, and Afghanistan; and the author of ten nonfiction books. His most recent book is *The Dragonhead.*

MARIO VARGAS LLOSA is the author of such internationally acclaimed novels as *Conversation in the Cathedral, Aunt Julia and the Scriptwriter, The War at the End of the World, In Praise of the Stepmother,* and most recently, *The Feast of the Goat.* His nonfiction books include several collections of essays and literary criticism: *The Perpetual Orgy, A Writer's Reality, Making Waves,* which won the National Book Critics Circle Award in 1998, and *A Fish in the Water,* a memoir recounting his experiences as a candidate for president of Peru in the 1990 elections. He lives in London.

GORE VIDAL was born at West Point and is the author of twenty-two novels, including the American Chronicle novels (*Burr, Lincoln, 1876, Em-*

pire, Hollywood, Washington, D.C., and *The Golden Age*), five plays, and six collections of essays, of which *The Second American Revolution* won the National Book Critics Circle Award for criticism in 1982 and *United States: Essays, 1952–1992* won the National Book Award in 1993.

GARRY WILLS, who teaches history at Northwestern University, is the author of *Lincoln at Gettysyburg, Saint Augustine,* and *Venice: Lion City.* He has received the Pulitzer Prize, the National Book Critics Circle Award (twice), and the Presidential Medal of the National Endowment for the Humanities.

PENNY WOLFSON received a master of arts in nonfiction writing from Sarah Lawrence College. Her work has appeared in the *New York Times, The Atlantic Monthly, Exceptional Parent,* and in literary reviews. In spring 2003, St. Martin's Press will publish her first book, based on her essay "Moonrise," which also won a National Magazine Award in 2002. She lives in Dobbs Ferry, New York, with her husband and their three children.

Notable Essays of 2001

SELECTED BY ROBERT ATWAN

MARILYN ABILDSKOV
The Men in My Country. *Quarterly West,* no. 53.

DEBORAH Y. ABRAMSON
Proof: A Preface. *River Teeth,* Spring.

ANDRÉ ACIMAN
Barcelona. The Sophisticated Traveler, November 18.

FAITH ADIELE
Passing Through Bandit Territory. *Crab Orchard Review,* Fall/Winter.

JOEL AGEE
German Lessons. *Harper's Magazine,* February.

WILL AITKEN
Architecture of Loss. *The Threepenny Review,* Winter.

FOUAD AJAMI
The Sentry's Solitude. *Foreign Affairs,* November/December.

MARCIA ALDRICH
The Fine Art of Slumping. *Witness,* vol. 15, no. 1.

CYNTHIA ANDERSON
Cars. *Inkwell,* Spring.

ANTHONY AVENI
Is Harmony at the Heart of Things? *The Wilson Quarterly,* Winter.

NICHOLAS BAKER
No Step. *The American Scholar,* Autumn.

HELEN BAROLINI
Making My Bones. *The Massachusetts Review,* Spring.

M. GARRETT BAUMAN
Gravity. *New Letters,* vol. 67, no. 2.

JOHN BERGER
A Gratitude Hard to Name. *The Threepenny Review,* Summer.

ANNE BERNAYS
Remembering Mrs. McIntosh. *The Chronicle of Higher Education,* February 9.

MICHAEL BERUBE
Dream a Little Dream. *The Chronicle of Higher Education,* September 21.

ELAINE CROYLE BEZANSON
Black Ice: A Patient's Perception of Pain. *Regional Anesthesia and Pain Medicine,* January/February.

AKEEL BILGRAMI
Gandhi's Integrity. *Raritan,* Fall.

NORMAN BIRNBAUM
Up or Down to Oxford. *The Reading Room,* no. 3.

GREG BOTTOMS
Patron Saint of Thrown-Away Things. *Creative Nonfiction,* no. 17.

THE B·E·S·T AMERICAN SERIES ™

THE BEST AMERICAN SHORT STORIES® 2002
Sue Miller, guest editor • Katrina Kenison, series editor

"Story for story, readers can't beat the *Best American Short Stories* series" (*Chicago Tribune*). This year's most beloved short fiction anthology is edited by the best-selling novelist Sue Miller and includes stories by Edwidge Danticat, Jill McCorkle, E. L. Doctorow, and Akhil Sharma, among others.

0-618-13173-6 PA $13.00 / 0-618-11749-0 CL $27.50
0-618-13172-8 CASS $26.00 / 0-618-25816-7 CD $35.00

THE BEST AMERICAN ESSAYS® 2002
Stephen Jay Gould, guest editor • Robert Atwan, series editor

Since 1986, the *Best American Essays* series has gathered the best nonfiction writing of the year. Edited by Stephen Jay Gould, the eminent scientist and distinguished writer, this year's volume features writing by Jonathan Franzen, Sebastian Junger, Gore Vidal, Mario Vargas Llosa, and others.

0-618-04932-0 PA $13.00 / 0-618-21388-0 CL $27.50

THE BEST AMERICAN MYSTERY STORIES™ 2002
James Ellroy, guest editor • Otto Penzler, series editor

Our perennially popular anthology is a favorite of mystery buffs and general readers alike. This year's volume is edited by the internationally acclaimed author James Ellroy and offers pieces by Robert B. Parker, Joyce Carol Oates, Michael Connelly, Stuart M. Kaminsky, and others.

0-618-12493-4 PA $13.00 / 0-618-12494-2 CL $27.50
0-618-25807-8 CASS $26.00 / 0-618-25806-X CD $35.00

THE BEST AMERICAN SPORTS WRITING™ 2002
Rick Reilly, guest editor • Glenn Stout, series editor

This series has garnered wide acclaim for its stellar sports writing and top-notch editors. Now Rick Reilly, the best-selling author and "Life of Reilly" columnist for *Sports Illustrated,* continues that tradition with pieces by Frank Deford, Steve Rushin, Jeanne Marie Laskas, Mark Kram, Jr., and others.

0-618-08628-5 PA $13.00 / 0-618-08627-7 CL $27.50

THE B·E·S·T AMERICAN SERIES ™

THE BEST AMERICAN TRAVEL WRITING 2002
Frances Mayes, guest editor • Jason Wilson, series editor

The Best American Travel Writing 2002 is edited by Frances Mayes, the author of the enormously popular *Under the Tuscan Sun* and *Bella Tuscany*. Giving new life to armchair travel for 2002 are David Sedaris, Kate Wheeler, André Aciman, and many others.

0-618-11880-2 PA $13.00 / 0-618-11879-9 CL $27.50
0-618-19719-2 CASS $26.00 / 0-618-19720-6 CD $35.00

THE BEST AMERICAN SCIENCE AND NATURE WRITING 2002
Natalie Angier, guest editor • Tim Folger, series editor

This year's edition promises to be another "eclectic, provocative collection" (*Entertainment Weekly*). Edited by Natalie Angier, the Pulitzer Prize–winning author of *Woman: An Intimate Geography*, it features work by Malcolm Gladwell, Joy Williams, Barbara Ehrenreich, Dennis Overbye, and others.

0-618-13478-6 PA $13.00 / 0-618-08297-2 CL $27.50

THE BEST AMERICAN RECIPES 2002–2003
Edited by Fran McCullough with Molly Stevens

"The cream of the crop . . . McCullough's selections form an eclectic, unfussy mix" (*People*). Offering the best of what America's cooking, as well as the latest trends, time-saving tips, and techniques, this year's edition includes a foreword by Anthony Bourdain, the best-selling author of *Kitchen Confidential* and *A Cook's Tour*.

0-618-19137-2 CL $26.00

THE BEST AMERICAN NONREQUIRED READING 2002
Dave Eggers, guest editor • Michael Cart, series editor

The Best American Nonrequired Reading is the newest addition to the series — and the first annual of its kind for readers fifteen and up. Edited by Dave Eggers, the author of the phenomenal bestseller *A Heartbreaking Work of Staggering Genius*, this genre-busting volume draws from mainstream and alternative American periodicals and features writing by Eric Schlosser, David Sedaris, Sam Lipsyte, Michael Finkel, and others.

0-618-24694-0 PA $13.00 / 0-618-24693-2 CL $27.50 / 0-618-25810-8 CD $35.00

HOUGHTON MIFFLIN COMPANY   www.houghtonmifflinbooks.com